£2.55

Geography of The British Isles

Geography of The British Isles

Norman J. Graves
Head of the Geography Department
University of London Institute of Education

John Talbot White
Senior Lecturer in Geography
Rachel Macmillan College of Education

Fourth Edition

Ieinemann Educational Books
.ondon

Heinemann Educational Books Ltd
LONDON EDINBURGH MELBOURNE AUCKLAND TORONTO
HONG KONG SINGAPORE KUALA LUMPUR NEW DELHI
NAIROBI JOHANNESBURG LUSAKA IBADAN KINGSTON

ISBN 0 435 34275 4

First published 1971, Second Edition 1972. Third Edition 1974
Fourth Edition 1976
Reprinted 1977

Published by Heinemann Educational Books Ltd
48 Charles Street, London W1X 8AH

Photoset in Malta by Interprint (Malta) Ltd
Printed in Great Britain by Morrison and Gibb, London and Edinburgh

Acknowledgements

The authors would like to thank all those who directly or indirectly have helped in the preparation of this book. In particular they would like to acknowledge that some of the material in this book is based on work by Prof. T. W. Freeman (*The Conurbations of Great Britain*), Professor P. Hall (*World Cities*), Mr G. Manners (*South Wales in the Sixties*), Messrs C. B. Marshall and I. G. McIntosh (*The Face of Scotland*) Miss J. Mitchell (ed) (*Great Britain: Geographical Essays*), Professors F. J. Monkhouse and H. R. Wilkinson (*Maps and Diagrams*), Dr K. R. Sealy (*The Geography of Air Transport*). Other sources of information which we would like to acknowledge with thanks are: British Rail, the British Airports Authority, the Port of London Authority, the Mersey Docks and Harbour Co., the London Brick Company, the Readers' Digest Association, the Central Statistical Office, Goldsmiths' College Geography Department, the town councils of Blackpool, Brighton and Great Yarmouth, the Irish Tourist Board, the Town and Country Planning Association Crawley Development Corporation, British Iron and Steel Federation, National Coal Board, Imperial Chemical Industries, Gas Council, Central Electricity Generating Board, Institute of Petroleum, Scottish Hydro-Electric Board, British Trawler Federation, White Fish Authority, Forestry Commission, Public Record Office, Geographical Field Group, National Parks Commission, the Department of Geography, University of Durham, the Geography Department, Northumberland College of Education, the Town Councils of Hexham and Berwick-upon-Tweed, National Farmers Union, Water Resources Board, Mr Brian Styles and the City of Birmingham Planning Department.
The authors and publishers would like to thank the following for permission to reproduce photographs:

Aerofilms 1.4, 2.3, 3.2, 3.7, 6.3, 8.1, 9.10, 9.11, 15.6, 17.23, 19.2(a), 19.4; *John Alexander* 13.17; *Birmingham Planning Department* 8.3, 8.4; *Brighton Corporation* 19.1; *BOAC* 16.7; *BP* 11.6, 13.10, 13.11; *British Railways Board* 15.10; *British Steel Corporation* 10.1; *Central Electricity Generating Board* 13.28, 13.30; *Director of the Institute of Geological Sciences* 14.8; *Esso* 13.14; *Fairey Surveys Ltd* 1.5, 7.14, 11.7 15.5; *Handford Photography* 7.8, 13.21; *ICI* 12.3; *Irish Tourist Board* 19.5; *Lithograve* 6.2, 8.7; *Liverpool Corporation* 5.9; *London Brick Company Ltd* 14.11(b); *Mersey Docks and Harbour Company* 5.3; *Adolf Morath* 11.3; *NASA* 1.1; *National Coal Board* 13.5, 13.6, 13.7; *Planair* 4.3; *Terence Soames* 10.2; *Harold White* 14.11(a); *White Fish Authority* 18.3, 18.5;

Contents

Preface

In this book, destined for the upper forms of secondary schools, we have abandoned overt regional studies and concentrated on certain themes through which we have attempted to teach in some depth the skills and concepts associated with geography. If we have concentrated on urban areas, industry, sources of power and communications, it is because sc many of the problems facing people in the British Isles today are precisely those associated with the growth of urban areas and the changing pattern of industry. However, such a book cannot hope to be comprehensive so that the various themes are accompanied by sample or case studies rather than by a region by region treatment of the ideas developed. The physical aspects of geography are brought in where they seem relevant, rather than as a series of introductory chapters detached from the main themes.

Wherever possible use is made of primary source material: maps photographs and statistical tables. These are the heart of the book and supply the base material on which teachers will develop their own class-room exercises. Suggestions are made in each chapter for such exercises almost all of which will be answerable from the evidence provided in the text and illustrations. For convenience, the exercises in each chapter have been broken down into two or more groups, the questions in each exercise referring to the text which immediately precedes them. Inevitab ly, the questions differ in degree of difficulty and teachers will have to judge which questions are appropriate for the classes they are teaching Some of the more obviously difficult questions have been marked by an asterisk.

N. J. G
J. T. W

Preface to the Fourth Edition

We have been given the opportunity in this edition to update not only the statistics (when available), but also any maps and diagrams which reflect changes which have occured since 1971 particularly administrative changes and changes in policy. We have also added some material on urban structure (Chapter 7) networks (Chapter 16), and land use (Chapter 17).

* More difficult exercises are marked with an asterisk and may be omitted if necessary.

Part I

Types and Problems of Urban Areas

Chapter One

The Growth in Urban Population

A. Population and Size of the British Isles

The British Isles, shown on Fig. 1.1, are a group of islands consisting of two large islands, Great Britain (England, Wales and Scotland) and Ireland, and a number of surrounding islands such as the Isle of Man. The main political unit, as shown in Fig. 1.2 is the United Kingdom which consists of Great Britain and Northern Ireland, the south of Ireland being an independent state called the Republic of Ireland, or Eire. Each country is divided into counties such as Lancashire, Kent, Northumberland. The areas and populations of various parts of the British Isles are given in Table 1.1.

Table 1.1

Country	Area (km²)	Population (1973)
England	130,374	}49,175,000
Wales	20,765	
Scotland	78,775	5,212,000
Northern Ireland	14,120	1,547,000
Republic of Ireland	68,895	3,029,000
United Kingdom (including islands)	244,034	55,934,000

Source: *Annual Abstract of Statistics.*

You can compare Table 1.1 with Table 1.2 which gives figures of areas and populations of some other countries in Europe.

Table 1.2

Country	Area (km²)	Population (1973)
France	547,026	52,346,000
Netherlands	33,812	13,400,000 (Est)
Spain	504,750	35,000,000 (Est)
Greece	131,956	9,000,000 (Est)
Sweden	449,964	8,144,428
West Germany	248,601	62,201,000

Source: Europe Year Book, 1975.

Fig. 1.1 Satellite photograph of Western Europe and the British Isles

These two tables show you how the United Kingdom's area and population compare with some of our European neighbours.

We think of Great Britain as a very crowded island in which towns join up to form huge sprawling built up areas, in which it is nearly impossible to find a quiet country lane without meeting the inevitable motorist. It is perhaps difficult to realize that in 1086, that is twenty years after William the Conqueror arrived in England, the population of the whole of Great Britain was only about 2.0 millions. Subsequent growth of population in England and Wales was slow. In 1348 it was about 3.75 millions; in 1700 about 5.5 millions, and in 1750 about 6.5 millions. When the first census of population was taken for Great Britain, it revealed a population of 10.5 millions. Table 1.3 shows what has happened since that time.

Table 1.3 Great Britain

Date	1801	1861	1921	1961	1971
Population (millions)	10.5	23.1	42.8	51.3	53.8

By modern standards, England was nearly an empty land in the Middle Ages. The rapid growth in the population which occurred in the 19th century was partly due to a falling off in the death rate owing to improved medical care and sanitation. It was made possible by an increase in the *national income* or *national product*.

The *national income* is the sum total of all incomes earned in the country. You can easily understand that since people earn incomes because they produce goods and services, the more goods and services they produce the greater will be their incomes. In the United Kingdom, the increases which have occurred in the national income

Table 1.4 Europe: Gross National Product in 1972

Gnp (Gross national product)	$ millions	Per capita gnp $ thousands
The six original members of E.E.C.		
West Germany	231	3.7
France	176	3.4
Italy	108	1.9
Belgium	32	3.3
Luxembourg	1	2.9
The Netherlands	42	3.1
	Total 590	3.05 (mean)
The 3 newer members of E.E.C.		
United Kingdom	140	2.5
Ireland	5	1.7
Denmark	19	3.9
	Total 164	2.7 (mean)
The Nine	754	2.9 (mean)

Source: U.N. Statistical Year Book.

in the 19th and 20th centuries were largely due to the development of industry and trade on a larger and larger scale thereby enabling the country to support an increasing population. For, although a smaller proportion of the working population worked on the land as the years went by, food was purchased abroad from such countries as Canada, the U.S.A. and Australia in exchange for the manufactured goods which were being produced in ever increasing quantities. Thus, although very few people work on the land in the United Kingdom today, the population is generally well fed, whereas in a country like India where most people work on the land, many live near to starvation level.

The relative position of the gross national products of various countries of the European Economic Community is shown in Table 1.4.

1. *What is meant by the terms: (a) Great Britain, (b) United Kingdom, (c) British Isles, (d) Republic of Ireland?*

2.* *Study the following list of political and administrative divisions:*

Republic of Ireland	*Powys*	*Tyrone*	*Channel Islands*
Greater London	*Scotland*	*Wales*	*Great Britain*
Outer Hebrides	*Humberside*	*Cork*	*Isle of Man*
Northern Ireland	*Galway*	*Surrey*	*Strathclyde*
United Kingdom	*England*	*Antrim*	*British Isles*

With the help of atlas maps showing the British Isles and counties:

(a) Arrange the list in a series of sets such that a major unit contains all the minor units which can be fitted within it.
For example:

Set 1	*England*	*Set 2*	*Scotland*
	Greater London		*L. . . . .*
	Yorkshire		*O. . . . . .H. . . . . .*
	Surrey		

(b) State which sets will include other sets. For example the set for Great Britain will include the sets for England, Scotland and Wales.

3. *(a) Figure 1.2 shows some of the main ferry services (A to H) between Great Britain and neighbouring countries. Using an atlas to guide you, indicate in your note book the two towns linked by these services in each case and the approximate distance between them and the seas which they cross. For example:*
A – Newcastle to Bergen – 648 km – North Sea
B – Harwich to . . . .
If the ships' average speed is 30 km per hour, how long will each crossing take?

(b) Give the approximate latitudes and longitudes of:
(i) Edinburgh, (ii) Glasgow, (iii) Liverpool, (iv) London.

(c) Name the rivers shown on the map.

Fig. 1.2
The British Isles

4. (a) *From Table 1.1 work out the average* density of population *for each country by dividing the number of people by the area. For example, in England and Wales:*

$$\text{Average density of population} = \frac{49,175,000}{130,374 + 20,765}$$

$$\text{or approximately} = \frac{49,000,000}{151,000}$$

$$= \frac{49,000}{151}$$

$$= 325 \text{ people per square kilometre}$$

(b) *Arrange the list of countries in decreasing order of population density.*

5. (a) *Study Table 1.1 and Table 1.2. What do you notice when you compare the figures for:*

(i) France and the United Kingdom
(ii) Germany and the United Kingdom
(iii) The Netherlands and Scotland
(iv) Greece and England

(b) Is there any obvious relationship between a country's area and its population?

6. (a) From Table 1.3 and the text state how many times greater was the population of Great Britain:
(i) in 1801 compared with 1086 (about 7.0 centuries)
(ii) in 1971 compared with 1801 (about 1.5 centuries)

(b) What was the rate of population growth per century:
(i) between 1086 and 1801
(ii) between 1801 and 1971

(c) Draw a column graph to show Great Britain's population in 1801, 1861, 1921, 1961, 1971 (1 cm = 10 million people).

7. (a) What was the first cause of the rapid growth of population in the United Kingdom in the last 150 years?

(b) What made it possible for this increased population to be fed?

B. Distribution of Population in the British Isles

One of the interesting problems which geographers often study is that which is concerned with the *distribution of population* in any given country. Why is it for instance that most of the population of Australia may be found in the coastal belts of that huge island-continent? Similarly in the British Isles we shall try to find out just where the population is distributed and what factors have influenced this distribution. In discussing these factors we need to make a distinction between 1. *negative factors*, and 2. *positive factors*.

1. Negative factors

These factors are those which in some way or another tend to discourage people from settling in an area. It may be that the relief is mountainous, that the climate is too cold or bleak, that the soils are thin and poor, that there are few mineral resources. For example, there are few people in Central Australia because the climate is so dry that people and animals find it difficult to obtain a water supply – and without this they cannot live.

2. Positive factors

These factors are those which encourage people to settle in and develop an area. Thus gentle relief, good soils, warm and moist climatic conditions will tend to encourage agricultural settlement. Similarly a supply of minerals may stimulate the development of industry and therefore lead to the growth of population in a given area, as for example the supply of coal in various parts of Yorkshire led to the development of various textile and metal industries. You may, however, object that a thickly populated town like London seems to depend on none of the advantages mentioned above. We shall look into this in Chapter 7. Of course, these factors change with time; for example due to improved technical know-how, deserts may become populated, and equatorial rain forests cultivated.

Fig. 1.3 shows the *distribution of population* in the British Isles. It is a very generalized map showing the broad pattern of *population density*. It is not of course accurate in detail; no map on such a scale could be, but it shows up clearly the two extremes of population distribution, that is the areas where there are many people per square kilometre and the areas where there are very few. The two photographs in Fig. 1.4 and Fig. 1.5 show aspects of these two extremes as seen from the air. In Fig. 1.6 one of the factors affecting the distribution of population is illustrated.

The map in Fig. 1.3 leaves out a good deal of very important information. For example we calculated on p. 6 that the average density of population in England was about 325 people per square km, but on the map all high density areas are shown as being over 205

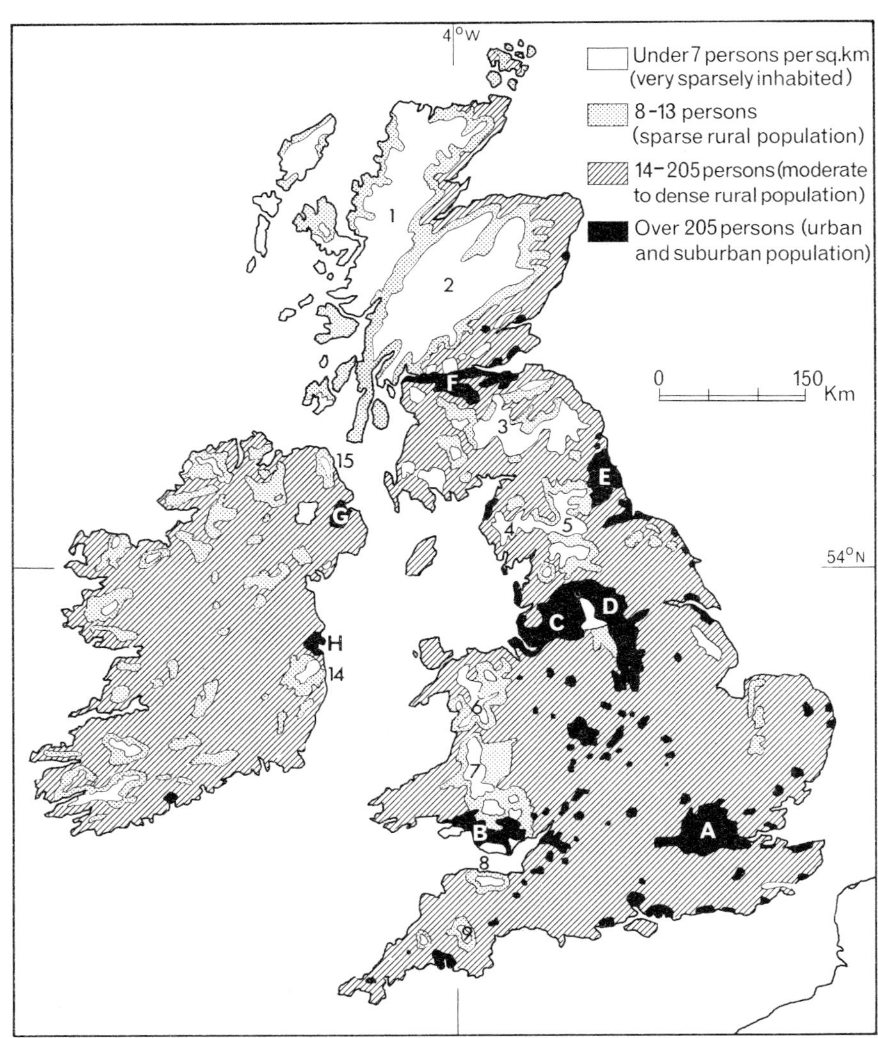

Fig. 1.3 The British Isles: population density

Fig. 1.4
Moorland scene in the Southern Uplands

Fig. 1.5
Central London

people per square km. In fact most of these areas will have population densities well above this figure. Inner London, for example, has a density of population of 10,837 per square km! Further the map suggests, but does not show, that 80 per cent of the United Kingdom's population is classed as 'urban population', i.e. population living in towns. Table 1.5 indicates how Britain stands in comparison with some other countries.

Over and above this about 33 per cent of the total population of England and Wales lives in six big urban areas called conurbations – these are: Greater London (7.3 millions), South-East Lancashire (2.8 millions), West Midlands (2.8 millions), West Yorkshire (2.1 millions), Merseyside (1.7 millions), Tyneside (1.2 millions). In Scotland 35 per cent of the population lives in Central Clydeside (1.7 millions). In Ireland the Dublin urban area has 0.7 million people and the Belfast urban area 0.5 million. Thus population in the British Isles and in particular in Great Britain is much more concentrated in certain areas than would appear at first sight. We shall now work out in some detail what this population distribution is and how relief has influenced it.

8. *Study Fig. 1.3 and an atlas map of the British Isles and*

(a) name the areas of dense population labelled A to H

(b) on an outline map of Great Britain plot in the correct place circles which are proportioned to the size of each conurbation. The drawing of these* proportional circles *may be done as follows:*

(i) find the square root of each conurbation's population,
e.g. Greater London: 7.3 millions
Square root of 7.3 = 2.702
(This number may be obtained by using a square root table or by using logarithms)
e.g. Tyneside: 1.2 millions
Square root of 1.2 = 1.1

(ii) The square roots now represent the radii of the circles to be drawn. Since 2.702 and 1.1 are the largest and smallest values for the conurbations a scale in centimeters may be appropriate. If we try 1 unit of radius = 0.5 centimeters, then: Greater London's radius = 2.702 × 0.5 = 1.351 cms or 1.4 cms approximately.
Tyneside's radius = 1.1 × 0.5 = 0.55, or 0.6 cms approximately. Thus Greater London and Tyneside may be represented by the circles shown in Fig. 1.7.

It is necessary to find the square root of the population because the area of a circle is proportional to the square of the radius ($A = \pi r^2$). Your sketch will begin to look like Fig. 1.8 and it should have a scale as shown on Fig. 1.9.

(c) Which parts of the British Isles are very sparsely populated? (Mention large areas, e.g. North Scotland.)

Table 1.5

Country	% of population classed as urban
Australia	82
United Kingdom	80
Canada	70
U.S.A.	70
Japan	64
Netherlands	60
France	56
U.S.S.R.	48
Italy	45
Switzerland	42
Norway	32
Kenya	5

(Source: Hall P., *World Cities*)

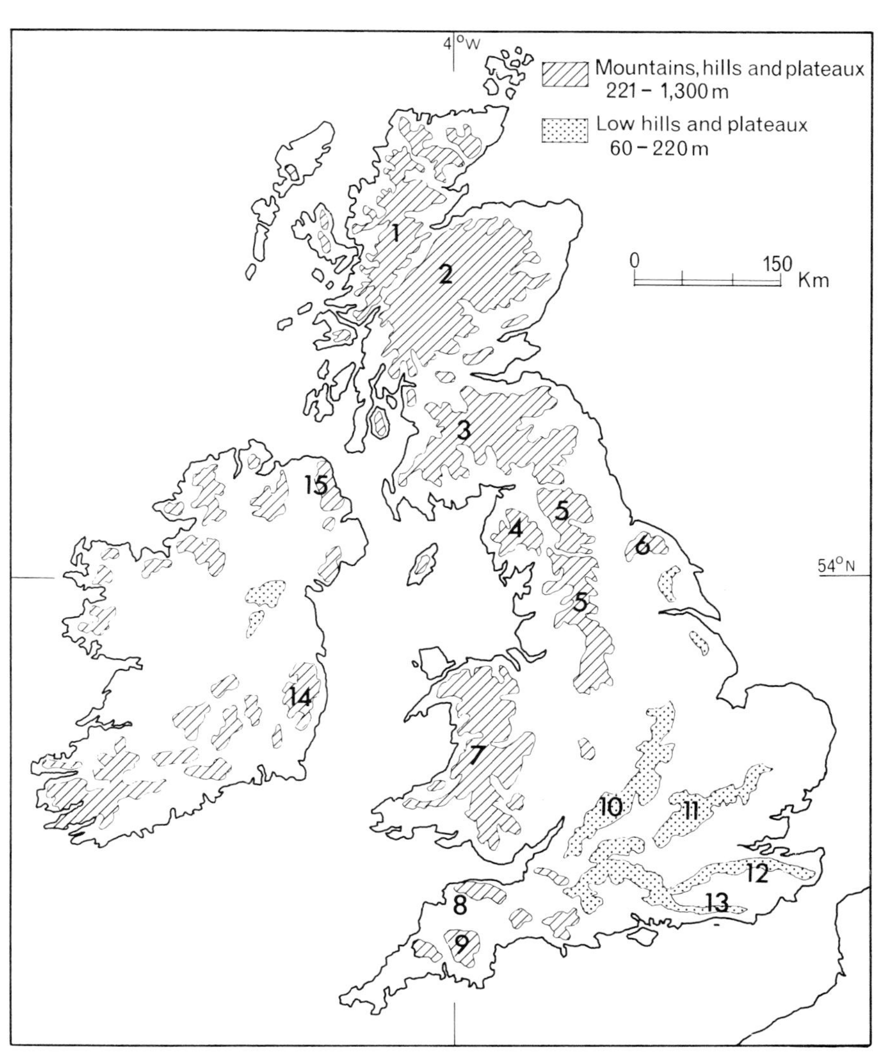

Fig. 1.6 The British Isles: relief

Fig. 1.7 Proportional circles to represent population

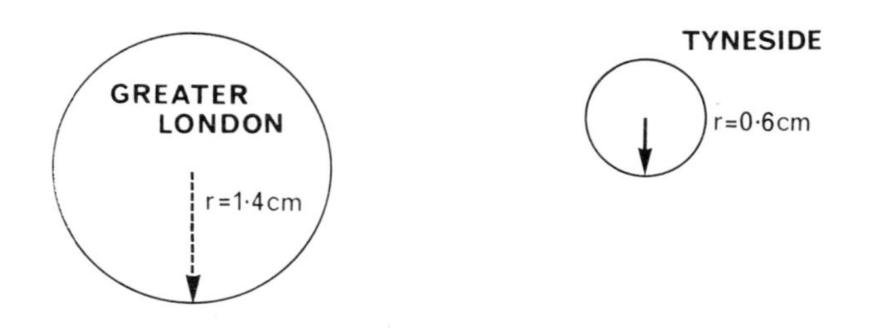

9. (a) *Using the physical map of the British Isles from your atlas, name the areas of highland marked 1 to 15 on Fig. 1.6.*
   (b) *Which of these areas are (i) very sparsely populated, (ii) moderately populated?*
   (c) *Suggest reasons to explain your answer to (b).*
   (d) *Which areas of relatively low land are sparsely populated?*
10. (a) *Basing your answer on the photographs in Figs. 1.4 and 1.5 describe carefully a typical area of (i) low population density, (ii) high population density.*
    (b) *Which of these two photographs suggests where 80 per cent of the British population live?*
11. (a) *From Table 1.5 draw column graphs to show the percentage of the population living in towns (use 1 cm for 10 per cent).*
    (b) *Which of these countries are important industrial countries?*
    (c) *What connection is there between an industrial country and the percentage of its population living in towns?*
12.* *Indicate in what way Fig. 1.3 may be misleading.*

Fig. 1.8

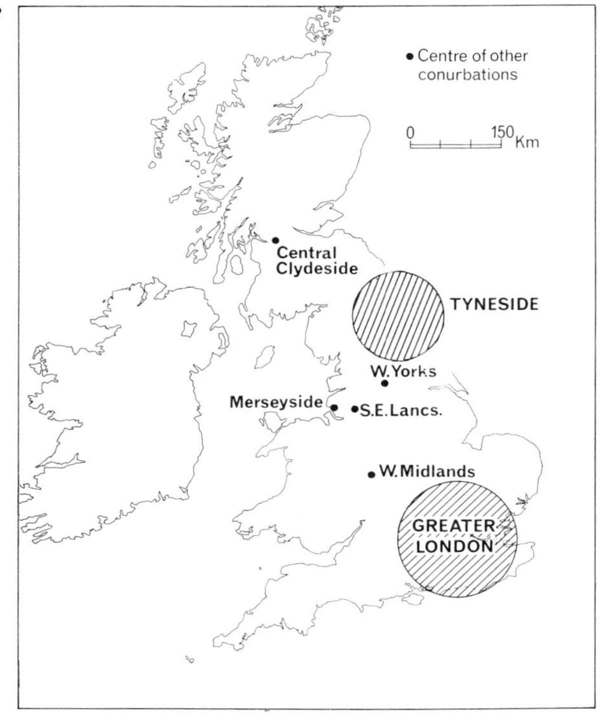

The pattern of urban living which is revealed in the text and in the map (Fig. 1.3) has not always been the case in Great Britain. To go back no further than 1801, only 16.9 per cent of the population in England could be classed as urban. But by 1891 this had changed to 53.7 per cent, and in 1931 it had reached 80 per cent. This is why the following chapters are concerned with various types of towns, for we may as well learn something about the places 80 per cent of the population have to live in.

REVISION EXERCISES

13. ***The United Kingdom forms a political unit governed from London. What are the names of four similar political units surrounding the U.K.: one to the west, one to the north-west, one to the south and one to the east? (See a map of Europe in your atlas.)***

14. ***What is the average density of population in England and Wales and how does this compare with other parts of the British Isles?***

Fig. 1.9 Proportional circle scale

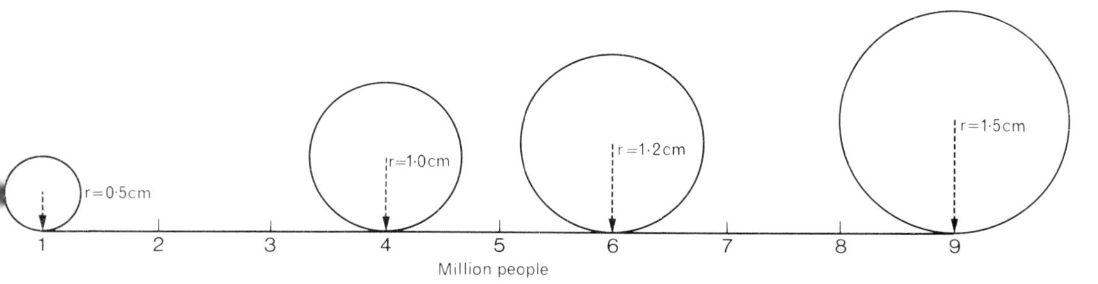

15. ***Describe the distribution of population in the British Isles (Fig. 1.3).***

16. ***What changes have occurred in the proportion of the population living in towns in England since 1801?***

17. ***In which conurbations do over 33.3 per cent of the people in England and Wales live? (Fig. 1.3 and atlas.)***

18. ***In what way has high relief influenced the distribution of population in the British Isles? Is this a negative or a positive factor?***

*19.** ***What positive factors do you think have encouraged people to live in towns?***

*20.** ***What does Table 1.4 tell you about the relative positions of the United Kingdom's gross national product (or gross national income) and gross national product per head of populations within the European Economic Community (E.E.C. or Common Market)?***

Fig. 1.10

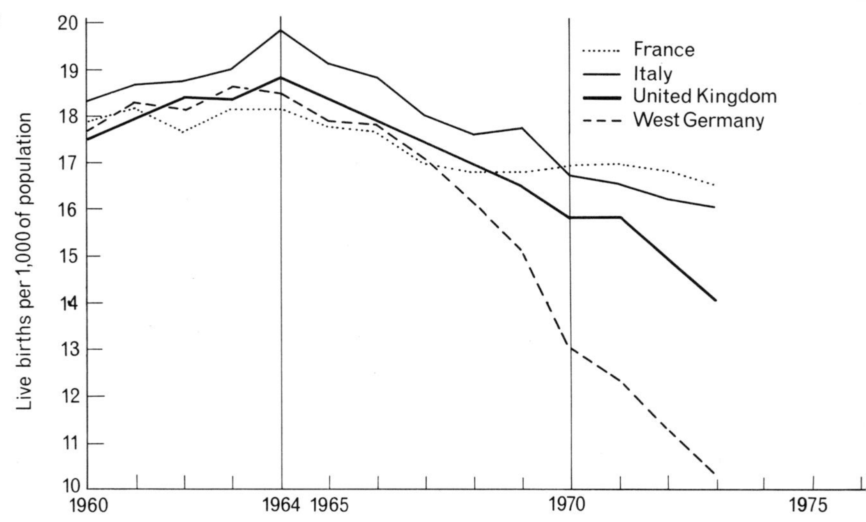

21.* *State what Figure 1.10 tells you about the respective birth rates of four countries in Western Europe. Could you safely predict what will happen to the total populations of France, Italy, United Kingdom and West Germany on the basis of the information in the graph? Give reasons for your answer.*

22.* *In which countries is the demand for teachers in the late 1970's likely to fall heavily?*

23.* *How may demographers (those who study population) decide whether a person should be counted as belonging to the urban or to the rural population?*

Chapter Two

The Market Town

A. Origins

The growth of the population of the British Isles is closely connected with the growth of *urban areas*. Many of the problems we face today are due to this growth, the loss of *rural land* and the depopulation of the countryside. To understand such problems, we need to study the origin and growth of towns and cities. Even the largest, such as London, had small beginnings.

Some places on the surface of our land have proved more convenient than others as meeting places. Situated at cross-roads, at river crossings, by gaps through hills, they have developed as natural meeting places. If we study the reasons for people needing to meet each other, we are, in some way, studying the growth of towns. Think, for a moment, of the reasons why you like living in a town or, if you live in the country, why you like visiting the town. It is often to buy things, whether they be goods, or services or entertainment. The shops are one of the great attractions: in earlier days, the market. Thus market towns were the first important '*central places*' to develop.

The word '*market*' is derived from the Latin 'mercari', to trade. A market is a place where people who wish to sell things meet people who wish to buy things. Many towns grew up around market places. Often they were granted market rights by the Crown: between the years 1199 and 1483, the right to hold a weekly market was granted to 2,800 places. Your local town hall or library can usually tell you when your own town gained its market charter. Many towns still retain the word 'market' in their name, such as Market Harborough in Leicestershire. The word 'chipping', which is Scandinavian in origin, also indicates a market, as in Chipping Norton.

The old market place is still to be found in the centre of many towns, suggesting that the town grew up around the market activities. But market day may no longer see the place full of cattle, sheep, poultry, fruit, cheeses, butter and other produce, as it once did. More and more the functions of the old market have been taken over by the modern shopping centre. In place of the market held once a week, we have the shops, as a market, open for six days of the week. It is interesting that the most modern stores are frequently called 'supermarkets'. The decline of the old markets is due to several factors but the growth of permanent shops in place of temporary stalls is one of the most important. Of 21 places in Worcestershire

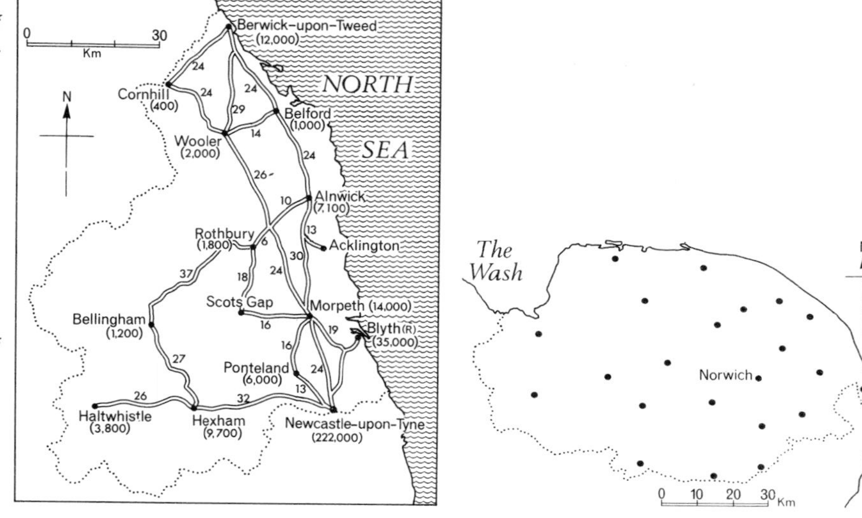

Fig. 2.1 Market towns of Northumberland. The following still have retail markets: Berwick, Alnwick, Hexham, Haltwhistle, Newcastle, Morpeth, Blyth (Road distances in kilometres)

Fig. 2.2 Market towns of Norfolk

that once held the rights of weekly market, only 8 are shown a market towns in modern gazetteers and only 5 retain their livestoc market, according to the *Atlas of Britain*. Fig. 2.1 shows the marke towns of one English county, Northumberland, in some detail whils Fig. 2.2 shows the pattern of market towns in Norfolk. These ar two of the largest counties in England (5,141 and 5,259 square km respectively), one in the north with a considerable area of hill lan and the other in the east with no hill land. The map of Northumber land shows that of the fifteen places named only seven retain thei retail produce market, whereas all but one have some sort of live stock market. The population of the towns is quoted and it will b seen that it is in the smaller towns that the retail produce marke is dying out.

Also shown on Fig. 2.1 are the distances between the markets. Th average distance apart is about 24 km. They are unevenly sprea over the county whereas the pattern of markets in Norfolk is muc more regular. Even in Norfolk, there are more markets in the easter half than in the western half of the county, perhaps indicating tha the eastern half is more fertile and more populated. The fact tha there are 22 markets shown in Norfolk as against 15 in Northumber land, a county of comparable size, may suggest that Norfolk is o the whole a more fertile county, but we would have to have muc more information about the types of markets before we could com to any justifiable conclusion.

1. *Make a list of the towns you can find in the encyclopaedia o gazetteers (such as the handbooks of the motoring organizations with the words 'market' and 'chipping' in their names.*
2. *Suggest reasons:*
   (a) Why the markets of Norfolk are more evenly spaced than thos of Northumberland.

(b) *Why there are large areas of west and north-west Northumberland without markets. Reference to an atlas map will help with this question.*

3. (a) *What is the shortest distance shown between markets in Northumberland?*
   (b) *What is the longest distance shown between markets in Northumberland?*
4. (a) *How would people have travelled to market before the invention of the internal combustion engine?*
   (b) *Can you estimate how long it would have taken them to travel an average of 12 km to market?*
5. *Why have the small, local markets declined and, in many cases, ceased?*

B. Hexham: a market town

One of the market towns shown in Fig. 2.1 is Hexham, with a population of nearly 10,000 people. Its livestock market is one of the most important in northern England. Sales take place at the auction marts four days a week and cattle are brought from as far away as Ireland via Liverpool docks. As many as 2,000 head of cattle have been auctioned in one day. In one day, I saw lorries from Wooler in the north, Carlisle and Penrith in the west, Northallerton and Knaresborough in Yorkshire. Many special firms have grown up by the markets supplying farm machinery, fertilisers, seeds, feedstuffs and, not least, advice and services to farmers. Even the inns have special licensing hours for people attending market.

The old market grew up at the gates of the Abbey and probably started under the protection of the abbot and monks. The market cross, which is still to be seen in many towns, has now gone but on market days the place is still crowded with stallholders selling a great variety of produce. The car parks are full and the bus station busy. Information from the bus timetable has been mapped in Fig. 2.5, showing all the bus routes and the frequency of buses from outlying places to Hexham. Bellingham, for example, has eight buses a day whereas Kirkheaton has only one bus a week, on Tuesday, the main market day. Towns like Hexham which supply services for the surrounding areas are sometimes known by geographers as *central places* or *service centres*.

Fig. 2.3 is an aerial view of the town taken by an aircraft approaching from the east. The simplified map of the town centre, Fig. 2.4, will help you to identify the main features of the place. The Seal, for example, is the large open space in the background while the open fields in the right foreground are shown on the map as car parks. The air photograph was taken before the car park was constructed.

Fig. 2.3 Hexham in Northumberland

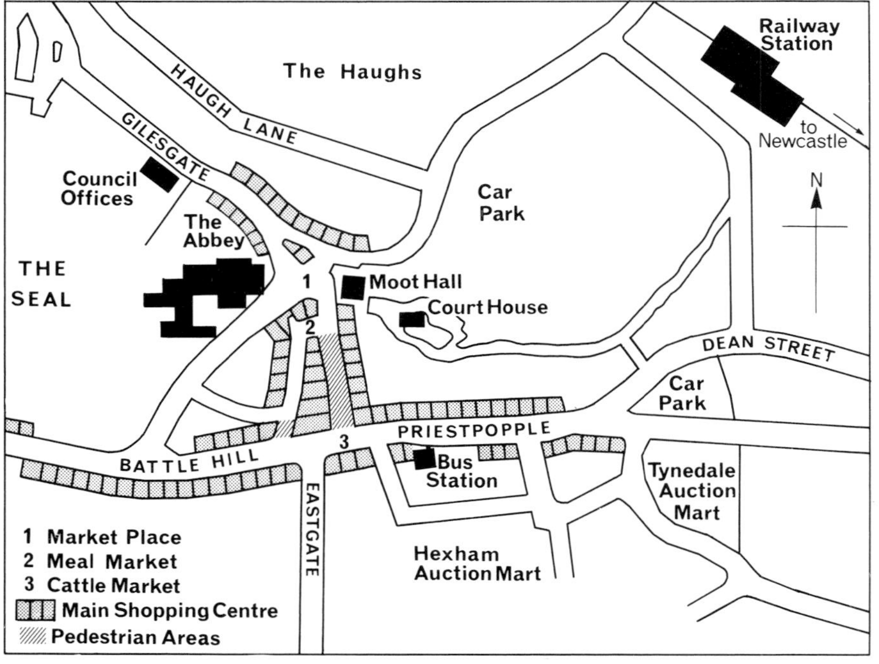

Fig. 2.4 Hexham

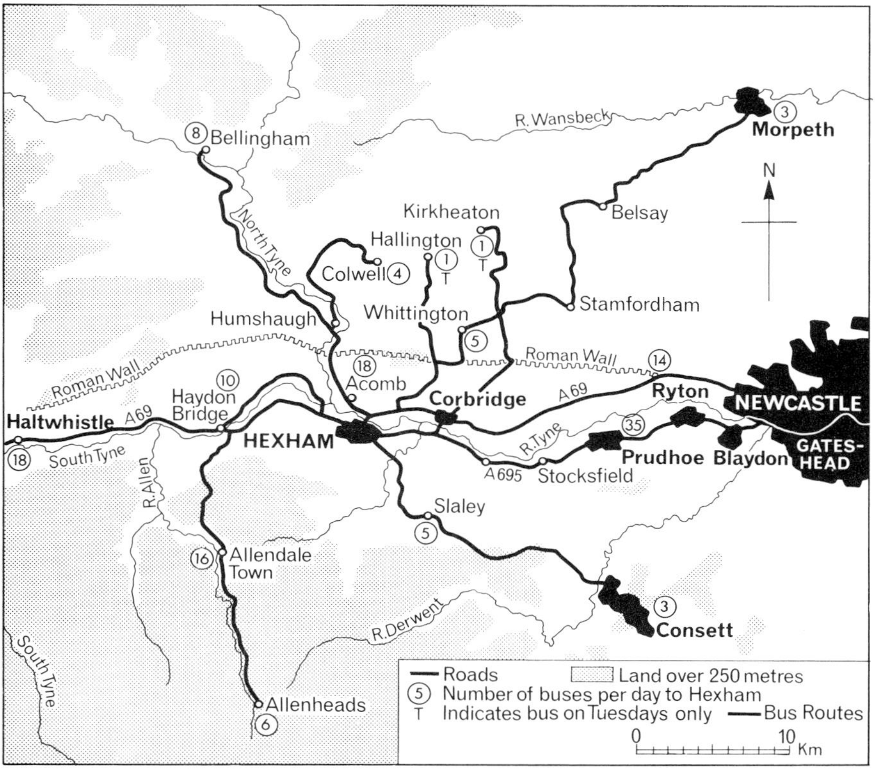

Fig. 2.5
Hexham: communications

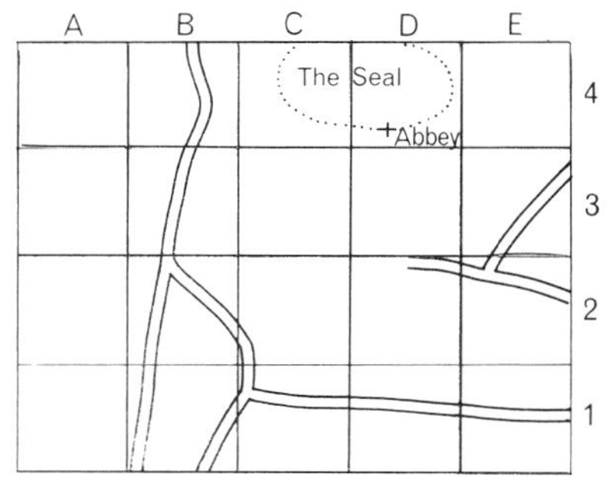

Fig. 2.6
Map drawn from Fig. 2.3

6. *Make your own copy of the aerial photograph as in Fig. 2.6, or make a tracing of the original and on it indicate:*
   (a) the Abbey
   (b) the old market place in front of the Abbey
   (c) the congested area of the old town
   (d) the section of the main road called the Cattle Market
   (e) the two modern auction marts, including the pens for the livestock
   (f) the railway yards by the station
   (g) a new housing estate
   (h) allotments and market gardens

7. *Having studied the photograph, can you now suggest reasons why the town council is now planning to move the cattle and sheep market, from its site on the main road down to the flat land by the railway station?*
8. *Why have the fields in the photograph been transformed into car parks shown on the map?*
9. *What do you notice about the position of the main shopping centre?*
10. *Using Fig. 2.5 decide:*
   (a) Which are the five busiest bus routes to Hexham?
   (b) What distance do people travel to market from (i) Bellingham, (ii) Allenheads, (iii) Kirkheaton?
   (c) As the land over 240 m is often affected by snow and icy conditions, which bus routes are most likely to be affected in winter?

REVISION EXERCISES

11. ***With the aid of an atlas, make a map of Northern England showing the area that supplies Hexham livestock market, based on information given in this chapter.***
12. ***If there is a livestock market in your own area, make a study of it, using some of the methods shown in this chapter.***
13. ***Are there any street names in your area that show that markets were once held there? If there are what are these names?***
14. ***If there is a street market surviving in your area, make a study of the type of produce that is for sale and list especially the produce that is brought in from the countryside, what we might term farm produce.***
15. ***If you have a map available on a scale of 1/2500 make a study of your local shopping centre. First of all, mark in those buildings that have become shops, as has been done for Hexham (Fig. 2.4). Then make a count of all the shops and classify them according to the goods they have for sale.***
    For example:

Grocers	***6***	***Hardware***	***1***
Butchers	***2***	***Chemist***	***1***
Confectioners	***5***	***Bakers***	***2***

16. ***Find out more about the origin of markets and market towns from a good encyclopaedia.***

Chapter Three

The Growth of Cities

A. County Towns and Cathedral Cities

A simple comparison of the population figures for the market towns mapped in Northumberland and Norfolk in the previous chapter shows that, in terms of population, some towns are much more important than others. Hexham, with 10,000 inhabitants, is typical of many Northumbrian market towns; but Blyth, with 36,000, is considerably bigger and Newcastle-upon-Tyne is by far the biggest city in the county, with more than 0.25 million people.

In Norfolk, some of the market towns are very small, varying from just over 2,000 at Watton to 9,000 at Dereham and 13,000 at Thetford. In contrast, Kings Lynn has nearly 30,000, Great Yarmouth over 50,000 and Norwich over 121,000 inhabitants. In this chapter, we shall start to enquire why certain towns and cities grow more quickly, and achieve greater importance than others.

Of the towns named above having greater populations, Kings Lynn, Great Yarmouth, Blyth and Newcastle-upon-Tyne are all ports and their growth is partly due to their port facilities and shipping activities. The question of ports will be dealt with later in Chapter 5. The two outstanding places, Norwich and Newcastle-upon-Tyne, the biggest in their respective counties, are both county towns, the centres of administration for the counties, and offer many more services to a wider area than the simple market town, such as Hexham. They have larger shopping facilities, entertainment, education, welfare services and government. They each have a cathedral.

Before going any further in our study of these special *central places* we must have a closer look at two words that have cropped up several times and can lead to confusion, the words *town* and *city*. The word *city*, in its origin, is associated with places of special status, such as the seat of bishops and towns that have received 'city charters' from the Crown. In Scotland, many important towns have the status of 'royal burgh'. One of the most important buildings associated with cities is the cathedral (the word is taken from the Greek 'cathedra', meaning a bishop's chair). The origin of many cities is linked with the growth of the Christian church and many cathedrals were built during the 12th and 13th centuries. Some cathedral cities are now comparatively unimportant, but most cathedrals were built in places that have been of importance for many centuries, at the meeting of routeways, in areas of great fertility, at natural meeting places for many people. The location of English cathedral cities is shown on Fig. 3.1. There is a tendency now to use the word *city* to mean a place of special importance, of greater importance than the usual *town*. It is very difficult to draw a hard and fast line between them.

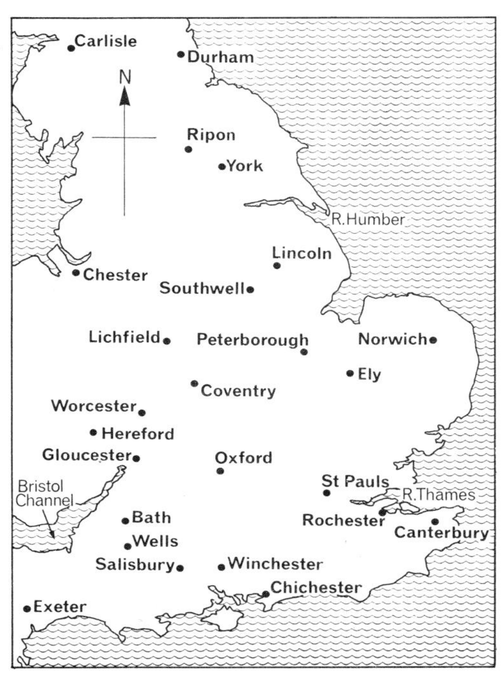

Fig. 3.1 The older English cathedral cities

B. The City of Durham

A fine example of an historic *city* which is still a 'central place' of great importance is Durham. With a population of over 23,000, it was by no means the largest place in the former County of Durham; there are several ports, such as Sunderland and South Shields, and industrial towns, such as Darlington, that are greater in size. But Durham is in the centre of the county and its administrative offices are situated there. This makes it the *county town* of Durham.

The aerial photograph, Fig. 3.2 shows the centre of the city, with its magnificent cathedral, the castle, the market place and the university buildings in close proximity. The city has a natural defensive *site* created by the deeply-incised meander of the river Wear. This natural defensive *site* was supported by a wall; the castle protects the one weak spot, the approach along the narrow neck of land from the north.

Before the by-pass of the A1 was constructed, the Great North Road went through the city. The steep narrow streets caused traffic jams and made life in the old city unpleasant. Since the air photograph was taken, a new footbridge has been built to the east and a new main road-bridge has been opened across the narrow neck of the 'peninsula' just to the north of St Nicholas' Church by the market place. The map of the city centre, Fig. 3.3 will help you to identify the buildings and bridges mentioned so far. Traffic across the old bridges used to be controlled by a policeman sitting in the market place with television cameras showing him the traffic approaching each bridge. The by-pass to the west and the new by-pass being opened up to the east have made this less necessary but the many services offered still make this a very busy place. Local people not only come for shopping, for the university, for the cathedral and to use the many facilities of the city but also for the annual Durham Miners' Gala. This is one of the great festivals of the year when miners from all over the county take over the city from early morning to late at night, with brass bands and dancing in the streets and a fair down by the river.

The problems faced by a medieval city, confined within old walls, with the need for modernization and expansion are very great. There is a need to preserve the past, not only for its own sake but also for the tourist trade it brings in. But the city authorities have to give

Fig. 3.2
The central core of Durham from the north

the citizens the employment possibilities and the facilities they require in the present time. Fig. 3.4 shows the pattern of recent growth. Much of it is due to rapid expansion of the University (which even uses the Castle) and to the clearance of poor-quality housing from the older, central areas. Also, new industrial and commercial enterprises have been stimulated by the government in an attempt to compensate for the decline of traditional industries, such as coal-mining.

Fig. 3.3 Durham (left)

Fig. 3.4 The development of Durham (right)

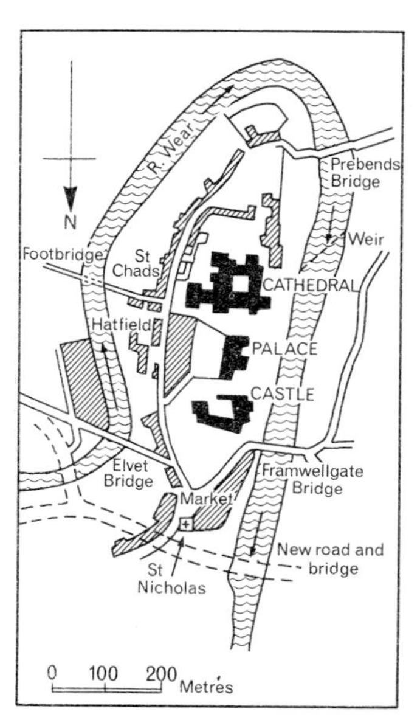

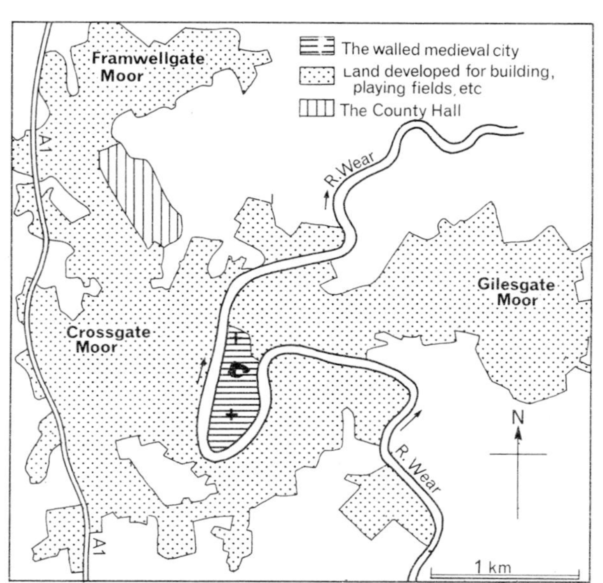

1. *Using methods similar to those used in the analysis of Hexham, study the aerial photograph of the City of Durham (Fig. 3.2) and identify the following features:*
   (a) the Cathedral
   (b) the Castle
   (c) the market place
   (d) St Nicholas' Church
   (e) the river Wear (and mark with an arrow the direction you think the water is flowing)
   (f) the bridges.
2. *How far is it (a) from east to west across the heart of the old city on the line of the cathedral?*
   (b) from Elvet Bridge to Framwellgate Bridge?
3. *Why was the castle built on the north side of the old city?*
4. *What proof can you find in this chapter that there was once a wall round the city?*
5. *How far is it now from the Cathedral to the furthest point of the built-up area shown in Fig. 3.4?*
6. *Compare the size of the old city with the size of the new adminis-*

trative area in which the new County Hall has been built. What do you notice in the comparison?

7. *Why do you think Durham has grown so strongly towards the west and north-west?*

8. *Suggest reasons why there has been less growth of the city to the north and south along the river Wear.*

9. *With the aid of an atlas, draw your own map of the County of Durham showing the county boundary, the coast, the river Wear and the City of Durham, the main road system and rail links as far as they are shown in the atlas. Add a scale to the map.*

0. *As a result of drawing the map of the County, do you think the City of Durham is well-situated as the administrative centre of the County? If your answer is 'no', where would you have established the county town?*

1. *What do you understand by the phrase 'the site of a city'?*

:. Canterbury

ome historians suggest that the idea of cities was introduced into ıe British Isles by the Romans. Certainly, many cities can trace ıeir history back to the Roman period; many have actual remains f Roman walls, roads and buildings. The *sites* that the Romans hose for their administrative and military rule in Britain were so ell chosen that many have remained important ever since. Their oad system that linked the main centres (see Fig. 3.5) shows many imilarities to the present pattern of main roads. The A2, for example, nce Watling Street, is still one of the busiest routeways in the

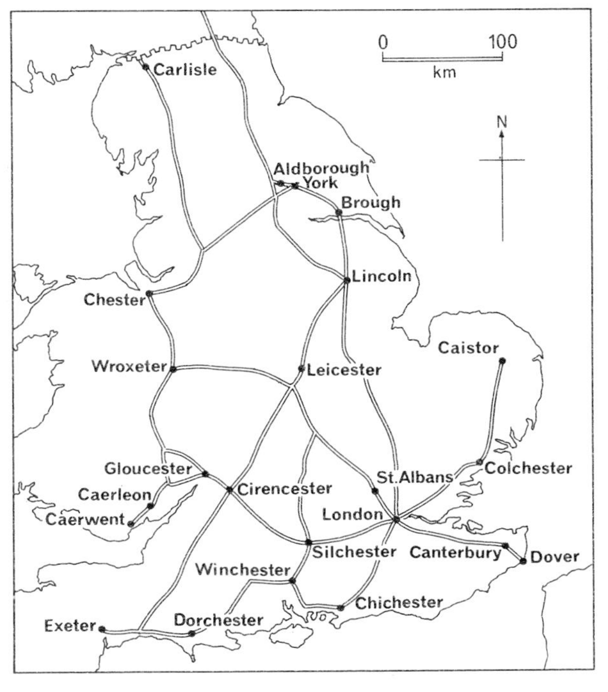

Fig. 3.5 Roman capitals, legionary fortresses and 'colonies'

country; though many parts of it are being by-passed by the construction of the M2.

It was on the great highway from the Channel ports to London that we now call the A2 that the City of Canterbury grew up. (See Fig 3.6.) Now a population centre of more than 32,000 people, it grew

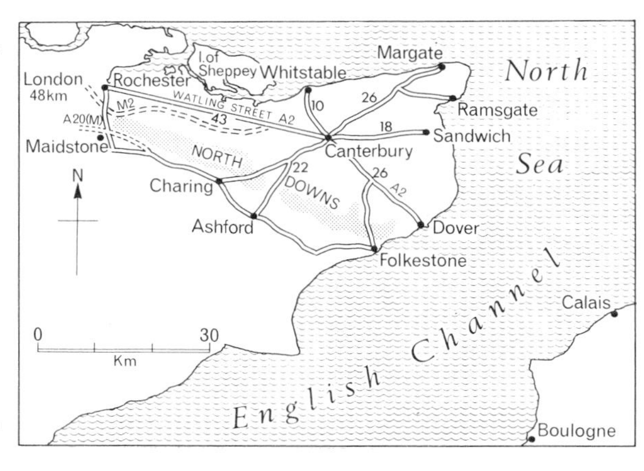

Fig. 3.6 The position of Canterbury

Fig. 3.7 Canterbury from the north

up on a Roman site at the crossing of the river Stour, to the north of the gap that the river cuts through the North Downs. It grew quickly into one of the most important centres of Christian culture in the British Isles and a centre of pilgrimage after the death of Thomas à Becket in the great cathedral. Unlike Durham, little remains of its castle but much of the medieval wall remains, round which many car parks have been situated, on what was once the moat. It is not the *county town* of Kent, but it was chosen as the site of the new University of Kent. It is a sufficiently important central place to need new shopping and entertainment facilities; these are being catered for in new developments taking place in parts of the old city that were destroyed by bombing in the last war. The aerial photograph, Fig. 3.7, shows many of these features, which are also indicated on the map of the city centre, Fig. 3.8. The redevelopment of historic cities like Canterbury can change the character of the place, 'spoil' it in many peoples' view. A multi-storey car-park may be useful but it looks out of place alongside a cathedral. A new shopfront can alter the look of a street. Individual buildings such as the Cathedral and the Castle are protected as *listed buildings* by the Department of the Environment. Under new legislation large areas of towns are protected as *conservation areas*. Canterbury within the walls is one such area. So is the old centre of Durham (Fig. 3.2).

12. How far is it round the walls of the city?

13. Name one of the ancient gateways to the city.

14. What proof is there on the map that there was once a castle in the city?

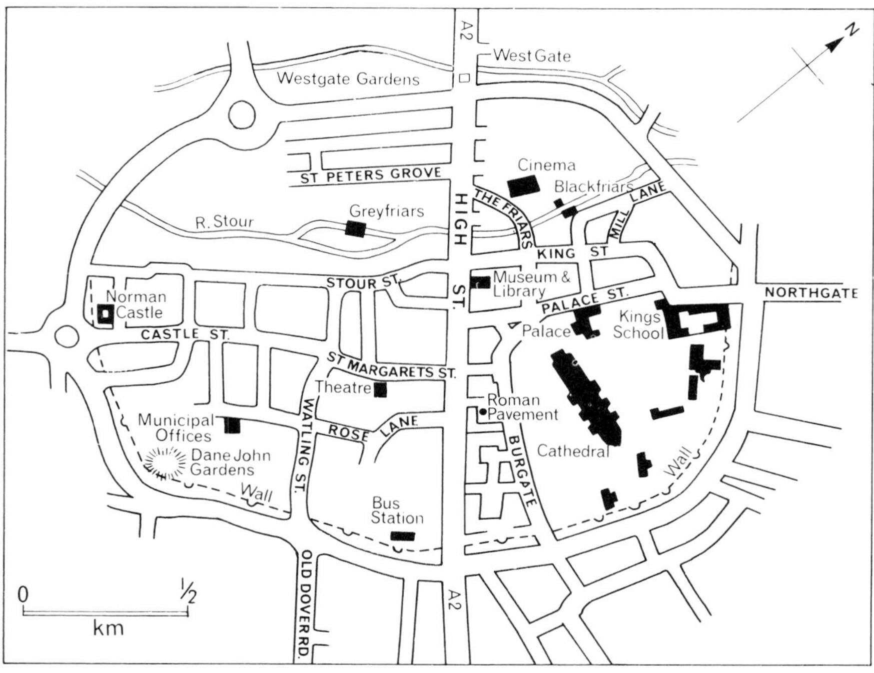

Fig. 3.8
The walled city of Canterbury

15. *What proof is there that the city originated at least as early as the Roman period?*

16. *Suggest some of the reasons that led to the growth of Canterbury as* a central place.

REVISION EXERCISES

17. ***All the towns and cities studied in detail so far have been situated by rivers. Suggest reasons why rivers are important in the siting of towns and cities.***

18. ***List the 'services' that*** **central places** ***like Durham and Canterbury offer to their own inhabitants and the people from surrounding districts. Many have been mentioned in the last two chapters.***

19. ***In many cities, the following important buildings and open spaces are found close together:***

    (a) Town Hall
    (b) Market
    (c) Castle
    (d) Cathedral or Abbey
    (e) Technical College or College of Further Education
    (f) University.

    Make a diagram with your own school at the centre and show the distance you must travel to the nearest of each of the above buildings and spaces. Fig. 3.9 shows an example of this exercise from a London school.

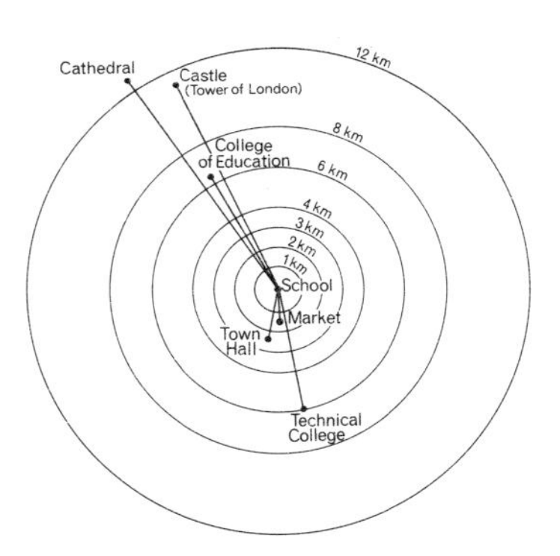

Fig. 3.9
Link diagram for a London school

20. ***Here are six more*** **central places** ***similar in type to Durham and Canterbury:***

    (a) York
    (b) Lincoln
    (c) Chester
    (d) Gloucester
    (e) Winchester
    (f) Norwich.

    With the aid of an encyclopaedia or one of the guides of the motoring organizations, find out the present population figures for each of these centres. How do they compare with Durham's 23,000 and Canterbury's 32,000?

21. ***Select a county town of your own choice and make a special study of it to find out what services it provides. (a) One of the***

six cities mentioned in 20 above may be used. A good encyclopaedia will help to give you a start; guide books may be obtained from the Town Clerk of the place concerned.
(b) In what way has it changed since about 1500 A.D.?

2. *Which of the older cathedral cities shown on Fig. 3.1 are no longer important* central places *and have small populations below 15,000?*

Chapter Four

Capital Cities

A. Capitals and Nations

Among the many towns and cities that are found throughout th
British Isles are a few that have developed to such an extent that the
act as *the central place* for an area even greater than a county. B
reason of their special position, their historic growth and the service
they offer, they have become administrative centres of entire regior
of the British Isles.

The most obvious example is London itself, the largest city in th
land and the *capital* of the United Kingdom. This will be studied i
detail in Chapter 7. But there are other cities that may be said t
be *capital cities*. The United Kingdom, with the Union Jack as it
flag, was the result of the Act of Union in 1707 when the crowns c
Scotland and England finally merged as one. The 'kingdoms' tha
comprise the United Kingdom still preserve much of their sense c
separateness and many areas still use languages other than Englis
in their day-to-day lives. Recent years have seen the revival c
nationalist feeling and demands for greater independence, especiall
in Scotland and Wales. Even small areas such as the Isle of Man an
the Channel Islands jealously guard those aspects of their lives th
make them independent of England, in such matters, for exampl
as tax laws.

Even within the most populated country, England, there are co
siderable differences in speech between people in different regio
and a person from the West Country may have difficulty in unde
standing someone from Yorkshire. The regions have their roots i
the old Saxon kingdoms, such as Wessex, Mercia and Northumbri
but few people seriously consider themselves as anything other tha
English. Nevertheless, certain cities of England, such as York, we
once capitals of independent kingdoms. Fig. 4.1 shows the separat
nations or parts of nations that became united into our prese
Kingdom, together with the 'capital' cities. Table 1.1 shows th
population and size of the same areas.

B. Edinburgh: its Growth

Edinburgh is one of several cities that have been the *capital* of th
independent kingdom of Scotland. Situated just south of 56 degre
North, it is one of the most northerly capital cities in the world.

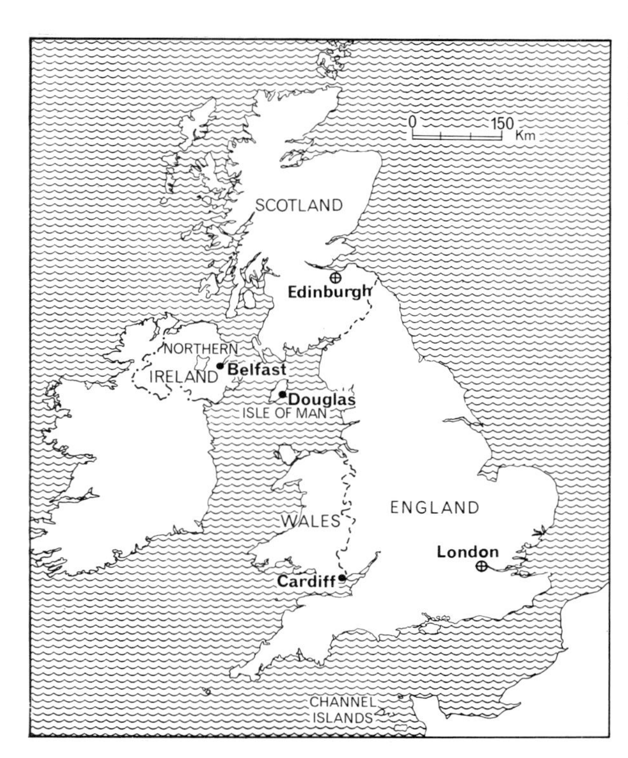

Fig. 4.1 Political divisions of the United Kingdom

ies in the Central Lowlands of Scotland on the south side of the Firth f Forth. On atlas maps it often appears to be a port. In fact, the ity grew up on a sheer-sided outcrop of volcanic rock two miles rom the sea: the port of Leith developed to serve Edinburgh.

The Castle Rock offered a fine *defensive site* which guarded the asiest route into Scotland from the south-east. In the beginning, the ity or burgh occupied only the flat summit of the Castle Rock. Then he city grew down the one gentle slope, to the east. The high street hat developed is still the main street of the Old Town and is known enerally as the Royal Mile, joining the great Castle to the Royal 'alace of Holyrood at its foot. The Palace was built on what was nce a monastery: that is why the lower end of the Royal Mile is alled Canongate. The Old Town was a walled city and the danger of ttack, especially from the English, forced the city to grow upwards ather than outwards. The tall, many-storied buildings of the high treet are now being carefully renovated and developed to preserve he unique appearance of the Royal Mile.

The overcrowding of the Old Town eventually forced the burgh o grow outside the old walls: the marshy ground to the north was ridged in the 18th century and a new town was planned and built n farmland with wide, straight streets, crescents, squares and eleant houses. In spite of the usual traffic problems and the developlent of Princes Street and George Street as main shopping centres, le New Town still retains its elegance and calm and much of it now a conservation area.

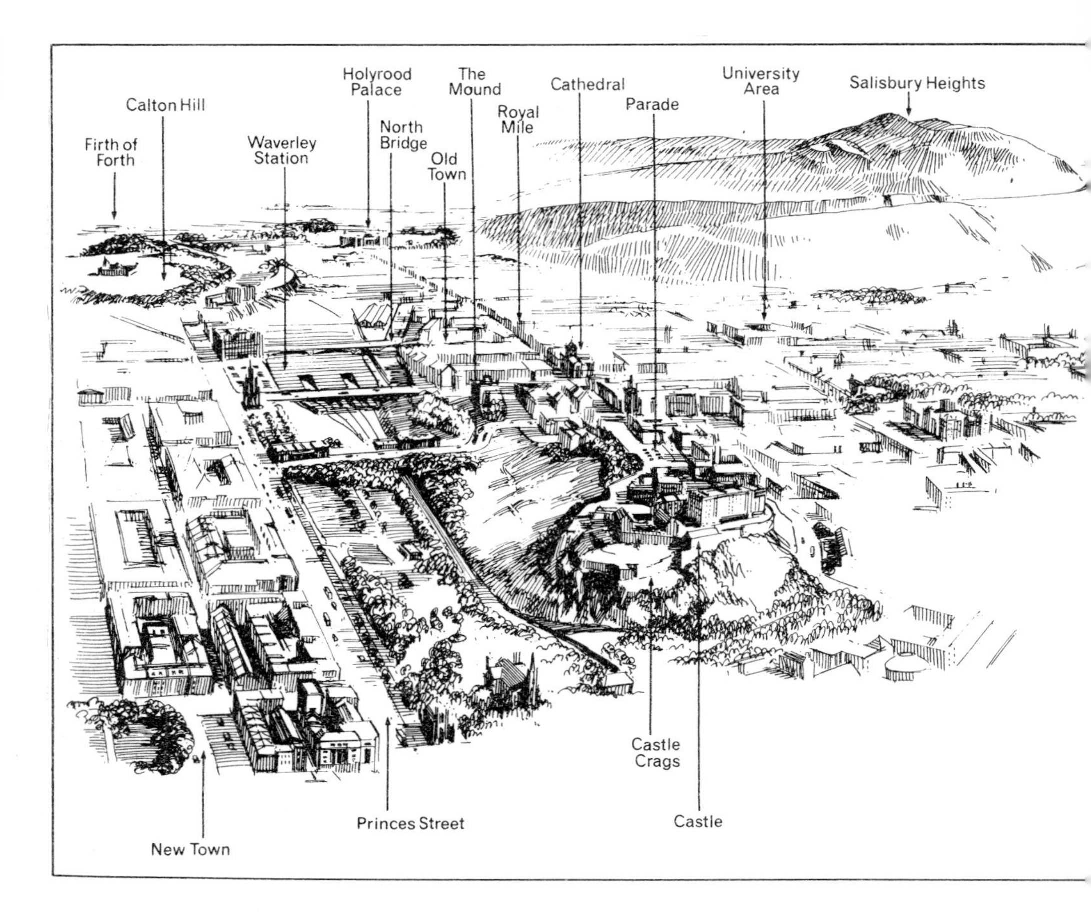

Fig. 4.2 Sketch of central Edinburgh

The 19th century saw the railway arrive and two railway station were built in the marshy ground between the Old and New Town New industries and housing areas grew with the railway an Edinburgh and Leith grew into one urban area.

This brief history of the scottish Capital can be followed dram tically in the aerial photograph, Fig. 4.3, which is taken from th west end of Princes Street. The simplified plans of the city centr Fig. 4.4 and Fig. 4.5 will help you to identify the main features of th photograph.

1. *Either by using the 'frame' method, as with Hexham, or by mear of a sketch (with tracing paper laid over the photograph), identi the following stages in the growth of Edinburgh: (See Figs. 4.2, 4.*
   (a) The Castle
   (b) The Royal Mile
   (c) St Giles Cathedral (on the Royal Mile)
   (d) Holyrood Palace
   (e) The North Bridge
   (f) Princes Street
   (g) Charlotte Square
   (h) Waverley Station
   (i) Princes Street Gardens
   (j) The monument to Sir Walter Sco
2. *Princes Street Station is now empty and there is great debate*

Fig. 4.3
Edinburgh from the west

to the use of the site. *If you were the planner, how would you use the site? See fig. 4.4.*

3. *Is the Royal Mile really a mile in length?*
4. *What other outcrops of rock, apart from the one on which the Castle stands, are to be seen in the photograph?*
5. *Can you identify any* industrial area *in the picture?*
6. *What differences can you see between the Old Town (along the Royal Mile) and the New Town?*

C. The Functions of Edinburgh

The Royal Burgh of Edinburgh has developed as the administrative centre of the whole of Scotland. We have met the combination of castle, cathedral and university in other cities such as Canterbury and Durham. Scottish Law and the Scottish Kirk are quite independent of the English Legal system and the Church of England, and both the Law Courts and the Assembly Hall (of the Scottish Kirk) are in Edinburgh. It is the insurance and banking centre (the banks print their own notes), the printing and publishing centre and the home of the most important newspaper, *The Scotsman*. Most of these important functions are concentrated in one part of the city which is illustrated in Fig. 4.5. The government offices are in St Andrews House but a house has been developed for H.M. Secretary of State for Scotland in Charlotte Square which is shown in Fig. 4.4.

Fig. 4.4 Edinburgh: the old and the new

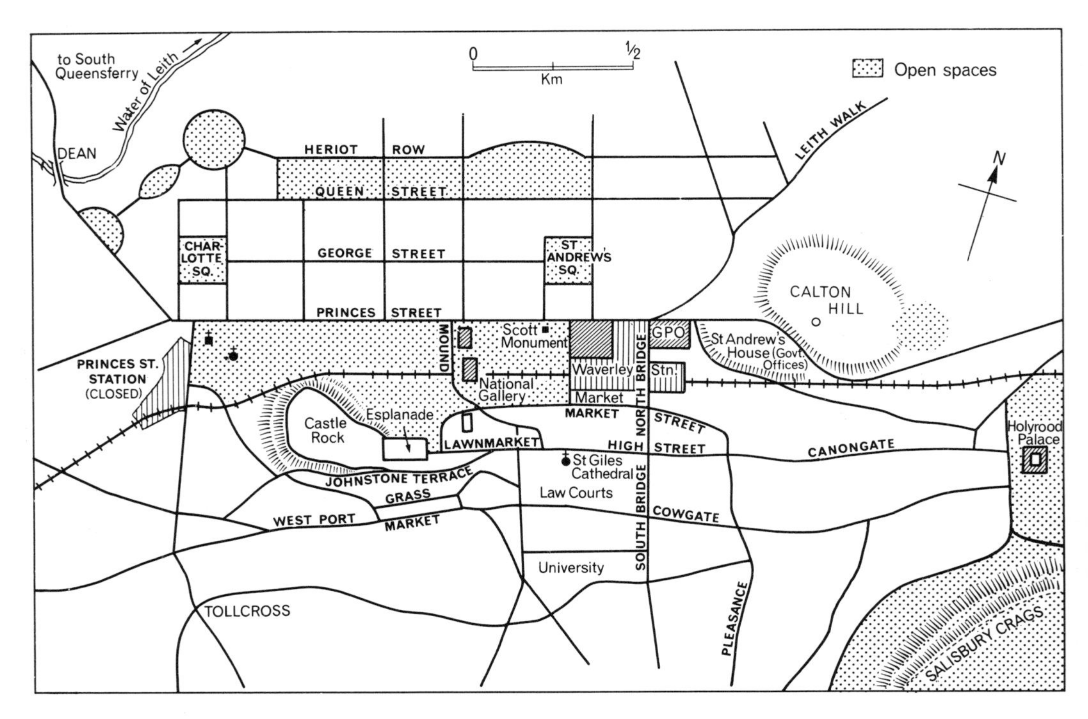

7. *Make a list of those buildings shown in Fig. 4.5 which are directly related to Edinburgh's* function *as a* capital city.

Because of its attractions as a *capital city*, the variety of employment it offers, especially to professional and clerical workers, the excellence of its schools, colleges and university, its cultural attrac-

Fig. 4.5 Edinburgh: public buildings

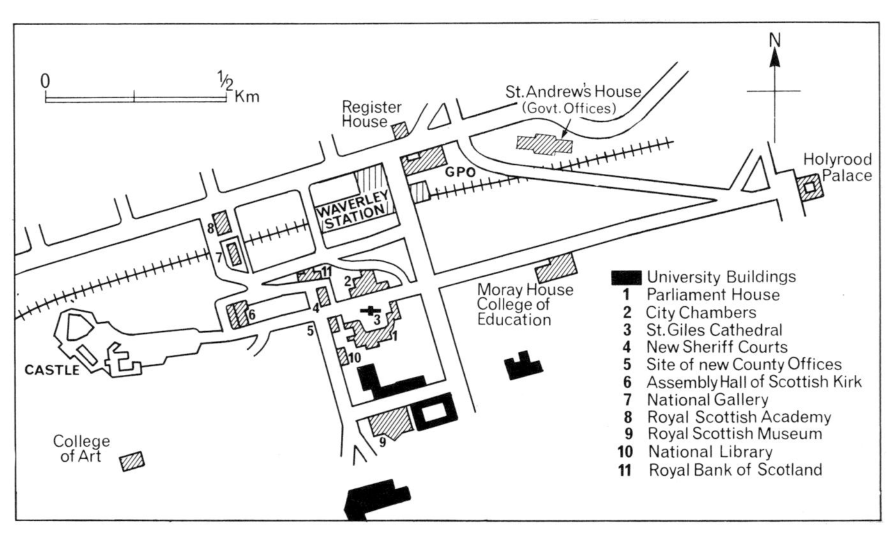

tions and its shipping facilities, Edinburgh acts as the centre of a network of road and rail routes which not only bring visitors from long distances but also daily workers. The building of the new Forth Road Bridge alongside the existing Forth Railway Bridge has made the north shore of the Firth of Forth much more accessible: already, more than 100,000 vehicles cross the road bridge each month.

Table 4.1.

Edinburgh City Employment, 1971	
Food, drink and tobacco	6.9%
Engineering & Electrical	4.7%
Paper, printing, publishing	4.0%
Construction	6.9%
Distributive Trades	14.2%
Transport and Communication	5.5%
Insurance and Banking	6.5%
Professional & Scientific Services	22.0%
Public Administration	5.9%

(Source: Dept. of Employment, Scotland)

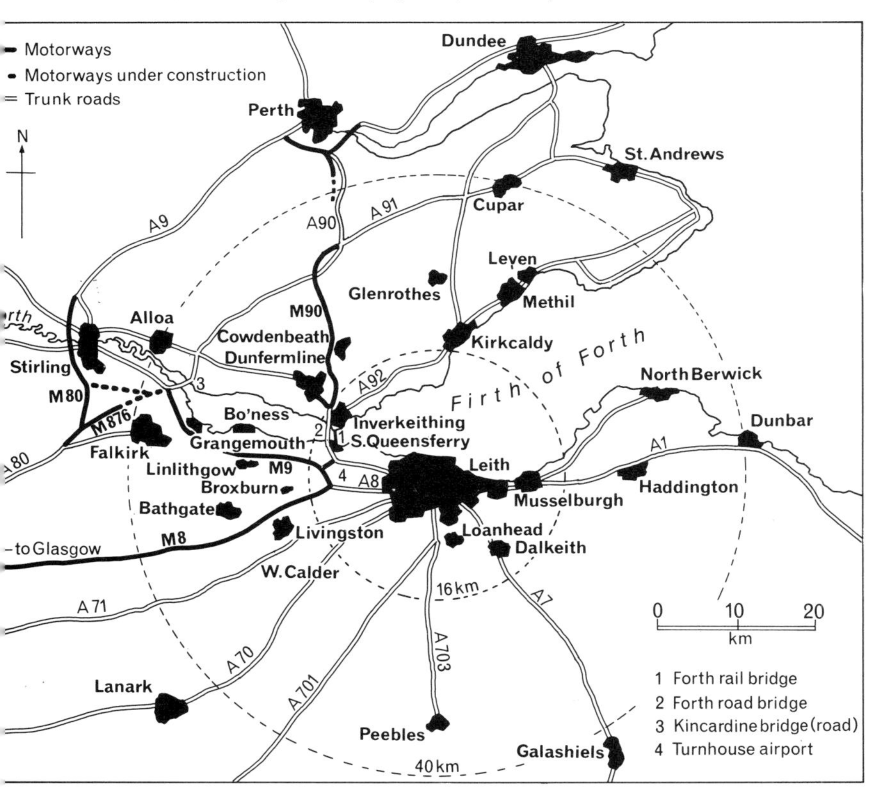

Fig. 4.6 Edinburgh: road routes

Edinburgh is now a *city* of half a million people with important industries associated with brewing, bakeries, printing, publishing, engineering and light service industries: these industries, and the growth of Edinburgh, have stimulated traffic in Leith Docks which is a port with world-wide connections.

Although the influence of Edinburgh is nation-wide, the area of its greatest influence, especially regarding its employment for people living outside the city, is shown in Fig. 4.6. Table 4.1 shows the main categories of employment in the city.

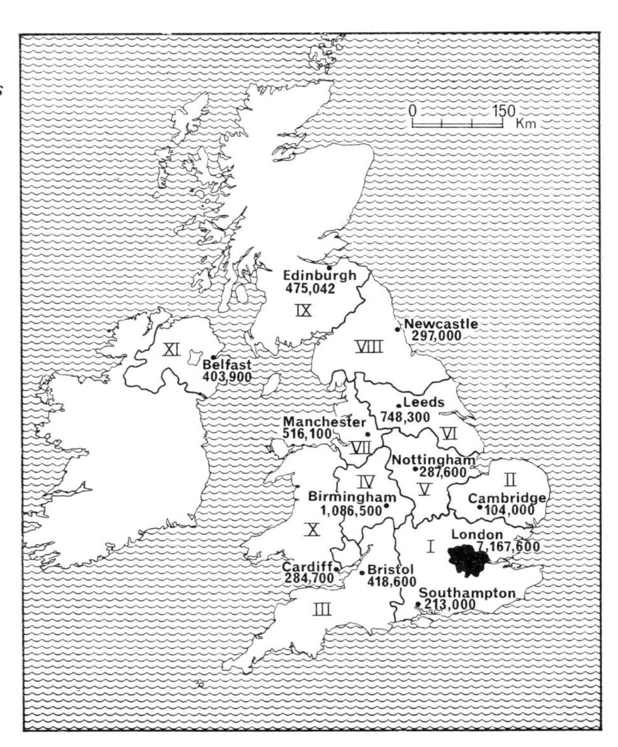

Fig. 4.7 The economic planning regions and regional capital populations (1974 estimates).

8. *Study the figures of employment in Edinburgh. They show the percentage of the total number of people employed in various types of work. Shop assistants come under 'Distributive Trades' not under 'Food, Drink and Tobacco'. (A manufacturing group.)*
   (a) What are the two most important categories of employment?
   (b) The first four categories may be grouped together as 'industrial'; what percentage of the total is employed in industry?
   (c) The last three categories may be grouped as administration and commerce; what percentage of the total is employed in administration and commerce?
9. *Study Fig. 4.6 and answer the following questions:*
   (a) How far is the centre of Edinburgh from the new road bridge at Queensferry?
   (b) Before the new bridge was built, what was the distance from Edinburgh to the nearest road bridge across the Firth of Forth?
   (c) According to the inner circle marked on the map, Kirkcaldy is 16 km from the centre of Edinburgh. How far is it, in fact by road?
   (d) Is Dunfermline nearer by road to Edinburgh than Kirkcaldy or farther away?

(e) Suggest reasons why the shore by Queensferry was chosen as the site *for the new road bridge.*

D. Regional Capitals

In recent years there has been an increased emphasis on planning the future of Britain's economy. The growth of cities, the rapid industrial development of certain areas such as the South-East and the Midlands, the comparative decline of the older industrial areas of the North has meant that each region has its own special problems and that unemployment varies very much from region to region. The Government has divided the country into *regions*, each with its own Economic Planning Group and each with its own administrative capital. The most complex region is that of the South East and, while London is the administrative capital, it seems likely that the larger region will be divided into smaller ones with other *regional 'capitals'* such as Cambridge and Southampton. Table 4.2 shows these *regions* together with Wales, Scotland and Northern Ireland for comparison. The regions and their capitals are all shown on Fig. 4.7.

Table 4.2 Economic Planning Regions of Great Britain

	Area/Economic Planning Region	Population 1973 (thousands)	Area (km^2)
	Great Britain	55,934	229,852
I	South East	17,316	27,414
	Greater London	7,281	1,596
II	East Anglia	1,739	12,565
III	South West	3,878	23,660
IV	West Midlands	5,163	13,013
	Conurbation	2,785	696
V	East Midlands	3,448	12,179
VI	Yorkshire & Humberside	4,831	14,196
VII	North West	6,755	7,992
	S.E. Lancs	2,730	983
	Merseyside	1,621	389
VIII	Northern	3,295	19,349
IX	Scotland	5,212	78,767
X	Wales	2,749	20,763
XI	Northern Ireland	1,548	14,121

Source: *Britain 1975*, H.M.S.O.

REVISION EXERCISES

10. ***Which* Economic Planning Regions *in England have***
(a) a greater population than Scotland?
(b) a greater area than Wales?

11. ***What is the* regional *capital of (a) Yorkshire and Humberside and (b) of the East Midland?***

12. ***In which* Economic Planning Region *do you live?***
(a) Which is your regional capital?
(b) How far are you by road from your regional capital?

13. *There are now Regional Plans published for most of the regions shown on the map. Find out what the plan for your own region says about its future development.*
14. *In what way do Edinburgh, Cardiff and Belfast differ from all the* regional capitals *shown on Fig. 4.7?*

Chapter Five

The Great Port: Liverpool

A. The Nature of Liverpool's Main Function

The towns we have studied in this book have been examples of settlements in which one *function* tended to give the town its main character. For instance, Edinburgh is dominated by its *administrative function* as the government centre for Scotland, Hexham by its *function* as a market for the surrounding area, and Canterbury by its cathedral which attracts many visitors. Such towns are called *central places* in the sense that they tend to be centres performing services

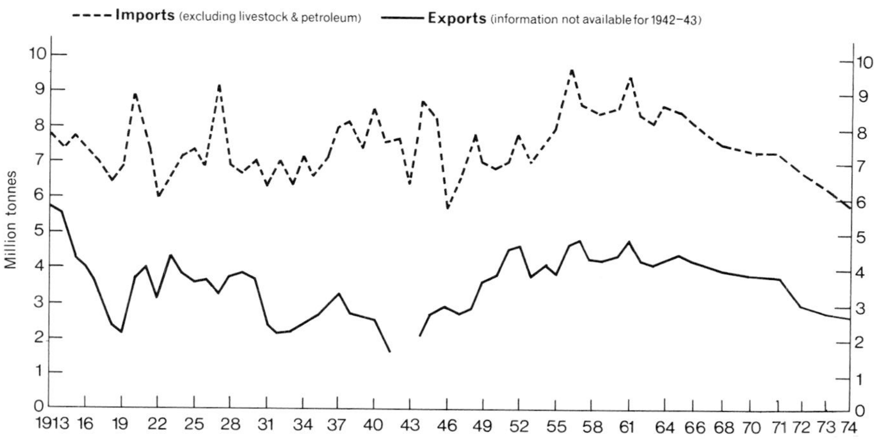

Fig. 5.1 The port of Liverpool: exports and imports

for surrounding areas – Liverpool is hardly a town in the centre of an area (see Fig. 1.2), and yet it acts as a *central place*, this time one in which its function as a port tends to distinguish it from other large towns. Table 5.1 and Fig. 5.1 show what has happened to Liverpool's trade in recent years.

This table tells us something of the port of Liverpool's trade, but not enough. Let us now look at some of the details (Tables 5.2 and 5.3).

Table 5.1

Year	Imports* (million tonnes)	Exports (million tonnes)	Year	Imports* (million tonnes)	Exports (million tonnes)
1962	15.1	4.3	1969	18.5	4.3
1963	16.2	4.2	1970	18.7	4.0
1964	15.3	4.3	1971	22.3	4.0
1965	17.7	4.4	1972	18.9	3.0
1966	18.9	4.2	1973	20.0	2.8
1967	17.4	3.9	1974	21.5	2.7
1968	19.1	4.2			

(Source: *Mersey Docks & Harbour Co. Annual Report*)
*Including petroleum

Table 5.2
Main imports of Liverpool 1972

Type of Import	Thousands of tonnes
Flour, grain, peas etc.	403
Animal feeding stuff	588
Fruit (fresh)	108
Sugar, glucose, molasses, etc.	965
Ores and scraps	1,642
Wood and timber	217
Cotton (raw and waste)	116
Oil seeds	173
Oil fats, resin, gums	302
Non-ferrous metals	179
Petroleum	12,434

(Source: *Mersey Docks & Harbour Co. Annual Report*)

Table 5.3
Main exports of Liverpool 1972

Type of Export	Thousands of tonnes
Pottery, glass and glassware	146
Iron and steel (incl. tubes and pipes)	550
Machinery and parts of machinery	378
Chemicals, drugs, dyes	726
Soap, oils, fats and resins	185
Vehicles	78

(Source: *Mersey Docks & Harbour Co. Annual Report*)

Fig. 5.2 gives some indication of the changes which have occurred in recent years in the types of goods imported to and exported from Liverpool.

The principal countries trading with Liverpool are shown in Table 5.4.

The docks required to handle the huge volume of cargo are illustrated in the map in Fig. 5.4 and in the photograph in Fig. 5.3.

The whole of this area was controlled by the Mersey Docks and Harbour Board, a body set up as long ago as 1857 to manage the docks on either side of the Mersey estuary. It was transformed into

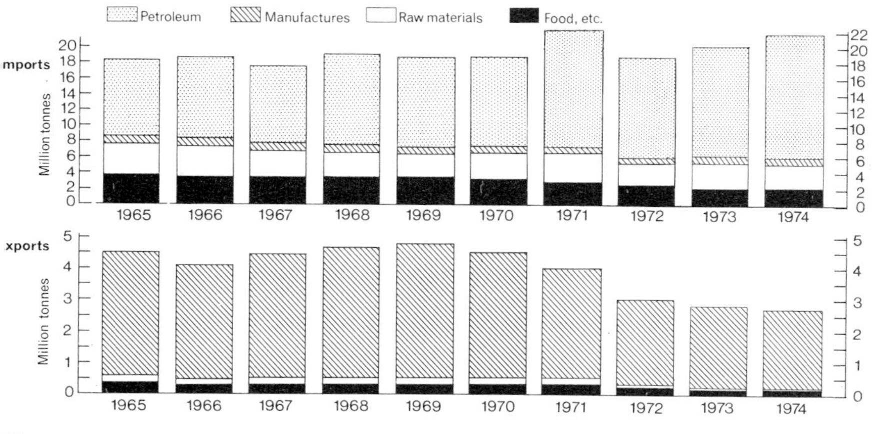

Fig. 5.2 Analysis of foreign imports and exports (exports scale four times greater than imports scale)

(Source: *Mersey Docks & Harbour Co. Annual Report*)

Table 5.4 Some areas trading with Liverpool 1972

Imports	(thousand tonnes)	Exports	(thousand tonnes)
U.S.A.	431	U.S.A.	148
Canada	717	Australia	76
Australia	281	Republic of S. Africa	178
South America: East Coast	1,069	W. Africa	409
South America: West Coast	112	New Zealand	182
West Indies	141	India, Ceylon and Pakistan	208
Malaysia and Singapore	254	Europe	434
Pakistan, India and Ceylon	239	West Indies	183
Mauritius	222	Canada	119
West Africa	686	Hong Kong	62
Europe	1,244	South America: East Coast	210
		South America: West Coast	98

(Source: *Mersey Docks & Harbour Co. Annual Report*)

a Statutory Company in 1971. Today more than 34,000 vessels are dealt with each year, in docks and basins having a total water surface area of about 184 hectares.

The most important fact to learn about shipping is that it costs a great deal of money to run a ship. Consequently ship-owners try to make their ships do as much work as possible; this means carrying cargo between ports rather than spending time in port waiting for cargoes to be discharged. A good port, from the ship-owners point of view, is one where his ship will spend the least possible time. Hence ports such as Liverpool are trying all the time to improve the speed of loading and unloading ships to ensure a quicker 'turn-round'. This can be done by using not only continuous flow methods, as when oil is pumped out of a tanker, but also mechanical means of general cargo handling, such as conveyors, fork-lift trucks and mobile truck-mounted cranes, such as the one illustrated in Fig. 5.5. Another way of handling cargo quickly is to put the goods into standard sized containers which can easily be handled by cranes and gantries and packed in the minimum of space in specially

Fig. 5.3
Liverpool docks
from the south

Fig. 5.4
The port of
Liverpool

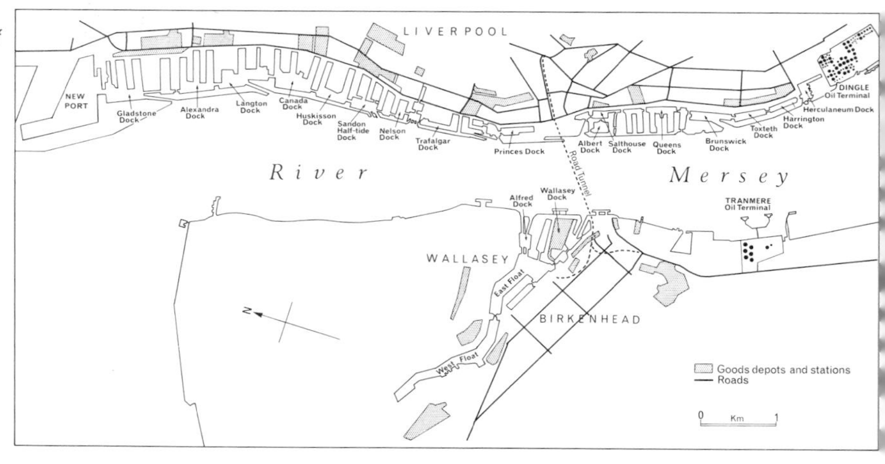

designed ships' holds. A new container terminal has been built in Liverpool as in other ports of the U.K.

The Mersey Docks and Harbour Co. is also responsible for seeing that ships get safely in and out of the dock basins. The need for these will be understood when it is realized that the *tidal range* may be as much as 10 metres. Thus, in medieval times and later, ships were often stranded on the mud near the Mersey's banks at low-tide, or if moored in deeper water they were exposed to very fast tidal currents. The first docks basin was built in 1715 and since that time the number of such basins has increased and continues to increase. Keeping a deep water channel open to allow ships to penetrate to the docks at all states of the tide is another task of the Mersey Docks and Harbour Co., as well as the provision of pilots, with expert knowledge of local conditions, to bring ships into harbour. This latter task is a delicate one with huge tankers drawing 13 metres of water. Weather hazards also cause trouble to ships entering Liverpool, but radio communication and radar help by giving pilots additional information, about their own position and the positions of other ships.

Fig. 5.5 Mobile truck-mounted crane

1. *From Fig. 1.2 and/or an atlas, describe the position of Liverpool (a) in words, (b) by a simple sketch map.*
2. *Study Fig. 5.1 and state:*
   - *(a) (i) what the general level of imports was like in the period 1955–74 compared with the pre-war period 1928–37; (ii) whether the fluctuations in imports in the post-1949 period are greater or smaller than the fluctuations in imports in the period 1919 to 1940.*
   - *(b) Whether the general level of exports is higher or lower in the post-war (1939–45) years than in the pre-war years.*
   - *(c) When were exports highest?*
   - *(d) In which direction is Liverpool's main trade, inwards or outwards?*
3. *From Table 5.1:*
   - *(a) State approximately what the ratio is between exports and imports.*

(b) *Why do the figures shown on Fig. 5.1* not *agree with those in Table 5.1?*

4. (a) *Study Fig. 5.2. (i) what is the essential difference between Liverpool's imports and her exports? (ii) which import has been most obviously increasing between 1965–74? (iii) what trends are noticeable among the exports?*
   (b) *Study Tables 5.2 and 5.3. (i) what are the two main food imports? (ii) what are the two main raw material imports? (iii) what are the two main exports?*
5. *In terms of weight the gap between imports and exports is large; in terms of money the gap is likely to be much smaller – why is that?*
6. (a) *With which area does Liverpool do a great deal of trade? (see Table 5.4)*
   (b) *To which association of nations do many countries with which Liverpool trades belong? Suggest why this should be so.*
   (c) *Compare Tables 5.2 and 5.4 and suggest some of the countries from which the main imports may come.*
7. *Study Fig. 5.4.*
   (a) *On which side of the Mersey are most of the dock basins?*
   (b) *The first docks were built near Princes dock – where have the most recent docks been constructed? Give reasons for your choice.*
   (c) *Why are there lock gates to the entrances to the Docks?*
   (d) *What kind of cargo is unloaded at Tranmere and Dingle?*
   (e) *What three possible ways – (i) of crossing the Mersey are available to people wishing to go from Liverpool to Birkenhead? (ii) of taking important goods away from the Liverpool docks?*
8. *Study Fig. 5.3.*
   (a) *Which group of docks are shown between the two dock entrances? (compare the map in Fig. 5.4)*
   (b) *What is the probable purpose of the sheds on the quayside?*
   (c) *Describe the various stages in getting a piece of imported cargo away from Liverpool.*
   (d) *From the photograph, which method of transport seems the most used to take imported cargo away from the docks.*
   (e) *What was the probable state of the* tide *when the photograph was taken?*
9. (a) *Why is it important for ships to have a quick 'turn-round'?*
   (b) *What methods may be used to ensure this?*
10. *Why do incoming ships need pilots?*

B. The Town of Liverpool

So far we have looked at the workings of the port of Liverpool, but we have learnt little about a town which in 1700 had a population of about 5,000 which rose to 25,000 in 1760 and to 54,000 in 1790. Today Liverpool is a town of over 600,000 people. The author Daniel Defoe, who travelled widely in England, noticed this growth in

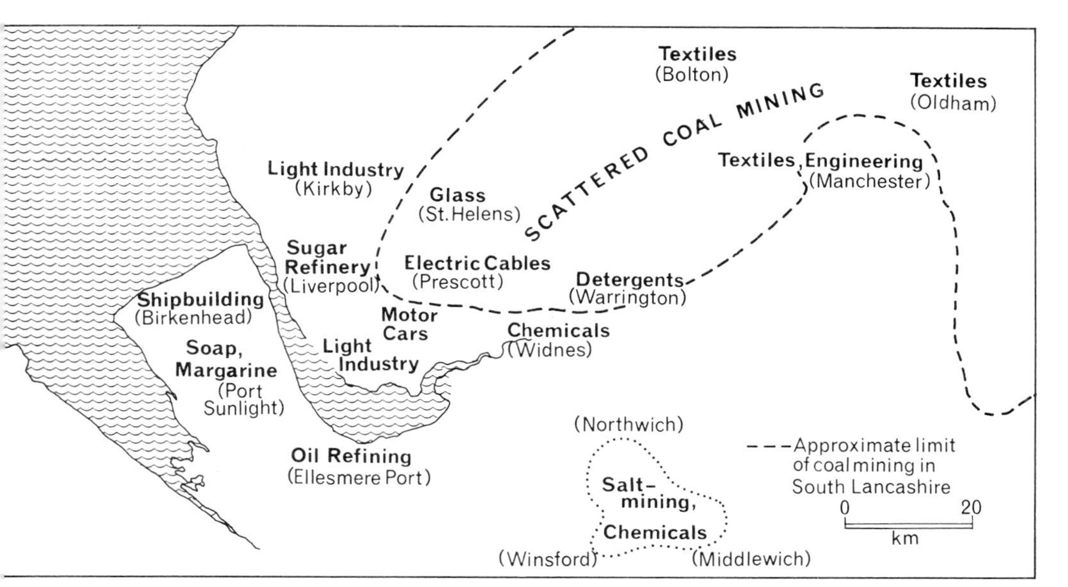

Fig. 5.6 Some manufacturing industries in Merseyside and north Cheshire

Liverpool. In 1725 he wrote, 'The town has now an opulent, flourishing and increasing trade, not rivalling Bristol in the trade to Virginia and the English Island colonies in America only, but is in a fair way to exceed and eclipse it, by increasing every way in wealth and shipping. They trade round the whole Island, send ships to Norway, to Hamburg, and to the Baltick, as also to Holland and Flanders; so that in a word, they are almost become like the Londoners, universal Merchants'.

It seems clear from Daniel Defoe's account why the population of Liverpool grew in the 18th century. But what was it made the shipping trade grow so much? If you look at lists of cargoes you will find that among them were coal and salt exports, whilst sugar from the West Indies and later cotton provided some of the main imports. It is also unfortunately true that many merchants grew rich by trading in slaves, until this trade was made illegal in 1807. The map in Fig. 5.6 gives you some indication as to why some of this trade was possible. Once growth in trade had started, it went on growing in the 19th century, with imports of raw cotton and exports of cotton cloth increasing rapidly.

The land area around a port with which the port trades is called its *hinterland*. Thus Liverpool's 18th- and 19th-century *hinterland* was essentially South Lancashire and Cheshire. Today Liverpool with a population of 607,000 has a *hinterland* which is wider still.

The extent of a port's hinterland is in part dependent on how easy it is to transport goods and people from the port to the surrounding areas. Fig. 5.7 shows that today Liverpool is linked to most parts of Britain by road, rail and air. In the past the Leeds to Liverpool canal was instrumental in developing Liverpool's trade with the Yorkshire industrial area. Rail connections between Liverpool, the Midlands and London are electrified and as Table 5.5 shows, services for passengers are frequent and rapid.

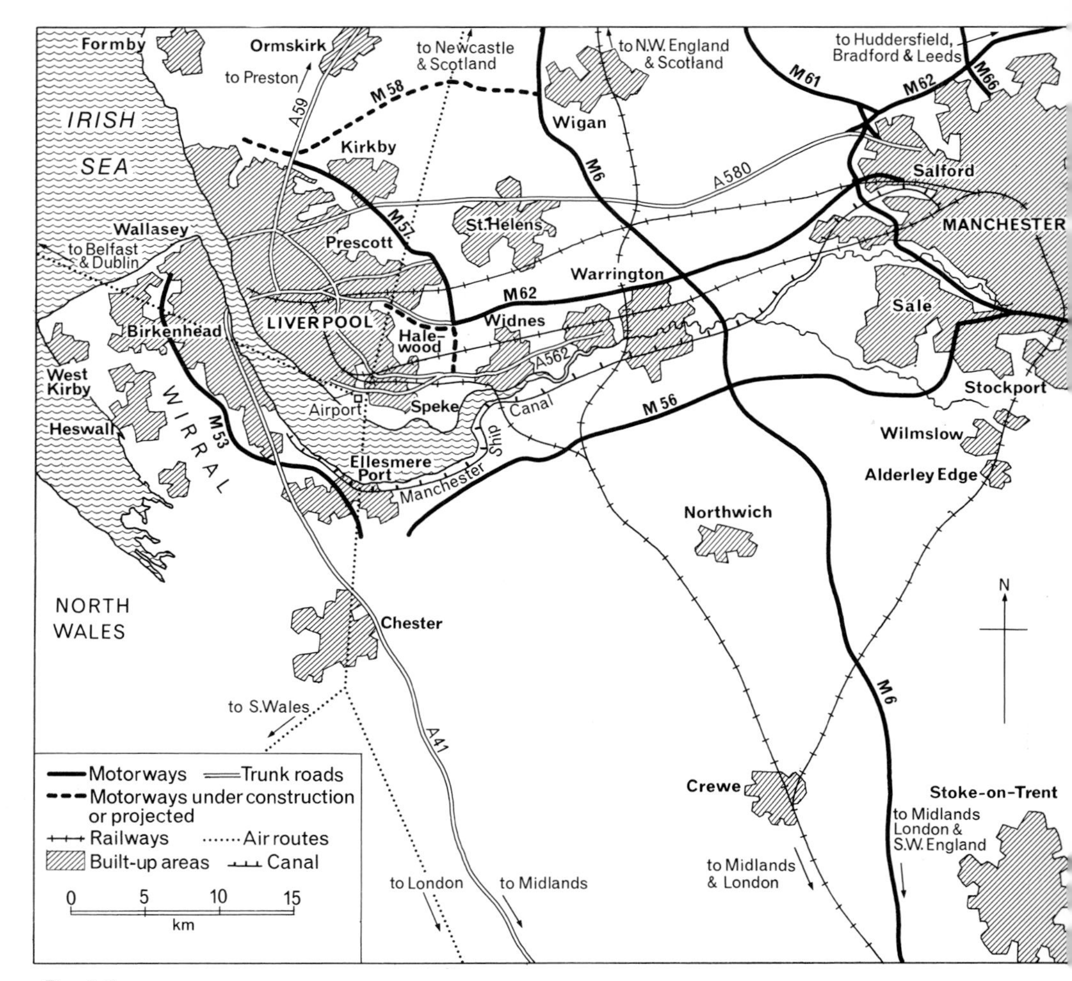

Fig. 5.7
Liverpool: communications

Table 5.5
Typical week day rail service between London and Liverpool

Euston	Liverpool	Liverpool	Euston
00.50	04.08	00.30	04.57
07.45	10.20	07.25	10.50
08.30	11.23	07.55	10.27
09.15	12.35	08.30	11.15
11.00	13.40	09.18	12.05
11.15	14.35	09.25	12.51
13.00	15.45	10.15	13.05
13.15	16.35	10.30	13.10
14.30	17.15	12.30	15.10
15.00	17.45	14.30	17.10
15.15	18.35	15.25	18.55
16.50	19.28	16.30	19.15
17.00	19.43	17.25	20.50
17.15	20.37	18.30	21.25
18.10	20.42		
18.30	21.15		
19.15	22.37		

The growth in Liverpool's trade resulted in a parallel growth in local industries and services – for example grain imports needed to be ground to flour, sugar had to be refined, vegetable oils turned into soap and margarine, petroleum broken down to petrol and other refined oils. Further, ships' cargoes had to be bought and sold, often on credit. Ships had to be charted and insured, cargoes had to be insured. Thus around the port's main function there developed what are known as (a) *port industries* (b) *commercial activities*. Examples of the *port industries* are the Unilever works at Port Sunlight making soap and margarine from imported vegetable oils, the Shell oil refinery at Stanlow, the Tate and Lyle sugar refineries in Liverpool's dockland. Examples of *commercial activities* are the offices of such shipping lines as the Cunard Company, such insurance offices as the Standard Marine Insurance Company and of course the main banks are represented in the town. Once these activities take root they tend to stay in the town even though their business often expands to cater for other areas. Thus the Liverpool and London and Globe Insurance Company, now caters for a much wider area than the Liverpool area but its head office remains in Liverpool. All this *economic growth* could not take place, as we saw on p. 4, without an increase in population. But Liverpool being a port has attracted population not only from the surrounding country districts, but also from overseas. Thus in present day Liverpool one finds families which originated not only from South Lancashire and Wales, but also from Ireland, Jamaica and Hong Kong. This is why one often hears that Liverpool is a *cosmopolitan city*. It also explains why Liverpool has a large Roman Catholic population.

One problem which is common to many British cities is that economic growth is not steady. Old industries decay and die and new industries develop, but not always at the same time or at the same rate. Thus it is difficult to ensure, without doing anything special about it, that all workers who seek employment will always find it. So the local government and the national government have sought to create local employment by attracting new industries to the Liverpool area to ensure a steady growth in the number of jobs available. This has been done by offering industrialists convenient *sites* within the city boundaries as shown in Fig. 5.8, or by offering *sites* in newer satellite towns such as at Kirkby shown in Fig. 5.9.

Some of the new factories are closely related to Liverpool's *function* as a port. For example Goodlass Wall & Company which manufactures all kinds of paints and varnishes on the Speke industrial estate, requires the port of Liverpool to import some of its raw materials and to export some of its finished products. In contrast Bird's Eye Frozen Foods (part of the Unilever group of companies) which has a factory on the Kirkby industrial estate does not depend on Liverpool's port. Similarly the Ford Motor Company's factory at Halewood (near Speke) is more dependent on the railway linking it to Ford's other large factory at Dagenham than on the port, though it does export some of its products.

Thus, though the impetus for Liverpool's growth originally came from its *port function* and though this is still very important, like many other towns its economy is becoming more and more diversified. It does also combine the *functions* of cathedral city and University town. Like other towns, Liverpool has its problems of redevelopment, for many of its houses, buildings and streets were built in the 19th century and are now inadequate by modern standards. We shall not study such problems here as we shall be concerned with them in Chapters 6, 7, 8 and 9. It is important to remember, however, that though we have been learning about the town of Liverpool, the urban area stretches on either side of the river Mersey and that many people who work in Liverpool, live on the Wirral peninsula in such towns as Birkenhead, Hoylake, West Kirkby and Bebbington.

11. (a) What impressed Daniel Defoe when he visited Liverpool in the early 18th century?

(b) What were some of the original reasons for the increase in Liverpool's shipping trade in the 18th century?

(c) Which industries originally contributed to Liverpool's export trade? (see Fig. 5.6)

Fig. 5.8 Speke Industrial Estate

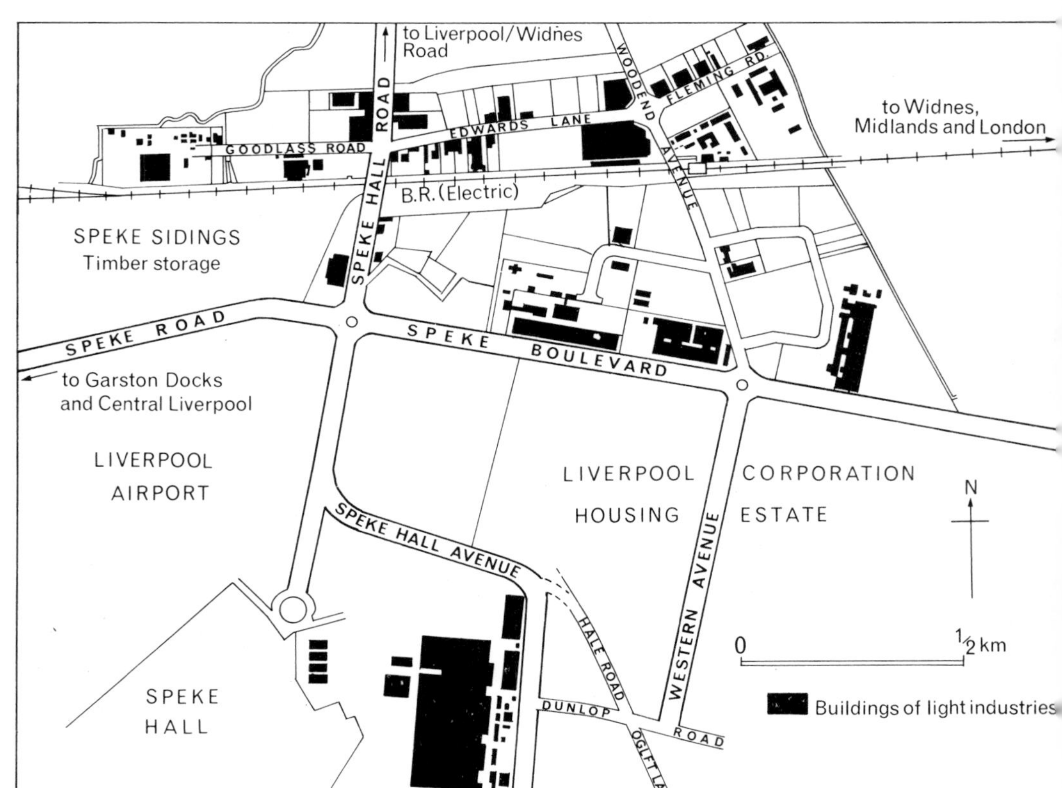

Fig. 5.9 Kirkby Industrial Estate, Lancashire

12. (a) *What is meant by the* hinterland *of a port?*
    (b) *The term* hinterland *can never refer to an area fixed for all times. This area tends to vary. Why is this?*
    (c) *How could you set about delimiting the* hinterland *of a small port like Immingham or Dover?*
    (d) *In what ways have the services of Liverpool been made more speedily accessible to its* hinterland *recently? (see Fig. 5.7)*
13. *Study Table 5.5.*
    (a) *Approximately how long does the rail journey from Liverpool to London take?*
    (b) *If the journey is 300 kilometres long, what is the average speed of the trains?*
    (c) *The air journey from Liverpool to London only takes about 45 minutes; how much faster is this than the train journey? What are the special disadvantages of short air journeys such as travelling to London bearing in mind (i) airport locations, (ii) weather conditions in winter?*
14. (a) *What is meant by a* port industry*?*
    (b) *What are the advantages of a port location for such industries as oil refining and flour milling.*
    (c) *Would a port location for such industries always be a sensible choice in a country like the U.S.A. or the U.S.S.R.? Give reasons for your answer.*
    (d) *Why is it not necessary in Britain to site an oil refinery in an interior location?*
15. (a) *In what ways are the* commercial activities *of Liverpool linked to its function as a port?*
    (b) *Why is it that one very important* commercial activity *in Liverpool and its surrounding area is warehousing?*
16. (a) *What is it meant when it is stated that Liverpool's population is* cosmopolitan*?*
    (b) *How can you account for the large percentage of Liverpool's population which follows the Roman Catholic faith, whereas in Britain in general, the percentage of Roman Catholics is lower?*
17. (a) *Study Fig. 5.8 and list the advantages which an industrialist might have in taking up a factory* site *on the Speke Industrial estate. Are there any disadvantages to such a* site*?*
    (b) *(i) what are the advantages of the Kirkby industrial estate as shown in Fig. 5.9? (ii) in what way can you tell that this is largely a post-World War II 'new' town development?*
18. *What is meant by the statement on page 48 that Liverpool's economy is becoming more and more diversified?*
19. *What is the difference between Liverpool and the Merseyside* conurbation*?*

Liverpool took a long time to recover from the damage it suffered during World War II and from the economic depression which affected it in the nineteen thirties. Today, however, it seems to have acquired a new impetus and a new city is being fashioned in which port and town are being redeveloped.

REVISION EXERCISES

20. *(a) Describe the distribution of the Mersey Docks and Harbour Board's dock basins.*

    (b) What are the advantages of the position of Liverpool's docks?

21. *What are the main characteristics of the port of Liverpool's trade?*
22. *What makes a modern sea port efficient?*
23. *Make a list of various* port industries *known to you, stating in which port they are to be found.*
24. *Why were 'industrial estates' such as the Speke Industrial Estate built in the Liverpool area?*
25. *What problems does the River Mersey pose for the inhabitants of the Merseyside conurbation?*

Chapter Six

The West Midlands Conurbation*

A. The Nature of the Conurbation

Liverpool is a town which developed around its port, in which the port acted as a stimulus to economic growth. We are now going to study an urban area in which no single *function* can be said to have stimulated its growth: namely Birmingham and its surrounding area.

As in most built up areas in England, the density of buildings varies and there are some open spaces. The urban area covers some 700 square kilometres and houses a population of some 2.4 million. The position of this *conurbation* in the Midlands is shown on Fig. 6.1.

One question we must ask ourselves in this chapter is: how did

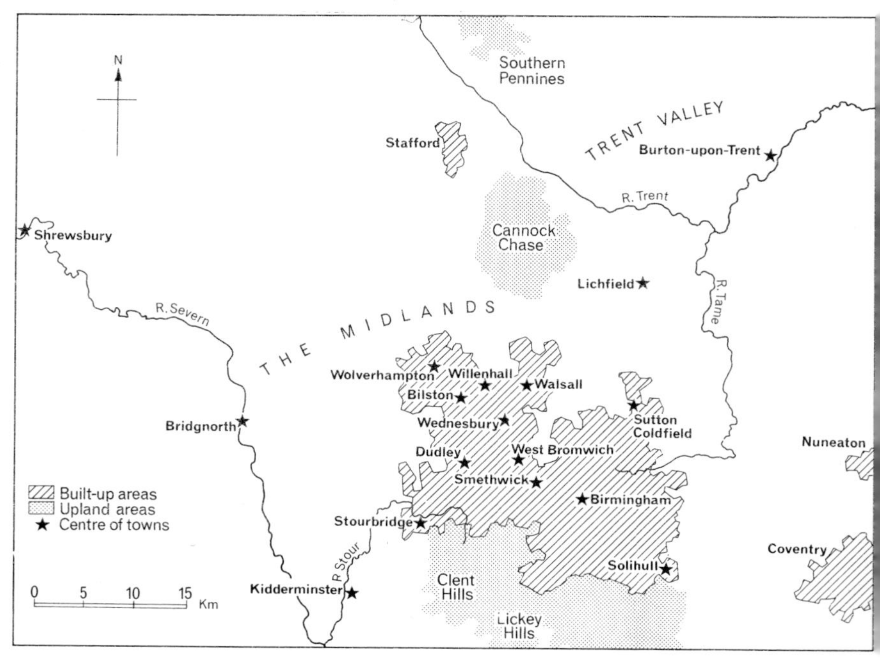

Fig. 6.1 The West Midlands Industrial Conurbation

*This is smaller than the new metropolitan county of West Midlands which includes Coventry (see Fig. 21.2).

Fig. 6.2 Central Birmingham

such a huge urban area come into existence? Before we attempt to answer this question let us first look at the area as it appears to-day. You will find some evidence from the two aerial photographs shown in Figs. 6.2 and 6.3.

These two photographs help to make clear a distinction between Birmingham and what has traditionally been known as the 'Black

Fig. 6.3 Walsall in the Black Country

Country', although the latter is not by any means as black as it once used to be. Birmingham is the biggest single urban unit in the whole *conurbation*, but the 'Black Country' consists of a series of urban areas stretching from Wolverhampton in the north-west to Smethwick in the south-east (see Fig. 6.1). Consequently the 'Black Country' has much less pattern about its urban areas. There has grown up an intimate mixture of old housing, old factories, new housing, cleared sites, old tip heaps, derelict land, and some new industrial buildings. As one 'town' runs into another, it is difficult to say precisely when one leaves Wolverhampton and enters Willenhall or when one leaves Wednesbury and enters West Bromwich. Only in some central shopping centres such as at Wolverhampton is the traveller conscious of being in a town which has a heart. One writer has stated, 'many of the towns lack well equipped shopping centres and consist of groups of factories and houses separated from one another by railways, canals and patches of derelict land; in other words, thousands of people live under industrial conditions but lack many of the distinct advantages of town life close to their houses and – in part at least – the Black Country has the character of a landscape of industrial villages'*. Birmingham on the other hand has a well defined centre and its citizens enjoy the advantages of a large town with cinemas, theatres, art galleries and concert halls. The approximate divisions between various uses to which the land is put are shown on Fig. 6.4 whilst the present day administrative boundaries are shown on Fig. 6.5.

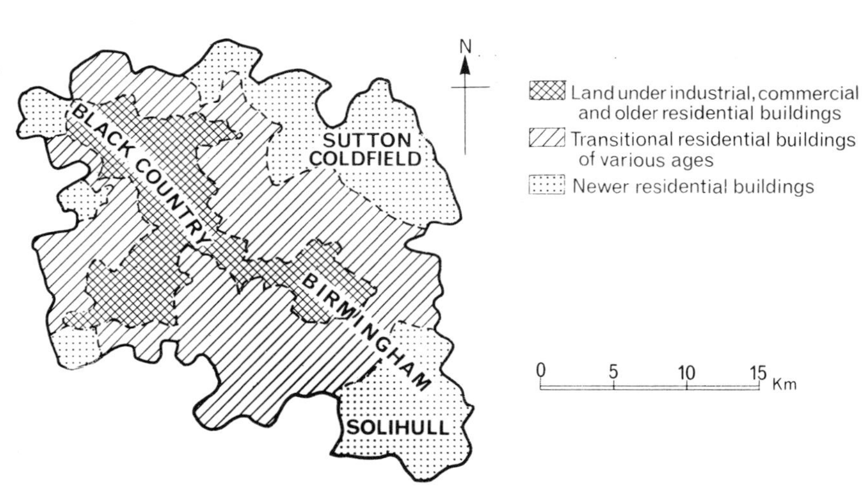

Fig. 6.4 Land use in the West Midlands Conurbation

The industries in which many of the people of the West Midlands *conurbation* work are very varied. The British Leyland Motor Corporation factories in Birmingham are the best known, but most of them are only assembly lines; the various parts to be assembled are made elsewhere in Birmingham and the Black Country. For example the Dunlop Company make tyres in a factory in north-east Birming-

* Freeman T. W., *The Conurbation of Great Britain,* M.U.P. 1959.

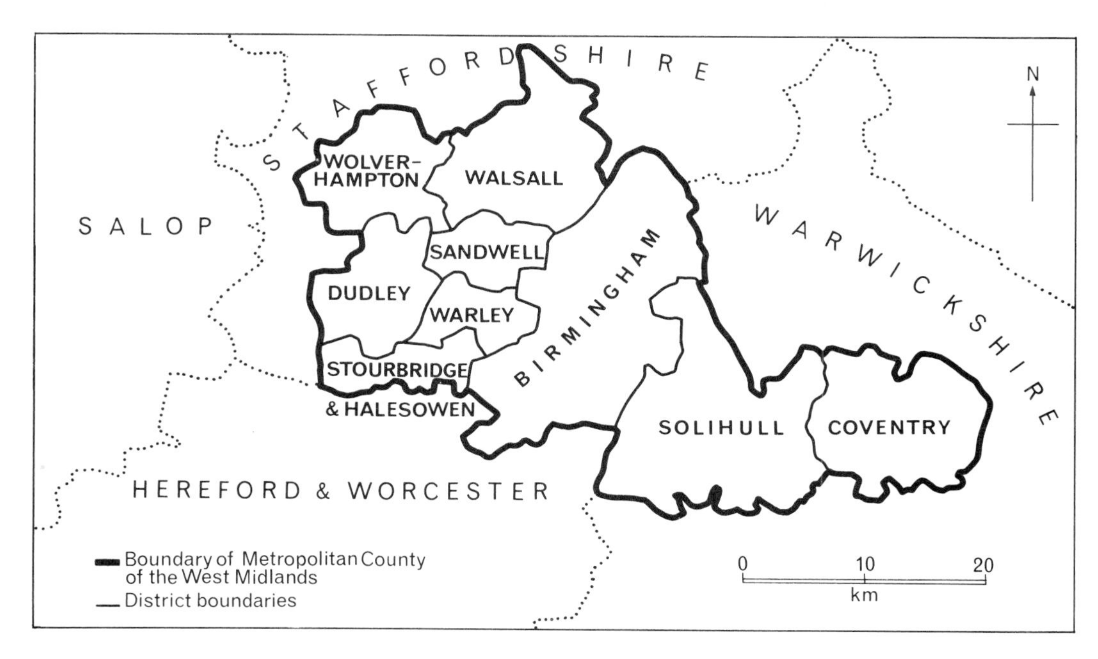

Fig. 6.5 Administrative divisions 1974 – Birmingham and the Black Country are part of the County of West Midlands

ham which they have called Fort Dunlop. About 20 per cent of the industrial population in the *conurbation* is employed in the motor industry. Besides the motor industry and its suppliers, there is also the manufacture of chocolate (Cadbury's at Bournville), the production of electrical goods (Lucas), the making of motor cycles (B.S.A.) and some older industries such as the manufacture of guns, hardware and jewelry. Most of the 'Black Country' industries are connected in some way with metals – iron and steel is produced at Bilston, locks and keys at Willenhall, nuts and bolts, screws and nails (Guest Keen and Nettlefolds) at Smethwick and springs at West Bromwich. Most aspects of engineering are represented in some form or other in the Black Country, such as the making of cranes and pumps. Thus, apart from the motor industry which is outstandingly important, the whole *conurbation* is not in any way linked to a particular function or industry.

1. *(a) Using Fig. 6.1 (i) state the approximate width and length of the* conurbation *from east to west and from north to south. (ii) How far away and in what directions are the towns of Stafford, Burton-on-Trent and Coventry?*
   (b) Using an atlas map, name two towns about 150 and 200 kilometres to the south of Birmingham respectively (Check your answers with the table on page 55).
2. *(a) Using the Figs. 6.2 and 6.3, state 3 ways in which the urban landscape of Birmingham differs from that of the Black Country.*
   (b) From Fig. 6.2 (i) what evidence is there that some of the buildings have been fairly recently built? (ii) Is the photograph an aerial

oblique *or an* aerial vertical·*photograph?*

(c) *What evidence can you find which supports the quotation from T. W. Freeman given on page 54?*

(d) *What does T. W. Freeman probably mean when he describes the Black Country as a 'landscape of industrial villages'?*

3. *What is the average density of population per square kilometre in the West Midlands* conurbation*? How does this compare with the figures given in Chapter 1 and Chapter 4 (p. 6 and p. 37)?*

4. (a) *How can you explain the shape of the 'industrial and commercial belt' of the* conurbation *shown in Fig. 6.4?*

   (b) *What do you notice about the position of the areas of recent residential buildings?*

   (c) *Which are likely to be Birmingham's better residential suburbs?*

5. *Get hold of newspapers or magazines and cut out the advertisements from firms with works in Birmingham and the Black Country. Make a list of these products.*

B. The Growth and Development of the Conurbation

The distances by road between Birmingham and several other important towns may be obtained from the chart below (in kilometres).

	LONDON	LIVERPOOL	BRISTOL	HULL	SOUTHAMPTON	GLASGOW	EDINBURGH	LEEDS	CARDIFF	NEWCASTLE-upon-TYNE	SHEFFIELD
LIVERPOOL	315										
BRISTOL	186	244									
HULL	269	205	325								
SOUTHAMPTON	123	346	120	352							
GLASGOW	630	341	586	392	667						
EDINBURGH	597	338	584	355	661	70					
LEEDS	304	117	310	88	358	336	306				
CARDIFF	246	262	70	358	189	592	590	334			
NEWCASTLE-upon-TYNE	438	246	456	187	502	229	170	147	478		
SHEFFIELD	256	117	262	98	307	384	357	53	286	198	
BIRMINGHAM	176	144	141	197	205	462	461	174	163	322	123

This chart and Fig. 6.1 show one of the advantages of the position of the *conurbation* with respect to the rest of England. This central position however, cannot be the only reason why the Birmingham area developed. Otherwise one might have expected a town like Lichfield (see Fig. 3.1 and Fig. 6.1) to have increased in size to a greater extent that it has in fact done. It would be dishonest to give one single explanation for the growth of Birmingham and the Black Country since all sorts of influences were at work in this area. We can only note how the area gradually grew in importance. Certainly at the time of William the Conqueror, there was nothing more than a ather small manor near the river Rea (a tributary of the Tame, see ˈig. 6.1) which could be forded at that place. It is possible that wing to the existence of this crossing place many people from the urrounding area came this way and it became profitable to establish *narkets* here.

In the early days people required simple articles for farming and or themselves. We know that by 1650 the making of nails, locks, its for horses, leather harnesses, were well established industries n the area. Later on in the 18th century, buttons, buckles and trin-ets of iron and brass were being made in Birmingham as well as uns, metal being cast in moulds of local sand. Clearly some form f heat energy was required for many of these industrial activities nd fortunately there was locally available a *coal seam* which out-ropped widely in the Black Country area called the 'Thick Coal' ecause it was often 10 metres in thickness and therefore easy to xtract. There were also ironstones, although at first the iron which hey made was often not up to the quality required by the manu-acturers of metal goods who had to import *pig iron* from elsewhere. Iowever, with improvement in *smelting* processes and the rise in he demand for iron, blast furnaces were set up in the Black Country. Jntil 1858, 182 had been built and the Black Country was described s 'a great workshop both above ground and below; at night it is urid with flames of the iron-furnaces: by day it appears one vast oosely-knit town of humble houses amid cinder heaps and fields tripped of vegetables by smoke and fumes'*.

The basis of all this industrial development was undoubtedly the *oalfield* which was for long known as the South Staffordshire Coal-ield and which now forms part of the West Midlands division of the National Coal Board's areas. The areas where *coal measures* (the ocks containing coal) appear on the surface are marked on Fig. 6.6. n fact coal is often mined where the *coal measures* are much deeper nderground, and today little coal is mined in the exposed coal neasures area either because it is not worth exploiting or because t has already been mined.

To help transport the raw materials of industry canals were built n the 18th and early 19th centuries, so that today the area possesses relatively dense network of old, narrow and little-used canals.

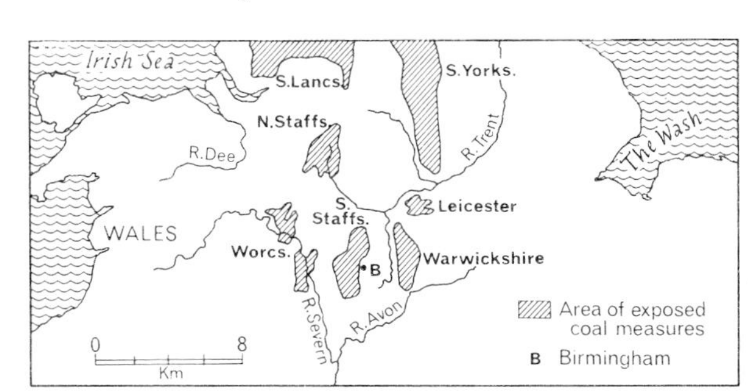

Fig. 6.6 Coalfields of Central England

Mackinder H. J., *Britain and the British Seas.*

Turnpike roads (i.e. paying roads maintained by a private company were also built and helped the growth of trade and industry in thi area. Later, after 1840, railways were constructed. As a result th older workshops and factories were built along roads or crowdec together along the banks of canals, whilst late 19th century industria growth tended to be along the railways.

With the decline in iron and coal resources, the heavy iron anc steel industry tended to contract, thus today the only major uni left in the industry is the British Steel Corporation's works at Bilston But the many metal-using trades remained since the metal usec could always be obtained from elsewhere. And as we saw earlier th number of such trades increased to include the cycle, motorcycle and motor car industry. In all these the value of the metal used i only a small proportion of the cost of the article produced. Most o the modern industries are *capital intensive* industries, that is industrie in which the capital cost of the equipment used is a major element i the cost of the product, as for example in an automated motor ca assembly plant.

6. (a) *Using the chart on page 56 state the distances between: (i) Birmingham and Bristol (ii) Birmingham and London (iii Birmingham and Liverpool (iv) Birmingham and Hull.*
   (b) *What do you notice about the position of Birmingham? How far is this position an advantage and a disadvantage to ar industrial town?*
7. (a) *How far would you say that the growth of: (i) Birmingham anc (ii) The Black Country were due to accidents of history?*
   (b) *What deliberate action was taken to facilitate the developmen of industry in Birmingham and the Black Country.*
8. (a) *When did the iron making industry dominate the Black Country.*
   (b) *Why did Mackinder describe the Black Country as it then was as 'a vast workshop both above ground and below'?*
   (c) *Why did the iron industry decline?*
9. (a) *What influence did the development of transport have on the location of industry in the West Midlands* conurbation*?*
   (b) *Why do you suppose many of the canals are little used today?*
10.* (a) *The manufacture of jewelry and of motor cars are two o Birmingham's industries. One is said to be* labour intensive *anc the other* capital intensive. *What is meant by these two terms?*
   (b) *Why is it necessary today for the industries of the West Midlands* conurbation *to be either* labour *or* capital intensive *industries?*

Conclusion

We have seen that the West Midlands *conurbation* has evolved fron a series of very small villages to a huge *conurbation* in the space of less than 300 years. The piecemeal growth of industry especially in the last 200 years has left a landscape which is not only ugly in parts, but which is a hinderance to future growth of development – consequently it is not surprising that such an area presents many problems for those concerned with the redevelopment of the area. We shall study some of these in Part II. One human problem which results directly from the fact that industry continues to grow, is that many immigrants from the West Indies and from the Indian sub-continent have settled in the area because work was available for them. This has occasionally led to friction between the established population and the new settlers. It is important to bear in mind that this sort of friction has often occurred in the past between Englishmen, until such a time as the newcomers have become accepted.

One difficulty which always arises when the population of a town grows is that of finding enough space to house everyone. Consequently it is often necessary today to seek land outside the present city boundaries to put up new houses, and even to set up a completely new town. For example the town of Telford, 48 km north-west of Birmingham is being developed to take up Birmingham's overspill population. The problem of urban growth is dealt with in Chapter 9.

REVISION EXERCISES

11. *What is meant by the word* conurbation*? Give examples other than those in the West Midlands.*
12. *How did the 'Black Country' acquire its name?*
13. *'The Birmingham and Black Country area has never had high long term rates of unemployment like north-eastern England because the area has adapted to changing economic conditions.' Describe in your own words what this sentence means.*
14. *Explain the following terms.*
    (a) Coal Seams
    (b) Coal Measures
    (c) Coalfield
    (d) Exposed Coalfield
    (e) Concealed Coalfield
15. *If you were going to set up an industry in Birmingham, would you set up a heavy or light industry? Give your reasons.*

Chapter Seven

The Functional Zones of Towns: London

A. The Growth of London and its Administrative Division

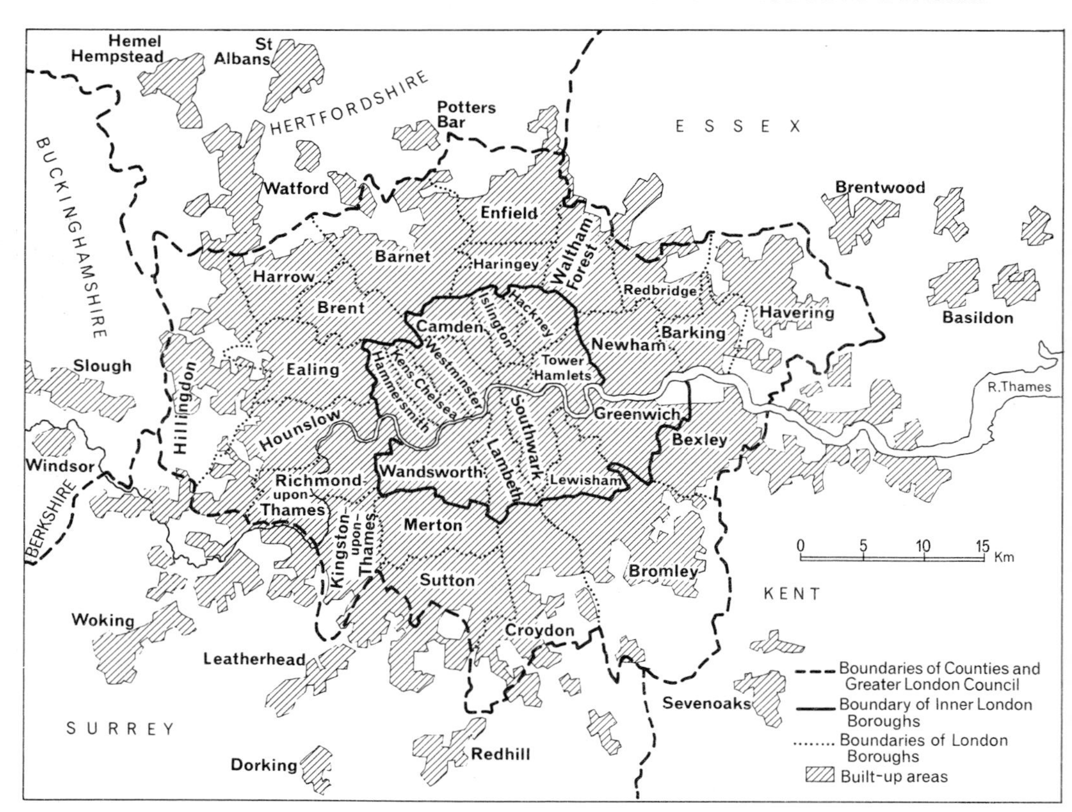

Fig. 7.1 Greater London

We are going to study a town which because of its sheer size can be considered as unique in the British Isles. Not only is London the largest single urban unit, but it holds a special position as the largest port, the biggest industrial centre and the capital of the United Kingdom. We shall attempt to discover how we can divide it up into different areas or *zones*. But before we do this we need to settle one question. What exactly do we mean when we write about London?

Probably most people who claim to be Londoners would say that London is the built up area which has its centre somewhere near

Trafalgar Square and which stretches northwards to Enfield, southwards to Croydon, eastwards to Hornchurch and Bexley and westwards to Hillingdon, as shown on Fig. 7.1. In fact such an answer would correspond to what is now the area ruled by the Greater London Council whose limits are also shown on Fig. 7.1 and whose total population is 7.3 millions. You will notice from the map that the Greater London Council area is, however, divided into a number of *boroughs* whose councils have a limited number of *services* under their control, for example library services, refuse collection and street lighting. There is one major difference between the inner and the outer *boroughs*; the outer *boroughs* are responsible for education within their area, whereas the inner *boroughs* which formed the old 'London County Council area' have handed their powers on education to the 'Inner London Education Authority'.

This political area known as Greater London was formed in 1965. As you may well imagine, London has gradually grown to this size, especially since 1850. Fig. 7.2 shows 4 stages in this growth of London:

1. The medieval city which in extent is approximately the size of the present city of London.
2. The area which was built up in 1850 and is mainly marked in north London by the sites of the main railway stations which could only be built on what was then the outskirts of the built up area, as in the cases of King's Cross, St Pancras, Euston, Marylebone and Paddington.
3. The area which was built up round about 1914.
4. The present day extent of the built up area.

Such a pattern tends to reveal a characteristic of most towns in industrial countries, namely their tendency to grow in a series of concentric rings, with buildings being thickest on the ground in the centre and more thinly spread in the outer areas and, in general, the older buildings being in the centre and the newer ones on the outskirts, though as we shall see this is not always true. Thus if you went to the 'West End' district of London you would find many brand new buildings, partly to replace those destroyed in World War II, but also because many *sites* have been used several times over, on each occasion a newer building more in keeping with the needs of the times having replaced an older building, a good example being the Post Office Tower. However, many older buildings remain and with a little training it is possible to discover, by looking at houses and buildings, in what period they were built and therefore the age of the part of London the observer is standing in. Neglecting the City which presents difficulties to the observer because many sites have been used several times over, in area number 2 in Fig. 7.2 the observer might see several houses in a terrace such as those in Gordon Square which were built in the early 19th century (Fig. 7.3). Here middle class houses tend to be built as town houses around a square, the centre of which the tenants would use as an open space for strolling in. There are several similar squares in London's West End district, like Hanover Square, Russell Square,

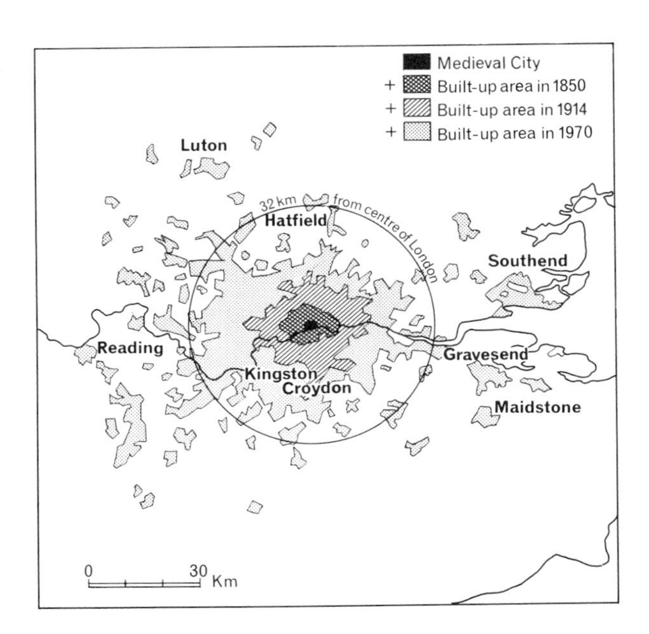

Fig. 7.2
The growth of London

Fig. 7.3
Georgian houses in Gordon Square, central London

Fig. 7.4
Early 20th century houses in Battersea, south-western London

Cavendish Square – similar styles exist in other English cities such as Abercromby Square in Liverpool. Many of the houses are no longer used as dwellings, but as offices or even classrooms for University students. Many are being pulled down to make way for more up-to-date buildings.

In area number 3 may be found houses built between 1850 and 1914 such as the example shown in Fig. 7.4. Here houses tend to become individual 'villas', with complete privacy from neighbours. Not only is there no common garden to stroll in, but the individual gardens are often separated by high walls.

In area number 4, we have the interwar type of suburban dwellings familiar to most of us – detached and semi-detached and terraced housing, usually consisting of 2 living rooms and kitchen downstairs and from 2 to 4 bedrooms upstairs with a bathroom and toilet. Small gardens extend both to the back and front. Such an area is shown in Fig. 7.5. It is with the building of such houses that the built up area of London more than doubled between 1918 and 1939. Working class houses were never as large or as well equipped as those shown in the previous photographs. A typical 19th-century working class dwelling in Battersea is shown in Fig. 7.6 and a 20th century council house estate is shown in Fig. 7.7.

Fig. 7.5 Interwar housing in a London suburb (Stoneleigh-Epsom)

Fig. 7.6 Later 19th century working class housing in Battersea now being demolished and replaced by blocks of flats.

Fig. 7.7 1960s council housing

1. (a) Using Fig. 7.1 calculate the distance from (i) the northern boundary of the borough of Enfield to the southern boundary of Croydon; (ii) the western boundary of the borough of Hillingdon to the eastern boundary of the borough of Havering.

(b) (i) what would be the area of Greater London if it were a rectangle with the two sides calculated in (a). (ii) the actual area is 1,590 square kilometres – what is the per cent error due to the approximation calculated in (b) (i)?

(c) which boroughs still have large areas of open land?

2. The following is a list of the areas, population and rateable values of the boroughs of Greater London. The rateable value is the estimated value of a property's income on which local 'rates' (i.e. taxes) are levied. For example, if a property has a rateable value of £200 and rates are levied at 50p in the £1, then the owner will pay £100 in rates each year. The way in which rateable value is estimated is not always clear, but the valuation officer responsible

Name of Borough	Population (1974)	Rateable Value in £ m. 1974	Area (hectares)
Barking	157,800	27	3,551
Barnet	302,140	56	8,849
Bexley	217,210	28	6,372
Brent	275,150	49	4,370
Bromley	305,530	45	15,706
Camden	194,440	103	2,146
Croydon	332,880	64	9,526
Ealing	292,510	54	5,483
Enfield	264,790	46	8,024
Greenwich	215,040	30	4,859
Hackney	213,020	36	1,926
Hammersmith	177,560	34	1,595
Haringey	234,690	34	2,996
Harrow	204,660	32	5,022
Havering	245,610	36	11,820
Hillingdon	235,030	52	10,903
Hounslow	207,380	46	5,854
Islington	188,160	50	1,471
Kensington and Chelsea	176,900	67	1,180
Kingston-upon-Thames	138,620	28	3,712
Lambeth	299,380	56	2,691
Lewisham	358,710	32	3,432
Merton	176,640	30	3,752
Newham	231,300	35	3,710
Redbridge	237,180	35	5,593
Richmond-upon-Thames	170,940	29	5,588
Southwark	248,230	50	2,846
Sutton	168,210	26	4,293
Tower Hamlets	153,360	40	1,997
Waltham Forest	232,580	31	3,922
Wandsworth	294,000	40	3,549
Westminster	226,240	312	2,134
City of London (Not part of Greater London Council)	5,190 *	245	271
G.L.C.	7,281,080	1,834	

(Municipal Authorities Year Book).

* Population of those actually living within the city (the night population); some 400,000 work within the city.

usually takes into account the size of the house, its gardens; its situation, the amenities in the local area, e.g. whether it is in a pleasant open situation or whether it is next to a noisy dirty factory.

(a) Ignoring the City of London, state (i) which borough has the greatest population. (ii) which borough has the greatest area. (iii) which borough has the smallest population. (iv) which borough has the smallest area. (v) what figure represents the typical size of the population of a London borough. How does that compare with the population of Hexham (page 17) and Liverpool (page 45)?

(b) (i) have the boroughs with small areas a relatively small or relatively large population? (ii) therefore which boroughs tend to have a high density of population, the large area or small area boroughs? (iii) what is the general position in Greater London of the boroughs with a high density of population?

(c) (i) which borough seems to have an abnormally high rateable value*? (ii) which boroughs seem to have a* rateable value *which is fairly high (above £50 m)? (iii) what is the general position of the boroughs with a high* rateable value*? (iv)* trace a map of the London boroughs (or enlarge Fig. 7.1) and draw columns in each London borough to represent the size of its* rateable value *(use 1 mm to represent £1 m – you will have to break the column for Westminster).*

3. *Compare Fig. 7.1 with Fig. 7.2.*

   (a) With which administrative boundary does the area built up by 1914 approximately correspond?

   (b) With what administrative boundary does the area built up in 1970 approximately correspond?

   (c) Why then do you suppose that the administrative boundaries of London change from time to time?

4. *(a) What differences would you find between central and suburban London (i) in the density of buildings? (ii) in the age of buildings?*

   (b) What exceptions would you find to what you have stated under (a)?

5. *What contrasting style of houses would you find in various parts of London? (See Figs. 7.3, 7.4, 7.5, 7.6, 7.7.)*

B. Functional Specialization in Different Areas

So far we have been concerned to establish that *zones* of different ages can be recognized in London. Earlier, it was stated that buildings were being replaced and that some houses had been changed into offices. We must understand why this tends to occur in almost every city in the world. In the first place if a city grows it is because more people wish to work and live within it. Once a town begins to thrive many firms are attracted to it because of the advantages it offers in labour supply and as a market for the firm's goods and services. The business of firms is conducted by their offices which need to contact suppliers of raw materials, customers, insurers, shippers, sometimes government departments if permits or certificates for import and export are required. Obviously the nearer the various offices are together the easier the business may be conducted. Consequently, such offices tend to be found grouped together in the *central business district* of the town. Thus the City of London is the main *central business district* of the London Area. Now it might well be argued that such a district need not be central but, in practice, such districts have grown up in the centre of town because of the central position they occupied with respect to the market formed by the town's inhabitants. Clearly as the *central business district* expanded, so it had to take over land and buildings which were once given over to dwellings. There was usually no difficulty about this, since the firms who took over these areas could afford to pay prices or rents that the private individual could rarely afford. Thus little by little the private householder was squeezed out of the central area and either his house was converted into an office, or it was knocked down and a new purpose built office building was substituted. Occasionally private owners resist and an unusual association of buildings is found in a *central business district* as in the case illustrated in Fig. 7.8. In London the main *central business district* is so specialized in large scale business transactions that it does not cater for all the services a citizen might require. Thus there are a large number of subsidiary *central business districts* catering for local needs – especially shopping centres which often include local administrative services and entertainment; for example such *central business districts* exist at Lewisham Clock Tower, Holloway Road, Camden Town, Bromley, Kingston-upon-Thames, Wood

Fig. 7.8 Central Croydon from the south-west

Green and so on. Still smaller in size is the local shopping 'parade' which usually consists of a small group of food shops, a newsagent and possibly a chemist. Thus in general it is possible in London to recognize 3 broad categories of *central business districts*; (i) a highly specialized one the city (ii) a large local shopping centre (iii) a small local shopping centre.

However, having established this, we will still not understand what the various specialized districts of London are, unless we bear in mind that because it is the *capital city* of the U.K. it performs services for the whole country as well as for London. The government offices in the Whitehall area make evident this national *function*, as do the huge offices of the large firms with branches and factories all over the country, such as the offices of the Imperial Chemical Industries. Recently many such office buildings have been placed out of London to overcome some of the congestion they were causing. Thus the national insurance offices, are now located in the Newcastle-upon-Tyne area. Others have been set up at nearer towns such as Dorking. The various specialized districts of inner London are shown on Fig. 7.9. The widespread industry of Greater London is shown on Fig. 7.10. The industrial areas tend to be long and narrow in shape.

Fig. 7.9 Central London

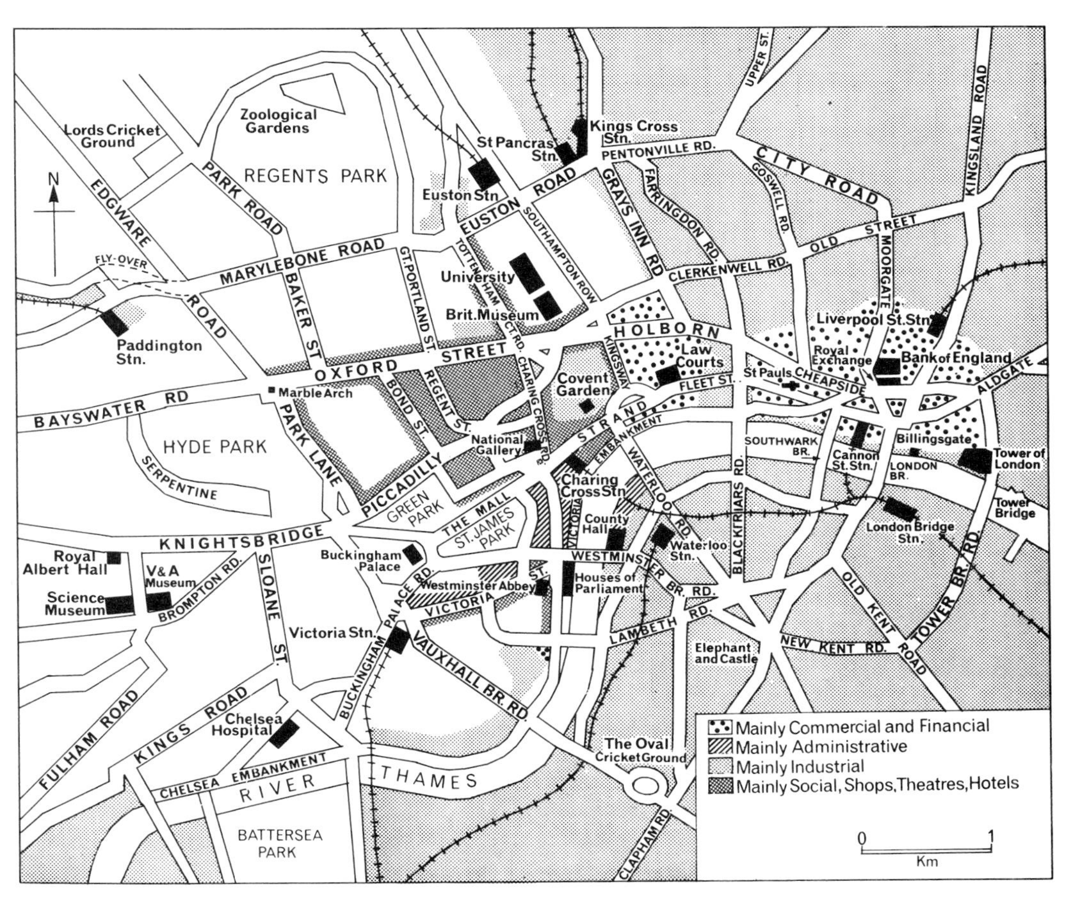

You may wonder whether London would have had so many industries or grown so large had it not also been on a navigable river. Fig. 7.11 enables you to compare London's dock system with the main industrial areas, whilst the diagrams and maps in Fig. 7.12 and 7.13 indicate how important is London's port in relation to the trade of the whole country. In fact it has been estimated that 25 per cent of the U.K. trade is generated within 50 km of London and that 50 per cent is generated within 160 km of London. Thus the port of London is well placed to serve this trade – but remember that it is also because the port of London exists that trade has been able to develop. Hence if London wants to keep or expand its import-export and *transit trade*, it needs to provide facilities which, as we saw in the case of Liverpool, enable ships to do a quick turn round. So the Port of London Authority is going ahead with modernization schemes which enable ships, for example, to be loaded directly from the side instead of by crane, for *container* handling and for lorries and cars to drive straight into the holds of ships with their loads. The possibility of expanding London's trade is very great for, within the triangle formed by Birmingham, Paris and the Ruhr towns in Germany, about 66 per cent of North-west Europe's manufacturing industry is located, and it is industry which is basically responsible for generating trade. The trade of the Port of London is shown in Table 7.1.

Table 7.1 Port of London Trade (in million tonnes)

		1970	1971	1972	1973	1974
Imports	Foreign	32.57	31.84	32.84	32.15	27.67
	Coastwise	16.32	14.75	11.90	13.13	13.97
Exports	Foreign	6.32	6.08	5.41	6.89	6.31
	Coastwise	3.75	3.44	3.06	3.64	2.90
In Transit		1.46	1.31	1.30	1.43	0.66

6. *Why are industries and business firms attracted to large centres of population?*
7. *(a) Why do the offices of various firms tend to congregate together?*
   (b) Give the name of a street in a town you know where there is a group of offices.
   (c) In what ways have the property firms responsible for the rebuilding of certain areas of London recognized the fact that offices tend to group together?
   (d) What name is given to the office and shopping area of a town?
8. *(a) Originally many central areas of London and other towns were inhabited. Today office workers often have journeys to work of 1 hour from their homes. How was it that people were forced to live far from their work?*
   (b) In the extreme case of the City of London, what is (i) the night population (ii) the total day population (see table, page 64) (iii) the ratio of the night to the total day population.

(c) *Enquire of the time taken for the journey to work of ten of your friends' fathers or mothers. What is the average time taken? What is the most frequent or most typical time for the journey?*

(d) *What problems does the inflow of people to central London pose for the transport authorities?*

9. (a) *In some small towns there is only one* central business district. *In London there are many. Why is this?*

(b) *Within London, business districts are of unequal importance. Name 3 business districts you know personally and arrange them in order of importance. State in each case what are the functions of that particular district.*

(c) *The City of London specializes in financial services – that is in arranging loans to finance trade of various kinds. Suggest how the city came to be concerned with this sort of service.*

10. *Study Fig. 7.9*

(a) *What are the main functions of (i) the West End district between Piccadilly and the National Gallery (the Leicester Square area)? (ii) the West End district around Oxford Street? (iii) the area north of the city around Clerkenwell Road? (iv) the area around Hyde Park?*

(b) *Why is it likely that most of us could not afford to pay rent for a house or flat around Hyde Park?*

(c) *Which side of Central London is the more industrial?*

11. *Fig. 7.10 is a map of the distribution of the main industrial areas of London – examine this map carefully and*

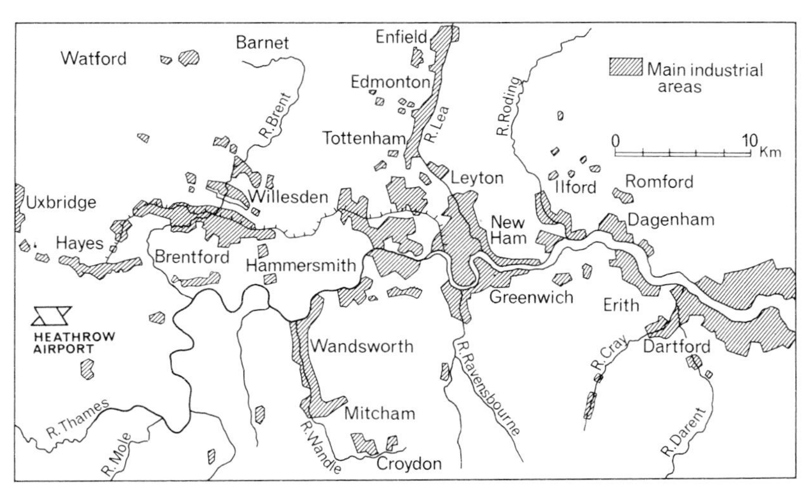

Fig. 7.10 London's industrial areas

(a) *State what you might notice to be the position of the main industrial areas in relation to waterways. (i) in east and south London (ii) in west London.*

(b) *One industrial area developed mainly on or near the Great West Road – which area is that?*

(c) *Many of the industries along Thames-side are power stations, gas works, sugar and grain mills. Why are they so sited?*

(d) *Many industrial locations along rivers, such as alongside the Wandle or the Cray, were not put there because water transport was available since the rivers are not navigable. Suggest reasons why industrialists might have found cheap sites for their factories along these rivers.*

12. *Using Fig. 7.11*
    (a) *Give the names of the main docks in London downstream from the city.*
    (b) *(i) what tends to happen to the size of the dock basins as one travels downstream? (ii) give reasons for what you find.*
    (c) *(i) if goods had to be brought into London from abroad and taken away quickly by lorry to Birmingham, to which docks would it be best to send them? (ii) if goods came in at Tilbury and they had to go to Rochester by road, which way would you route the lorry driver?*

Fig. 7.11 The Port of London

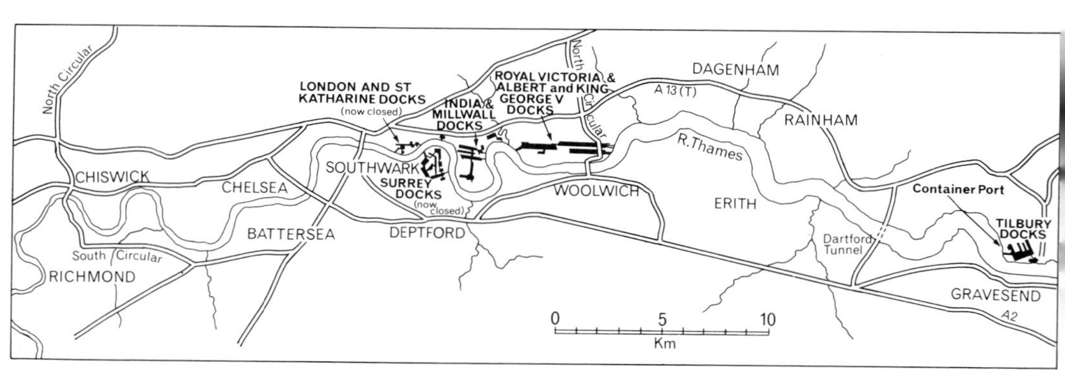

13. *From Table 7.1*
    (a) *What is the approximate ratio between London's export and import trade by weight of goods?*
    (b) *What is the approximate ratio between London's export and import trade by value of goods?*
    (c) *What does the great difference between the two ratios suggest about the nature of London's imports compared with her exports?*

14. *Study Fig. 7.12 (a) and 7.12 (b) and*
    (a) *Make a list of the ports of the U.K. in order of importance (i) for exports. (ii) for imports.*
    (b) *(i) what strikes you about the position of Airports in relation to many sea ports? (ii) would Airports have been in the same relative position if the figures had been based on weight of goods instead of value?*
    (c) *What has happened to the imports and exports of London and Liverpool relative to Southampton, Felixstowe and Dover. Can you explain these changes between 1970 and 1974?*

15. (a) *What do Figs. 7.13 (a) and (b) tell you about the Port of London's hinterland for exports and imports?*

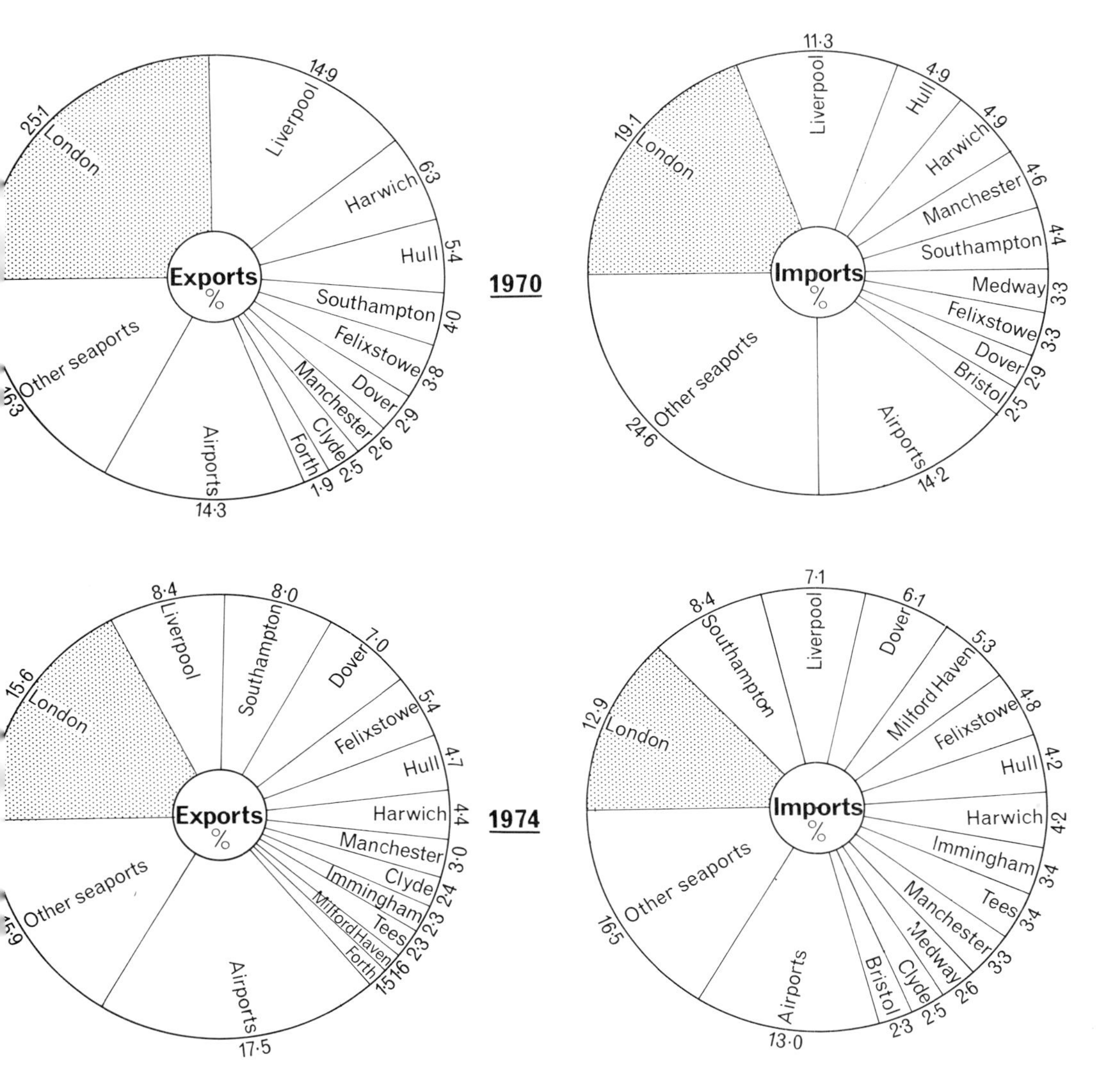

Fig. 7.12
(a) Exports and (b) Imports (by value) of the principal ports as a percentage of the U.K. total for 1970 and 1974

(b) *Name the regions 25 per cent or more of whose exports pass through the Port of London.*

(c) *Why is it that London has a large share of the exports of many British regions?*

16. (a) *Using an atlas draw a sketch map to show London in relation to the positions of Birmingham, Paris (France) and Dortmund (Germany). This map should show the coastline of south and south-eastern England and of northern France, Belgium and the Netherlands. Put in the towns Calais, Lille, Antwerp, Brussels, Amsterdam, Rotterdam, Dusseldorf and Duisburg.*

(b) *Is London in a good position to develop its trade? Why has this trade not developed since 1970?*

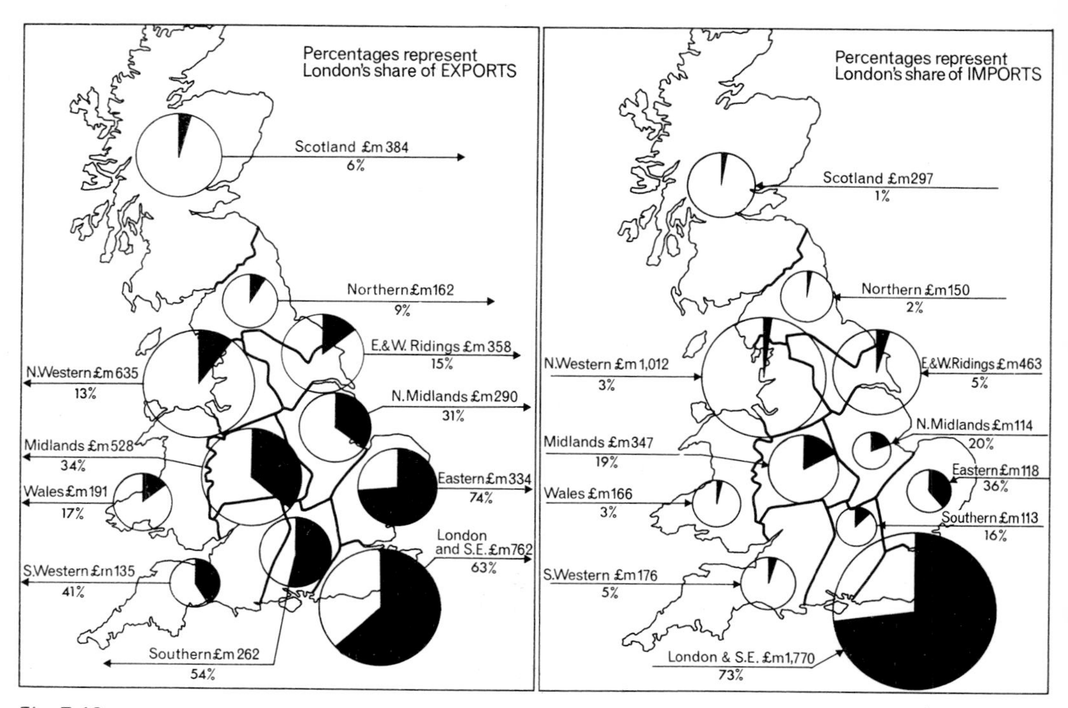

Fig. 7.13
Importance of the Port of London to each region of Great Britain (a) exports and (b) imports by value
(Port of London Authority)

C. Theories about Urban Structure

If you look at Fig. 7.2 again, you will notice that the historical growth of London results in the existence of a series of concentric rings on the map, with the older areas in the centre and the most recently built areas on the outskirts. This kind of pattern led the American E. W. Burgess to suggest in 1923 that many towns would tend to have an *urban structure* of the same kind. This particular theory is illustrated in Fig. 7.15. Broadly his idea was that as a city expanded, so the central area would become essentially the *central business district*, this would be surrounded by a *zone of transition* where former large residential houses are being broken up into flats or used as offices or as small workshops like in parts of Islington in London. This zone would be followed by one in which small working class houses and flats would dominate, since working people would need to live fairly close to their work in the city centre or in the zone of transition. A London example might be Wandsworth. Beyond the *working class zone* would lie the houses of the 'middle classes' who could afford to live somewhat further from the city centre in newer and more spacious accommodation. Still further out would lie the 'commuter belt' of those who could afford to live in the semi-rural areas surrounding the city. Examples of the last two in the London area would be Bromley and Sevenoaks (see Fig. 7.1).

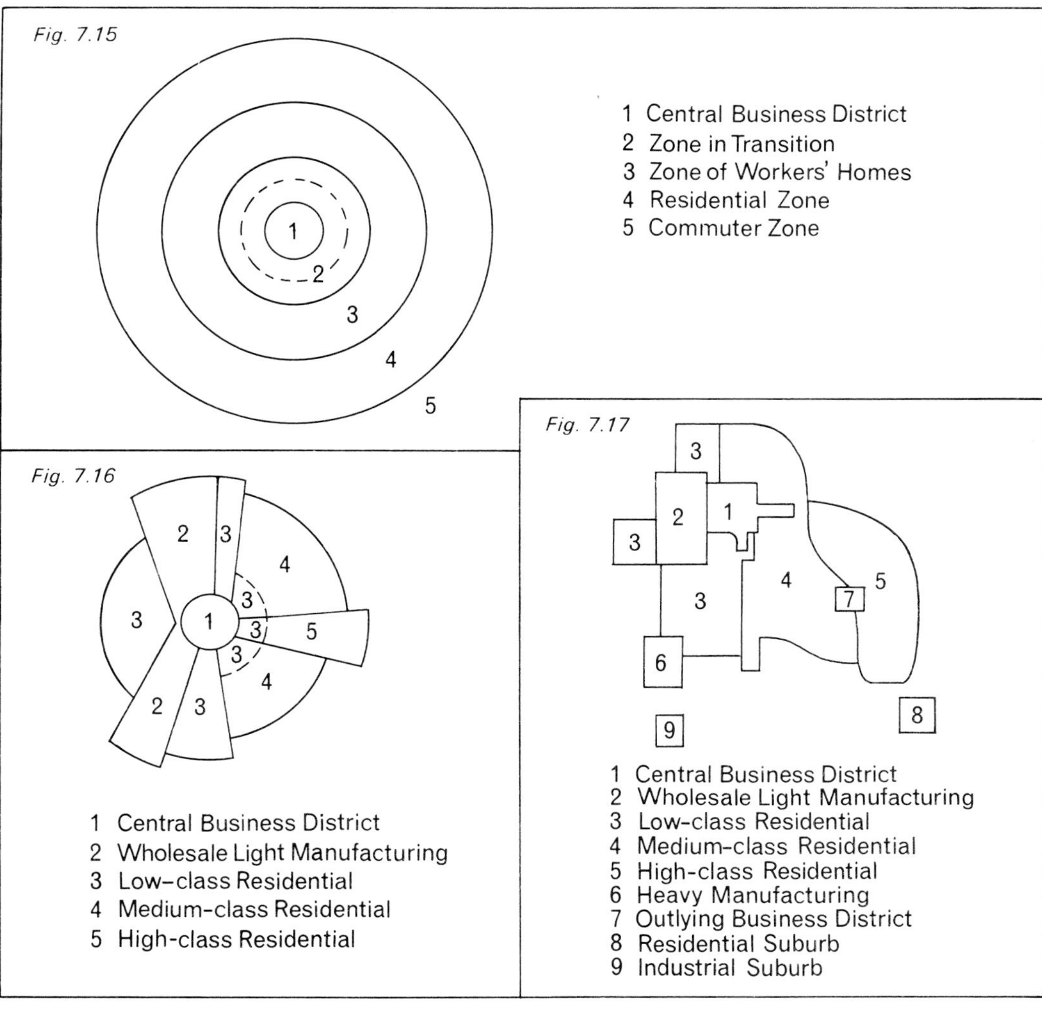

Another American, Homer Hoyt, suggested that the influence of transport routes would tend to make cities develop sectors rather than concentric rings. His model which was suggested round about 1939 is illustrated in Fig. 7.16. It is a mixture of concentric rings cut up by sectors which extend outwards from the city centre. We can find examples in London: the industrial areas extending along the Lea Valley in Fig. 7.10 could be thought of as part of Sector 2 in Hoyt's model, whilst the high class residential areas extending from Westminister through part of Camden to Barnet (Fig. 7.1) could be an example of a Sector 5 type of development. Two other Americans, C. D. Harris and E. L. Ullman, suggested that many towns could look like Fig. 7.17. Basically the main idea here is that, while there is some order in the way cities grow and develop (for example district 3 is farther out than district 2 which itself lies beyond the central business district), yet cities do not conform to the neat patterns

Fig. 7.15 (top) Concentric theory of urban structure (after Burgess)

Fig. 7.16 (above left) Sector theory (after Hoyt)

Fig. 7.17 (above right) *Multiple nuclei theory (after Harris and Ullman)*

Fig. 7.14
Central London and Southwark

a
y
b

suggested by Burgess and Hoyt. The very fact that we can find examples in London which seem to illustrate both theories, suggests that London's urban structure is not a simple one.

In general most of the models of urban structure tend to assume for simplicity that the town for which they provide a model exists on a flat plain where the physical environment is uniform. In fact, few cities really exist in such conditions. Some are on the coast (see Chapters 5 and 19) and so cannot be circular, some are on hilly ground and this affects the shape of the town and the types of functions as hills are often prized as good residential areas. Rivers and their flood plains often cross towns, and as we saw in the case of the Lea Valley, flood plains have low land values and are often taken up by industrial premises, consequently an industrial belt may follow a flood plain. Thus, whilst cities may tend to look like one or other of the models shown in Figs. 7.15, 7.16 and 7.17, they will seldom exactly resemble them.

Conclusions

London, as we have seen, is many things; a port, a financial centre, a shopping centre, an entertainment centre, but also a residential area. All these *functions* have a *geographical* or *spatial* aspect. Sometimes for physical reasons, as in the case of the docks, sometimes for economic reasons as in the case of the *central business district*, similar *functions* tend to cluster together. So we tend to have in London as in many other large towns, *functional zones* such as the city, the Whitehall administrative zone, the West End high-class shopping centre, and so on. We must remember that these zones are never purely one-function zones; rather does one function stand out, for if you keep your eyes open when you walk in a town, you will find many mixed uses of any particular area, for example, residential use in the Clerkenwell industrial area of central London.

One problem which is affecting central London is the tendency for factories and offices to migrate to the suburbs and even to areas outside London. When companies or public corporations wish to expand their business and to make access to their sites easier, they tend to choose new 'out-of-town' locations where land and rents are cheaper and roads and railways are less congested. Further, the Government has encouraged the movement of officies to suburban or country locations to limit the number of office workers who commute each day from the suburbs to the City and West End. If this change were to go on too quickly without other redevelopments, then central London might become a dead city.

REVISION EXERCISES

17. ***What proportion of the population of the U.K. (look up chapter 1) lives in London?***

18. ***What proportion of the total area of the U.K. is the London area?***

19. *What is meant by the term Greater London*
   (a) In every day speech?
   (b) As an administrative area?

20. ***Why do rateable values differ from one part of London to another?***

21. ***Why are the inner London boroughs generally smaller in size than the outer London boroughs?***

22. ***Why is it sometimes difficult to tell the period during which a particular area of London was built?***

23. ***What are the main* functional zones *of London?***

24. ***Write a brief account of the nature of the Port of London's trade and of its hinterland.***

25. ***Study Fig. 7.18. What trends do you notice in total import and export traffic, and what changes are occuring in the composition of this traffic?***

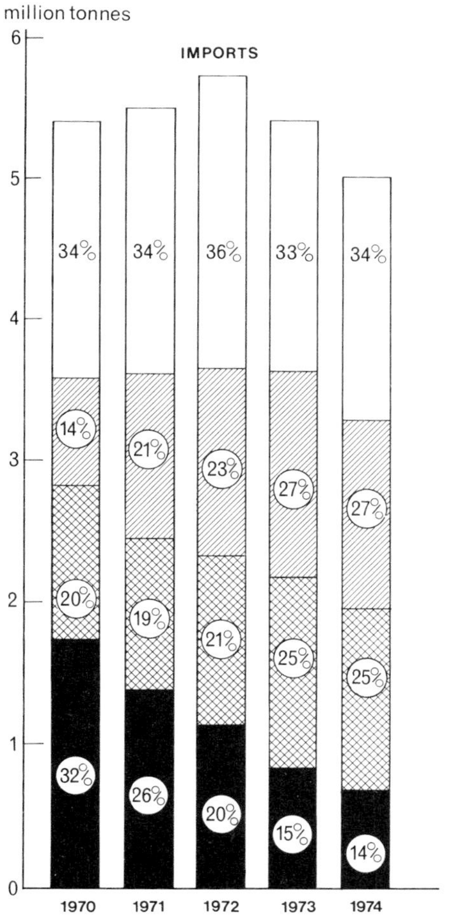

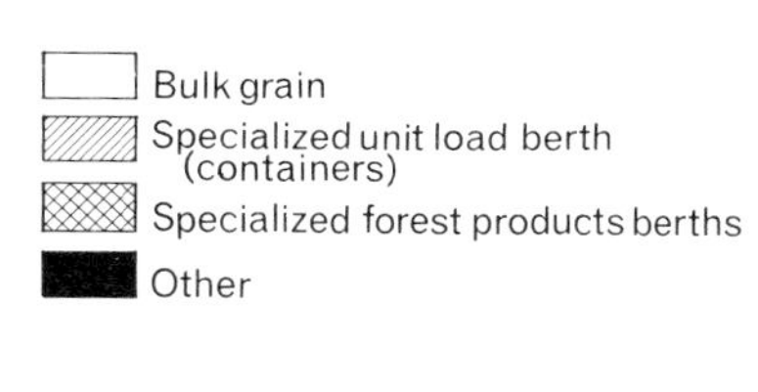

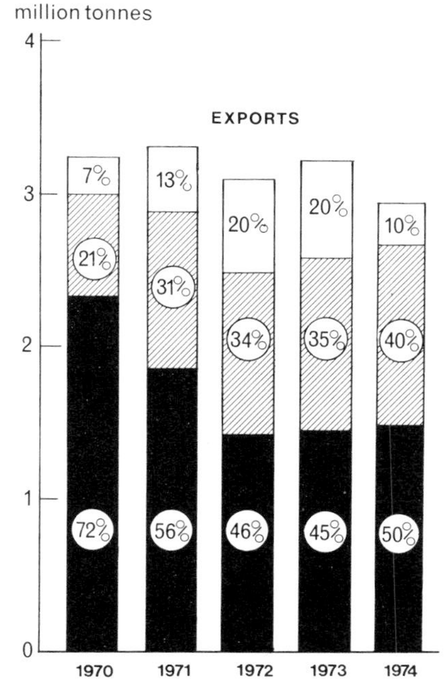

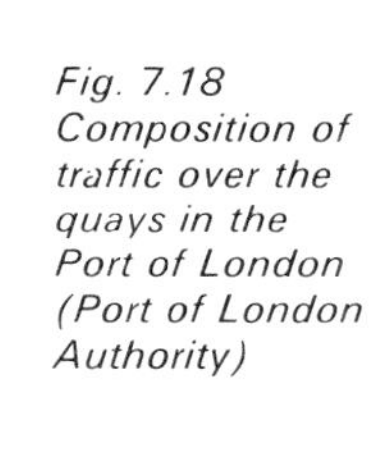
Fig. 7.18 Composition of traffic over the quays in the Port of London (Port of London Authority)

26. ***(a) Study Fig. 7.14 and state which functional zones the letters a, b, c, and d stand for.***
   (b) What is shown by the letters X, Y, Z?
   (c) Can you identify: the Oval, London Bridge railway station,

the Thames bridges, Regent Street, Aldwych, the Kingsway, the Elephant and Castle roundabout, the Blackfriars to Elephant and Castle railway track? (Fig. 7.9 will help).

27. *From the maps in this chapter and from your knowledge of London or your own town draw a sketch map to show how you would divide it up into rings, sectors or districts. Label each district according to its main function. Does your map look anything like Burgess's, Hoyt's or Ullman's and Harris's models? Why do you think your map differs from theirs?*

Chapter Eight

Rebuilding City Centres and the Traffic Problem: Birmingham

A. City Centres

As we have seen in Liverpool, London and many of the other towns we have examined, city centres have a tendency to change in character over the years. In some cases, where the town is small and growing very slowly, the change in the central areas may be limited to the replacement from time to time of an old building by a new one, or a group of small shops may be bought up by a big supermarket chain and a new supermarket is set up in its place, perhaps simply by knocking down walls and making three shops into one. In other cases, however, towns have grown fairly rapidly in the last 150 years and the *central business district* has expanded in a rather haphazard manner, leaving blocks of older residential building here and there. These may be decaying rather badly and not be worth patching up. Further, even the commercial heart of the town may consist of a medley of buildings, some very old, put to a variety of uses from industrial workshops to warehouses, shops and office buildings. Such an untidy *townscape* inevitably arose from many years of unplanned growth. Individual shopkeepers, industrialists and other businessmen were, in general, allowed to develop their businesses where they wished with a minimum of control and the result was, in many cases, something like that shown in Fig. 8.1.

Strangely enough, one of the problems of inner areas, namely that of old decaying houses, arose because of some attempted measure of government control. During World War I (1914–18) and in later years, attempts were made to protect poorer tenants against large increases in the rents of certain dwellings by freezing the rents then charged. The argument was simple: accommodation was expected to be in short supply because of lack of new building and because some houses and flats might be destroyed by enemy action. If rents were allowed to go up as a result of this shortage, many people with low incomes might find it difficult to pay such rents. Therefore as a special measure rents were pegged at their existing level. In effect the Rent Restriction Act prevented landlords' in-

Fig. 8.1
The centre of old Birmingham

comes from rising. Now, what had been expected to be a temporary measure lasted for a very long time, for the supply of new accommodation after World War I did not increase sufficiently quickly to make it easy for people to find relatively cheap housing. Thus governments maintained rent restriction until many years after World War II which itself further decreased the supply of houses. The consequence was that many rents in the 1950s remained at a level fixed in 1914 or in the 1920s and 1930s, although by then the price of almost everything else had risen. For example it is estimated that in the mid-1950s prices were in general three times what they had been in 1939. Thus many landlords were either unable and in most cases unwilling to spend money on properties which brought in an income which was insufficient to repay them for the costs of repair or improvement. So many houses were allowed to get into a state of decay which caused them to become uninhabitable, thereby making the housing shortage worse.

However, quite apart from this special problem, buildings have a limited useful life. There comes a time when the cost of repairing and improving a building year by year is such that it is a better proposition to knock it down and replace it with a new one. A large proportion of the buildings in city centres had reached this stage in the years which followed World War II. Fig. 8.2 shows how extensive was the area of housing in Birmingham which was considered to be in need of replacement in 1948. Further as we saw in the case of London, if a town is growing rapidly, the rents in the city centre become very high because many business firms are usually competing for accommodation. It follows from this that if a landlord owns

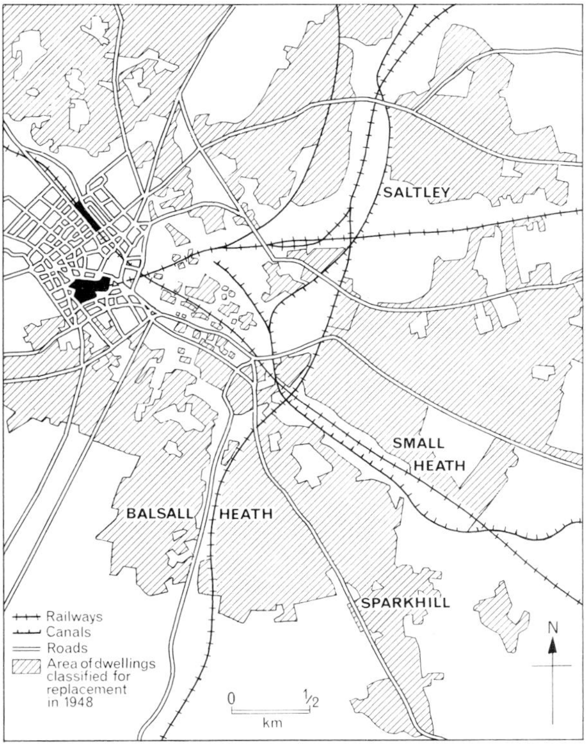

Fig. 8.2 Central Birmingham and the inner residential areas

an area of land in a central area and this is occupied by a low building with one or two storeys, he could make a lot more money by knocking down the low building and building a high one, thereby allowing him to offer more high priced accommodation, probably as offices. Hence there is a tendency for older buildings to be replaced by taller blocks which yield more useful space in a given area. This is also the reason why modern car parks in city centres are multistorey car parks. Both these features are shown in the photograph (Fig. 8.3) of that central part of Birmingham known as the Bull Ring.

The problems which arise in the inner areas of a city are:

1. The rehousing of thousands of families living in old decaying houses, many of which are over 100 years old.

2. The reconstruction of commercial areas with the aim of providing more and better accommodation for firms wishing to set up in the city centre.

3. The remodelling of transport networks.

However, as we have seen, allowing individuals or firms to set up shop, or build where they please often results in a *townscape* which is hardly beautiful and may create all kinds of extra problems, for example the supply of *services* (water, gas, electricity, sewage, schools) may be insufficient or the roads may become choked with traffic. This is why Acts of Parliament (the Town and Country Planning Acts of 1947, 1971 and 1972) were passed to ensure that all redevelopment of city centres and all new development elsewhere

Fig. 8.3 The Bull Ring and car park

should be properly planned by the civic authorities in consultation with all the public bodies which provide services, and with business firms intending to redevelop in the area.

If we again study the case of Birmingham, we find that, following the passing of the Town and Country Planning Act of 1947, the authorities made an intensive survey of the city which lasted four years. On the basis of this survey a Development Plan was prepared and submitted to the Central Government authority (Ministry of Housing and Local Government) for approval. This plan was finally

Table 8.1

Type of Land Use	Area in hectares	
	1951	1971
Residential	10,763	11,684
Industrial	1,499	1,872
Railways and Railway land	543	560
Waterways and associated docks and depots	108	112
Business and shopping	119	361
Civic buildings	422	636
Educational establishments	119	275
Public open spaces	533	1,271
Open spaces not available to general public	1,617	1,980
Other areas	4,758	1,886

(City of Birmingham Planning Dept.)

approved with modifications suggested by the Ministry of Housing and Local Government and in the light of objections, in 1961. The objectives of the plan were:

1. To allocate areas for housing, to improve housing conditions by the redevelopment of parts of the central areas.
2. To increase the area of open spaces within the city.
3. To allocate *sites* for schools in the light of the development of housing areas.
4. To make land available for industry.
5. To improve the road system and ensure a smooth flow of traffic.

The areas of Birmingham allocated to various uses in 1971 are shown in Table 8.1.

Modern planning is flexible. Any plan which is devised is reviewed at the end of a five year period, with a view to taking into account changed conditions – for example an unexpected growth in population, or new requirements for industry, or a changed pattern of traffic flow. It is also necessary to amend plans in the light of changes in public policy. Consequently in 1974 the former county borough council of Birmingham put forward a new Structure Plan which foresaw the following changes in policy:

1. There will be much more emphasis on the retention and improvement of housing rather than the redevelopment of whole areas. The new urban renewal policy is shown in Fig. 8.6(b) where, over and above the comprehensive redevelopment areas shown in detail in Fig. 8.6(a), two kinds of areas are marked:

   (a) the *renewal areas* which are close to the existing redevelopment areas, in which houses built mainly between 1875 and 1914 would be renovated to make them suitable for present-day occupation;
   (b) the *general improvement areas* which are in clusters further afield and in which not only would houses be improved, but other facilities would also be provided such as schools, health centres, open spaces for recreation, in order to raise environmental quality.

2. Public transport is to be encouraged since it is now agreed that attempting to provide facilities for all who wish to use private cars in the city seems only to cause greater traffic difficulties and a decline in the quality of the environment. A consequence of this policy is to restrict the availability of parking spaces in the city centre.

3. There will be a tendency to adopt measures which result in the saving of energy. Thus the use of private cars is again to be discouraged on this score.

Structure Plans are less rigid than the former development plans. They provide long-term aims and guidelines and are put into operation by more specific short-term plans.

1. *What is meant by the term* townscape *used on p. 79?*
2. *Why is the* townscape *shown in Fig. 8.1 described as untidy?*
3. *(a) Why were rent restriction laws passed?*
   (b) How did rent restriction cause the decay of many houses in cities?
   (c) Would owner-occupied houses decay for the same reasons?
4. *Why is it necessary to pull down old houses and replace them by new ones even when they are not rent-controlled?*
5. *(a) Make a grid of vertical and horizontal lines at 2 cm intervals on a piece of tracing paper in a frame which is the same size as the frame of Fig. 8.2.*
   (b) Place the grid over Fig. 8.2 and count the number of grid squares which have half their areas or more covered with shading (i.e. areas with dwellings needing replacement).
   (c) (i) what proportion is this of the total number of squares? (ii) work out the total area shown on the map and then the approximate area needing new dwellings.
   (d) Why is it that there is apparently little housing needing redevelopment in the area near the railway stations?
6. *Explain why apparently quite serviceable buildings are demolished in city centres.*
7. *Give at least two reasons why the unplanned development or redevelopment of towns would probably be unwise in the 20th century.*
8. *(a) What British Act of Parliament makes local authorities responsible for planning the development of the areas under their control?*
   (b) In the case of Birmingham, (i) what steps did the planning authority take to get an approved development plan, and (ii) what were the main aims of the plan?
9. *Supposing you were responsible for redeveloping a block of land for industry, shops and private dwellings, what offices would you have to consult to ensure that proper services were provided?*
10. *(a) From Table 8.1 work out (i) the percentage of land allocated to residential, industrial, business and shopping uses in 1951 and in 1971, (ii) those land uses in which the biggest proportional increases were envisaged by the development plan.*
    (b) Why do you suppose there has been an important increase in the acreage of land allocated to 'open spaces'?

B. Planning and the Traffic Problem

Redeveloping city centres cannot take place without a very thorough investigation of the likely movement of people and goods. When towns are small the total traffic attracted to the city centre is small and at the worst may cause a little congestion at certain times of the day on certain days of the week. Through traffic may be diverted by *by-pass roads* away from the city centre. When a town is large, however, the problem assumes altogether different proportions. In the first place only a small proportion of the traffic is *through traffic*, so that building by-passes only takes a relatively small quantity of traffic from the city centre. In the second place the number of people moving into the *central business district* (C.B.D.) to work every day is very large and creates congestions at the beginning and at the end of the working day. In the third place people also move into the C.B.D. to shop in the bigger departmental stores. In the fourth place if private cars are used by workers and shoppers, these must be parked during the hours between entering and leaving the C.B.D. Last but not least, lorries and vans delivering goods to the city centre must be able to stop and unload without causing traffic blockages.

Let us examine each of these aspects of the traffic problem in turn, beginning with the one presented by day time shoppers. The main difficulty here lies in finding a way of parking cars without choking the roads in the C.B.D., for, a double line of parked cars in a road has the same effect as if the road were suddenly halved in width. The result: existing traffic can only squeeze through slowly. In some of the new towns like Basildon, where the city centre could be planned from the beginning, the ingenious idea was developed of making the main shopping centre a pedestrian area. This idea was adopted by Birmingham which has converted many of its central streets into pedestrian precincts (Fig. 8.4). The shopper

Fig. 8.4 Pedestrian shopping precinct in Birmingham

can walk about in the shopping precinct without fear of motor traffic and he is forced, if he has come by car, to leave his car in a special car park provided near the shopping area. Such car parks also serve to get commuters' cars off the streets of the C.B.D.

These have to be sited in strategic positions in the C.B.D., but if possible off main roads so that cars slowing down to enter car parks do not cause obstructions to the free flow of traffic. Fig. 8.5 shows the position of some existing car parks for the

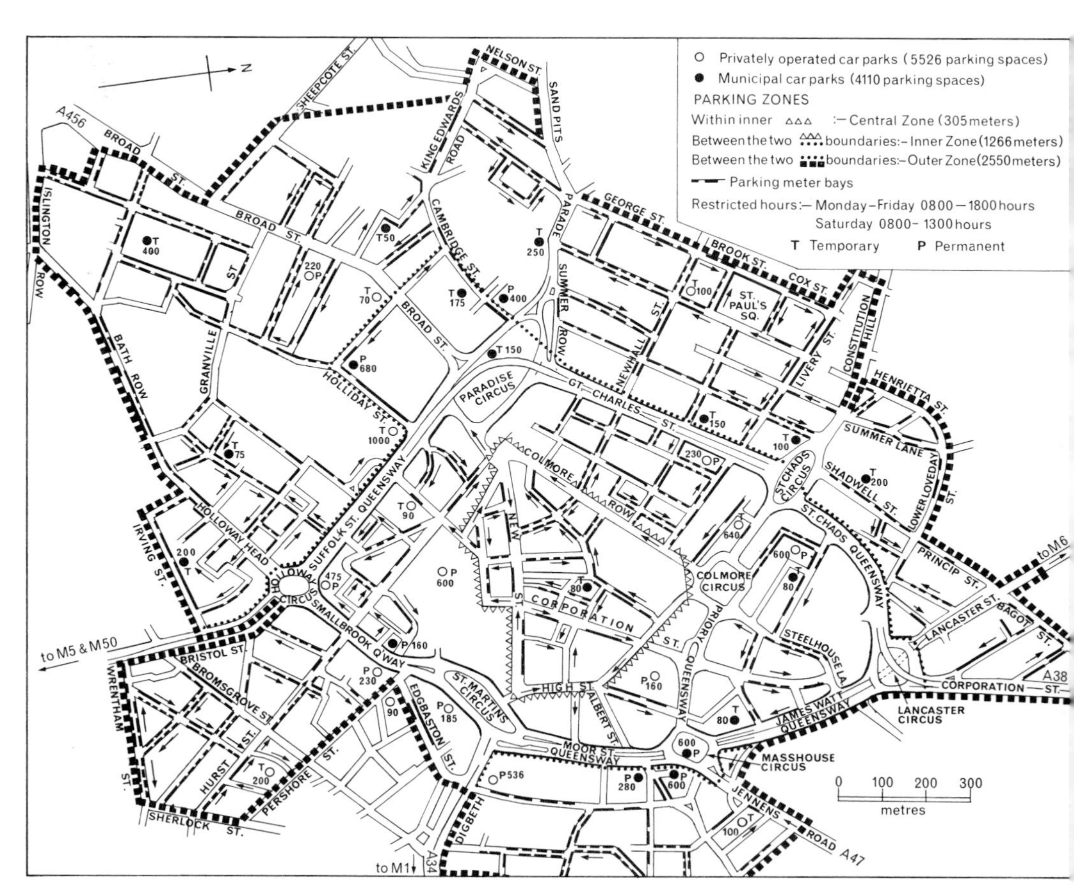

Fig. 8.5 The central business district – car parks and Ringway, 1972.

central area of Birmingham. In some cases access to the car park is gained by a tunnel which leads down from the central reservation of dual carriageway so as not to impede traffic flow. (See Fig. 8.3.)

Such car parks are not cheap. Each parking place may cost between £300 and £450. A total of 9,440 parking places existed in 1973. Some of those provided are shown in Table 8.2(a).

The movement of traffic in and out of the C.B.D. during the morning and evening rush hours is, however, dependent on the capacity of the roads into the C.B.D. and the extent to which the streets in the central area become choked. Now the capacity of roads

Table 8.2(a) Parking Places in Central Birmingham

Location	No. of Places
Edgbaston Street Underground Park (for market traders only – not on map)	130
Bull Ring Multi-Storey Park	600
Bull Ring Parking Floors	500
Smallbrook Ringway Park	160
Pershore Street Park (not on map)	230
Holliday Street Multi-Storey Park	700

Source: City of Birmingham Planning Dept.

may be increased by widening them. But this is enormously expensive. Not only must the land be bought to make the widening possible, but buildings may have to be knocked down and people or firms rehoused elsewhere. Very often this can only occur in areas of old buildings 'ripe' for development. Further, street widening often involves the relaying of sewers, water mains, gas pipes, electricity and telephone cables. As we can see every day in our towns, in spite of the expense, street widening goes on, although you can understand why it sometimes appears to be a slow process.

Whether the streets in the C.B.D. become choked depends on how quickly cars can get to their destination and be parked off the streets before other cars come into the area. Fig. 8.5 shows the old street pattern of central Birmingham on which has been superimposed an *inner ringway* now complete. Before the ringway was built, as cars came into the central area from North, South, East and West, they met at various street intersections and in the process of crossing each other to reach their ultimate destination, caused traffic chaos. The inner ringway with its underpasses enables vehicles to cross one another without meeting and therefore without needing to slow down or stop, and it enables motorists who, for example, might wish to go from Bristol Street (south of the map) to Livery Street (north of the map) to do so without using the streets of the Central Area, which are free to be used by purely local traffic.

The congestion caused by lorries and vans delivering goods may be overcome by the provision of special delivery bays within buildings receiving the goods. Commercial vehicles can then drive straight into a covered unloading area and thereby not impede traffic flow. In the same way pedestrian footpaths are being set out in such a way that they connect up with the commercial buildings which they serve, but only connect up with the roads at bus stops or at crossing points.

Just as the *inner ring road* is meant to relieve congestion in the city centre, so the *middle ring road* will do the same for the areas immediately around the C.B.D. The path of this *middle ring road* is shown in Fig. 8.6(a) in relation to the districts to be redeveloped. Whereas the *inner ring road* is completed, work on the *middle ring road* is about half completed. Work can only proceed as each area is demolished and rebuilt – such work is scheduled to take twenty years, the rate at which it is being done is limited by the finance becoming

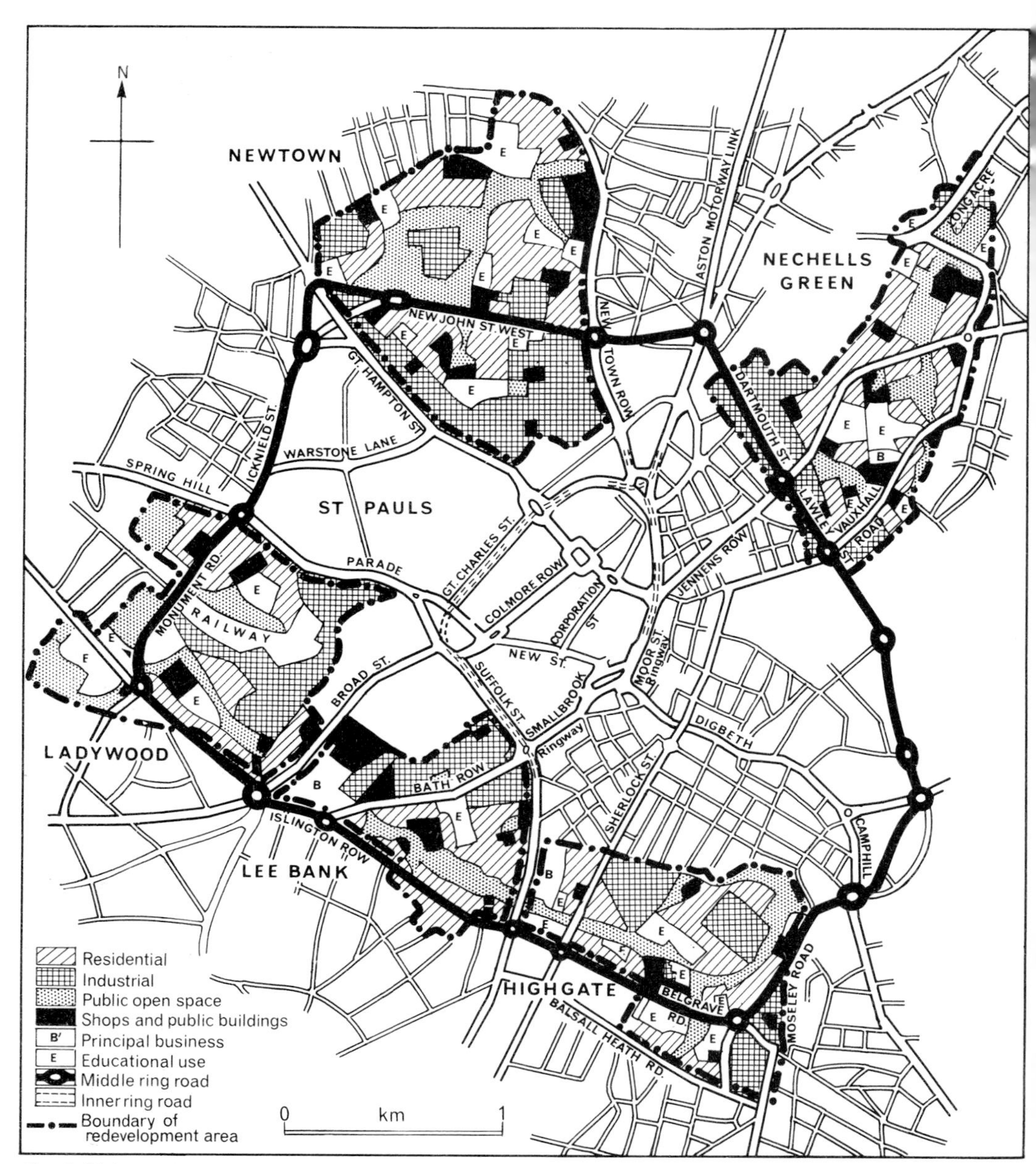

Fig. 8.6(a) The middle ring road and redevelopment areas (Phase 1)

available for each redevelopment scheme. Such finance not only comes from government sources but also from private organizations wishing to take up sites on the development area. Over and above this, the *middle ring road* is planned to pass through areas not immediately scheduled for redevelopment, for example between the Newtown and Nechells Green redevelopment zones and under the tracks running to New Street Station. It follows that the acquisition of such land and buildings as are necessary to allow the construction of the *middle ring road* is likely to be a long and expensive process. The present policy of limiting the inflow of motor cars to the city

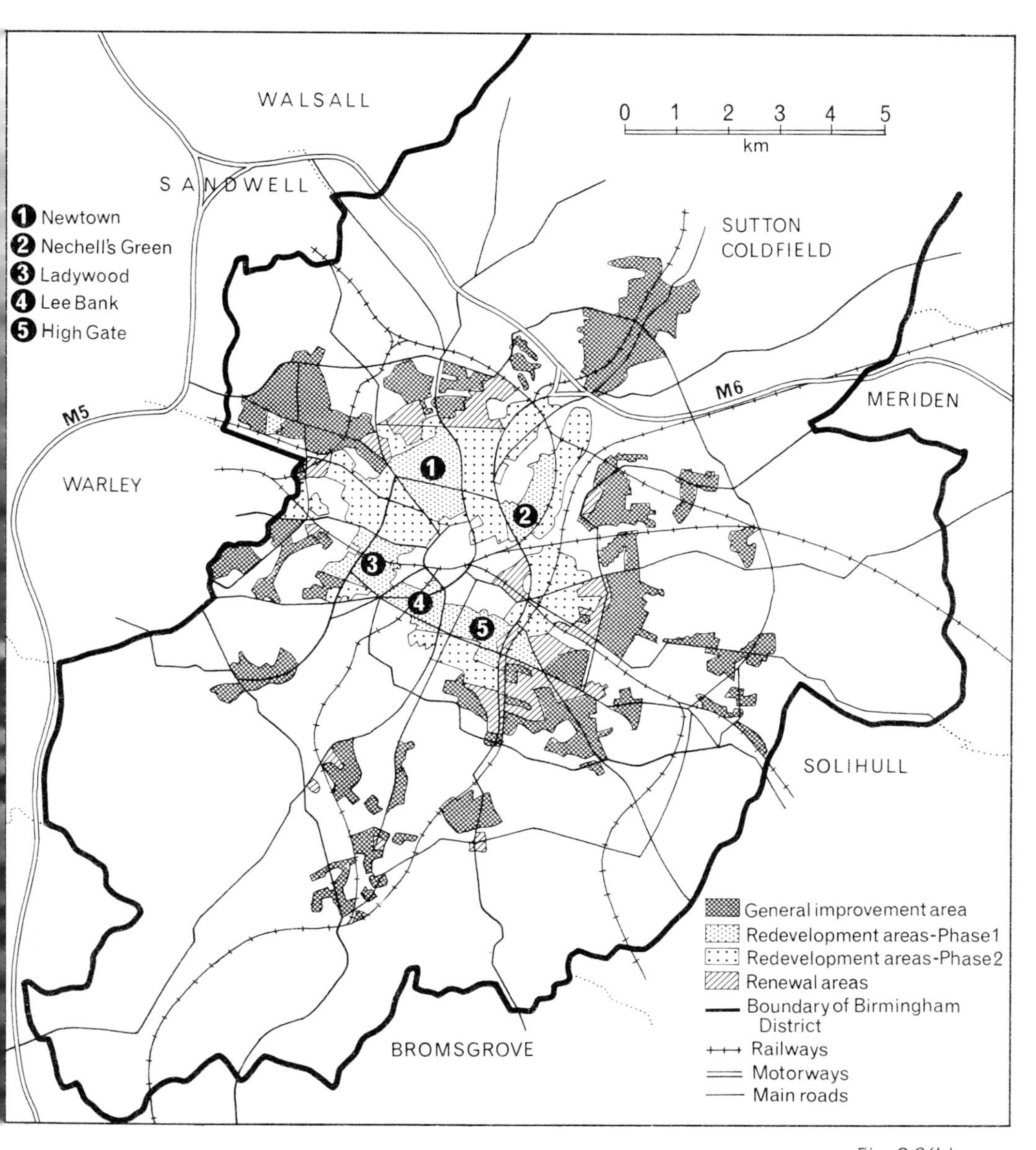

Fig. 8.6(b) Redevelopment and urban renewal (Phase 2)

centre applies particularly to the commuter rather than to those who wish to park temporarily for business, shopping or entertainment. Consequently the pricing of parking meter bays and of car parks is designed to discourage long term parking during normal working hours. For example, as shown in Fig. 8.5, there are 3 parking zones – central, inner and outer – and parking meter charges are as shown (overleaf) in Table 8.2 (b).

Similarly, car park charges are adjusted according to the location of the car park and the time for which parking occurs.

Redevelopment in the five areas shown in Fig. 8.6(b) is complete and has created a landscape similar to that of the Ladywood area

Table 8.2(b) Cost of parking in Birmingham (in pence)

Duration	Central Zone	Inner Zone	Outer Zone
24 minutes	2	—	—
48 minutes	4	—	—
1 hour	5	5	—
2 hours		10 p	5
4 hours	Not allowed	Not allowed	10
No. of Meters	305	1,266	2,550

shown in Fig. 8.7. Land use in the areas concerned before and after redevelopment is given in Table 8.3. Phase 2 of redevelopment is now proceeding (Fig. 8.6(b)) in the inner areas.

Area	Total Redevelopment Area (hectares)	Population A (B)	No. of Dwellings A (B)	Education: No. of Schools A (B)	Education: Area (hectares) A (B)	Industry (hectares) A (B)	Public Open Space (hectares) A (B)
Nechells Green	106.8	12,537 (19,072)	3,635 (5,885)	10 (12)	10.8 (3.2)	24.8 (25.2)	16.8 (1.6)
Newtown	159.6	15,400 (28,125)	4,467 (9,349)	14 (15)	16.0 (5.2)	47.6 (47.6)	24.1 (2.6)
Ladywood	115.6	12,448 (24,418)	3,609 (7,558)	9 (9)	10.0 (1.8)	24.8 (24.6)	20.0 (0.8)
Lee Bank	76.8	6,531 (14,797)	1,894 (4,492)	5 (7)	5.1 (1.4)	16.0 (17.7)	10.0 (0.08)
Highgate	94.4	10,080 (16,484)	2,924 (4,886)	15 (8)	12.8 (2.4)	21.4 (21.4)	15.6 (3.9)
Total	553.2	56,996 (102,896)	16,529 (32,170)	53 (51)	54.8 (14.0)	133.2 (136.4)	86.4 (8.8)
			Unfit Dwellings before Redevelopment 24,670				

(A) After Redevelopment
(B) Before Redevelopment

Source: City of Birmingham Planning Dept.

Table 8.3 Land Use in the Five Comprehensive Development Areas (Phase 1)

The aim is to create residential neighbourhoods with (a) all necessary local services, (b) housing separated from industry, (c) road layout designed so that through traffic by-passes the residential areas (d) open spaces, and (e) the grouping of certain social facilities, e.g. schools, churches, community centres, in a central area so that these can be both useful and attractive to look at.

Not all people or firms can be rehoused in these central areas, and many are being given dwellings and factory sites in outlying areas or overspill new towns outside the city boundaries, or in expanding towns such as Tamworth, Staffordshire.

11. (a) *What is meant by the term* through traffic*?*
(b) *Why is it that the bigger a town is, the smaller is the proportion of the total traffic which is* through traffic*?*

12. *What are the main causes of traffic congestion in the central areas of older English towns?*

13. (a) *What are the advantages of* pedestrian shopping precincts *(i) to the pedestrian (ii) to the motorist?*
(b) *What complementary facility must be provided with a* pedestrian precinct *(i) for the shoppers (ii) for the vans delivering to the shops?*
(c) *Draw a sketch plan for a traffic-free shopping area showing how motor vehicles would gain access to the car parks and to unloading bays of shops.*

14. (a) *Study Fig. 8.5 and describe the position of the car parks in relation to the* inner ring road. *What are the advantages of the sites of these car parks?*
(b) *What do the plans for two of the future car parks suggest about the relative development of road and rail transport for passengers?*

15. (a) *Why are car park spaces so expensive to provide in Central Birmingham?*
(b) *If a car park space costs £400, over how many years will this cost be recovered if the hourly charge is 10p and the space is occupied on an average 5 hours out of 24 during each day.*
(c) *If the figures in (b) are representative, how much money will the Bull Ring Multi-Storey Park collect in one day?*
(d) *Suggest what changes in the extent to which a central car park might be used (i) during a normal week day (ii) on a Saturday.*
(e) *If on a certain day of the week the demand for car park spaces far exceeded the supply of these, what measure could the car park authorities take to discourage motorists from bringing their cars into the city centre?*
(f) *If parking charges may be varied from one car park to another, which of the existing car parks shown on Fig. 8.5. might well charge a lower price? Give reasons for your answer.*

16. (a) *What are the advantages of the* inner ring road *(i) to motorists entering the C.B.D. (ii) to local traffic?*
(b) *Why are underpasses essential if the ring road is to serve a useful purpose?*
(c) *How would a motorist entering the C.B.D. by Bristol Street get to the car park near Snow Hill without using the local streets?*

17. (a) *Why is the widening of main arterial roads in towns a slow and costly process?*
(b) *What in particular is likely to delay the completion of Birmingham's* middle ring road *in the eastern part of its course? (See Fig. 8.6)*

18. *Study Fig. 8.6*
   - *(a) Name the five areas which have been redeveloped.*
   - *(b) Suggest why these areas were redeveloped rather than areas further out from the centre.*
   - *(c) State how far it is true that in each area housing has been separated from industry.*
   - *(d) State in how many areas the principal business district is in or near to the centre of the neighbourhood unit.*

19. *From Table 8.3:*
   - *(a) (i) calculate the* density of population *per hectare for the total redevelopment area before and after redevelopment. (ii) why has there been a fall in the density of population in these areas? (See Fig. 8.7 and the last column in Table 8.3.)*
   - *(b) (i) what is striking about the area allocated to schools before and after redevelopment? (ii) although the number of schools has not increased very much what evidence is there that the school population has increased or decreased? Are school conditions likely to be less or more crowded after redevelopment?*
   - *(c) The area used for industry has not changed much. Does this mean that approximately the same labour force will be used in these areas? Give reasons for your answer.*

Conclusion

In this chapter we have examined some of the problems involved in the redevelopment of city centres and inner areas. We have noted

Fig. 8.7 The Ladywood redevelopment area of Birmingham

hat any scheme for redevelopment must be preceded by a survey of he existing towns: its land use and the pattern of its traffic to estimate he future demands upon land for buildings and transport. Once this as been achieved a structure plan is prepared by the local authority ased on the findings of the survey and on town planning principles which have been evolved. In general development must

1. Provide modern buildings for business purposes in the C.B.D. which are usually tall because of the scarcity of land.

2. Plan a road system which will (i) separate 'through' from local raffic and (ii) use underpasses and flyovers so that vehicles do not ross one another on the same level.

3. Separate pedestrian traffic from vehicular traffic by providing, or example, shopping precincts.

4. Provide plenty of off-street parking for business vehicles, hoppers' vehicles and delivery vans, but discourage commuter ehicles.

5. Arrange for the gradual rebuilding or renovation of areas of ld housing and industry so as to develop a neighbourhood unit which is not only pleasant to look at but also provides the services which its inhabitants need.

There is a growing body of opinion which feels that providing nore and better roads in city centres will merely encourage more notor traffic and that the only solution is to use the price mechanism nd other encouragements such as bus lanes to make public transport nore attractive to the commuter. Experiments are going on with a dial-a-ride' system whereby small buses will call at a person's house o pick up passengers and take them to a main transport road.

The physical redevelopment or renewal of the inner areas of cities oes not by itself dispose of all the problems found in such areas. These areas tend to be those where houses are in multiple occupancy, where old people live who may find life difficult to cope with, where ncomes may be lower than average, where immigrants may congregate, where unemployment may be above average and where chools may offer poorer facilities. The cumulation of these handiaps means that social problems often abound in such areas and hese need to be solved just as much as the physical problems of a lecaying environment.

REVISION EXERCISES

0. ***Why is the redevelopment of town centres necessary?***

1. ***Why is it that the larger the town, the greater are the difficulties of redeveloping its centre?***

2. ***Why did town centres develop in a haphazard manner in the past?***

3. ***What is the purpose of the Town and Country Planning Acts?***

4. ***Why are development plans reviewed every five years?***

5. ***Why is it necessary for highway engineers to carry out a traffic survey before they plan a new road system?***

Chapter Nine

Green Belts and New Towns

A. Green Belt

In previous chapters we have studied the origin and growth of town and cities because the great majority of people in the Unite Kingdom live in 'built-up' areas. Further, many people who live i rural districts travel daily to work in towns. The movement of peopl especially young people, from rural areas to urban areas continue the growth of cities has reached the point where the quality of lif within them is in danger. Opinions about this 'quality' differ ver widely. It may be argued that more people are moving into citie because the city has more to offer than the countryside in moder life. One thing is certain; it is becoming increasingly difficult to trav in cities, as we have seen in Chapter 8. Also, cities tend to grow out wards into the surrounding countryside and cover what was onc farming land.

As early as 1935, the then London County Council put forward scheme 'to provide a reserve supply of public open spaces and o recreational areas and to establish a green belt or girdle of ope space lands' around London and began to buy up land around th capital city to prevent that land being built on. Fig. 9.1 shows part of that first *green belt*, the North Downs near Sevenoaks to th south of London.

Since London's first pioneering steps, many other cities hav followed in the same path, putting forward proposals for green belt around their built-up area in which further building will be restricte Although up to the time of writing only five of the *green belts* hav received final approval from the government, they are all taken int careful consideration when new developments are being planne London's Green Belt has been extended provisionally to double it original extent.

Fig. 9.2 shows the present location of the *green belts* in Englan and Wales. In most cases, the belts do really form a continuous circl around a city, such as York and Cambridge. In others, the restricte area is planned to prevent the city growing in a certain directio such as Newcastle-upon-Tyne to the north-west. However, goo communications, especially motorways and railways, attract in dustry and urban development and the routeways that lead throug

Fig. 9.1 The North Downs near Chevening

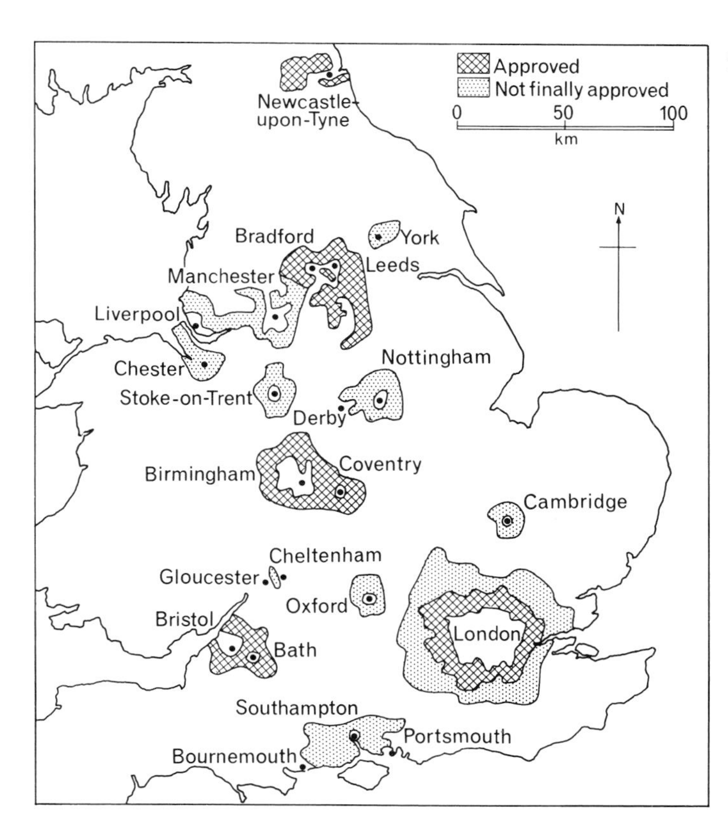

Fig. 9.2 The green belts

the *green belts* tend to break the ring of protected land. The Government is under constant pressure to give permission for development in such areas. It is difficult to think in terms of *green belt* along the line of the Ml and the electrified railway via Watford to the Midlands.

Some planners think that the idea of *green wedges* is better than *green belts*. The growth of Copenhagen is based on this concept. This keeps green areas close to the city centre and yet enables expensive communication systems to be fully used. The comparison is best shown in a simple diagram; see Fig. 9.3.

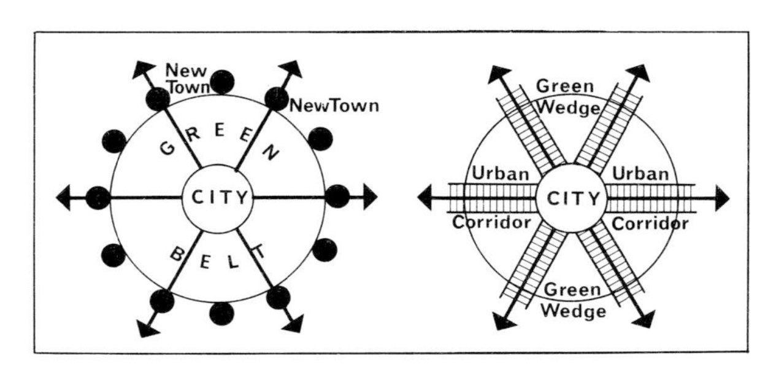

Fig. 9.3 Green belts and green 'wedges'

The same concept is extended to a wider area in the planning document *Strategy for the South East* where the areas of future growth are planned as a series of *corridors* along the major road and rail network, such as the M1, M2, M3, M4 and M23 motorways.

1. *Can you suggest why the areas around cities in which building is restricted should be called* green belts*?*
2. *What uses of the land can you identify in the photograph of the London* green belt*, Fig. 9.1?*
3. *Which* green belt*, apart from the one round London, is now approved by the Government?*
4. *Are the* green belts *spread evenly throughout England and Wales or are they concentrated in certain regions?*
5. *Can you suggest why there is hardly any* green belt *shown in either Wales or in the South West Peninsula?*

B. New Towns

Recent governments of this country have talked of building as many as 400,000 new houses each year. So if certain areas are restricted such as *green belts*, then others must be found for this new building quite apart from new factories, schools, hospitals and the like. One possibility is to rebuild old areas within the city boundaries; this is known as *urban renewal* and is associated especially with slum clearance and the construction of new town centres such as Birmingham and Coventry (see Chapters 6 and 8).

The other possibility is to let building 'leap-frog' over the *green belts* and build away from the established centres. But if these buildings consisted entirely of houses, the people living in them would have to travel even further to get to work and the traffic problems would be even worse. So it has become official policy to select certain areas for new building that will not only supply good, modern housing, but also factories, offices, shops and schools to serve the new housing areas. This is the basic idea behind the growth of new towns, for which the United Kingdom is now famous.

The idea of a *new town* is not so new. We saw, in Chapter 4, how the new town of Edinburgh was built 200 years ago. The purpose behind new towns is not just to give people a new place to live and work but a better place to live in, with more space and fresh air, less travelling, less worry, more leisure. The New Towns Act was made law in 1946 and the first New Town Corporation was set up at Stevenage in Hertfordshire with the task of building a new town for people from the London area. Stevenage now has 6 'neighbourhoods' with 10–20,000 people in each and more than 35,000 of the inhabitants are employed in the new town itself. Building is still going on.

In the following year, 1947, five more new towns were started, Crawley, Harlow, Hemel Hempstead (all in the London ring), Newton Aycliffe (in County Durham) and East Kilbride in Scotland. The idea proved so successful that more than twenty new towns were built within the next sixteen years and the idea was copied by many other countries. Fig. 9.4 shows the new towns of what is called 'the London ring' while Figs. 9.5, 9.6 and 9.7 show the situation in the whole of the United Kingdom. Table 9.1 gives a list of *new towns*.

Fig. 9.4 The London green belt

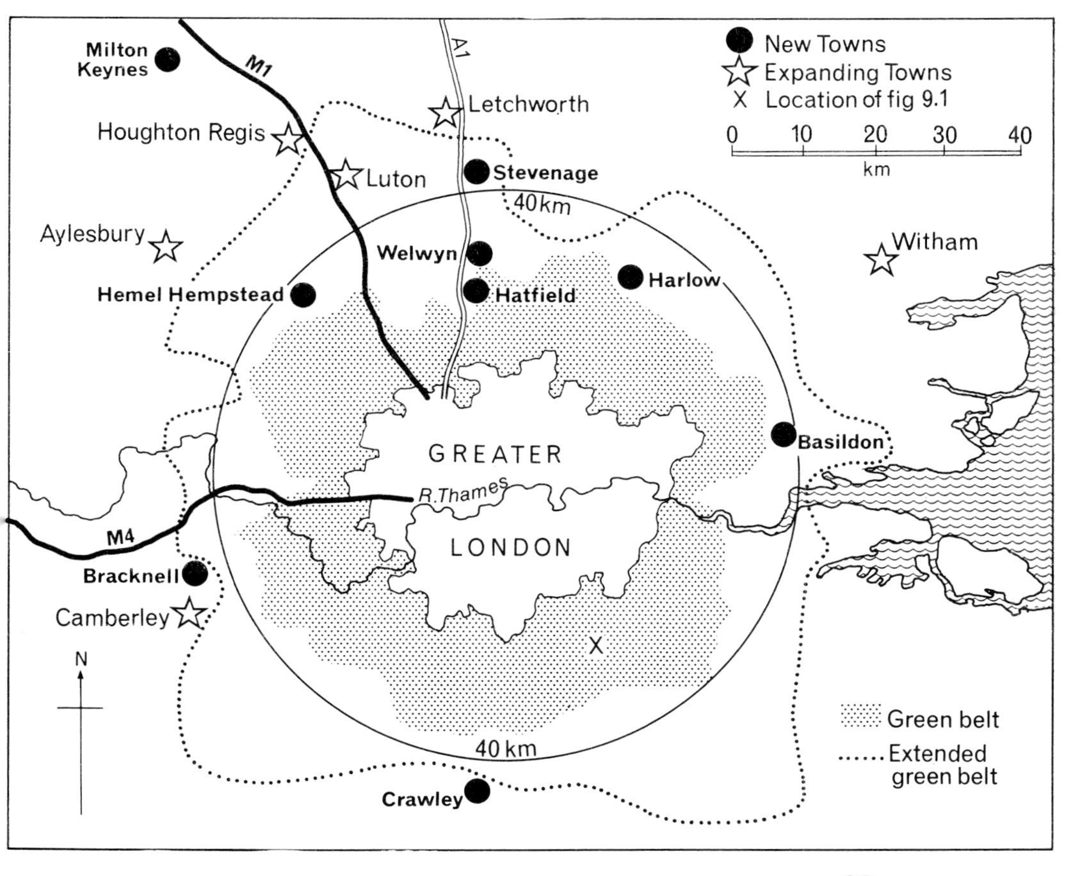

Fig. 9.5 Growth towns: England

You will notice that the maps show not only *new towns* but also *expanding towns*. A *new town* is governed by a special authority whereas an *expanding town* is governed by the existing local authority. Official policy now favours *expanding towns* rather than building entirely new ones, partly because of the enormous cost of building town centres with all the services that people require.

In fact, it will be quite difficult in the future to distinguish between *new towns* and *expanding towns* and it may be better to regard them all as 'Growth Areas' as in the map of part of Scotland, Fig. 9.6.

Table 9.1 New Towns

New Town	Population in 1975	Date of Establishment
Basildon	85,000	1949
Bracknell	41,000	1949
Crawley	71,000	1947
Harlow	82,000	1947
Hatfield	26,000	1948
Hemel Hempstead	73,000	1947
Stevenage	75,000	1946
Welwyn	41,000	1948
Corby	54,000	1950
Cwmbran	43,000	1949
Telford	94,000	1968
Newton Aycliffe	25,000	1947
Newtown (Wales)	6,700	1967
Peterlee	26,500	1948
Redditch	50,000	1964
Runcorn	48,000	1964
Skelmersdale	39,000	1961
Washington	39,000	1964
Cumbernauld	38,000	1955
East Kilbride	71,000	1947
Glenrothes	32,000	1948
Livingston	22,000	1962
Milton Keynes	60,000	1967
Antrim	40,000	1966
Ballymena	50,000	1967
Craigavon	73,000	1965
Londonderry	84,000	1969
Irvine	50,000	1966

Source: Town and Country Planning.

At the time of writing, important new schemes for *expanded towns* are going ahead. For example, at Milton Keynes in north Buckinghamshire (in the vicinity of Bletchley) and another to join Preston and Chorley at the mouth of the Ribble in Lancashire. Another growth area is planned in the Tweed Valley to stretch from Galashiels to St Boswells. The size of these new schemes is a result of reconsidering the whole idea of *new towns*. It may be argued that the ring of *new towns* around London has only succeeded in creating a new suburban area still dominated and attracted by London itself. The new towns have been so successful in attracting new industries that some of the older towns, such as the 'cotton' towns of Lancashire, are now opposed to further new towns. The older towns feel that they need more industry, new housing and other facilities themselves.

6. *How many new towns can you identify in the ring around London? (Fig. 9.4.)*
7. *Name four expanding towns in the London ring. (Fig. 9.4.)*
8. *How far is it from the centre of London to (a) Crawley and (b) Bletchley? (Fig. 9.4.)*

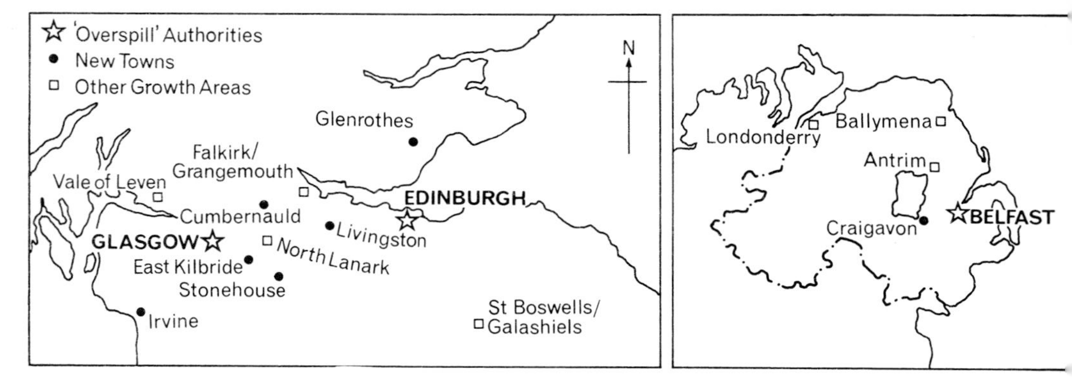

Fig. 9.6
Growth towns: Scotland (left)

Fig. 9.7
Growth towns: Northern Ireland (right)

9. *If London is the 'exporting authority' (i.e. the authority sending people to the new towns) for the ring of growth areas around London, name five other 'exporting authorities' throughout the country.*
10. *Apart from the London area, which part of the United Kingdom has the greatest concentration of* new *and* expanding towns*? (Fig. 9.5.)*
11. *Northampton has recently been selected as an important* expanding town. *Which 'exporting authority' is it nearest?*
12. *Table 9.1 shows the population of some of the* new towns *in 1975. Study the table and then answer the following questions:*
    (a) *How many of these towns are already larger than the old-established cities of Durham (20,000) and Canterbury (30,000)?*
    (b) *Which are the six largest new towns?*
    (c) *How 'old' is Stevenage? i.e. How many years is it since it was first established as a* new town*?*
    (d) *How 'old' is Washington?*
    (e) *How many* new towns *had been set up in the 10 years from 1946 until 1956?*
    (f) *How many new towns had been set up since 1956?*
13. *Can you identify any growth areas (whether* new *or* expanding towns *in Wales? (Fig. 9.5 and Table 9.1)*
14. *How many* growth areas *are shown in (a) Scotland, (b) Northern Ireland?*

C. Crawley New Town

Crawley, in Sussex, 48 km south of London, was one of the first *new towns* to be set up in 1947 and with a population of 71,000 has reached the target set by its planners.

The Master Plan for the town (Fig. 9.8) shows an industrial area and a town centre surrounded by residential areas. Each residential neighbourhood was planned to have a population between 5,000 and 8,000 and is separated from the other areas by main roads carrying the heavier traffic. At the centre of each neighbourhood is placed a primary school so that young children can reach it without crossing

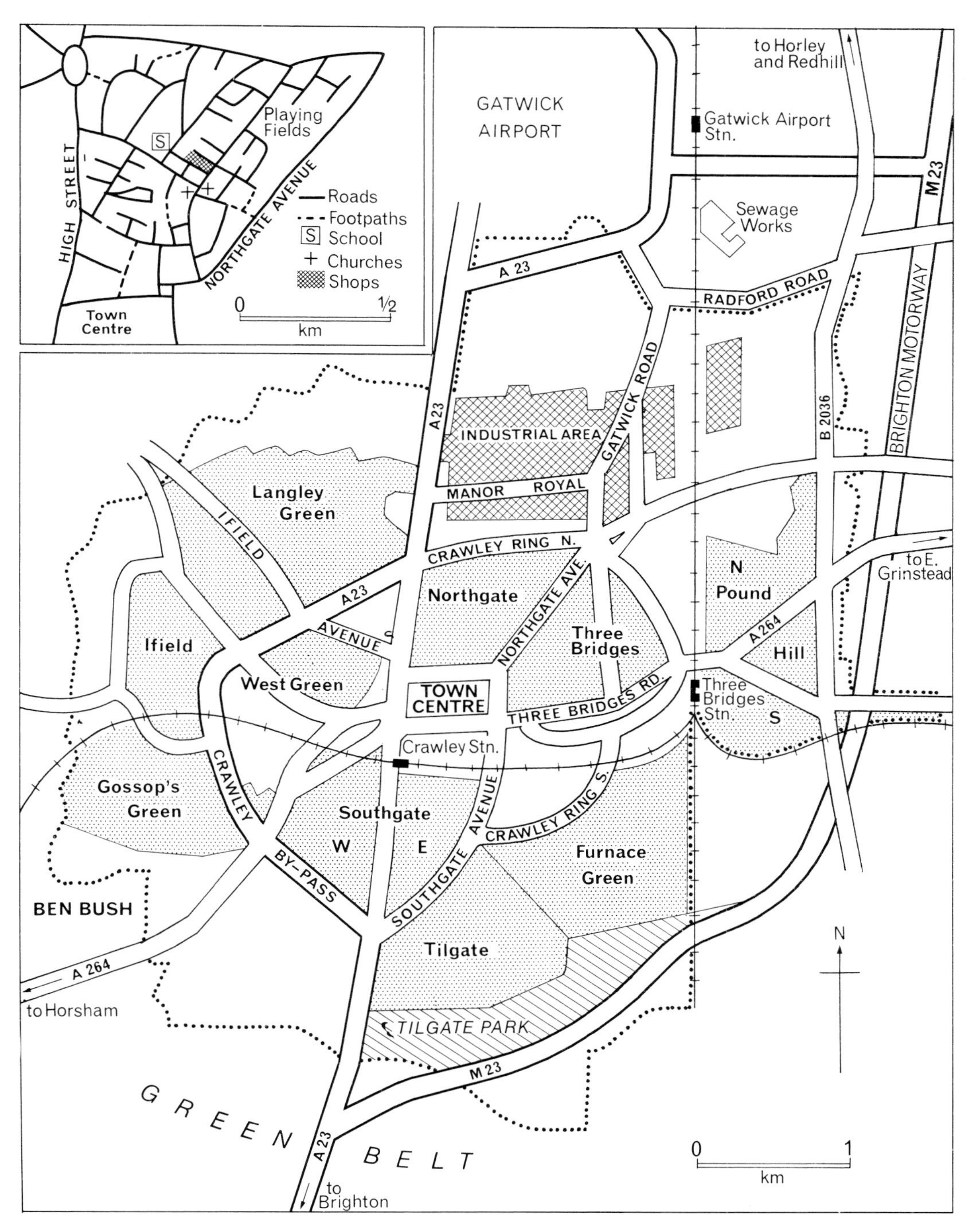

main roads. Also at the centre are shops for daily needs, the church, the public house and community centres.

A typical neighbourhood, that of Northgate, is shown in Fig. 9.9. Ten of these neighbourhoods have now been completed and the eleventh is being built now. Houses in the neighbourhoods are rented only to people who come to work in the Crawley area, which includes

Fig. 9.8 Crawley: town plan

Fig. 9.9 (inset) The Northgate Neighbourhood

the airport at Gatwick, the second 'London' airport but 41% now own their houses.

The main public buildings and the large and specialist shops are all in the town centre which is designed to separate pedestrians and traffic.

The industrial area lies on the London side of the town so that heavy traffic does not cross the residential areas and has good access to the main London to Brighton road and to the railway. The main industries are engineering, food and pharmaceuticals, plastics, printing and electronics. Gatwick Airport employs over 1,200 people from Crawley.

Crawley is now officially 'of age' with its own borough council and mayor since 1974. Its target population has been doubled. A new park and nature centre has been opened at Tilgate.

Fig. 9.10 shows an aerial view of the *new town*. In contrast to it is Leigh in Lancashire (Fig. 9.11), an older industrial town built up

Fig. 9.10 Crawley new town from the south-west

in the 19th century on the traditional industries of coal mining and cotton manufacture. Leigh has changed a great deal in recent years with the comparative decline of coal and cotton industries but it still bears the marks of its past. A comparison of the two photographs will tell you a great deal about the thinking that went into the planning of *new towns*.

15. *On the evidence of the photographs alone (Figs. 9.10 and 9.11), make as long a list as possible of the ways in which the new town is an improvement on the old town. For example (a) in the old town, mills, factories and houses are mixed up together whereas (b) in the* new town *the factory estate is developed in a special area away from the houses.*
16. *Analyse the air photograph of Crawley (Fig. 9.10) using the method of frame and grid as before (with Edinburgh and Durham in earlier chapters) and identify the following:*
    (a) the old church (has it a spire or tower?)
    (b) the old market street
    (c) the new shopping precinct

Fig. 9.11 Leigh, Lancashire from the west

(d) *the old railway station (is there a train in?)*
(e) *the new bus station (how many buses can you see?)*
(f) *the neighbourhood of Northgate lying to the north of the town centre (the photograph is taken from the south-west looking north-east).*

17. *Why is the industrial estate situated to the north of Crawley?*
18. *Why is there a primary school at the centre of each neighbourhood?*
19. *How have the planners of Crawley tried to make life safer for pedestrians?*
20. *Can you suggest reasons why the target population has been doubled after 28 years?*

REVISION EXERCISES

21. ***What is the purpose of a* green belt *round a city?***
22. ***What is specially 'new' about a* new town*?***
23. ***In what ways does the plan of a* new town *try to cut down the distance that people travel in their daily lives?***
24. ***In what ways does a* new town *tackle the problem of traffic congestion?***
25. ***There have been complaints that new towns do not have enough facilities for young people. If* you *were designing a* new town, *what public buildings would you put in the town centre?***

Part II

The Changing Distribution of Industry

Chapter Ten

The Distribution of Industry

A. Old and New Patterns of Distribution of Industry

1. The degree of specialization of occupations in a given area

There was a time when it was possible to look at a map of Great Britain and say with confidence that certain regions were dominated by certain industries or products. West Yorkshire was associated with the woollen textile industry, South Lancashire with cotton textiles, Clydeside with shipbuilding, South Wales with iron and steel and tin plating, Nottingham with bicycles, Leicester with hosiery, and so on. To some extent, some of these old established industries remain in the areas in which they developed, but only in a few cases do they really dominate the areas concerned. They have evolved, changed in character, spread elsewhere, been swamped by other industries, so that most industrial areas are areas of mixed industries. Let us take the case of the Glasgow area which has long been associated with the shipbuilding industry (see Chapter 11). If we examine the occupations of the working population of the Western area of the Lowlands of Scotland we find that nearly 50 per cent of the working population are non-industrial, one third of the working population being engaged in commerce, administration or the professions. Employment Statistics for 1969 gave a breakdown of the industrial occupations as shown in Table 10.1.

Table 10.1

Occupational Group	Numbers in thousands
Engineering, Electrical, Vehicles	49
Food, Drink and Tobacco	30
Textile and Clothing	24
Shipbuilding and Marine Engineering	15
Paper Printing and Publishing	18
Metal Manufacture	13
Chemicals	4
Others	11
Total	164
Non-Industrial	197

Source: Dept. of Employment and Productivity

Even if we consider the figures for Middle and Lower Clydeside, which includes most of the heavy industry, the two dominant groups, (engineering and electrical, shipbuilding and marine engineering) accounted for considerably less than half the total number of people employed in the area.

Let us take another area which has for over 100 years been thought of as the coal, iron, steel and tin plating region of the United Kingdom: south Wales. Tables 10.2, gives a list of the standard occupational groups as devised by the Department of Employment and Productivity. For each group four sets of figures are given:

Table 10.2

Occupational Group*	Total Nos. employed in Great Britain (thousands) (1)	% of total employment in Great Britain (2)	Total Nos. employed in S. Wales† (thousands) (3)	% of total employment in S. Wales (4)
Agriculture, Forestry & Fishing	421	1.9	5.2	0.8
Mining & Quarrying	361	1.6	37.3	5.5
Food, Drink & Tobacco	728	3.3	14.0	2.1
Coal & Petroleum Products	40	0.2	4.7	0.7
Chemical & Allied Industries	425	1.9	13.4	2.0
Metal Manufacture	518	2.4	62.7	9.2
Mechanical Engineering	956	4.3	20.9	3.0
Instrument Engineering	159	0.7	1.7	0.2
Electrical Engineering	795	3.6	24.3	3.6
Shipbuilding & Marine Engineering	177	0.8	1.2	0.2
Vehicles	789	3.6	18.7	2.7
Other Metal Goods	563	2.5	19.5	2.9
Textiles	555	2.5	8.1	1.2
Leather, Leather Goods & Furs	44	0.2	0.8	0.1
Clothing & Fottwear	418	1.9	12.2	1.8
Bricks, Pottery, Glass, Gement, etc.	299	1.3	6.8	1.0
Timber, Furniture, etc.	287	1.3	6.4	0.9
Paper, Printing & Publishing	568	2.6	9.8	1.4
Other Manufacturing Industries	344	1.6	16.8	2.5
Construction	1,338	6.0	47.5	7.0
Gas, Electricity & Water	335	1.5	11.8	1.7
Transport & Communications	1.501	6.8	44.6	6.5
Distributive Trades	2,691	12.1	69.2	10.1
Financial, Business, Professional & Scientific Services	4,214	19.0	90.9	13.4
Catering, Hotels, etc.	784	3.5	23.9	3.5
Miscellaneous Services	1,329	6.0	55.5	8.1
National Government Service	583	2.6	19.1	2.8
Local Government Service	960	4.3	35.1	5.1
Total employees in employment	22,182	100.0	682.1	100.0

*(1968 Standard Industrial Classification)

†South Wales is taken to be the counties of Gwent, South, Mid and West Glamorgan.

Source: *Annual Abstract of Statistics 1974* (figures for 1973) and Department of Employment and Productivity 1968 Standard Industrial Classification.

1. The total number of people employed in that group for the whole of Great Britain.

2. The percentage of people employed in that group in the whole of Great Britain.

3. The total number of people employed in that group in South Wales.

4. The percentage of people employed in that group in South Wales.

Now such a table enables us to judge the relative importance of various occupations in Great Britain as a whole and in South Wales in particular. It tells us much more than the two photographs in Fig. 10.1 and Fig. 10.2, for though these show us two aspects of industry in South Wales, heavy industry and light industry, we cannot tell from these how typical they are of the whole area. From the table, however, we can see that 'Metal Manufacture' (which includes iron and steel) accounts in 1973 for 9.2 per cent (column 4) of the number of people employed in South Wales, and so is clearly fairly important compared with for example, 'Shipbuilding and Marine Engineering' which only accounts for 0.2 per cent of the working population of South Wales. Thus column 4 of the table is an indication of extent of specialization that exists in South Wales. This column tells us that some specialization occurs in 'Mining and

Fig. 10.1 The Margam and Abbey works of the British Steel Corporation near Port Talbot

Quarrying' and 'Metal Manufacture' since between them these two groups account for about 14.7 per cent of the employed population. This means that a serious decline in the demand for coal and steel would cause a good deal of unemployment in such an area. At the same time this also means that about 85.3 per cent of the employed population are *not* employed in 'Mining and Quarrying' and 'Metal Manufacture' – so that a picture of South Wales as essentially an area of mines and quarries and steel works would at least be 85.3 per cent inaccurate.

2. The location quotient

Supposing, however, that we wanted to find out to what extent any one of the occupation groups listed in Table 10.2 was localized in South Wales rather than in any other area. In other words, how could

Fig. 10.2 The Treforest industrial estate

we work out how far South Wales stood out as an area of Great Britain for 'Metal Manufacture'? Now according to Table 10.2 we have the percentage of people employed in that group for the whole of Great Britain (column 2: 2.4 per cent) and the percentage employed in that group for South Wales (column 4: 9.2 per cent). The greater the percentage for South Wales compared with the percentage for Great Britain as a whole, the greater will be the extent to which this particular occupational group is localized in South Wales. We can work out a number by dividing 9.2 (the South Wales percentage) by 2.4 (the percentage for Great Britain) which is known as the *Location Quotient* as shown below:

Location Quotient for 'Metal Manufacture' in South Wales

$$= \frac{9.2}{2.4} = 3.8$$

It follows from this that if the percentages are the same then the *Location Quotient* will be equal to 1. For example:

Location Quotient for 'Electrical Engineering' in South Wales.

$$= \frac{3.6}{3.6} = 1$$

This means that South Wales does not employ proportionately more people in that group than Great Britain as a whole.

If, however, the percentage for South Wales is smaller than that for Great Britain, then the *Location Quotient* will be less than 1. For example:

Location Quotient for 'Agriculture, Forestry and Fishing' in south Wales

$$= \frac{0.9}{1.9} = 0.47$$

This means that farmers, forestry workers and fishermen are relatively unimportant in South Wales and proportionately less important than in Great Britain as a whole.

The advantage of such a calculation is that it is objective. It does not depend on personal judgement or on incomplete evidence such as a few photographs. It can tell us that as long as the *Location Quotient* is above 1, then there is some degree of localization of the industry in the area concerned, and the higher the figure, the greater the degree of localization. This quotient is based on labour statistics It does not tell us how far output of any particular goods is concentrated in a given area.

In the case of South Wales, if *Location Quotients* are worked out for all 24 occupational groups listed, it is found that in eleven cases the Quotient is above 1, but in only two cases is the Quotient very high, namely in 'Mining and Quarrying' and 'Metal Manufacturing' in all others it is between 1 and 2.

3. Specialization and the service industries
If we look at columns 2 and 4 of Table 10.2 we can see a number of occupational groups where the percentages are fairly close to one another, i.e. where the *Location Quotient* is around 1. For example: Financial, Business, Professional and Scientific Services, Transport and Communications, Distributive Trades, Gas, Electricity and Water. This is the *services* group, where people are employed to perform *services* for all the people living in the area: school teachers, doctors, bus and coach drivers, water supply engineers, and so on. It is reasonable to expect that the proportion of people carrying out these services would not vary widely from one area of the country to another. Consequently there is a fairly even distribution of such *service* occupations throughout Great Britain, though of course concentrated in the urban areas. A few *service* industries are found concentrated in the main commercial centres – for example, London has a high *Location Quotient* for 'Insurance, Banking and Finance', and for 'Public Administration and Defence' reflecting its *function* as a capital city. But these tend to be exceptions to the general tendency in *service* occupations.

Now one tendency which has been found to be true in most areas of the world is that as a country's economy develops and grows so the *service industries* grow and become an increasingly important part of the economy. To make the point clear, let us take two extreme examples: Botswana, a recently independent country in southern Africa, and the United Kingdom. In the first case the overwhelming majority of the population is engaged in agriculture, and the very few who are engaged in *service industries* are concentrated in the state capital Gaborone. Such a situation is largely due to the fact that so little trade and manufacturing takes place that there is little need for the services of banking, insurance, transport and public utilities. On the other hand in the U.K., the *service industries* account for nearly half of the numbers in employment, and these are distributed over a large number of towns and villages. The conclusion is that in an economy like the U.K.'s the very size of the 'services sector' of the economy helps to diversify the occupations in any given area.

1. (a) *Using Table 10.1 construct a bar graph to show the total numbers in industrial occupations in the Glasgow area. Use a scale of 2 cm to 40,000 workers. Make the bar 1 cm in thickness.*
   (b) *Divide this bar graph into eight different parts to correspond to the eight occupational groups listed in Table 10.1. Make each section proportional to the numbers in each group, e.g. Food, Drink and Tobacco will be 1.5 cm long* $(\frac{30,000}{40,000} \times 2 \text{ cm})$
   (c) *Label this bar graph 'The Industrial Occupations of Glasgow'.*

2. *Draw a circle diameter 8 cm and divide this circle into two sectors to show the percentage of the employed population in Glasgow which is in industrial and non-industrial occupations (see p. 106). Remember that the angles at the centre must be proportional to the percentage in each group.*
3. *What general conclusion do you come to about the distribution of occupations in such an old established industrial area?*
4. *From Table 10.2 draw a bar graph to show the distribution of occupations in Great Britain based on column 2. To simplify the task:*
   (a) combine all the percentages from 'Gas, Electricity and Water' to 'Local Government Service' and call this 'Services'
   (b) Leave as separate percentages 'Agriculture, Forestry and Fishing', 'Mining and Quarrying', 'Construction'
   (c) Combine all other percentages as 'Manufacturing Industries'.
   Use a scale of 2 cm to 20 per cent and make the bar graph 1 cm wide.
5. *From the bar graph drawn for question 4, what can you say about the distribution of occupations in Great Britain as between the various sectors of the economy?*
6. *(a) What is a* Location Quotient *meant to show?*
   (b) How is a Location Quotient *calculated?*
   (c) Calculate the Location Quotients *for South Wales for the occupational groups shown in Table 10.2. Arrange these in a table and check on what proportion of the 28 groups have* Location Quotients *of 1 or more.*

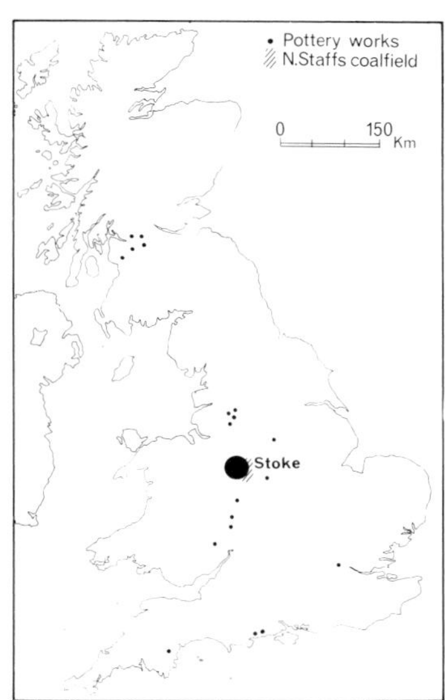

Fig. 10.3
The manufacture of pottery

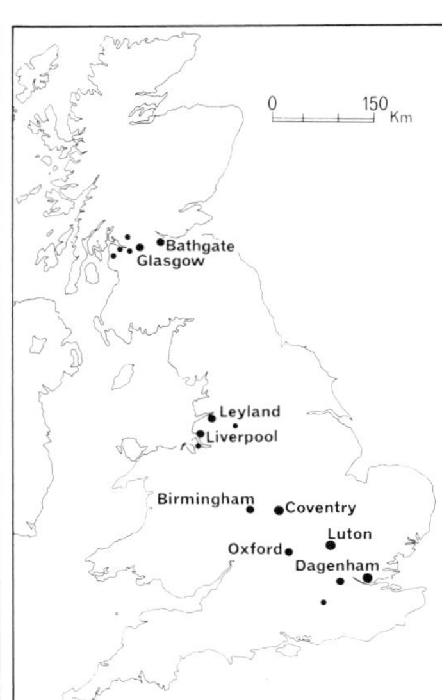

Fig. 10.4
Motor vehicle manufacturing

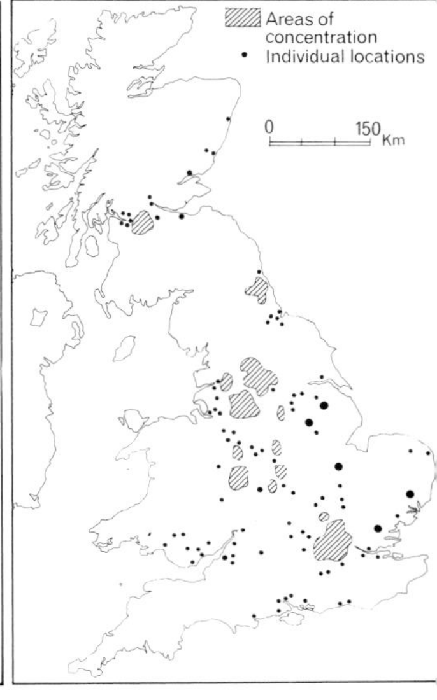

Fig. 10.5
Electrical and Mechanical engineering industries

(d) *Which occupational groups have a very low* Location Quotient? *What does this imply about these groups?*

7. (a) *Why is it that in Great Britain the* service industries *are such an important part of the economy?*

(b) *How does a large 'Service Sector' in an economy help to diversify the distribution of occupations in the country?*

B. The Location of Industry in the U.K.

1. The manufacturing belt

So far we have been finding out:

1. That it is possible to classify occupations into various types.
2. How the working population is divided among the various occupations.
3. That in any region or area of Britain there is a multitude of different occupations and that, today, seldom does one industry employ more than a relatively small proportion of the total labour force in an area.
4. How we can work out a *Location Quotient* which tells us to what extent an industry is localized in a given area.

We have not, however, looked at how industry is in fact distributed in Great Britain. The maps in Figs. 10.3 to 10.8 show the distribution of some of these industries. The map of the distribution of the pottery industry gives the impression that this industry is highly localized mainly in the area of Stoke-on-Trent.

The distribution of the motor industry (cars and commercial

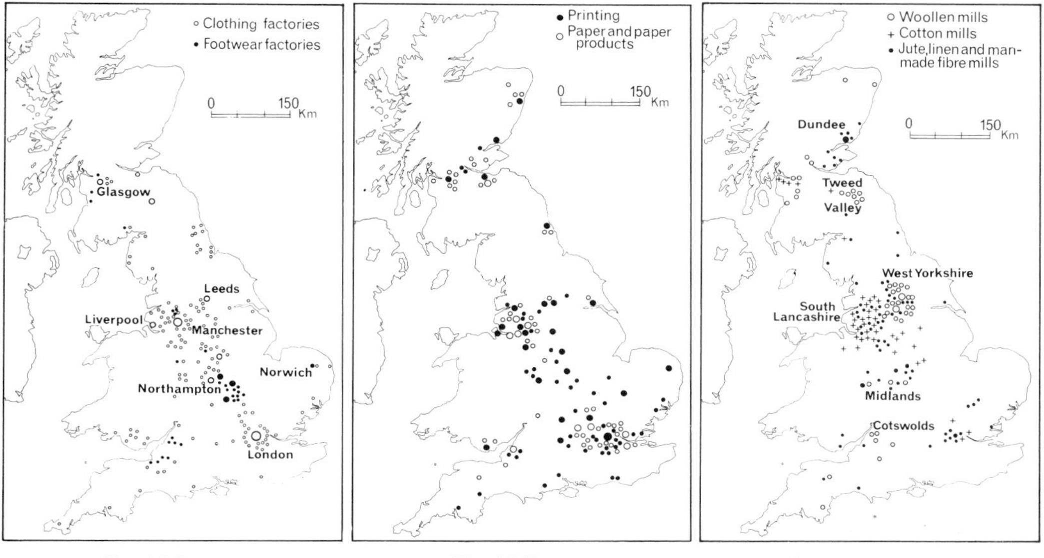

Fig. 10.6 Clothing and footwear industries

Fig. 10.7 Printing and paper industries

Fig. 10.8 Textile industries

vehicles) is more scattered, stretching from Dagenham (Ford) through Luton (Vauxhall – General Motors), Coventry (British Leyland Motor Corporation, Chrysler), Birmingham (B.L.M.C.), Liverpool (Ford), Leyland (B.L.M.C.) to Glasgow (Chrysler).

The map in Fig. 10.5 covers a wide area of industry (mechanical and electrical engineering) and shows a wide scatter of firms in these industries over Britain with notable concentration in certain areas. The same may be stated about the spread of such industries as Clothing and Footwear (Fig. 10.6), Printing and Paper Manufacture (Fig. 10.7), but a greater degree of localization is apparent in the textile industries (Fig. 10.8).

If you look carefully at these maps, especially at Figs. 10.4 to 10.7, you will find some pattern emerging about the distribution of industry in Great Britain. It is possible to distinguish a kind of *manufacturing belt* stretching from London through the Midlands to South Lancashire with another belt stretching across the Central Lowlands of Scotland. Within these belts are found almost all the types of industries which exist in Britain, though some firms in these industries are located outside the belts, for example Fig. 10.6 shows an important footwear industry in Norwich which is outside the London-Liverpool belt. It is important to bear in mind that the term *manufacturing belt* is being used in a general sense. It does not imply a continuous line of industrial firms, except in some of the bigger urban areas. There are vast stretches of open country between London and the Midlands and between the Midlands and south Lancashire.

The next step is to seek an explanation for this general pattern of industrial distribution, ignoring for the time being, the industries lying outside the belt.

We know from the work done in Chapters 5, 6 and 7 that Liverpool and Manchester, Birmingham and London developed as important towns some time back in history and particularly during and since the first industrial revolution (1750 onwards). They attracted people and capital and became what is called *growth points*. Glasgow became such a *growth point* in Scotland. Trade began to take place between these various towns; roads, canals and railways were built to cope with this trade. For example the Trent-Mersey canal was dug to allow china clay from Cornwall to be brought to the Stoke-on-Trent area for Wedgewood's potteries; the Liverpool to Manchester, London to Birmingham railways were built and eventually extended and linked to one another to carry both goods and passengers. Many manufacturers seeking sites for new factories, tended to favour those on or near canals, roads and railways so that they might use the transport facilities. Further, business men tend, on the whole, to prefer to work close to one another because they can share certain services which makes these cheaper. For example they may make use of the same banking facilities, the same water, gas and electricity supplies, whereas if they set up their factories in isolated sites, all these facilities would be much more expensive. Thus, for all these reasons, new industrial development was attracted to existing towns and to the

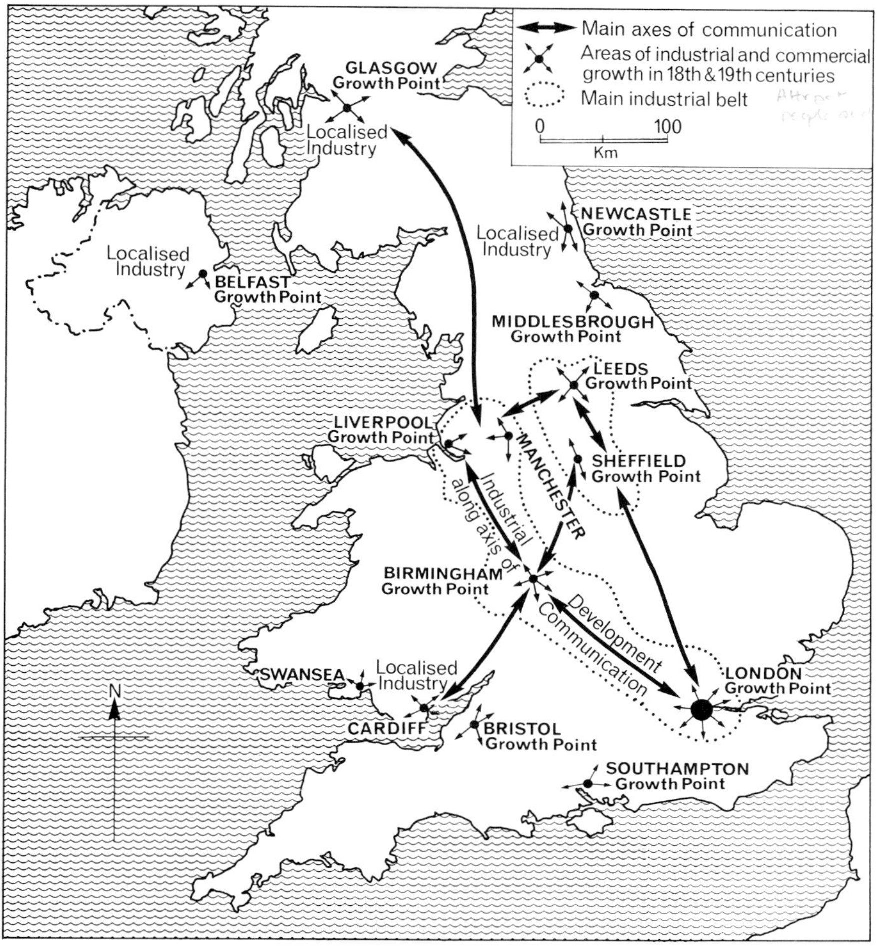

Fig. 10.9 Industry and communications

areas between them served by the canal, road and rail network. These points are summed up in Fig. 10.9.

2. The localization of industry

We have found out why once industry and transport get going they tend to attract one another and great belts of mixed industrial development arise. We have not, however, found out why some industries are apparently highly localized. The Pottery industry in the Stoke-on-Trent area, the Textile industry in South Lancashire and West Yorkshire, the Iron and Steel industry in South Wales, the Shipbuilding industry along Clydeside and so on. It is important here to understand an important distinction between

(a) the *localization of industry*, i.e. why a majority of works or factories in an industry are found in a given area, and

(b) the *siting of a factory*, i.e. why a particular firm or factory within an industry has chosen a particular *site*.

For example, the existence of many woollen textile mills in the

Bradford, Halifax, Huddersfield area is an example of the *localization* of an industry. But the location of the Ford Motor Company's main works at Dagenham is an example of the *siting* of a factory. Whilst it is always important to choose a good *site* for any establishment, it is not always necessary for all other establishments in the industry to be in the same locality. Fig. 10.4 shows quite clearly that there is no tendency for the motor industry to be localized in one area. What then causes *localization* when it occurs?

In many cases it will be found that it is usually the older and the heavy industries which become localized and it is necessary to go back into history to understand how this happened. Let us take the case of the Lancashire textile industry. When, during the early part of the industrial revolution, it became possible to use machinery to spin yarn and weave cloth, this machinery was powered by big mill wheels driven by falling water. Now since some textile workshops existed in the South Lancashire area in the 18th century, industrialists who wished to use the new machinery moved into the valleys where they could use water power and soft (lime free) water. Later, in the 19th century, when the steam engine provided a more powerful and more easily controlled form of power, it happened that a coalfield existed locally which could provide the fuel to raise steam. So new factories were built in or near such towns as Bolton, Bury, Rochdale and Oldham in the southern coalfield area and Blackburn and Burnley in the northern coalfield area. (See Fig. 10.10.) There

Fig. 10.10 *Localization in South Lancashire*

were other advantages to South Lancashire as a location for a textile industry using cotton as a raw material. The port of Liverpool could be used for importing the raw material and food. The Cheshire salt field (see Chapter 13) provided a raw material used in the early bleaching processes and an important chemical industry grew up near Widnes and Warrington which served the textile industry. Further a textile machinery manufacturing industry developed in the Manchester area. Thus in time the group of industries, warehouses, transport facilities which existed in South Lancashire and Cheshire became closely linked to one another. It is not surprising therefore that even though eventually most mills came to use electric power in the 20th century, most of them remained in the South Lancashire area, although they no longer needed to be near a coalfield. This tendency for an industry to continue growing in the area where it first began is called *geographical momentum*.

However, if we examine the location of factories producing new fibres (Fig. 10.11) for the textile industry, we shall see that there is

Fig. 10.11 The production of synthetic fibres

not the same concentration or *localization* in the areas of South Lancashire and West Yorkshire. Man-made fibres are those made by a series of chemical processes, using either wood pulp as in the case of the viscose and acetate fibres such as rayon, and petroleum products in the case of the synthetic fibres such as 'nylon' and 'terylene'. All the factories producing these fibres have been set up in the 20th century and most of them since World War II. Consequently none of these were dependent on steam as a source of power, neither were heavy raw materials required. Consequently there was no necessity for these new factories to be in any particular part of the U.K. You must remember, however, that the factories shown on Fig. 10.11 are those producing fibres. The majority of those producing cloth from man-made fibres still tend to be located in the old textile districts mainly in South Lancashire. This is because pure cotton cloth has to a large extent been replaced by cloth made of man-made fibres or mixtures of man-made and natural fibre. For example more shirts are of nylon or terylene. Many of the Lancashire textile mills have been adapted to use these man-made fibres. In fact, the companies producing the man-made fibres have in many cases bought the old textile firms. Courtaulds, for example, one of the biggest producers of man-made fibres in the U.K., are owners of spinning, weaving, dyeing, printing and knitting factories.

Some industries are localized simply because they rely on heavy raw materials which it would be expensive to carry far on land. Iron and steel works tend to be near coal or iron ore or near the coast if they rely on imported supplies. Brickworks tend to be near the source of the clay used to make them. But those highly localized industries are tending to be the exception rather than the rule.

3. The factors influencing industrial location

Let us now look at the individual *site* chosen for a factory. What was it that led the management of the Ford Motor Company to choose Dagenham; or why did the De Havilland Aircraft Co. choose Hatfield (Herts); or why did some furniture companies set up their works in High Wycombe (Bucks)? Of course in many cases, if the firm is a very old one, its location may be no more than an accident of history. The original owner may have been able to expand on a site which was large enough; what was once a small workshop became a large factory.

But we are more concerned with the choice of new *sites*, since this is the problem likely to face most managements in the future. The following costs have to be borne in mind:

1. The cost of purchasing or renting the land on which the establishment is to be built.
2. (a) The cost of transporting raw materials to the factory.
   (b) The cost of transporting the finished product to the market customers.
3. The cost of labour used in the factory.
4. The cost of power used.

Over and above this, decisions on location have to be based on such facts as whether gas, water, sewage and electricity services are already provided, whether roads or railways are near at hand, whether it may be possible to move into an existing building.

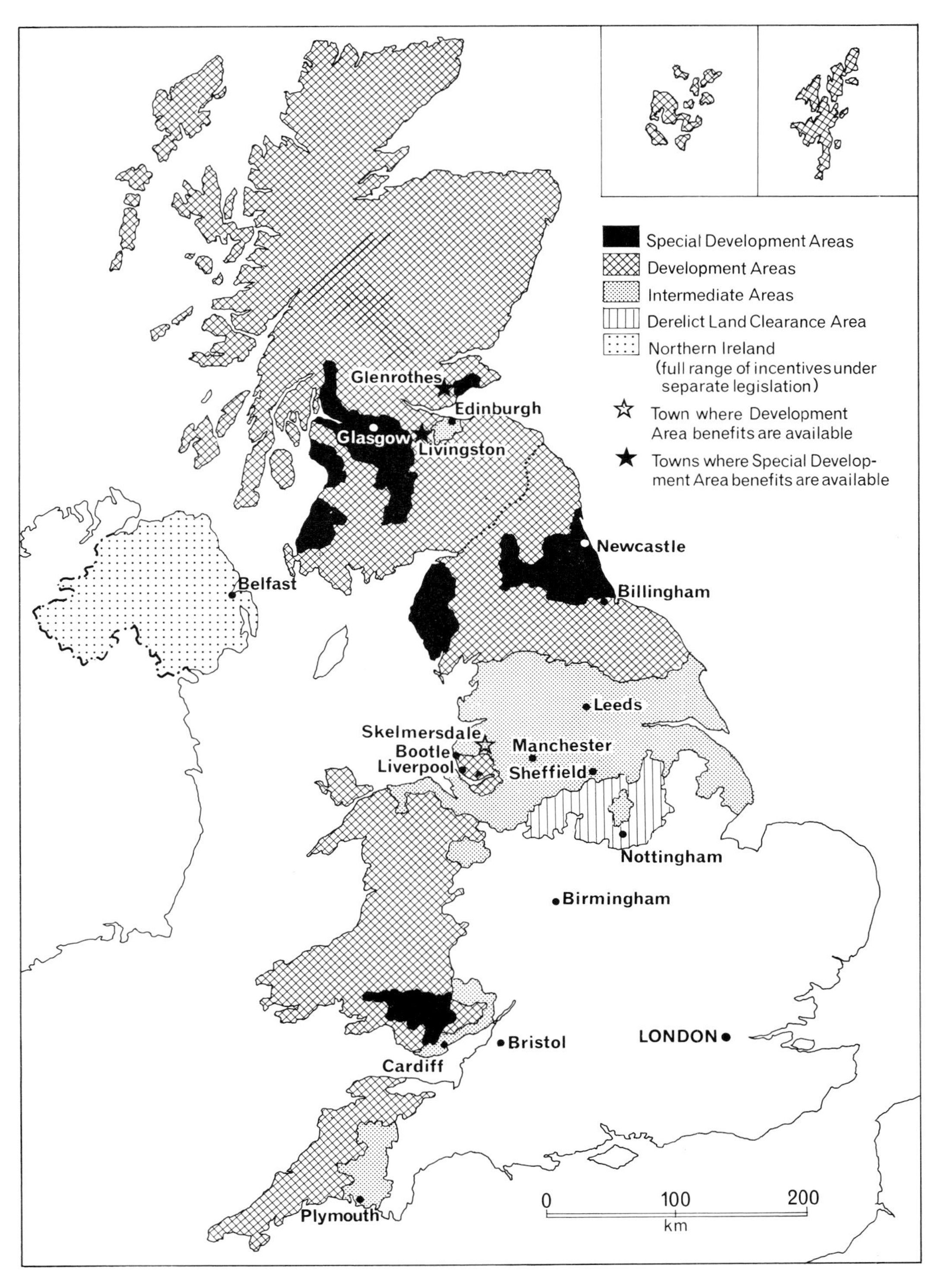
Special Development Areas
Development Areas
Intermediate Areas
Derelict Land Clearance Area
Northern Ireland
(full range of incentives under separate legislation)
Town where Development Area benefits are available
Towns where Special Development Area benefits are available
Glenrothes
Edinburgh
Glasgow
Livingston
Newcastle
Belfast
Billingham
Leeds
Skelmersdale
Bootle
Manchester
Liverpool
Sheffield
Nottingham
Birmingham
Bristol
LONDON
Cardiff
Plymouth
0
100
200
km

Fig. 10.12 Regional development

Except in the case of industry using heavy raw materials, the cost of transport of raw materials is not the overriding factor, for in most cases the value of the goods produced is much greater than the value of the raw materials and their transport, the best example of this being that of factories making precision instruments. On the other hand, there is a great advantage in being located in or near a large urban area to which the products may be sold and from which labour may be obtained, and where *sites* with services may be easier to come by. Many new factories are therefore to be found near large urban areas. Further many modern light industries may not require a building specially designed to their requirements. A building of standard design may be adequate and the firm concerned puts in the machinery and other equipment it requires. Consequently many industrial estates have been set up providing both *sites* and services and some buildings for immediate occupation by firms. One such estate is shown in Fig. 10.2.

One of the difficulties of market based industrial development is that it has tended to reinforce the drift of population to the south of England. Firms have set up in south-eastern England because there is a huge market there and people have migrated to the south-east to work in the new industries. This is why Governments have attempted since 1945 to encourage firms to set up new factories in areas where old industries are declining. These areas are known as *Development Areas* (Fig. 10.12) and industrialists setting up there are given many advantages, such as cheap rentals for factories or factory sites and help with the cost of purchasing equipment. Such a policy also helps to diversify industry in the older industrial areas which in the past may have been dominated by heavy industry. The Government may also refuse to allow a firm to set up a factory in what it considers to be an already overcrowded area. By such a policy of discouraging certain locations and encouraging others, the Government is attempting to ensure:

1. A more even distribution of industry over the whole of the U.K.
2. A greater diversification of industry in the *Development Areas*.

To sum up, most industries today, unless they are heavy industries, have a wide choice of locations open to them. Which *site* a particular firm chooses is more often influenced by the availability of services, of labour and possibly the proximity of the market for its product, than by any other factors. It may however, be induced to go to a *Development Area* by an offer of a cheap *site* and other financial incentives. In many industries, like the soft drinks industry, distribution costs are the main costs and therefore the industry must be located near its market.

C. Trends in British Industry

In the first part of this chapter we examined employment in Great Britain and in South Wales. Another way of looking at British industry is to look not at employment but at the value of output. This is shown in Table 10.3 which is for manufacturing industry only.

Industry Group	Output (£ million)			Percentage of total output	Output per head (£)		
	1970	1971	1972	1972	1970	1971	1972
Food, drink & tobacco	2,348	2,685	3,058	13.6	2,975	3,345	3,848
Coal and petroleum products	239	259	235	1.1	6,530	6,952	6,371
Chemicals and allied industries	1,694	1,838	2,070	9.2	3,981	4,462	5,147
Metal manufacture	1,464	1,289	1,371	6.1	2,541	2,352	2,680
Mechanical engineering	2,402	2,621	2,617	11.7	2,293	2,589	2,785
Instrument engineering	350	381	415	1.9	1,979	2,163	2,441
Electrical engineering	1,639	1,783	2,051	9.1	2,120	2,357	2,732
Shipbuilding and marine engineering	315	349	414	1.9	1,722	1,881	2,253
Vehicles	1,651	1,743	2,172	9.7	2,058	2,216	2,795
Metal goods not elsewhere specified	1,162	1,264	1,380	6.2	2,087	2,284	2,526
Textiles	1,145	1,206	1,317	5.6	1,754	1,960	2,242
Leather, leather goods and fur	80	91	111	0.5	1,740	2,002	2,396
Clothing and footwear	571	649	699	3.1	1,269	1,419	1,551
Bricks, pottery, glass, cement, etc.	684	836	942	4.2	2,308	2,871	3,213
Timber, furniture, etc.	536	655	791	3.5	1,997	2,416	2,916
Paper, printing and publishing	1,462	1,633	1,837	8.2	2,409	2,745	3,149
Other manufacturing industries	760	842	949	4.2	2,212	2,480	2,786
All manufacturing industries	18,502	20,123	22,427	100	2,304	2,551	2,918

Source: *Census of Production Reports* 1970, 1971, 1972 (1972 provisional results). Discrepancies between totals and their constituent parts are due to rounding.

Table 10.3 Manufacturing Industry: Net Output 1970–72

The percentage column for 1972 shows clearly which are the important groups of industries in terms of the total value of their outputs: food, drink and tobacco; mechanical engineering; vehicles and paper, printing and publishing all account for over eight per cent of the total value of the output of manufacturing industry. The column indicating value of output per head of those employed in the industry shows clearly which are the *capital intensive*, which are the *labour intensive* industries. For example, the value of output per head for the 'Coal and Petroleum Products' group is four times as great as that for the 'Clothing and Footwear' group. To see which industries are expanding and contracting, look at Table 10.4.

An *index of industrial production* is just a number which indicates whether output has gone up or down. For example, if the output of coal in 1970 was 142 million tonnes but the output in 1980 were to be

Industry Group	1948	1958	1968	1970	1972	1973	1948–73 Change (%)
All industries	50.5	67.5	97.2	100	102.4	109.8	117
Mining/quarrying	129.1	133.6	111.4	100	84.0	93.6	–28
Total manufacturing	47.8	65.5	95.8	100	102.0	110.3	131
Food/drink/tobacco	58.4	73.3	96.5	100	105.0	109.3	87
Coal/petroleum products	21.4	51.9	84.0	100	102.6	110.0	414
Chemical/allied industries	25.5	45.7	89.8	100	108.0	120.9	374
Metal manufacture	61.8	77.4	97.5	100	90.8	99.5	61
Engineering industries	34.7	55.6	91.1	100	100.5	112.3	224
Shipbuilding	110.3	111.6	95.1	100	91.8	95.1	–14
Vehicles (inc. aircraft)	39.0	78.7	101.1	100	101.6	101.6	161
Other metal goods	64.1	77.1	98.3	100	94.2	102.8	60
Textiles/clothing	73.4	76.1	98.9	100	104.6	109.6	49
Bricks, pottery, etc.	54.4	62.7	102.2	100	114.2	126.3	132
Timber, furniture, etc.	45.4	66.7	106.5	100	113.5	130.2	187
Paper/printing/publishing	42.7	69.8	96.2	100	101.9	112.8	164
Other manufacturing	30.5	45.4	95.7	100	104.6	111.3	265
Construction	56.3	68.7	103.5	100	105.2	107.5	91
Gas/electricity/water	31.4	54.5	91.6	100	111.2	117.8	275

Source: *Economic Trends*; *Monthly Digest of Statistics*

Table 10.4 Index of Industrial Production 1948–73 (1970 = 100)

160 million tonnes, then the index of production for coal for 1970 would be 100 and for 1980,

$$\frac{100}{142} \times 160 = 112.7$$

It is clear from Table 10.4 that, although industrial output has increased generally over the past years, certain groups of industries have declined. For example, mining and quarrying have declined largely because total coal production has decreased since petroleum and natural gas have been extensively used as fuels. 'Shipbuilding' is another industry which has steadily declined because foreign shipyards, particularly Japanese shipyards, have been able to produce cheaper ships more quickly. Similarly 'Metal Manufacture' and 'Vehicles' are groups of industries which are either in decline or not expanding. Again, the problem here is to produce steel and cars in competition with efficiently produced foreign goods. It seems that certain industries for which Britain was a pioneer have lost the momentum which they once had and are now relatively high cost producers. The problems posed are:

1. Which other industries should be encouraged to develop to take the place of the decaying industries?

2. How can labour be encouraged to move from declining to growing industries?

Unfortunately, developing industries tend to be capital intensive industries which do not need much manpower and certainly little unskilled manpower. Consequently, the future demand for labour is likely to be one for skilled workers in industry or for those offering an expertise in various service industries. But a great deal of investment in industry is required to create a demand for such skills.

8. (a) What is the great centre of the pottery industry in Great Britain? (Fig. 10.3)
   (b) Although the location of the industry was originally based on a local clay called Etruria Marl, what raw material did this industry use for its high quality products and where did this come from (see p. 114)?
   (c) Why would it not have been sensible to shift the industry elsewhere when clay had to be imported for making chinaware?
9. (a) Why would you expect the distribution of motor vehicles manufacturing and of engineering industries to be similar? (Figs. 10.4 and 10.5)
   (b) What area of concentration of the engineering industry is not also a motor manufacturing area?
10. (a) Why is there a wider scatter of clothing factories than of motor vehicle factories? (Figs. 10.4 and 10.6)
   (b) Which area in England shows a notable concentration of footwear factories?
11. Study Fig. 10.7.
   (a) What are the three main areas of concentration for the paper and paper products industry?
   (b) These areas are near to great ports; what are the advantages of these locations?
   (c) The printing industry is much more scattered; why is this? (Bear in mind who is likely to require printing services.)
12. (a) What are the centres of concentration of (i) the woollen textile industry (ii) the cotton textile industry (iii) the jute textile industry (Fig. 10.8).
   (b) What is meant by the localization of industry?
   (c) Why is the cotton textile industry localized but the man-made fibre industry (Fig. 10.11) much more scattered?
   (d) Which modern industries still tend to be localized?
13. Explain the term geographical momentum.
14. (a) Where is the manufacturing belt (i) in England, and (ii) in Scotland?
   (b) If the manufacturing belt is not a continuous belt of industry, what is it?
   (c) Does the manufacturing belt appear more of a 'belt' on a small scale or large scale map?
   (d) Why is there a tendency for industries to group together in such a belt? (Fig. 10.9 and p. 114)
15. Suppose Lyons decided to set up a new bakery in the S.W. suburbs of London
   (a) Which of the following is likely to be the most important reason why they did this (i) because it was easy to get flour into the area (ii) because the population of the district was growing (iii) because plenty of labour was available?
   (b) Fig. 10.14 is an example of the site chosen for a cosmetics works (i) does it have any advantage specific to a cosmetics works? (ii) as part of an industrial estate what advantages does it have?
16. (a) Why is it that if a completely free choice of location was given

Fig. 10.13 Textiles, mechanical and electrical engineering in Ireland

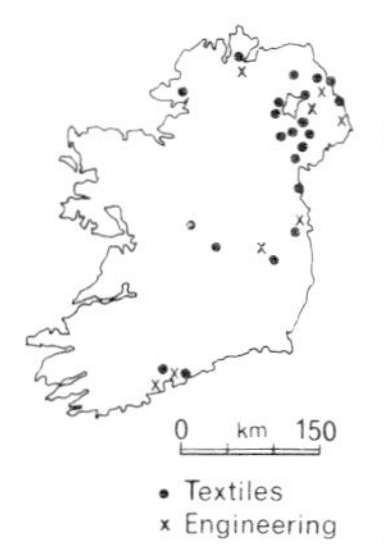

to all industrialists, south-eastern England would probably become even more overcrowded than it is?

(b) What measures are taken to ensure a more even spread of industry in the U.K.?

(c) What are the Development Areas *and where are they in England?*

17. *(a) From Fig. 10.13 what do you notice about the distribution of industry in Ireland?*

(b) Compare Fig. 10.13 and Figs. 10.5 and 10.8. What conclusion do you come to about the relative development of these two industries in Britain and Ireland?

(c) What are the main trends of British Industry in the 1970's?

Conclusions

In this chapter we studied some aspects of the distribution of industry in Britain. We have seen that we can measure the degree to which an industry is localized in an area by calculating its *Location Quotient*. This has shown us that today most areas are seldom completely dominated by one industry, though some areas are less diversified than others, and South Wales is one of these. Some areas called *Development Areas* are being encouraged to develop varied industries. We have also seen that the process of *localization* is less strong than it was in the 19th century due largely to most industries no longer being dependent on coal. However, the gradual growth of industry in England along main lines of communication has produced a *manufacturing belt* stretching from London to South Lancashire and West Yorkshire. Finally industrial location is now to some extent controlled by Government policy, and permission to develop new sites for industry must be given by the Department of Trade and Industry, and by the local authority's planning department.

REVISION EXERCISES

18. Large areas of Britain seem to have no industries. Why is this?

19. (a) If 3 per cent of the employed population in a given area were working in the vehicles industry, what would be the* Location Quotient *of the industry in that area? (See Table 10.2.)

(b) What does the figure you obtain tell you about the extent of the* localization of the industry *in that area?

20. If you were advising a printing firm about a site for its new works, would you suggest a site near a main road or near a main railway? Give reasons for your answer.

21. Which of the following countries would you expect not to have many* service industries *in their economies:
Canada, U.S.A., Tanzania, Saudi Arabia, U.S.S.R., Morocco, Paraguay, West Germany, Switzerland, Botswana, Thailand, Bolivia?

22. Do you think weather or climate has an effect on the location chosen for any industry in the U.K. If so, give examples.

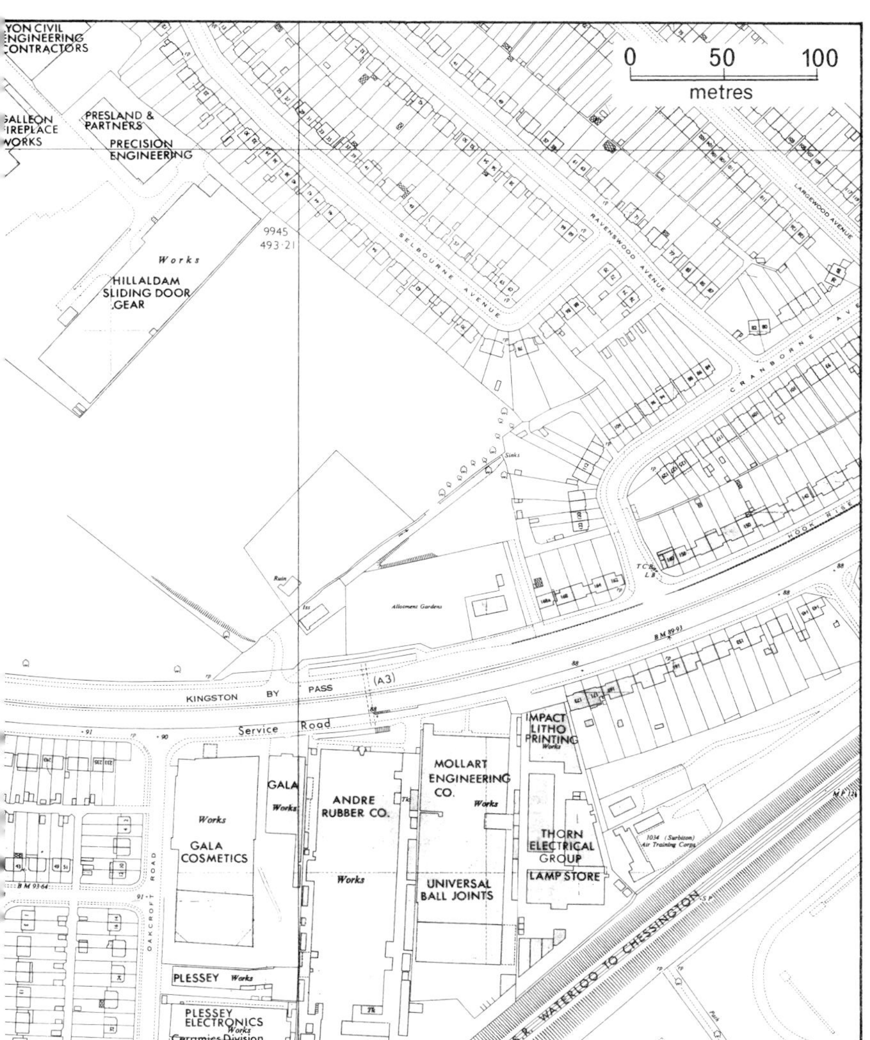

Fig. 10.14 Industrial development on the Kingston By-pass

23. ***Using Fig. 10.14, plan the site of a new electronic component works. State how big the building would be, what services you require and where you would lay the access road. Which local authority and government departments would you be required to consult?***

Chapter Eleven

Iron, Steel, and Shipbuilding

A. 'The Workshop of the World'

The British people are now essentially city dwellers. The gre magnet drawing people from rural to urban areas has been the possibilities of employment of various types. The growth of many of ou great cities is linked with the development of machine industrie The United Kingdom was the first great industrial nation and, in th 19th century, was known as the 'workshop and carrier of the world We were then the richest nation in the world. Being first in the fiel can be a disadvantage: many of our traditional industries are suffering severe competition from the newer industrial nations, with mor modern equipment and new techniques of production.

The 'workshop and carrier' of the world based its industrial supremacy on coal, iron and steel and ships, not forgetting the hard wor and inventiveness of its people. The production of steel is sti regarded as a useful index to the importance of an industrial natio Table 11.1 compares the steel production of the 'top five' nation in 1875 with those of today.

Table 11.1 Steel production

1875 (thousand tonnes)		1974 (million tonnes)	
United Kingdom	710	Common Market (inc. U.K.)	153
United States	380	Soviet Union	136
Germany	320	United States	132
France	210	Japan	117
Russia	10	China (estimated)	27

Source: *British Steel Corporation*

The British Steel industry is now part of the European Coal an Steel Community and future plans are discussed with our Commo Market partners. If you cannot visit a steel plant, the best alternative is to see one of the many films of steel-making. The great furnaces, in which steel is made, are scattered throughout the countr but are generally found on or near coalfields. Fig. 11.1 shows th distribution of the main plants. The British Iron and Steel Federation says, 'The ideal location for a steelworks would have eas access to raw materials and labour and be within easy reach o

1865	100
1875	710
1885	1,890
1895	3,260
1905	5,810
1915	8,550
1925	7,390
1935	9,860
1945	11,820
1955	19,790
1965	27,010
1970	27,870
1971	23,793
1972	25,000
1973	27,120
1974	20,800

Table 11.2 U.K. Steel Production (thousand tonnes)

Fig. 11.1 The principal steelworks of Britain

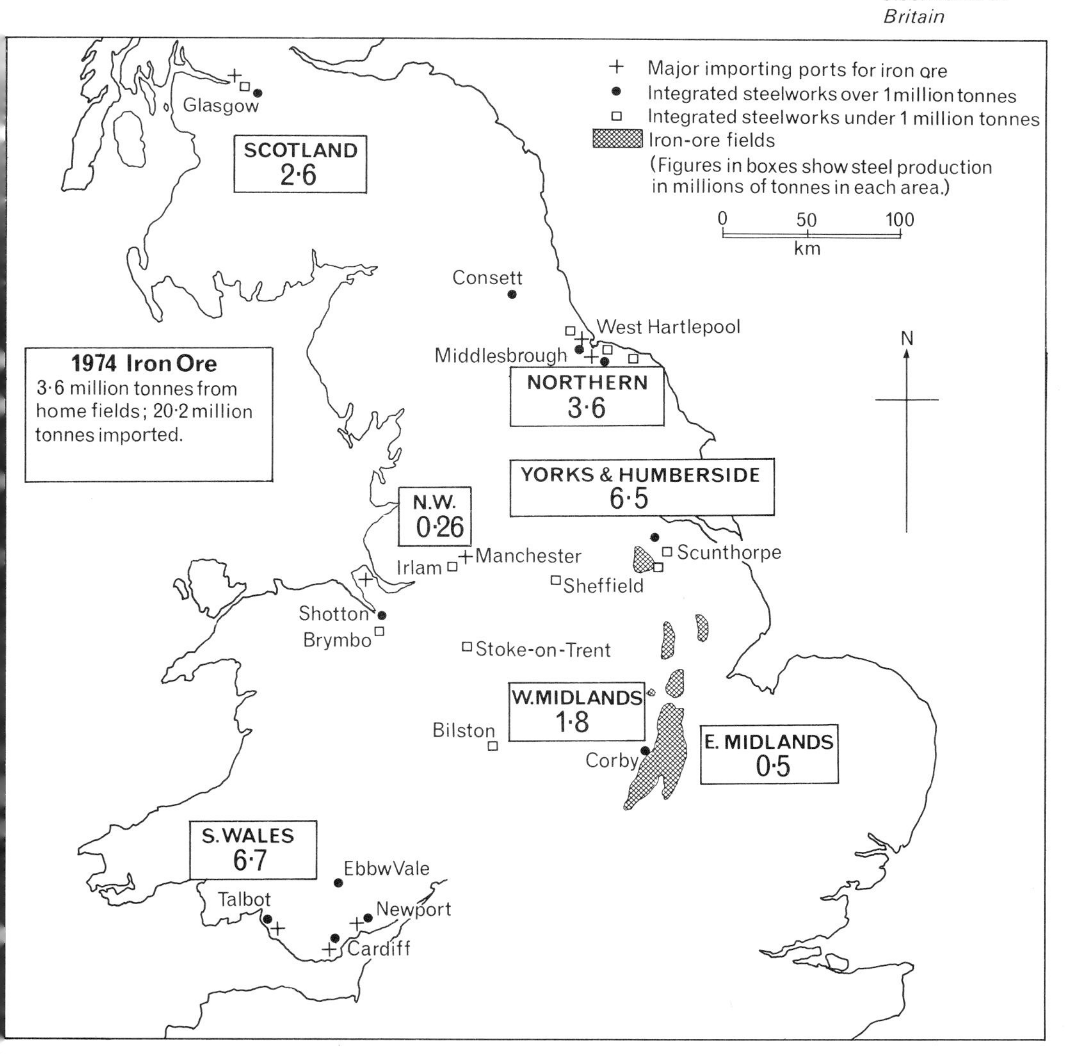

(Source: *British Steel Corporation*)

markets. On average, four tonnes of raw materials have to be brough into a works for each tonne of finished steel sent out'.

The British Steel Corporation intends to concentrate future outpu in five major centres, Clydeside, Teesside, South Wales, Sheffiel and Humberside. The 'Anchor' project at Scunthorpe in th Humberside region will be the largest of its kind.

The raw materials are basically iron ore, fuel for smelting (usuall coke), limestone as a flux, many specialist materials in small quanti ties for special types of steel, enormous quantities of water; moder techniques need further materials such as oxygen in bulk supply

The complex processes by which iron-ore is made into a variety o types of iron and steel is greatly simplified in Fig. 11.2 to act as

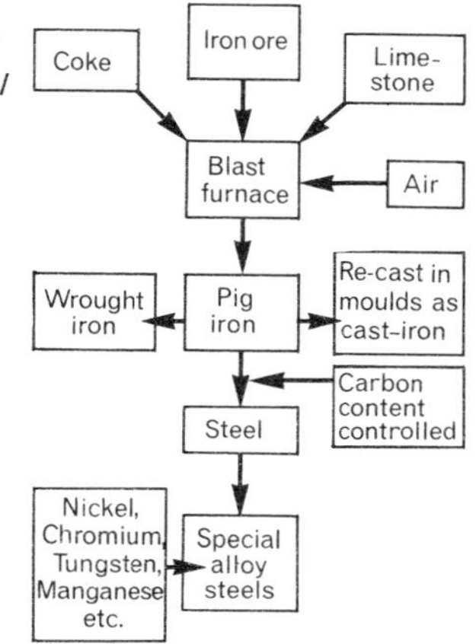

Fig. 11.2 Flowchart of iron and steel manufacture

Fig. 11.3 A walking drag-line excavating over-burden from an iron ore field in North-amptonshire

reference diagram when reading this chapter. If all the main processes are carried out in the same 'plant', it is known as an 'integrated' plant.

The United Kingdom has no shortage of coke and limestone but high-grade iron-ore is now in very short supply. Fig. 11.1 shows the main iron-ore fields in the country but the average iron content of home ores is 27 per cent whereas the average iron content of ores imported from abroad is 62 per cent. This means that more than twice the amount of 'pig iron' (iron ready for further use) can be made from imported ore than from home ores.

As our own resources are being used up and as they are of low-grade ore, the steel industry is becoming more dependent on imported ores. In 1974, we used 3.6 million tonnes of home ores and imported another 20.2 million tonnes. But our home supplies are vitally important in order to save foreign currency and in the event of international discord (such as supplies being cut off by war). Fig. 11.3 shows one of the opencast iron ore mines. Enormous walking draglines and earth-shifters remove the overburden (top layers of earth) and then remove the iron-ore itself. By law, the mining companies have to restore the land after mining so that it can be used for farming again. We cannot afford to waste land: but this process does make the iron-ore more costly to extract.

The importance of imported iron-ore gives an advantage to steel furnaces situated near ports and this trend is likely to continue. Indeed, special bulk carriers are now in service: the more ore a ship can carry at one trip, the cheaper the cost of carrying each ton will be. Some of the new carriers find it difficult to use some of the traditional iron-ore ports, in South Wales, for example. So the ideal location for a steel works outlined above must now take into account the need for a deep-water harbour.

With reference to Tables 11.1 and 11.2:

1. *Only two nations appear both in the 1875 list and the 1974 list. Which are they?*
2. *Under which name do Germany and France appear in the 1974 list?*
3. *Under what name does Russia appear in the 1974 list?*
4. *Which country in the 1970 list does not appear at all in the 1875 production figures?*
5. *What is the United Kingdom's position in the modern 'league table' of steel production?*
6. *In which ten years did steel production in the United Kingdom increase by the greatest tonnage?*
7. *In which periods did U.K. steel production actually decline?*
8. *Make a graph of U.K. steel production over the last hundred years. For this purpose, simplify the production figures to the nearest half-million.*

With reference to Fig. 11.1 and the text:

9. *What factors are taken into account when siting a steel plant?*
10. *Name four of the most important raw materials needed in the manufacture of iron and steel.*
11. *Which are the two most important steel-producing areas in the British Isles in terms of tonnage produced?*
12. *Which two areas are situated on local iron-ore deposits?*
13. *Why are most steel plants situated on or near coalfields? (A map of coalfields will be found in Fig. 13.1).*
14. *How many integrated steel plants does Britain have producing over 1 million tonnes of steel a year?*
15. *What advantages does a steel plant have by being situated near the coast?*
16. *How is it possible for Manchester, an inland city, to be a major port for the importation of iron-ore?*
17. *Why will Britain be increasingly dependent on imported iron-ore?*
18. *What does Table 11.3 tell you about British blast furnaces when compared with Table 11.2?*

Table 11.3

1873	683 furnaces.
1920	284 furnaces.
1973	79 furnaces.

(Brit. Steel Corp.)

B. South Wales

If we take the production figures for steelworks shown in Table 11.1 and put them in order of importance, the South Wales region comes out as the most important with an annual output of 6.7 million tonnes of steel just ahead of Yorkshire/Humberside with an output of 6.5 million tonnes. In this region are no less than 3 integrated steelworks, each producing over 1,000,000 tonnes per year. These plants are shown in more detail in Fig. 11.4. They are fed by coking coal

Fig. 11.4 Iron and steel plants in South Wales

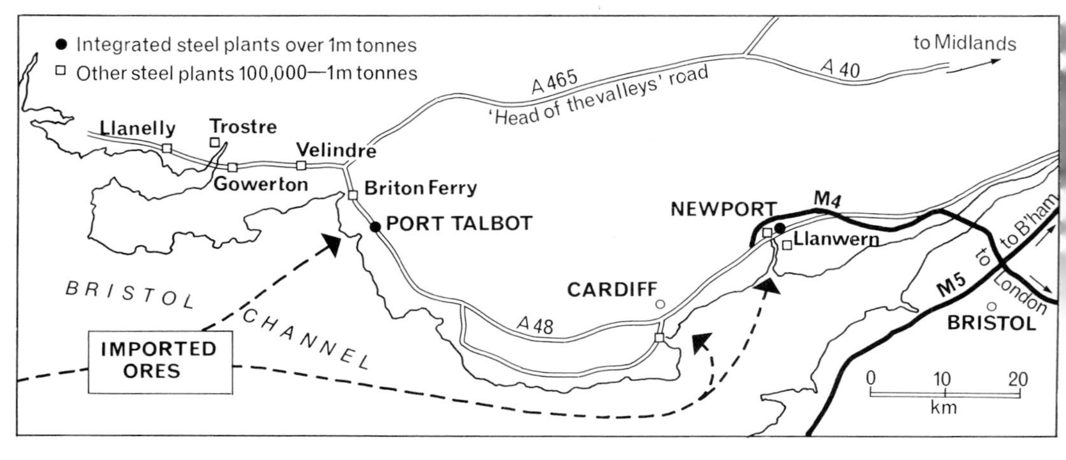

from the nearby coalfield (cf. Fig. 13.1), by imported iron-ore coming to the South Wales ports and by limestone from local geological outcrops. The Abbey Works at Margam (Fig. 10.1) even has coal shafts within its grounds, thus supplying fuel with the maximum of convenience and minimum transport costs.

This concentration of very large steel-works is the most recent stage of a long period of development and change in the steel-towns of South Wales, which now produce nearly 60 per cent of the sheet-steel of Britain and 100 per cent of its tin-plate (sheet steel is the basis of tin-plate). The steel industry grew up in the valleys where both coal and iron-ore were mined and this led to the growth of hundreds of small steel and tin-plate mills. The formation of the Steel Company of South Wales in 1947 and the construction of new modern plants at Margam (Port Talbot), which were then the most up-to-date in Europe, led to the closure of the smaller works. In the late 1970's, Ebbw Vale is to specialize in tin-plating together with Velindre and Trostre.

South Wales is linked via the A40 and the M5 motorway to the industries of the Midlands, much of its sheet steel going into the production of motor cars. Its links with London and the south have been improved with the new Severn Bridge and the M4 motorway. Yet the deep valleys of the South Wales coalfield made east-west transport difficult and the region is still somewhat isolated from the other industrial areas.

It is official government planning policy to encourage the movement of Welsh industry out of the valleys down towards the coast where new roads linking the main centres of Swansea and Cardiff are under construction.

Coal exports were once the main traffic of the South Wales ports, especially Cardiff, but the decline of the coal trade and the exhaustion of local iron-ores has led to the greater importance of imported iron-ore. The ports are handicapped by their inability to take big bulk-carriers so the steel companies have developed a new deep-water iron-ore terminal to take 100,000 tonne carriers (with a possible extension for 150,000 tonners) at Port Talbot. Other terminals have been developed at Immingham, Teesside and Hunterston on the Clyde.

19. *According to Fig. 11.1, what proportion of Britain's total steel output came from South Wales?*
20. *Suggest reasons why South Wales has the greatest concentration of steel plants in the British Isles.*
21. *Explain the difficulties which must be overcome if South Wales is to develop in the future as a major industrial region.*
22. *With the aid of motoring maps or a good atlas, make a map to show the position of the South Wales steel plants with their major road and rail links with Oxford, Bristol, Coventry, Birmingham and the London area and show the distances involved.*

C. The Uses of Steel

It has been said that the steel-using area of the Midlands makes everything from a pin to a steam-engine. Extend this to Tyneside and include a modern oil tanker weighing 250,000 tonnes deadweight and it gives some idea of the great variety of uses to which steel is put. In 1875, the year quoted in Table 11.1, nearly half the steel output of the United Kingdom was used in the railway industry. But in 1975 less than 2 per cent of our steel output was used by the railway industry, for rails, engines and rolling stock. The steel industry is always looking for new outlets for its products of wires, pipes, sheets and sections. The greatest user now is industrial plant, using 9 per cent of our output, while motor vehicles and aircraft use 11 per cent. Sheet steel covered with a thin layer of tin is the basis of most of our 'tins' while steel girders are still the basis of much construction work in modern buildings, cranes and bridges. Where strength and *stability* are required, steel manages to maintain its reputation against all the many new construction materials now available.

Fig. 11.5 shows a traditional use of iron and steel in Tyneside, an area closely associated with the early developments in iron and steel manufacture. Fig. 11.6 in contrast, shows one of the special drilling rigs made to withstand the gales in the North Sea while holding the drills searching for oil and gas. More than 9,000 tonnes of steel were used in the *Sea Quest*, a thousand tonnes more than in the new Tay road bridge.

One of the traditional users of steel plate is the shipbuilding industry. A special rail link runs constant supplies of iron-ore from the Tyne docks to Consett Iron and Steel works and, in return, carry a regular supply of sheet steel and sections to the shipyards of Wearside and Tyneside. In spite of which, only 3.5 per cent of our steel output is now used in shipbuilding.

Britain's leadership in shipbuilding, reflected in the quotation used earlier in this chapter, 'the workshop and carrier of the world', has been lost to other developing industrial nations. The decline of this industry is shown in the Index of Industrial Production (Table 10.4).

Fig. 11.5 The Tyne bridges at Newcastle

D. Shipbuilding

The famous ships of the Elizabethan period, the 'wooden walls' of England, were built largely of timber and were built in small shipyards on the south coast and on the river Thames. My grandfather worked on the boilers of a British warship at Deptford on the river Thames. But that was before the 1914–18 war. The size of modern ships and the use of steel in place of timber has lead to the concentration of the shipbuilding industry in deeper estuaries close to the coalfields. The great shipyards whose names are still household names in the world of ships are nearly all north of a line drawn between the Mersey and the Humber: Clydeside, Tyneside, Wearside, the Mersey, Belfast Lough, Barrow-in-Furness. (See Fig. 11.10.) Of course, small craft such as tugs, yachts, trawlers and *cobles* for inshore fishing are still made in a large number of small yards scattered throughout the country but the big tonnage is associated with the estuaries named above.

As recently as 1949, the yards of the north-east, in other words, the Tyne, the Wear and the Tees, produced more than half the tonnage launched in this country. Shipbuilding in this region dates back to the 13th century when ships were built to bring coal to the south, especially to London. The first steam-turbine engine was fitted into a ship on the Tyne in 1894. The tradition is a long one and Tyneside recently saw its largest-ever ship launched, over 250,000 tonnes. Clydeside saw the launching of the new Queen liner in 1967 and a super-tanker of nearly 200,000 tonnes was launched in Belfast Lough in the same year. Yet, in spite of this strong and continuing tradition, British yards have lost their leading position in the world. Table 11.4 shows the world tonnage of shipping launched in 1971.

Table 11.4 World Shipbuilding, 1973 (thousand tonnes)

Japan	15,673
Sweden	2,517
W. Germany	1,979
Spain	1,568
France	1,133
Norway	1,071
U.K.	1,017

(Whitaker 1975)

There are very many reasons for our comparative decline in face of the competition of Japan, Sweden and West Germany, some of them linked with problems of management and relationships with the unions. But, basically, the other nations have new or modernized shipyards, capable of turning out very large ships quickly, using up-to-date prefabrication and welding techniques. A recent report on the shipbuilding industry, carried out on behalf of the government, has made the main point that our shipyards and the companies are too small. It has recommended that yards operating on the same stretch of water should amalgamate to form single large units, so as to be in a better position to compete with other countries.

Several mergers have been announced recently and all the Tyneside yards now operate as one unit. This group even control yards outside the estuary of the Tyne. The estuary of the Wear now has two major groups and further amalgamation is likely.

The Clydeside yards are now combined into two groups, the Upper Clyde Shipyards and the Lower Clyde Shipyards. The Upper Clyde group is in severe financial difficulties but Clydebank has a future in producing oil rigs.

Not the least of the difficulties is the problem of launching large ships in comparatively narrow, shallow estuaries. It is possible to make estuaries deeper by dredging and, when necessary, by blasting. It is not so easy to widen an estuary. Many new devices have

Fig. 11.6 The Sea Quest drilling rig

been introduced to overcome the difficulty. When the *Queen Elizabeth II* was launched on Clydeside, people were warned not to be on the bank opposite because of the temporary flooding the wave might cause. Ships were traditionally launched at right angles to the water. Now the larger ones are launched at an angle. The largest will be launched sideways!

Wearside specializes in launching ships in sections that can be welded together later in specially constructed docks or even at sea. The Tyneside group are now busy with 250,000 tonners called Very Large Crude Carriers (V.L.C.C.'s). These new methods raise new problems but the ability to adapt to modern changes is the essential requirement of modern industry.

23. *Why are most of the great shipyards of Britain to be found north of the Mersey/Humber line?*
24. *Make a map of the British Isles and mark on it the estuaries on which the shipbuilding industry is concentrated: Tyneside, Wearside, Clydeside, Merseyside, Belfast Lough and Barrow-in-Furness.*
25. *Make a series of diagrams to show the problem of launching a ship 120 metres long into an estuary only 120 metres wide.*
26. *Find out the difference between rivetting and welding.*
27. *When a ship is launched in sections, why do the individual sections not sink?*

E. Wearside

Fig. 11.7 is an aerial view of one of the shipbuilding estuaries on the north-east coast of England, the Wear at Sunderland, looking upstream from the North Sea. The photograph not only reveals the river and the shipyards, but the northern suburbs of the city and Roker Park, the famous football stadium, and a modern coal mine right in the heart of the city. The main yards are mapped and named on Fig. 11.8.

Sunderland's industrial greatness has been closely connected with the mining and export of coal and the comparative decline of that industry has led to problems in shipping. Once there were 77 yards, building and repairing ships; now there are five, and those five are linked into two main groups. One yard concentrates on marine engines, another is producing prefabricated container cargo ships, like an 'off-the-peg' suit instead of one made-to-measure. The SD-14 general cargo ship and the B-26 bulk carrier (26,000 tonnes) are two such successful ventures. By making many ships of the same size and design, economies can be made in the yard and the ships sold for a competitive price. The Wear has been dredged down to 8 metres depth but yards upstream often have to dredge the river before a launching. Unfortunately, the river Wear cuts a gorge through solid rock, the Magnesian Limestone, and this is a major obstacle to a deeper channel. So the Wear has only about 5.6

Fig. 11.7
Wearside

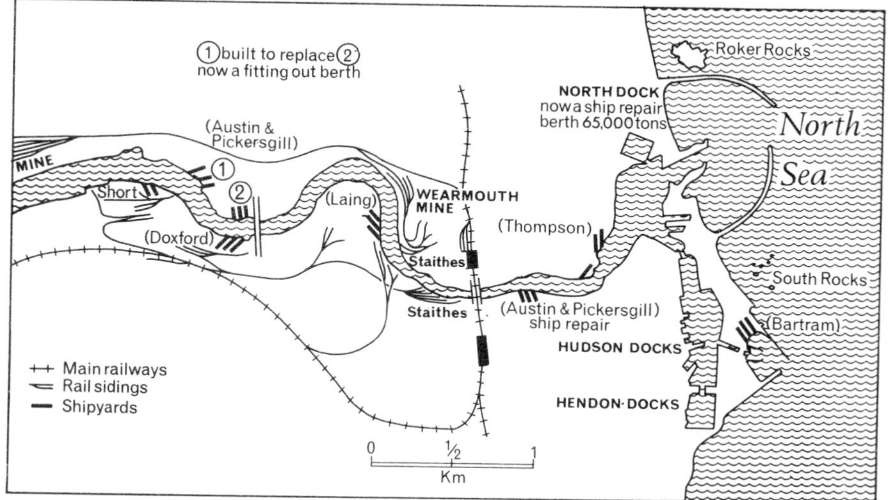

Fig. 11.8
Wearside

km of water deeper than 8 metres whereas the Clyde has 30 kilometres and the Tyne nearly 19 kilometres. The Austin and Pickersgill yard marked (1) on the map was built to replace the yard marked (2). Surprisingly, it is further upstream, towards shallower water, but the important feature is its alignment.

Some of the problems of the yards in maintaining regular orders to keep their skilled labour force permanently employed may be shown by Table 11.5.

Table 11.5 Wearside shipbuilding

	Ships	Total tonnage	Average tonnage
1840	251	64,000	av. 257
1905	95	342,000	3,608
1932	2	2,600	1,300
1952	26	170,000	6,000
1971	19	265,000	13,900
1974	15	246,000	16,400

(Shipbuilders and Repairers National Association)

So the problem of supplying a ship at the right price and the right time (it takes about seven months to build a 50,000 tonne section of a ship) is very difficult in this competitive industry.

28. Using the scale on Fig. 11.8, what is the width of the river Wear (a) by the bridge nearest the river mouth? and (b) opposite Short's Yard?

29. How far is the Austin and Pickersgill yard from the open sea? For this purpose, the lighthouses at the estuary mouth can be regarded as marking the open sea.

30. What advantages does the new Austin and Pickersgill yard (1) have over their earlier site (2)?

31. What problems does the nature of the banks of the Wear present to the company planning a new ship yard?

32. What dangers face shipping approaching the Wear estuary?

33. Why are railway sidings built in close association with the shipyards?

34. What part of the shipbuilding process is carried out in a 'fitting-out berth'?

F. Clydeside

Clydeside, birthplace of the Queen liners, has been the home of shipbuilding for at least 150 years and in 1967, the *Queen Elizabeth II* (the Q 4) was launched from John Brown's yard on the upper Clyde. This liner, the most modern in the world, 292 metres long, has a gross tonnage of 58,000 tonnes and has a draught of 10 metres. It carries over 2,000 passengers at a speed of 45 km/hour, and consumes 520 tonnes of fuel a day. Yet she is almost certainly the last of the great liners. Liners cannot compete with aircraft on the

North Atlantic crossing to New York and Montreal. In ten years, the Clyde's twenty shipbuilding yards have been cut to half that number: the 30,000 workers have been cut to 20,000. The discovery of oil in the North Sea has provided new sources of work with the construction of oil drilling rigs (Marathon), oil production platforms and oil rig supply vessels.

The map of the Clyde estuary (Fig. 11.9) shows the distribution of the main yards. The Upper Clyde group have experienced many difficulties. The yards on the lower Clyde, Lithgows and Scotts, have much more favourable conditions for building and launching big craft while the group above Clydebank will concentrate on ships of less than 100,000 tonnes. Two main groups have been formed, the Upper Clyde Group and the Lower Clyde Group. The many natural advantages of the Firth of Clyde with its great depth and long sheltered approach, often used for a ship's first trials, suggest that it will continue as a great shipbuilding centre. The oil-tanker terminal (see Ch. 13 B.) at Finnart on Loch Long will be capable of taking the

Fig. 11.9 The Firth of Clyde: a deep water entry to the British Isles

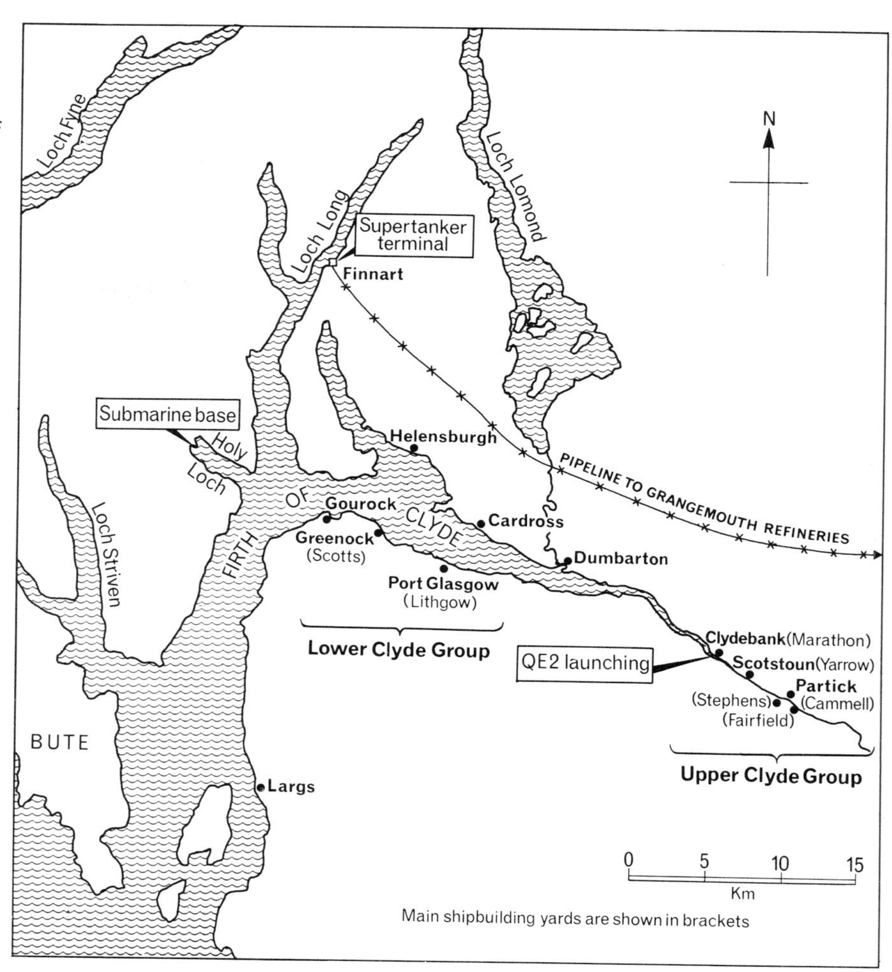

largest ships in the world. Holy Loch is the main base of the Polaris submarine fleet.

35. *What is the length of the Clyde shipbuilding zone from Fairfield's Yard to Scotts at Greenock?*
36. *How wide is the Clyde estuary (a) at Greenock? (b) at Largs?*
37. *What natural advantages has the Clyde as a shipbuilding centre?*
38. *Name three famous ships that have been launched on the Clyde.*
39. *Compare the size of the Queen Elizabeth II with the oil-tankers mentioned in Chapter 16 C.*

REVISION EXERCISES

40. ***Investigate the materials used in making modern steel and the processes they undergo. Some of these processes are closely-guarded secrets but a good encyclopaedia will help. The British Iron and Steel Federation publish some excellent pamphlets for schools including a simple guide to technical developments.***
41. ***Make your own list of the uses of steel and, where possible, the source of the object. For example, steel blades carry the manufacturer's name. So do steel girders which are found in the construction of many schools.***
42. ***What advantages does steel have over iron?***
43. ***What problems face British shipyards because of the increasing size of modern ships?***
44. ***Select one of the estuaries shown in Fig. 11.10 (apart from Wearside) and make a special study of it. The atlas will be helpful but the appropriate sheet of the 1:50,000 Ordnance Survey will be better for making a base map and the encyclopaedias (Brittanica and Chambers) will give further details.***

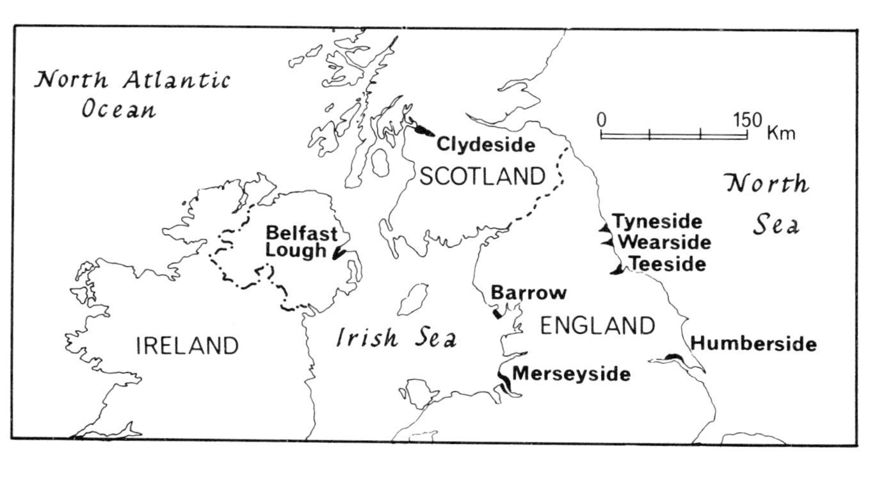

Fig. 11.10 The industrial estuaries

Chapter Twelve

The Chemical Industry

The chemical industry is one of the fastest-growing industries in Great Britain (see Table 10.4). The costliness of the production and the great size of the installations for the manufacture of chemicals, together with the competition with overseas companies, has led to the concentration of production in certain favoured areas dominated by a few very large firms. It is a difficult industry to study because of the difficulty of recognizing the product. We can all identify a motor-car or a radio set, a ship or a suit of clothes but it is not so easy to make a list of chemical products. The goods sold in a chemist's shop do have some relationship to the chemical industry, drugs, medicines, ointments and cosmetics being among the great range of products. But the importance of the chemical industry is better illustrated by the following list of the main divisions of the largest chemical company, the Imperial Chemical Industry, in the British Isles:

1. The Agricultural Division, concerned chiefly with various aids to farming such as fertilisers, weed killers, pesticides.
2. The Dyestuffs Division, concerned with making colour dyes, especially for textiles.
3. The Heavy Organic Chemical Division, concerned especially with oils, fuels, creosote etc.
4. The Mond Division, producing chlorine, caustic soda, salt and acids of all kinds.
5. The Nobel Division, concerned especially with explosives.
6. The Paints Division.
7. The Pharmaceutical Division, making medicines and veterinary products.
8. The Plastics Division, making such things as vinyl, PVC and polythene.
9. The Fibres Division, producing artificial fibres such as nylon, terylene etc.
10. Metal Industries, producing special non-ferrous metals.

This gigantic industry that affects every aspect of modern life developed from small localized industries producing colour dyes for clothing, tanning leather and making glass. One of the basic commodities was, and is, salt which was treated to produce sodium sulphate for use in soap manufacture and textile dyes. By the mid-19th century coal tar was found suitable for making dyes and paints

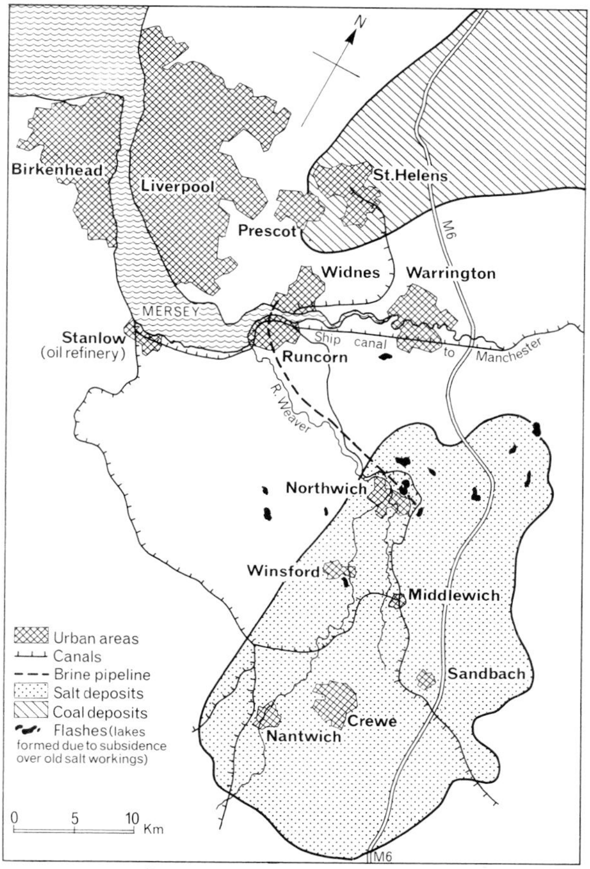

Fig. 12.1 Chemical manufacture in Cheshire and Merseyside

and coal remains one of the major raw materials in the industry. The traditional centres of the industry are still located where these raw materials are found in large quantities, such as the Mersey valley near to the Cheshire salt deposits and the S. E. Lancashire coalfield. Fig. 12.1 shows the location of salt deposits in the Weaver Valley. The salt is found in beds nearly 30 metres thick, sometimes near the surface (though the easily-accessible deposits have been worked out) and often at a depth of 65 metres, as, for example, at Winsford. Some of the salt is mixed with water and pumped as brine by pipeline to the chemical plants on the Mersey, such as at Runcorn. There is always a tremendous increase in demand for this salt during hard winters when local authorities have to try and keep the roads open. The Mersey area is also fed by canal transportation from both the salt and coal mining areas and its road links have been greatly improved by new motorway construction, especially that of the M 6. Because of their great size, cost and potential danger, the chemical plants themselves are located on comparatively cheap, low-lying ground near river estuaries. In the case of Merseyside, they have access to the dock facilities of Liverpool and the Manchester Ship Canal.

Four-fifths of chemical production is now based on petroleum as a raw material. Like coal, it mainly consists of carbon, but it is easier to handle and, although an imported material, relatively cheap. This has given additional advantages to chemical plants situated near to sea ports and to oil refineries. In some cases, new chemical plants have grown up alongside refineries and, in others, chemical factories have installed their own refineries. So close is the relationship now between the two that we may speak of the 'petro-chemical industry'.

One advantage of oil and many chemical products is that they can be transported by pipeline, especially suitable for inflammable and potential dangerous cargoes that are best kept off the road network. Hence we speak of a 'pipeline revolution', the rapid development of a network of large-bore pipes carrying both raw-materials and products from port to factory, from refinery to factory, from factory to port. Fig. 12.2 shows the main developments in the north-west region, associated with the Merseyside chemical industry. Notice the concentration of pipes from the oil refinery at Stanlow near the Manchester Ship Canal. Of particular interest is the Trans-Pennine pipeline completed in 1967 to link the chemical industries of Merseyside and Lancashire with those of Teesside.

Teesside is, in fact, now the largest concentration of chemical plant in the British Isles. At the Wilton Works alone, shown in Fig. 12.3, I.C.I. has spent £200,000,000 in developments over the last 20 years. The aerial view shows the enormously complex system

Fig. 12.2 Pipe lines in the North West region

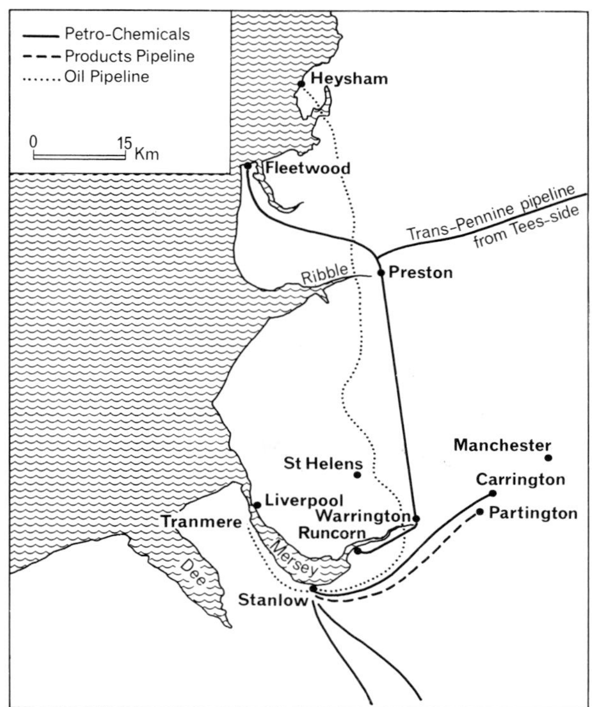

of buildings, towers, containers, pipes, road, rail and water links that have grown up on farming land on the south side of the Tees estuary. This site was first developed in 1946 on 800 hectares and linked with the already-established works at Billingham to the north of the Tees by a 16 km pipeline, as big as a London underground tube-tunnel, under the Tees estuary. Billingham developed between the two world wars, using local deposits of several raw materials used in chemical manufacture such as salt*, gypsum† and anhydrite‡. Coal was available from the Durham coalfield and limestone is found nearby.

*$NaCl$.
†$CaSO_4{:}2H_2O$.
‡$CaSO_4$

Fig. 12.3
The I.C.I. works at Wilton

The size of the Wilton works and the impact of the chemical industry on the landscape of Teesside can be assessed from the map, Fig. 12.4. When development is complete, the industry will take up nearly as much land as the main urban areas of Middlesbrough, Stockton and Billingham.

The existence of such a growth industry has led to a general 'boom' in Teesside life generally and especially in the port. Large new refineries to distill crude imported oil for chemicals have just been completed on reclaimed land on the north side of the estuary near the Seal Sands. New jetties have been built and the river widened to take tankers up to 60,000 tonnes. Further dredging will take place and the dredged material used to reclaim more low marshy land for future industrial development. Already, Teesside is the third largest port by volume of exports in the British Isles (after London and Liverpool). Its position opposite Rotterdam-Europort, now one of the most important petro-chemical areas in the world,

Fig. 12.4
Sites of industries on Teesside

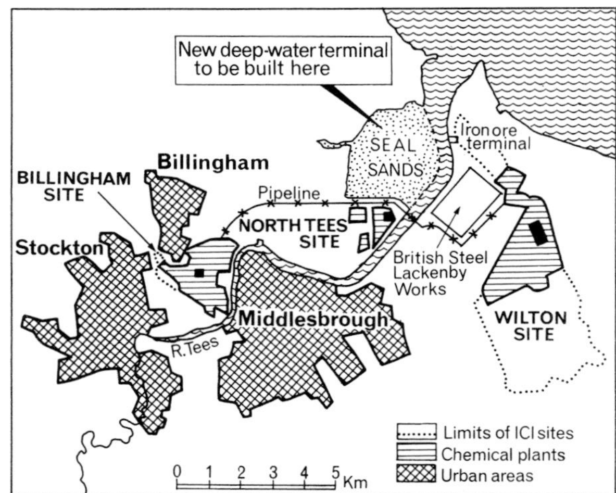

has led to a lot of industrial traffic between the two areas, including a container-cargo service. There are plans to make Seal Sands a new deep-water berth. Another plan already under way is the construction of a terminal dock capable of taking large bulk-carriers of iron-ore.

The potential importance of this area has been increased by recent discoveries of large deposits of potash, another important raw material in the chemical industry, in Eskdale in the nearby North Yorkshire Moors. Prospecting for oil has taken place in the same area (see Fig. 13.8) and recent borings have also found thick beds of salt.

The locational advantages of Teeside have attracted other heavy industries such as the steel plant at Lackenby and a bulk iron-ore terminal close by.

One of its major problems is to find new water resources for the chemical industry. Reference to the rainfall map of the British Isles (Fig. 14.1) will show that Teesside is one of the drier parts of the islands. After much debate and bitter opposition from naturalists and ramblers, Parliament gave permission for a new reservoir to be constructed among the moorlands of Upper Teesdale, above the waterfall of Cauldron Snout. This reservoir will produce the amount of water the chemical industry needs for a few years to come from the wet Pennine moorlands, at the cost of drowning large areas of unique wild alpine flowers, which are found nowhere else in the British Isles.

1. *Make a list of the advantages gained by the chemical industry because of its location on the river Mersey (See Fig. 12.1).*
2. *What is brine?*
3. *With the aid of a good encyclopaedia, find out the natural circumstances that led to large deposits of salt being found underground in Cheshire. Salt is usually associated with 'salt-lakes' in desert areas or with 'salt-pans' by the sea shore.*

4. *Suggest some of the difficulties faced by local authorities in the Weaver Valley where salt has been mined or pumped from underground.*
5. *From Fig. 12.2.*
   (a) What is the length of the pipeline from Heysham to Stanlow?
   (b) What advantages does a pipeline have over surface transport for chemical products?
6. *What do you understand by the term 'petro-chemicals'?*
7. *From Fig. 12.3.*
   (a) Make a list of factors that led to the selection of this site at Wilton for the development of a new chemical plant.
   (b) Using your own grid system (as in Chapter 2, when analysing aerial photographs), make an analysis of the Wilton site, marking in RS railway sidings OS oil storage tanks CH chimneys MR main road access RT refinery towers CT cooling towers
8. *With the aid of tracing paper with a kilometre grid on the same scale as Fig. 12.4 estimate the total area covered by the chemical plants of Teesside. Then estimate the area covered by the three main towns and compare the two results.*
9. *Select one of the raw materials mentioned, such as anhydrite, and find out more about it, especially its chemical constituents.*
10. *Make a list of the products of the chemical industry mentioned in this chapter.*
11. *With the aid of an atlas, draw a map of northern England to show*
    (a) Merseyside chemical area
    (b) Teesside chemical area
    (c) the rivers Mersey and Tees
    (d) the major urban areas of Liverpool, Manchester, and Teesside
    (e) the Pennines
    (f) a possible route for the Trans-Pennine pipeline using natural passes through the hills when possible
    (g) the site of the new reservoir on the moors at the source of the river Tees
    (h) the rainfall figures for Merseyside, Teesside and the Pennine Moors, choosing one figure for each area from the rainfall map (Fig. 14.1).

REVISION EXERCISES

12. ***Why is it easier to define the motor-car industry than the chemical industry?***
13.* ***A great deal of capital is required to set up a chemical plant. What does this sentence mean? Illustrate your answer by examples given in this chapter.***
14. ***Supposing you were asked to plan a new chemical works on the south coast of England; where would you place it? Give reasons for your suggested site.***
15. ***What are the advantages of pipe lines for the transport of the raw materials and finished products of the chemical industry?***

Part III

Power and Raw Materials for Industry

Chapter Thirteen

Fuel and Power Supplies

A. Coal Mining

Britain was once described in a textbook for French children as an 'island of coal'. The carbonaceous material has been mined in England, Ireland, Scotland and Wales and, as we have seen in the chapters on certain key industries, it is still a major source of power and of by-products. Our industrial supremacy in the 19th century was, to a large extent, based upon an abundance of cheap coal. A geography book produced for schools in 1905 started off with the statement that England was the richest country in the world. Coal production at that time was running at about 268,000,000 tonnes a year, the highest it has ever been as you will see from the statistical table, Table 13.2.

Coal has been mined in these islands since Roman times at least and as a result the most accessible coal seams have been worked out so that today, mining becomes increasingly more difficult and expensive. We are less dependent on coal as a source of power than we were because of the discovery of other sources of energy such as petroleum, natural gas and atomic energy. But coal is still of vital importance and we still come third in the world table of coal production, after the U.S.A. and the Soviet Union.

In its plans for the future, the National Coal Board, which controls the vast majority of coal mines in this country (some small private mines still operate), has to anticipate what the country's needs will be in future years. This has proved particularly difficult in recent years and Government estimates are changing constantly, largely due to the discovery of more sources of natural gas and the changing costs of various types of power. Table 13.1 shows the situation as foreseen by a government White Paper (a statement of official policy) at the end of 1967.

Table 13.1 Britain's Power Needs up to 1975: expressed in the equivalent of millions of tonnes of coal

Fuel	1957	1966	1970	1975
Coal	212.9	174.7	152.0	120.0
Oil	36.7	111.7	125.0	145.0
Nuclear & Hydro-Electric	1.7	10.2	16.0	35.0
Natural Gas	—	1.1	17.0	50.0
Total	251.3	297.7	310.0	350.0

(Source: Fuel Policy H.M.S.O.)

The table shows that the Government expected petroleum to be the most important source of power in 1975, and coal to be in second place. Both nuclear power and natural gas will grow very rapidly but coal still supplies over 33 per cent of our power and fuel. But these are plans and speculations and, no doubt, there will be many changes in plans over the next few years. One of the great values of coal is that it is a source of power that we find in our own country and do

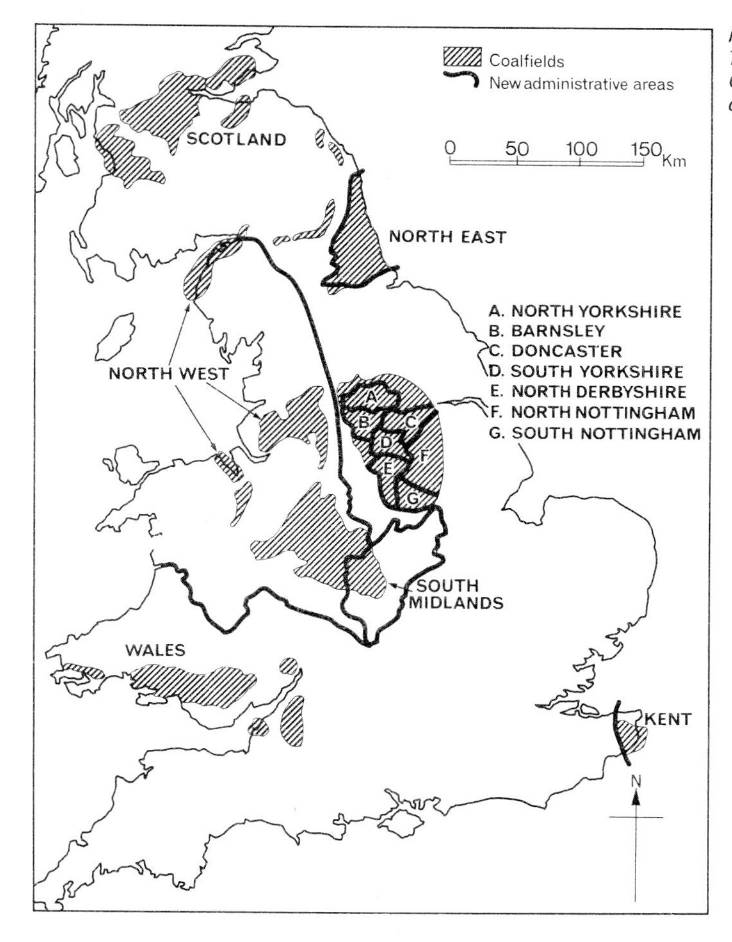

Fig. 13.1 The National Coal Board divisions 1974

Year	Saleable tonnes of coal	Manpower	Collieries	Output per man-shift (tonnes)
1947	185,000,000	707,500	958	1.1
1952	211,000,000	705,200	880	1.2
1957	207,000,000	707,700	822	1.3
1962	188,000,000	536,200	616	1.6
1967	164,000,000	409,700	443	1.8
1970/1	142,000,000	286,300	292	2.2
1974/5	124,000,000	246,000	246	2.2

(1971/2 Figures depressed due to industrial action). (Source: N.C.B.)

Table 13.2 National Coal Board Statistics (In this list of statistics, the saleable tonnes of coal have been simplified to the nearest million, manpower has been taken to the nearest hundred.)

not have to buy abroad, but most oil will have to be imported from other countries for some years yet. Natural gas and atomic power will be supplied from within our own frontiers.

A statement of the situation in the coal-mining industry is given in Table 13.2.

In April 1967, the National Coal Board completely reorganized its administration of mining in Britain and divided the collieries of England, Wales and Scotland into new Areas. A typical Area will produce about 10,000,000 tons of coal a year with a manpower of about 20,000. The new Area organization is shown in Fig. 13.1 which shows the boundaries of the areas superimposed on a map of the coalfields. This reorganization makes it difficult for us to compare new production figures for areas with the production figures for the old 'divisions', as they were called. For example, the coalfields now brought together under the North-West Area are referred to in many books and atlases as the Cumberland Coalfield, the Lancashire Coalfield and the Flintshire Coalfield. However, the new pattern will lay the foundation for the future of mining and, in this book, we are more concerned with the future than the past. This new map indicates which areas the Coal Board thinks will be most important in the future and which areas will be of less importance.

1. *Study Table 13.2 and answer the following questions:*
   (a) By how many millions of tonnes has coal production decreased in the 26 years, 1947 to 1974?
   (b) What has been the decrease in the number of men employed in coal mining?
   (c) Which figure has decreased more in proportion, the output of coal or the number of men mining it? The answer to this will need to be expressed in fractions or percentages that can be compared. For example:
   No. of tons coal decreased 21,000,000
   As fraction of 1947 output $\frac{21}{185}$
   which is approximately $\frac{1}{9}$ *or 11.4%*
   (d) (i) how many pits have closed since 1947? (ii) express this pit closure as a fraction or percentage of the 1947 figure.
   (e) (i) what column in the statistical table shows the greatest decrease in 20 years? (ii) what figures shows the greatest increase in the same number of years?
   (f) By what fraction or percentage has output per man-shift increased since 1947?
   (g) What was the average number of men per colliery (i) in 1947? (ii) in 1974?
2. *Using Fig. 13.1:*
   (a) How many Areas are there under the new reorganization?
   (b) In what part of Britain are the greatest number of Areas concentrated?
   (c) How many Areas are there in Scotland?

3. *If a typical Area produces 10,000,000 tonnes of coal a year, what is the approximate output of coal from*
   (a) Scotland,
   (b) North-east England?
   (c) the coalfield stretching from Yorkshire to Nottinghamshire and Derbyshire?
4. *Can you suggest reasons why the Areas of Doncaster, North Nottingham and South Nottingham do not have boundaries marked on the eastern side of the coalfield? Fig. 13.4 may help with this answer.*
5. *Which three Areas are nearest to Greater London*
   (a) by rail?
   (b) by sea?

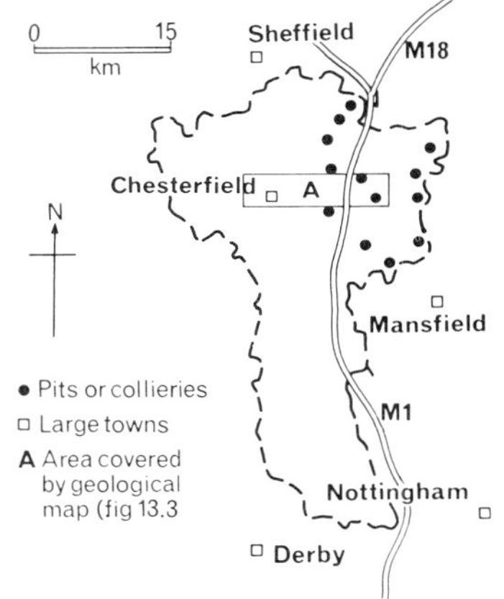

Fig. 13.2
The collieries of North Derbyshire

The most important aspect for coal as for all power sources is the unit cost of production and distribution. If coal is expensive as compared with oil or gas in producing the same amount of energy then users will turn to other power sources. So the National Coal Board has encouraged miners to move from the least productive pits to the more productive areas. It is possible that the mining industry will decline in many traditional areas and concentrate on others. This can mean hardship and upheaval for miners and their families and great difficulties for older men. The Coal Board helps in many ways, including making houses available for people moving to the 'new' areas.

We may understand more of the problems of mining if we take a closer look at one mining area. Fig. 13.2 shows the collieries in the North Derbyshire coalfield area and Fig. 13.3 is an extract from the Geological Survey of part of that area. Fig. 13.4 is a cross-section through the same area to show the underground structure of the rocks, especially the coal seams. Much of our knowledge of geology is derived from the studies made by mining engineers trying to find out what happens to coal seams underground. The part cover-

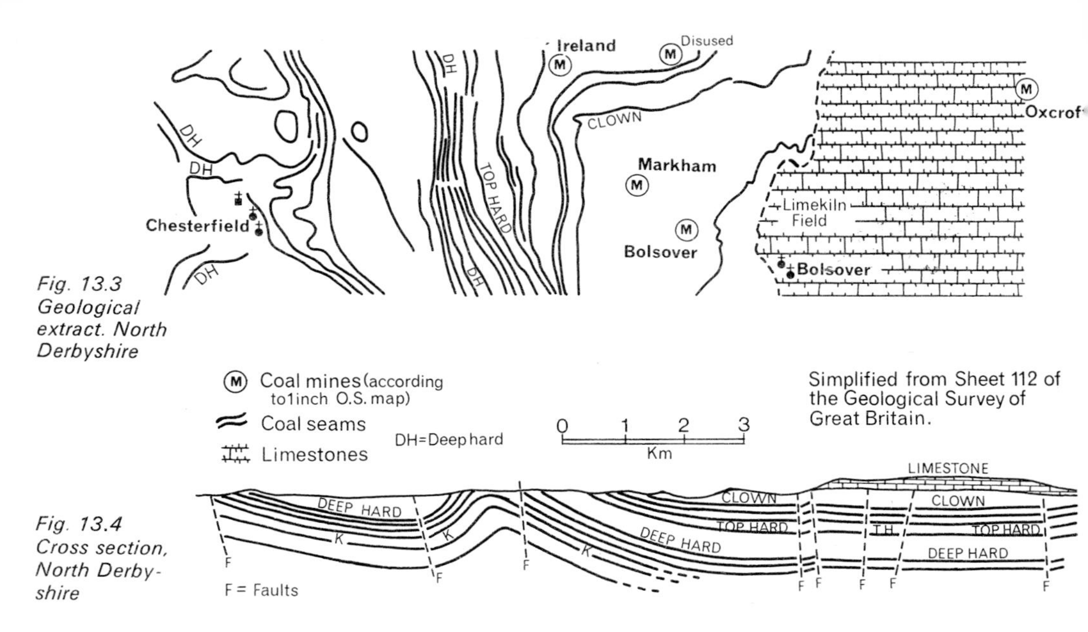

Fig. 13.3 Geological extract. North Derbyshire

Fig. 13.4 Cross section, North Derbyshire

ed by the geological map is indicated on the map of the whole area, Fig. 13.2.

The East Midland division, which includes the new Areas in Nottinghamshire and Derbyshire, is one of the most productive in the country and has reached a figure of over 2.9 tonnes per man-shift. This compares with 2.2 tonnes throughout the country as a whole. Stone Age implements have been found in old coal workings suggesting that coal was mined in prehistoric times, but it was the development of canals, giving cheap transport, that really opened the field up. Then George Stephenson cut through several seams whilst building the North Midland railway and this led to local coal being sent to the London area by train. One of the most important seams was the Top Hard coal which is named on the geological map, Fig. 13.3.

The very high productivity of the pits in the Nottingham and Derbyshire areas and the increase shown in output per man-shift in Table 13.2 is due to the modernization of the collieries. This is based upon the closure of pits with poor seams and concentrating on pits with good seams and reserves of coal, by developing new smokeless fuels and special fuels for certain purposes such as power stations, but most of all by mechanization and remote-controlled face-working. Already, by 1975, more than 93.5 per cent of coal was produced on power-loaded faces, the maximum technically possible. In the very latest collieries such as Bevercotes (shown in Figs. 13.5 and 13.6) coal will be mined and extracted without any miner undergoing the traditional sort of physical labour that is shown in Fig. 13.7. Even the pit-props that hold up the roof of the gallery are erected automatically by a machine. Of course, the older methods will carry on in older pits for a long time yet but the miner in a white coat is the symbol of the 1970's.

Fig. 13.5 Bevercotes Colliery

6. *How many collieries are there in the North Derbyshire Area (Fig. 13.2)?*
7. *Each important coal seam has a name given it by the engineers. Name two of them. (See Fig. 13.3.)*

Fig. 13.6 The control unit in Bevercotes Colliery

8. (a) *Each black line on Fig. 13.3 shows where the coal seam could be followed on the surface of the ground. This was once mined by open pits. It is very unlikely that coal is mined where the seams 'outcrop' (come to the surface) now. Why is this?*
   (b) *No active mines are to be found in the western part of the map around Chesterfield. Yet coal seams are shown there. Can you explain this?*
   (c) *Active mines are shown in the part to the east which is marked as Limestone. How is it possible to mine coal in limestone country?*
9. *What difficulties faced by the mining engineers are illustrated by the cross-section (Fig. 13.4)?*
10. *Staveley is a centre of the chemical industry run by the Coal Board itself. What two raw materials are available locally that would be useful in the production of chemicals? (See Fig. 13.3.)*
11. *What feature of the rock structure helps modern mining, especially in the eastern part of the section (See Fig. 13.4).*
12. *Enlarge a one kilometer stretch of the cross-section (Fig. 13.4) to the west of Bolsover and construct your own system of shafts and galleries to 'win' the coal.*

Fig. 13.7
The traditional way of hewing coal

B. Oil and Gas

*1. Petroleum or mineral oil**

It is not necessary, in this book, to stress the ever-increasing importance of petroleum. The number of vehicles on the roads using it both as a fuel and as a lubricant is a daily reminder of the fact that to some extent modern life runs on oil. Its use even as a source of fuel in power stations, in domestic central heating and, above all, as a source of raw materials for the chemical industry (referred to in Chapter 12) has meant that the use of petroleum is increasing rapidly. In terms of energy supply, it surpassed coal in 1971.

Up until the 1970's Britain has been almost entirely dependent on imported oil. In 1973 it produced 87,000 tonnes, for example, and imported no less than 110,000,000 tonnes. But exploration in the

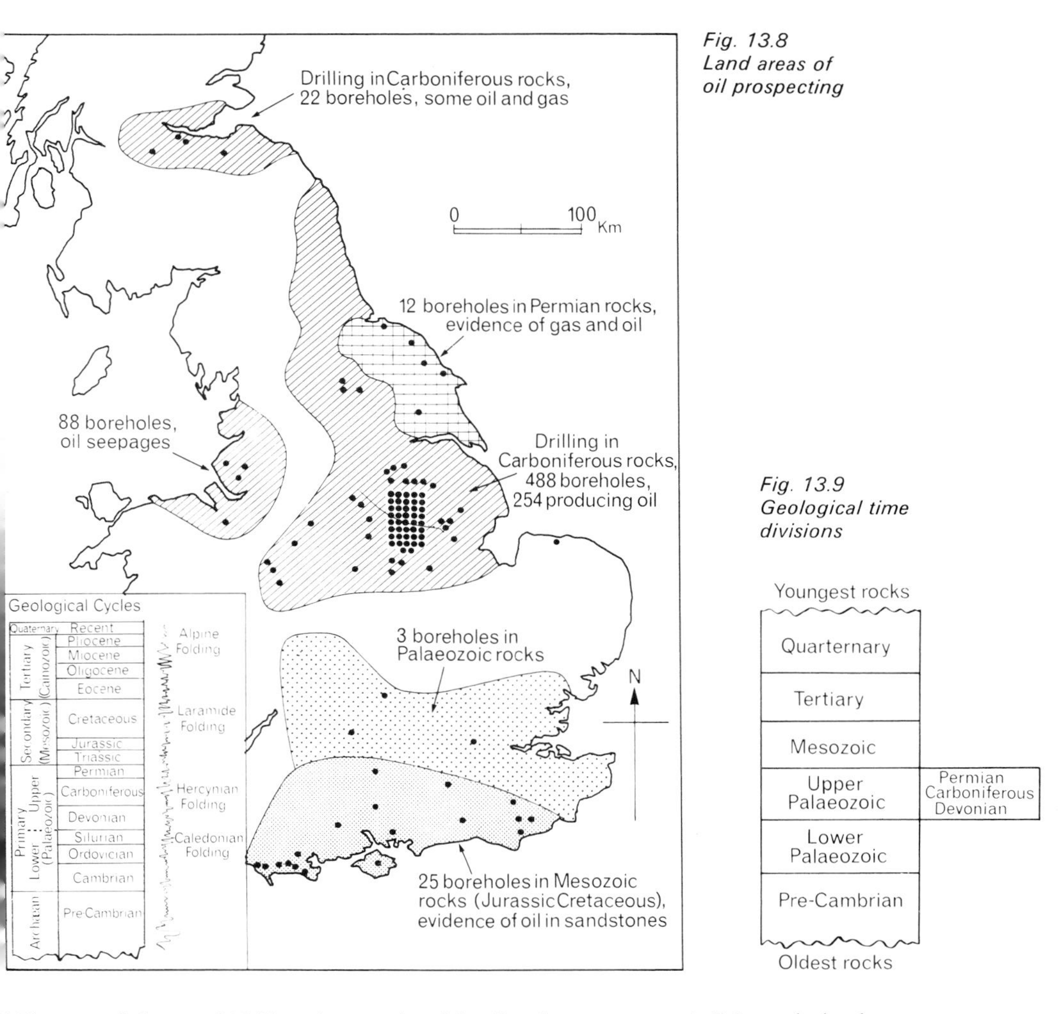

Fig. 13.8 Land areas of oil prospecting

Fig. 13.9 Geological time divisions

*The use of the word 'Oil' on its own is misleading because some 'oils' are derived from plants such as coconuts, cottonseeds, olives. These are called 'vegetable oils'. The oil derived from petroleum is a 'mineral' oil.

North Sea has revealed large deposits of oil as well as natural gas (see Fig. 13.16) which will make Britain self-sufficient in oil by the 1980's. It has already transformed the industrial scene in Scotland bringing new employment. The first oil came ashore by tanker in 1975 to the Isle of Grain refinery in the Thames Estuary. A 360-km pipeline brings oil direct to a terminal near Peterhead and then overland to refineries at Grangemouth. New refineries will be built further north. Exploration is also taking place inland (Fig. 13.8).

The references to the rocks may mean more if you refer to Fig. 13.9 which illustrates where the geological periods referred to in the prospecting map fit into the general history of the geology of the earth. The effects of such prospecting and drilling in the British Isles have been made known dramatically by press photographs of drilling rigs in the North Sea. The search for oil makes its own special landscape. The great superstructure of towers and drills is only necessary during the actual drilling operations: to support the drills that will bore down through the various rock layers until they reach the oil-bearing strata. Once the oil or gas have been discovered in sufficient quantities, the superstructures can be dispensed with and comparatively simple control units installed to regulate the flow of oil. Fig. 13.10 shows a new drilling rig set up near a cliff on the south coast while Fig. 13.11 shows an active extracting

Fig. 13.10 Oil drilling rig at Kimmeridge Bay in Dorset

Fig. 13.11 A pumping unit at Eakring in Nottinghamshire

well in the Midlands near Mansfield. The extraction of oil and gas needs a quite different surface structure from that of coal: the liquid and gaseous nature of the mineral oils and gases makes them easier to transport than solid coal. But the processing of oil, as we shall see, raises many other problems.

The fact that the United Kingdom still produces only a small proportion of the petroleum it requires means that we are importers of enormous quantities. So the effect of the petroleum industry on e British landscape is not so much in drilling rigs and oil wells ut in port facilities for handling the oil tankers that bring the il in, in the transportation of that oil from the ports inland and, ost of all, in the refining of the oil. Most of the imported oil is in rude' form and has to undergo many processes before it can be sed as a fuel, a lubricant and as raw material.

The first tanker was an ordinary cargo ship carrying barrels of erosine from the United States to London docks in 1861. The ship as a 224-tonner. Tankers of 250,000 tonnes have been launched in e Swan Hunter yards on Tyneside and in Belfast Lough and these re by no means the largest in the world. Ships of nearly 500,000 nnes are already on the oceans.

Before the Second World War, the usual type of oil-tanker weighd 12,000 tonnes and this size of craft could use most of the major orts of the United Kingdom. So the refining industry grew up in ssociation with the estuaries of the islands. The map (Fig. 13.12) ows the main refineries and the estuaries are named. Tankers f the general purpose type, weighing between 12,000 and 25,000

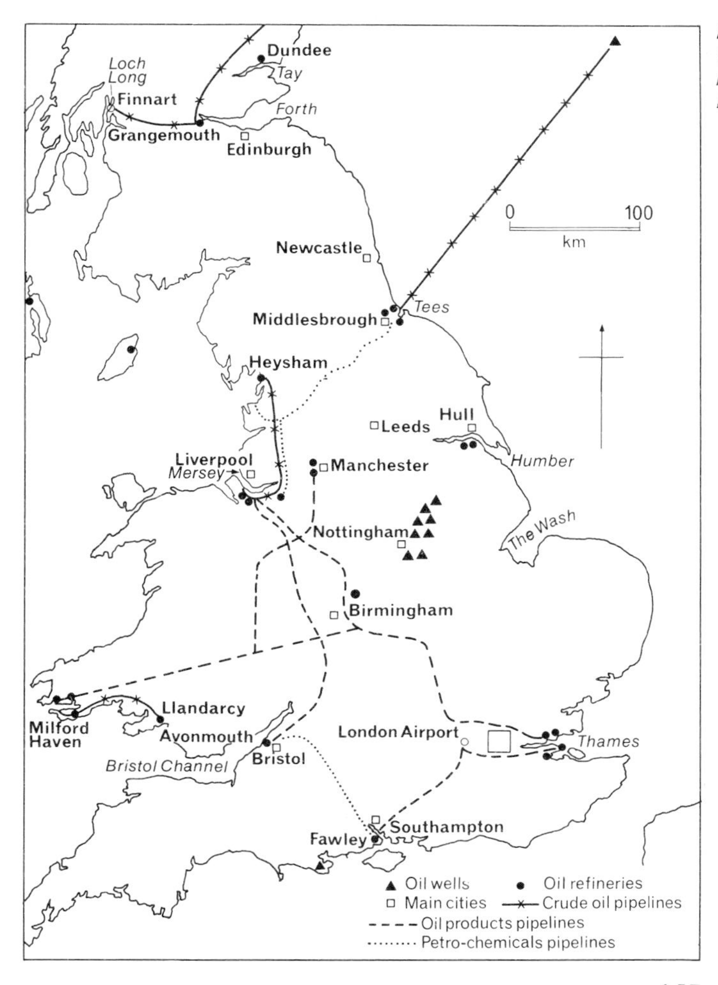

Fig. 13.12 The principal refineries of Britain

tonnes deadweight, are still being built and used to carry oil to th
refinery sites but the post-war expansion of the use of oil and pro
blems associated with the Suez Canal have encouraged oil compani
to order much larger vessels. It is much more economic to carr
cargoes of oil in very large tankers: each gallon of oil costs relativel
less to transport. The importance of this increase in super-tanke
is that there are few harbours that can accommodate such enormou
craft. The Thames and the Tyne have difficulty in keeping a depth
water of 8 metres for shipping. A 200,000 tonne super-tanker requir
more than 16 metres of clear water. So special tanker-terminals ar
being constructed to cope with these craft, at Loch Long in Scotlan
Milford Haven in Wales and Bantry Bay in Ireland. Their positio
are indicated in Fig. 13.13. The growth in the size of tankers is show
in Table 13.3 and in the following facts.

36 per cent of world oil is carried in ships of over 100,000 tonn
and 10 per cent in ships of over 250,000 tonnes. Britain has th
second largest tanker fleet in the world.

Perhaps this can be seen more dramatically in the overall length
the ships. By 1910, a 9,000 tonner was built 140 metres long. B
1930, a 22,000 tonne tanker was built, length 190 metres: by 1950,
28,000 tonner was 216 metres long. A 110,000 tonner built in 196
was 308 metres long: and the 326,000 tonner recently completed wa
345 metres long.

The problems involved in the use of super-tankers are not ju
those of finding harbours deep enough to take them but of gre

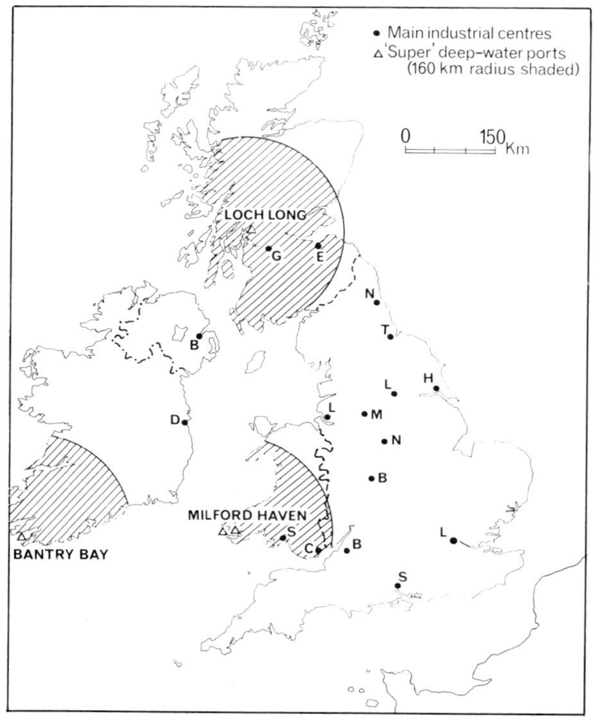

Fig. 13.13 Deep water terminals and the industrial centres

Table 13.3

Year	Weight of ship (tonnes)	Length (metres)
1910	9,000	140
1930	22,000	190
1950	28,000	216
1965	110,000	308
1967	191,000	340
1969	253,000	380
1971	326,000	345
1973	483,000	378

(Source: Institute of Petroleum)

navigation hazards. The loss of such a ship represents the loss of many millions of pounds and the possible pollution of long stretches of coastline with great loss of revenue to the holiday trade, to small craft owners and to wild life. Also, laying up a super-tanker due to a fall in world trade represents a great financial loss.

A British research unit is now studying the problems of navigating a 1,000,000 tonne tanker. A 250,000 tonner needs at least 16 km to slow down for docking purposes. How far do you need to slow down and stop a ship 4 times as big? One of the devices being tried out is a system of flaps that move out from the side of the ship.

The problem arises, how to transport the oil from the terminals to the refineries throughout the British Isles. Smaller tankers can be used. Another method, and one that is growing not only in Britain but throughout the world, is the underground pipeline. This has great advantages in safety, in keeping highly inflammable and explosive cargoes off the roads. Pipelines are not subject to traffic jams. But, of course, the laying of a pipeline across hilly country, of getting permission from farmers and landowners to cross their land is an expensive undertaking. Nor does a pipeline have the flexibility of a tanker-lorry. A pipeline cannot change direction as a vehicle can. But for carrying large quantities of petrol or petrol products across land, the pipeline is superior and by the 1970's a complete network of pipelines will cross the lowlands of England, Scotland and Wales. The main pipeline pattern is also shown in Fig. 13.12.

You will notice that nearly all the oil refineries shown in Fig. 13.12 are located on the coastline or near large estuaries. These installations are largely dependent on imported crude oil. They require large areas of cheap land. They are, to some extent, dangerous installations, the risk of fire and explosions being an ever-present hazard. They pollute the atmosphere with a variety of chemicals. For all of these reasons, they have to be sited carefully, not too near large areas of population. Yet they cannot be too far away because it is the large areas of population that use the refined products in factories and homes. Some of these considerations have led to large-scale opposition to the development of refineries near the tanker-terminal of Milford Haven, for this coastline has been designated

Fig. 13.14 The Esso refinery at Fawley on Southampton Water

as an Area of Outstanding Natural Beauty which should be preserve
for our enjoyment.

The United Kingdom is one of the most important refining area
in the world. Refining of mineral oil first took place at Pamphersto
in Scotland in 1884 and the Fawley refinery was functioning by 1921
The rapid growth of our refining capacity is shown in Table 13.4.

Table 13.4 Oil Refining in the U.K. (thousand metric tonnes)

1938	1,900
1950	11,000
1955	30,000
1960	49,000
1965	72,000
1970	93,000
1974	101,000

(Institute of Petroleum)

Fig. 13.14 shows an oil refinery. The processing of petroleum i
a highly complex procedure and it is not the function of this chapte
to discuss such technical matters. But it is useful to remind ourselve
of some of the main products from the 'fractioning' tower tha
dominates the refinery landscape. Apart from the storage tanks an
the innumerable pipes, the towers in which the crude oil is change
into a variety of more usable products are the main feature of th
oil refinery. Fig. 13.15 is a simplified diagram showing these products. Generally speaking, the crudest products are near the base
of the tower while the most refined products are near the top of th
tower.

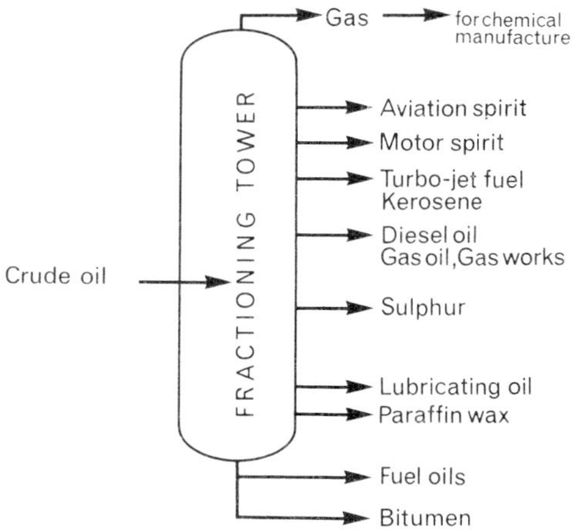

Gas → for chemical manufacture
FRACTIONING TOWER
Crude oil →
→ Aviation spirit
→ Motor spirit
→ Turbo-jet fuel Kerosene
→ Diesel oil Gas oil, Gas works
→ Sulphur
→ Lubricating oil
→ Paraffin wax
→ Fuel oils
→ Bitumen

Fig. 13.15 Products of a crude oil fractioning tower

13. *What is the function of the rigs found above oil wells?*
14. *Which area of the British Isles has been most intensively explored for oil? (Fig. 13.8.)*
15. *Why are most oil refineries on or near the coast, especially near estuaries?*
16. *What products from the fractioning tower (Fig. 13.15) of an oil refinery would be used for*
    (a) the motor-car?
    (b) the aeroplane?
    (c) roadmaking?
    (d) gas works?
17. *How long is the pipeline*
    (a) from Milford Haven to Llandarcy?
    (b) from Finnart to Grangemouth?
    (c) from the Thames to the Mersey?
18. *Describe the problems that faced the engineers who planned and constructed the pipeline from Teesside to the Mersey?*
19. *In what ways is oil (a) easier to handle than coal and (b) more difficult to handle than coal?*
20. *Name three methods of transporting oil.*
21. *Why is the Government keen to develop the search for oil and gas in the North Sea and our national territory in spite of the difficulties?*
22. *What difficulties will the increasing size of oil-tankers make for the British oil-refining industry?*
23. *Make a series of scale drawings of the tankers shown in Table 13.3 and on the same set of drawings put in the length of a full size football field, 110 metres long.*

2. Gas

A new 'craft' has appeared off the shores of eastern England in recent years so unusual that boatmen have been making extra money at holiday time by taking holiday-makers out to see it. We have already seen a photograph of this new attraction in the chapter on steel (Fig. 11.6). It is the drilling platform that enables the oilmen to drill through the rocks off-shore in their search for new sources of fuel. We have seen that *Sea Quest* weighs over 9,000 tonnes, being constructed almost entirely of steel. Another drilling platform called *Orion* stands on legs 118 metres high. The legs can be raised or lowered to suit the depth of water. The sheer size of such a rig can be judged in Fig. 11.6 by the size of the ships alongside it.

Discoveries of gas trapped in the rocks below the surface of the Netherlands encouraged the oil companies and the British Government to start searching for oil and gas in the same rocks that run under the North Sea. For this purpose, the nations bordering the North Sea agreed on boundary lines which would give each nation an area to explore. Britain, having a long North Sea coast was allocated a large part of the western half of the North Sea and that area was divided by the Government into small blocks and companies were invited to buy the right to drill in these allocations. No one could be sure whether they would strike it rich or not but the first successful strike took place quite soon, in 1965, off the Humber Estuary; hopes grew and more drilling was stimulated. The first gas was landed by pipeline in 1967 to feed into the special gas main.

Enough gas is already being extracted from the 'fields' shown on Fig. 13.16 and landed at newly-constructed terminals on the east coast to supply the vast majority of our gas requirements. All this dramatic change in our power supplies has happened in only ten years.

The limit of exploration is a line running approximately down the middle of the North Sea. This line has been agreed by an international convention and the areas to the east of it belong to the countries bordering the eastern shores of the North Sea.

Fig. 13.16 also shows the main area of the sea that was divided into small blocks, each of which was let out to various oil and gas companies who wanted to participate in the search for new sources of power: the successful 'strikes' have been indicated. Pipelines have already been constructed (and more are under construction) to bring the gas ashore. These pipelines link up with the main pipeline running north-west from Canvey Island which was originally constructed to bring imported natural gas into the most densely populated parts of the country.

As natural gas is much richer (gives more heat) than the usual 'town gas', made at the old gas works from coal, having 90 per cent methane content (as against 50 per cent in town gas), all the household burners and other equipment have to be changed. Canvey Island was the first place in which this technical change took place. Meanwhile, the Gas Council has set up special plants to make it possible to use the two types of gas together.

In January 1967, more than 1.5 million tons of coal were used to manufacture gas, the most important raw material in the gas industry. It is unlikely that coal will ever be used to the same extent in future, as the estimated reserves of the North Sea natural gas field

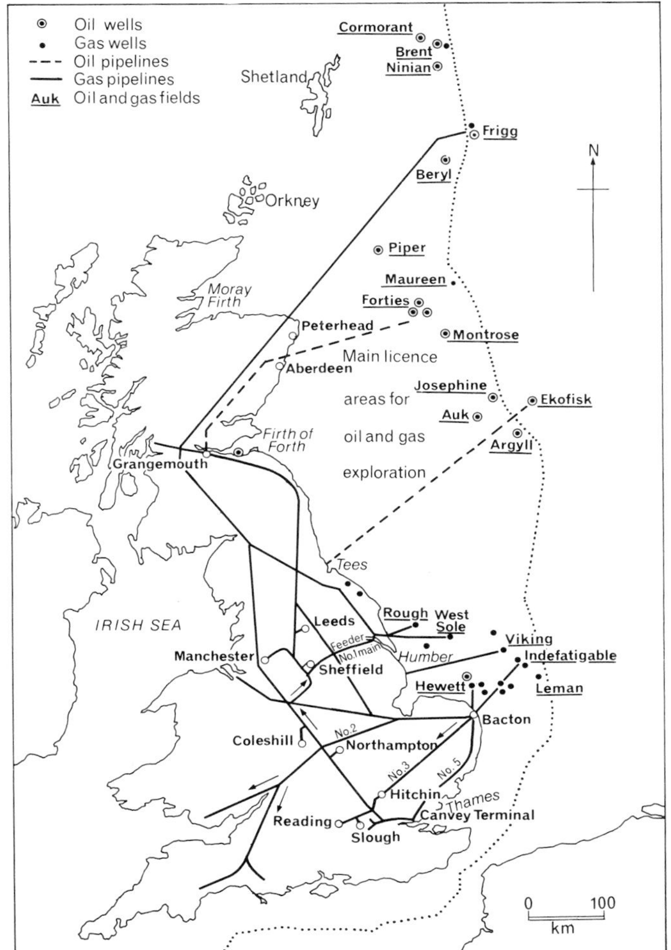

Fig. 13.16 North Sea gas and oil

would enable a consumption of over 3,000,000 cubic metres a day for the foreseeable future, which is just about the present consumption of gas in the United Kingdom.

Of course, the demand for gas is increasing every year. In 1961, gas sales reached 2,650 million therms. By 1974/5 they had reached 13,018 million therms.

Fig. 13.17 shows the sort of new installation that is needed in the control and use of natural gas, at Hitchin in Hertfordshire (Fig. 13.16).

Whether the new sources of gas will mean cheaper fuel for our homes and industry is doubtful. The cost of installing new pipelines and apparatus, of changing all our equipment and installing special plants means that gas will not be cheaper for some years. In the long run, it may prove a source of comparatively cheap power. Perhaps it will mean the end of the old gas holders. But the storage of gas remains a great problem. The Gas Council wants to store it underground in suitable geological formations. It is safer below ground

Fig. 13.17
A control unit for natural gas at Hitchin

than above and can be kept indefinitely until it is needed (e.g. during especially cold weather). Fig. 13.18 shows the type of geological structure that is quite common in south-east England that is suited to oil storage. The sandstone strata could hold the gas in its pores, the gas being trapped beneath by water and the Wealden Clays and it could not escape upwards because of the layer of Gault Clay above it. It could only escape through the wells specially provided. Such a system of storage needs very little apparatus above ground. A greater volume of gas can be stored, too, in liquified form.

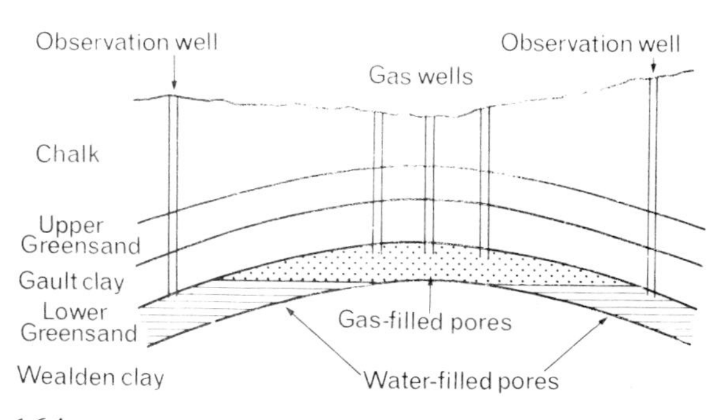

Fig. 13.18
The underground storage of gas

24. *What problems have faced the oil men in drilling for oil and gas in the North Sea?*
25. *What other countries have a North Sea coastline?*
26. *How is the natural gas from the North Sea wells being brought ashore?*
27. *What advantage does natural gas have over coal-gas?*
28. *Why was the first natural gas terminal built on Canvey Island on the Thames estuary?*
29. *With the aid of an atlas map of England, suggest which ports and towns are most likely to become more important industrial areas as a result of the discovery of North Sea gas.*
30. *In what other seas off the coast of Britain are licenced areas available for oil and gas exploration?*
31. *Estimate, with the aid of the scale on Fig. 13.16, the total length of pipelines for transporting natural gas.*
32. *What advantages does the underground storage of gas have over the older gas holders that are still to be found in many towns?*
33. *What dangers are involved in the transport and use of gas?*

C. The Electricity Supply Industry

In a recent statement to the Press, the Chairman of the National Coal Board said, 'In the end, the key to all markets for coal is the demand from the power stations'. Perhaps the meaning behind his remark will be made clear by the figures of coal users. (Table 13.5.)

Table 13.5 Main Users of Coal in 1974/5 (million tonnes)

Power stations	71.5
Coke Ovens	20.2
Industry general	19.2
House coal	14.2

(Source: N.C.B.)

The overwhelming importance of the electricity power station as a user of coal will be likely to grow as more domestic users go over to other forms of heating than solid fuels. British railway trains have moved out of the 'steam' age to use electricity and oil. The discovery of natural gas has reduced drastically the amount of coal burnt to produce gas. So the problems of the coal industry would be enormous if power stations turned to other fuels. Already several thermal stations are using oil; five in Southern Scotland changed from coal-burning in one year recently. In mountainous areas, hydro-electric stations using water power have been constructed, while in many parts of the country enormous new stations, based upon nuclear power, are being constructed and many are already contributing electricity to the national grid of power lines.

At the moment, then, the main power stations in Britain are on or near the coalfields and, of those coalfields, the most important is the York-Notts-Derby coalfield. Indeed, the valley of the river Trent below the town of Burton has been described as 'the powerhouse of England'. Along that valley is now the largest concentration of generating capacity in Great Britain.

Fig. 13.19 shows this concentration of power stations, all of which are conventional coal-burning stations. Their total output of electricity is over 11,500 megawatts. This figure achieves more meaning when you compare it with the total English output of electricity in 1975 which was about 58,500 megawatts. The station at West Burton generates 2,000 megawatts, one of six such giant installations now in use. A power station now being constructed on the Isle of Grain on the Thames Estuary will produce 3,300 megawatts. Yet, at one time, it was thought that the Bankside power station that dominates the Thames in London was enormous and that produces a mere 300 megawatts.

Fig. 13.21 is an aerial view of the West Burton power station while it was still under construction. It illustrates among other things the great loss of agricultural land to industrial use. However, the use of this photograph, together with the map of the Trent valley (Fig. 13.20) may help to explain why this area has become the powerhouse of England.

The power stations of the Midland Regions and of the North East Regions which stretch as far north as the Scottish Border are all of the conventional thermal type i.e. based upon raising steam to drive a turbine, which, in turn, drives the generators. But, as we have pointed out already, coal is not the only fuel for the production of electricity. The map of the North West region of the C.E.G.B. covering much of Lancashire, Cheshire, the Lake District and north Wales (Fig. 13.22) shows a very different pattern of generation.

34. Make a pie graph (divided circle) to show users of electricity based on Table 13.5.

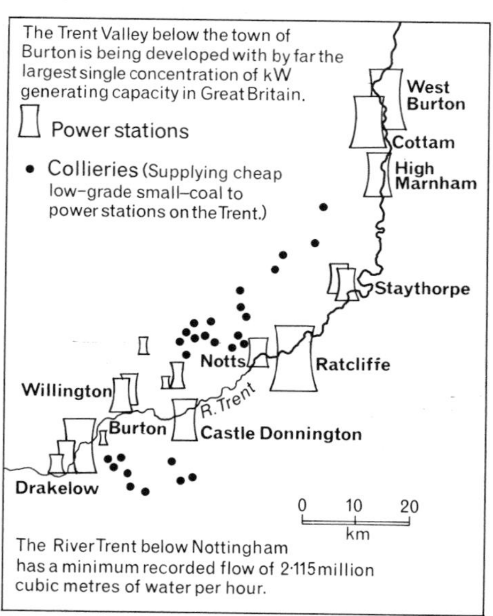

Fig. 13.19 Power generation in the Trent valley (below left)

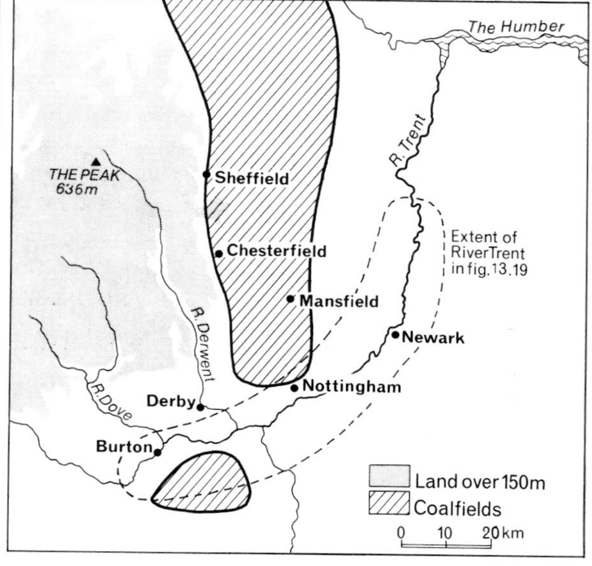

Fig. 13.20 The Trent valley (below right)

35. *Each one of the power stations shown on Fig. 13.19 is situated by the banks of the river Trent. What does this fact suggest about one of the greatest needs of a power station?*
36. *The symbol used on the map is a cooling tower. The cooling towers also dominate the photograph. What is their function?*
37. *What other raw material used for generating electricity is available near the Trent valley?*
38. *British Rail, the C.E.G.B. and the Coal Board have all combined to build a special computer-operated 'merry-go-round' rail link to supply small coal constantly to the station. Identify the 'merry-go-round' in the photograph and suggest reasons why this system will benefit the power station. (Fig. 13.21.)*

Fig. 13.21 West Burton power stations Nottinghamshire

39. *Apart from cooling towers and the rail-link, what other buildings can be seen at West Burton? (Fig. 13.21.)*
40. *Make your own plan of West Burton power station, indicating the main buildings and their uses and showing where the key materials of coal and cooling water are obtained, to include the river Trent and the railway. Use Fig. 13.21 to draw your plan.*
41. *Where does the water in the river Trent come from?*
42. *What problems arise for the River Board Authority because of the existence of so many power stations along the river, using the river?*
43. *In order to illustrate the enormous size of these power stations (they have been described as 'cathedrals of power') make a series of drawings based on the following facts:*

Height of the Dome of St Paul's Cathedral	*110.6 m*
Height of West Burton cooling towers	*113.6 m*

Height of Post Office Tower in London	*188.2 m*
Height of West Burton chimneys	*197.0 m*

Use a scale 1 cm to 10 m.

44. *How many power stations in the North West region are of (a) the conventional steam type; (b) the internal combustion type; (c) the hydro-electric type (using water direct); and (d) the nuclear type (using atomic energy)?*
45. *Can you explain the concentration of coal-burning stations in the centre of the region? (Reference to the Coal Board map Fig. 13.1 will help with this answer.)*

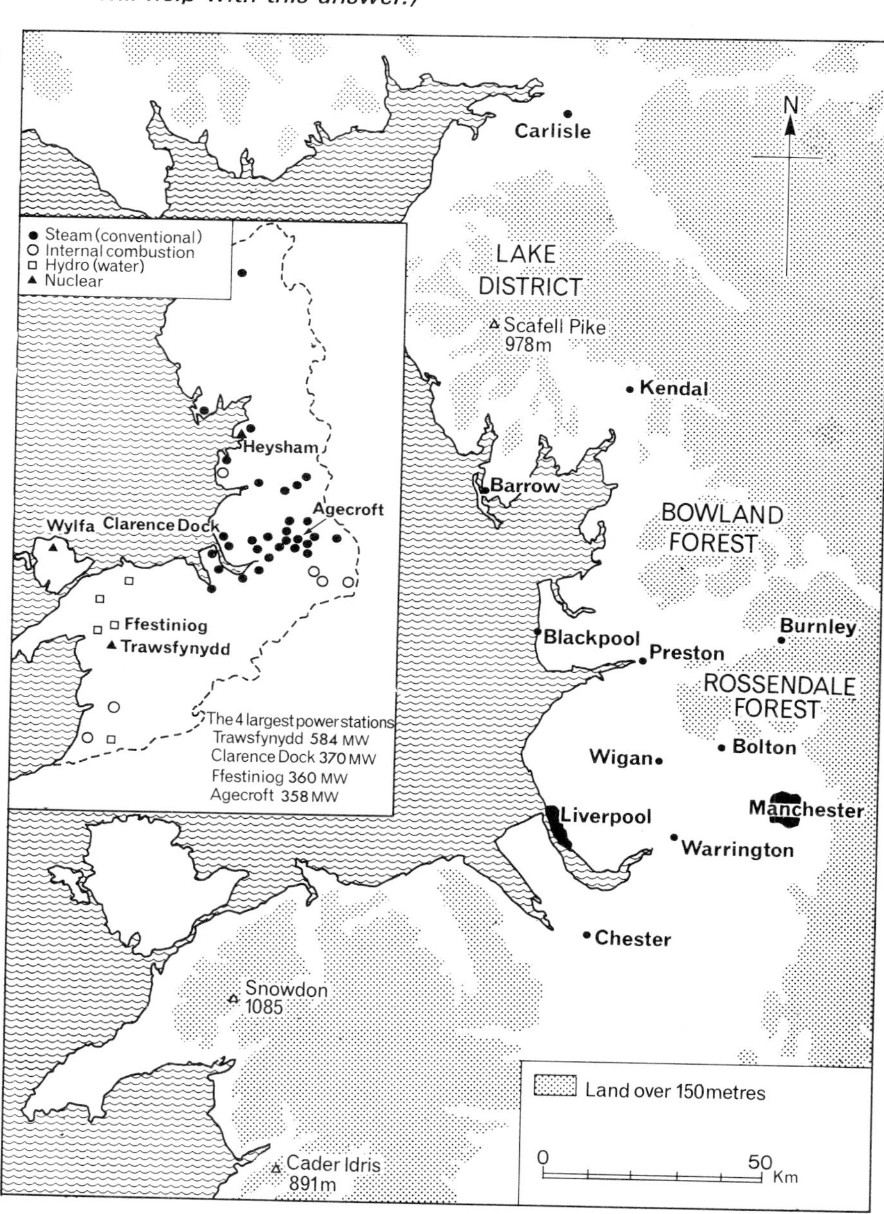

Fig. 13.22 The North West region of the C.E.G.B.

46. *What type of landscape are the Hydro-electric stations situated in? You may need to refer to an atlas to answer this question.*
47. *Can you suggest reasons for the siting of the new nuclear station at Wylfa on the north shore of the Isle of Anglesey when it is so far from the industries and cities that will use its power?*
48. *Which type of power station produces the most electricity in the north-west? Is its output bigger or smaller than that of West Burton on the Trent?*
49. *How is the electric power from the stations in the mountains of North Wales transmitted to the industrial areas of Birmingham and Manchester that will use the power? (Fig. 13.22.)*
50. *Can you see any single advantage that power stations using water from mountain streams and lakes will have over those using coal in the future?*

The supergrid

The answer to exercise 49 is fairly straightforward and it is illustrated well in the next two maps, Fig. 13.23 showing the main supergrid network in England and Wales and Fig. 13.24 showing the estimated power flow along that supergrid network in the winter of 1970/1. The main problem for the electrical supply industry is to get power at the right time to the right place. So cables capable of transmitting 400 kilovolts have to be constructed across the landscape taking electricity from the power stations to the cities. But the climate differs very widely from one part of the country to another: it can be freezing in London and quite mild in Bristol on the same day. And the C.E.G.B. cannot afford to build power stations costing millions of pounds of public money unless the power is needed. Even

Fig. 13.23 The Supergrid (left)

Fig. 13.24 The power flow (right)

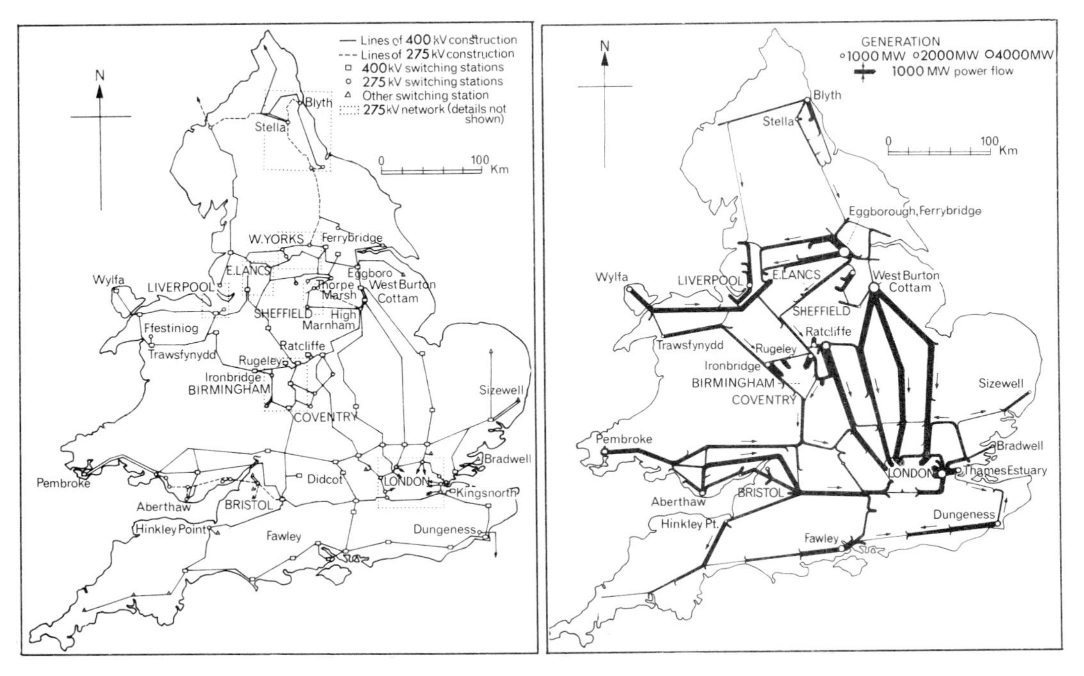

from hour to hour, demand for electricity can change dramatically: Fig. 13.25 shows the changes taking place during a favourite television programme. It is not the TV that uses so much power but the cup of tea in between!

So the Electricity Boards must be able to store power, they must be able to bring it in from other areas if the demand goes up sharply and the chance of a breakdown occurs (you know what happens at home if you put too many electrical gadgets on at once) and they must be able to step up or step down the voltage from one supply to another. This accounts for transformer stations and sub-stations as well as the power stations themselves.

The overall organization of the National Grid is shown in Fig. 13.26. Notice the similarity between the control centres and the Regional Capitals mentioned in Chapter 4. You will notice in Fig. 13.23 a supergrid cable line pointing across the Channel from Dungeness. We even borrow power from France when we need it. By means of the supergrid, there is a direct link with hydro-electric power stations in the Alps. The link between the Kent coast and northern France was laid down in 1961. Fig. 13.27 shows the main features of this international link. There is also supergrid connection with the two power authorities in Scotland.

Fig. 13.25 Demand for electricity during a peak T.V. viewing period

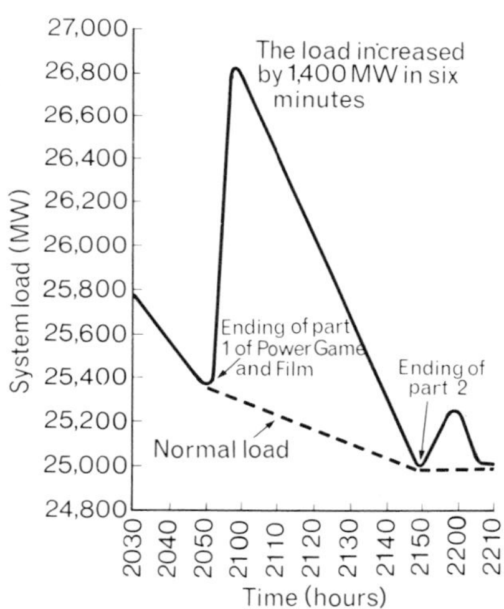

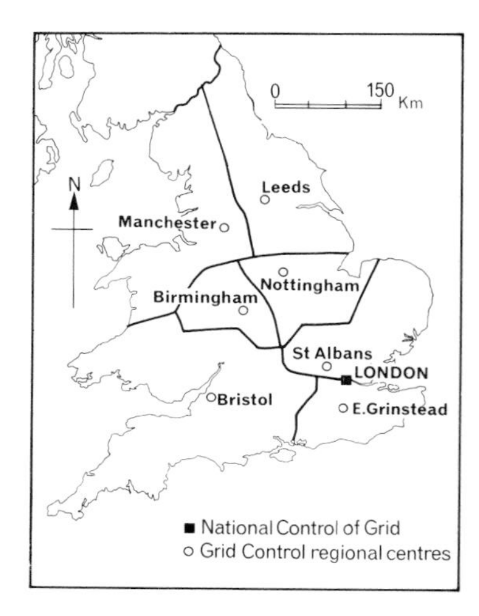

Fig. 13.26 Regional organisation of the National Electricity grid

Fig. 13.27 The 55 km cross-Channel power link

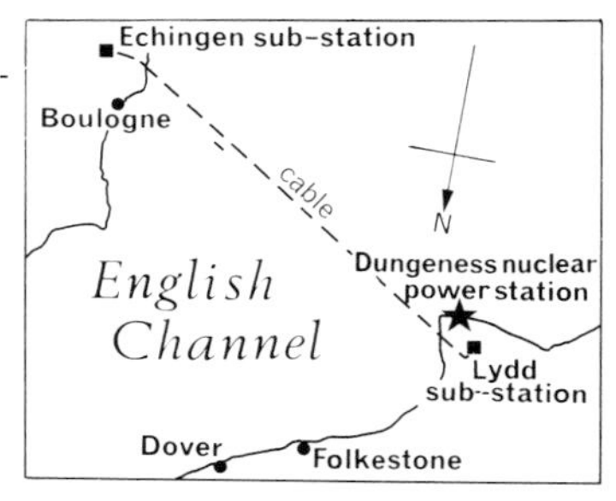

This is a matter of great controversy but, at the time of writing, the cost of one mile of underground cable is fifteen times as great as a mile of overhead pylon line. In other words, we can have underground cables but we must be prepared to pay more for our electricity if we wish to preserve the countryside, for example, in the Lake District and other National Parks.

Nuclear power

Britain produces more nuclear power than any other nation. By 1975, we were producing 3,462 megawatts from nuclear stations, one-third of the worlds nuclear power output. We export nuclear power stations and our expert knowledge about them. Our technical experience will enable us to build new nuclear stations that will produce electric power at a lower cost. Because of the element of danger due to their special type of fuel (radioactive material) and to their enormous demands on water for cooling purposes, these stations must be very carefully situated. Fig. 13.29 shows their location.

The success of the nuclear power programme needs a lot more research into new and cheaper methods of harnessing atomic power. The station at Wylfa will produce power at a unit cost above that of the most up-to-date thermal stations in the Trent valley but estimates for the new reactor at Hinkley 'B' (i.e. the second station on the same site, adjacent to Hinkley 'A'), suggest that the unit cost of the nuclear electricity will be lower than that produced by coal-fired stations. It is on this expectation that the Government has decided on an expansion of the nuclear power programme. New sites will be decided upon and by 2000 nuclear power may contribute about 75 per cent of our total energy needs. Another benefit from the latest reactors is that their water demands are no greater than for conventional plants and could, therefore, be sited inland where sufficient lake or riverine water is available. Safety has also been improved and stations may be situated nearer to larger centres of population: this will enable power lines to be shorter.

The pace of change of technology is likely to be even greater than it has been since the beginning of the nuclear power programme in 1955. Research now being carried out at Dounreay on the north coast of Scotland may lead to the development of yet another type of nuclear power plant even more efficient and cheaper than those now being built.

Fig. 13.28 shows the new nuclear station at Trawsfynydd in North Wales. This station is unusual in that it is not on the coast. It is located in the Snowdonia National Park where large amounts of water are available from lake storage and the heavy rainfall of the mountain area. Its isolation is a safety factor but its building was strongly opposed by many interests, especially those people who felt that such an industrial site was out of place in an area of such beauty that it has been designated as a National Park (see Chapter 20 for a fuller discussion of these areas).

Fig. 13.28 Trawsfynydd power station in North Wales

51. *What factors have influenced the location of nuclear power stations?*
52. *Can you suggest reasons why there is no nuclear power station situated on the east coast from the Wash northwards to the Moray Firth?*

Fig. 13.29 Nuclear power stations in the British Isles

Fig. 13.30 Ffestiniog pump storage scheme

53. *Which estuary in the British Isles has the greatest concentration of nuclear power at the moment? (Fig. 13.29.)*
54. *Compare the photograph of the nuclear station in Fig. 13.28 with that of the conventional thermal (coal-fired) station of West Burton (Fig. 13.21) and comment on the differences you notice in the buildings.*
55. *Do you think it is correct to call nuclear energy 'the power of the future'? Give reasons for your answer.*

Iydro-electric power

Ve have seen already that the North-West regional board obtains ome of its power supplies from hydro-electric stations in north Vales and the Lake District. Water has one great advantage over ther sources of power: it is comparatively inexhaustible. It can e used over and over again. Once coal or oil or gas is burnt, that's t! So hydro-electric developments take place where there is a large, egular supply of water, where a dam can be built safely to control nd store that water (cf. Chapter 14 Section A on water supplies) o as to feed a controlled 'head' of water to drive the turbines in he power stations. Fig. 13.30 shows the new storage section of the I.E.P. station of Ffestiniog. The idea of pumped storage is that uring off-peak hours when electricity is not needed, the power is sed to pump water back again up-hill into the main storage area, so hat the same water can be used many times to provide power. The ain-bearing clouds, the moorland scene, the natural rock-basin all ontribute to the suitability of the site. The same water supply will e used by the nuclear power station at Trawsfynydd.

The major region for hydro-electric development in the British sles, however, is the Highland zone of Scotland where there are ast areas of moorland of poor agricultural potential, high rainfall nd deep rock-basins and valleys carved out by ice which are uited to water storage. Long finger-lakes left by the melting glaciers f the past Ice Age make natural reservoirs. In 1943, the North f Scotland Hydro-Electricity Board was set up to harness the power of the mountain zone, to provide modern power to over a millior people scattered in small towns, farms and crofts and to produc surplus power to 'export' to the industrial centres of the Scottish lowlands, especially Glasgow and Clydeside. By 1965, over 50 per cent of the potential power had been harnessed and recent estimate suggest that nearly 90 per cent has now been controlled. The firs power schemes were used for the smelting of aluminium at Kinloch-leven. The total output of the H.E.P. stations in this region in 197 was 1,887,000 kW (i.e. 1,887 megawatts). That sounds a lot of powe until you compare it with the output of West Burton. That on thermal power station will produce from coal twice as much powe as all the Highlands of Scotland.

The Loch Tummel Scheme Fig. 13.31 is representative of thes power developments. Rainfall in the area varies from 1,400 mm to 1,750 mm annually (much of this in the form of winter snow) and a series of finger-lakes act as natural storage areas. The lakes and rivers that feed them are linked by a series of tunnels and aqueducts so that they make one system with most of the water flowing from Loch Ericht via Loch Rannoch to Loch Tummel. There are severa small power stations in the catchment area but the biggest ones are situated near Loch Tummel at the end of the water system. The nine power stations have a capacity of nearly a quarter of a millior kilowatts and the power supply is conveniently near the lowland cities. The complexity and importance of power cables to carry electricity to the houses and factories that use it is well illustrated by the map (Fig. 13.32) of the rural area north of Aberdeen in north east Scotland. It compares the total length of power lines in 194 with those in 1958.

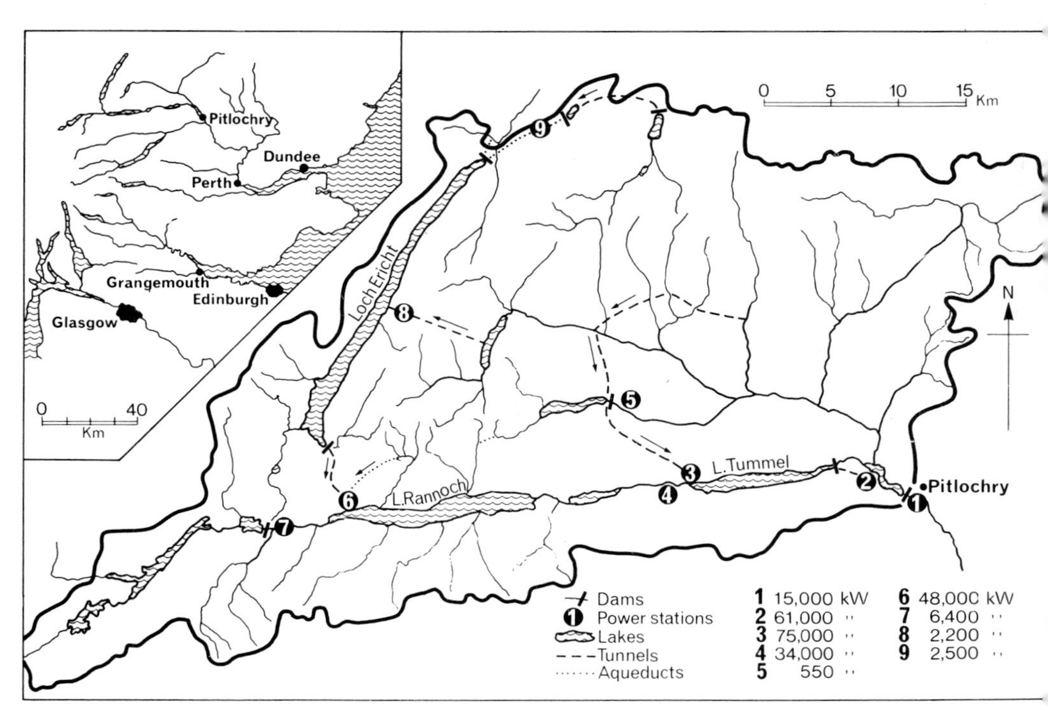

Fig. 13.31 The Loch Tummel scheme

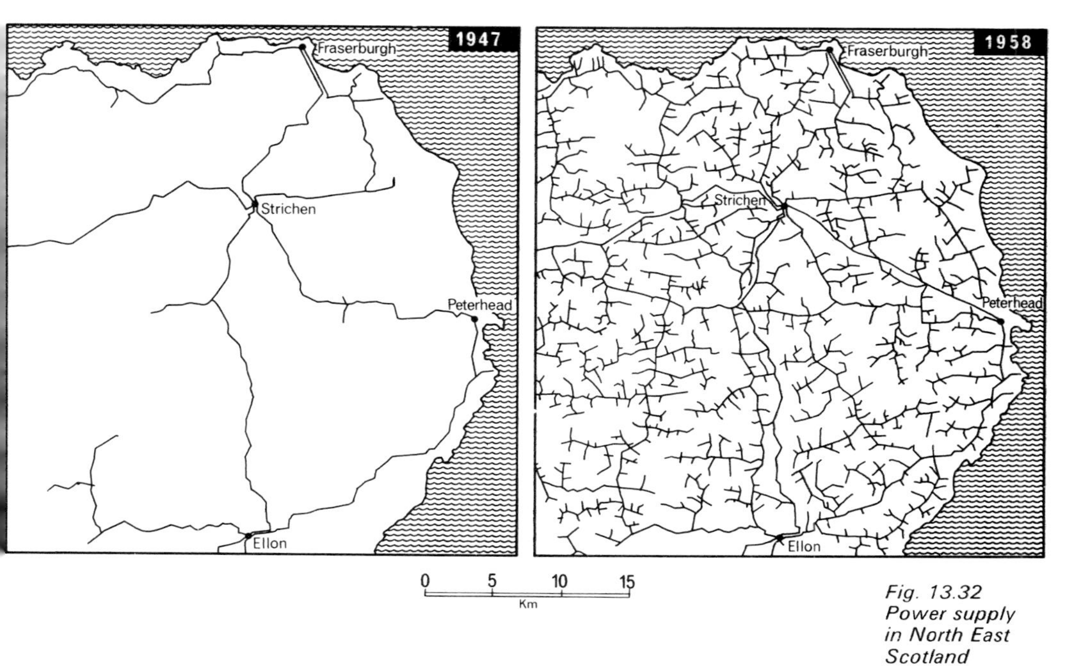

Fig. 13.32 Power supply in North East Scotland

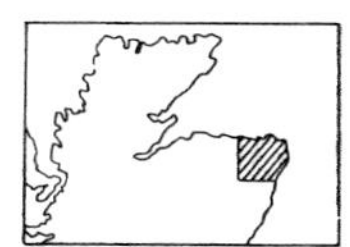

Earlier in this section, the phrase 'head of water' was used. It is not the total fall of water that decides the site of a power station: indeed, a high waterfall may present the engineer with great problems. What he wants is a large volume of water with a controlled fall. In fact, the larger rivers of Britain are, as yet, untouched from the point of view of power. Dams on the Thames or the Severn or the Trent would supply more power than the Highland schemes but dams on lowland rivers would lead to the loss of much larger areas of good land under the storage reservoirs.

56. *Why is the area shown in Fig. 13.28 of the Ffestiniog storage scheme well suited to hydro-electric development?*
57. *What is meant by* pumped storage*?*
58. *What advantages does water have over coal, oil or gas as a source of power?*
59. *Which region in the British Isles has the greatest development of hydro-electric power potential?*
60. *Draw a simple diagram to show the method by which flowing water is turned into electricity.*
61. *How many dams have been built in the Loch Tummel catchment area to control the waters?*
62. *By what methods have the hydro-engineers made all the lochs and rivers of the Tummel area into one system of continuous flow?*
63. *How far is the terminus of the Tummel system at Pitlochry from Glasgow? (Fig. 13.31.)*
64. *What figures of rainfall have been recorded in the Scottish Highland zone?*
65. *How important is hydro-electricity in the total power supply of Great Britain?*

Hydro-electric developments in the Highlands have brought great benefits to the sparsely-settled region; not only because of the supply of electricity to isolated farms and villages, but due to new roads, houses and employment possibilities.

REVISION EXERCISES

66. Why are power and fuel supplies more important to the U.K. today than they were 200 years ago?

67. (a) What is the main form of power used by industry today?
(b) What would happen if electrical power were to fail for a whole day all over the U.K.?

68. Draw up a table similar to the one below showing the respective advantages of coal, petroleum and gas as fuels.

	COAL	PETROLEUM	GAS
Use in the home			
Use in Industry			
Transport			

69. (a) You are asked by an oil company to become their geographical consultant on the siting of a new oil-tanker terminal in Great Britain. Where would you put it and why?
(b) Draw plans for the terminal showing where you would place the jetties, the storage tanks; what depth of water you would have at low tide – do not forget to put a scale to the map.

70. It would be possible to store gas underground near Winchester in Hampshire. Local people have resisted the carrying out of such a scheme. Do you think their attitude is reasonable?

71. Which type of electricity power station has the lowest transport costs for its fuel?

72. You are designing a hydro-electric power scheme for Wales. What sort of an area would you choose (a) to build four dams, (b) to site your power station? Give reasons for your answers.

73. (a) Would it be possible to generate large amounts of hydro-electrical power from (i) the river Thames (ii) the river Itchen (near Winchester) (iii) the river Wey (near Guildford) (iv) the river Severn (near Gloucester)?
(b) What might be the disadvantages of using the Thames as a source of hydro-electric power?

Chapter Fourteen

Water Supplies and the Raw Materials of the Construction Industry

A. Water Supplies

Water would seem to be a very usual, undramatic material and its supply a story connected with engineering, rainfall and rivers. In fact, the problems of water supply have caused such high feelings in recent years, that they have led to bomb attacks on reservoirs and pipelines in the Welsh Mountains. Naturalists have organized nation-wide petitions against the flooding of a special area of the Pennine Moors, farmers have prevented surveyors from looking over land that they feared would be lost to them as farming land, and the loss of control of its own water supplies to a new North of Scotland Water Board has aroused such wrath in the Orkney Islands that some people there are anxious to secede from the United Kingdom! Water, then, is dynamite!

Before we can understand some of the dramatic episodes above, we must look at the general situation in the British Isles regarding water. These islands have always enjoyed a reputation for wetness; the dampness of the climate has been given as one of the causes of bronchitis, which is also called the 'English disease'. It seems difficult to accept that we are short of water. Let us look at some simple facts.

In 1971 each one of us used on average 0.3 of a cubic metre (or 300 litres) of water each day. That gives a total consumption of about 16.5 million cubic metres supplied to the whole population by water boards. At the present rate of annual increase, the water boards are anticipating a consumption of at least 0.45 cubic metres (or 450 litres) per head per day by the year 2000 A.D. With a projected population of about 66.5 millions this gives a total water consumption of about 30 million cubic metres, nearly double the present figure.

So much for the consumption of water. Its supply, whether from rivers, springs or wells, depends ultimately upon the rainfall or other forms of precipitation such as snow, hail and sleet. The precipitation in England and Wales (i.e. the total amount of moisture falling on the land surface) in an average year is 73 million m^3 per day which is far in excess of even the expected consumption of the year 2000 A.D.

The figure 73 million m^3 per day is less impressive when we realize that it is only an average figure estimated, perhaps, over the last forty years. In fact, many years are much wetter than others: some places are much wetter than others; some parts of the year are much wetter than others. The total precipitation that falls is not actually available for immediate use. Some of the water runs off in the form of streams and rivers and this is available for use: but not all of it, otherwise the river would dry off below the point of extraction and fish and other forms of life would suffer. Also, no water would be left to remove sewage and waste. The water authority for London (The Metropolitan Water Board) is controlled by Parliament in the amount of water it can extract from the river Thames for just these reasons.

Some of the water seeps into the ground and penetrates deeply into the joints and fissures of rocks creating an *aquifer* i.e. a water-bearing layer of rock, such as the chalk under London. This water is in a natural storage and finds its way to the surface in the form of springs: or it may be reached by sinking wells.

Some of the water is lost quite quickly by evaporation, i.e. by return to the atmosphere. Even on a cool day in winter, wet pavements eventually dry in the wind, showing that the water has returned to the atmosphere.

The problem of water-supply is greatly intensified when we look at the overall distribution of precipitation throughout the United Kingdom. Fig. 14.1 gives the total precipitation recorded in an average year at many places in the islands. A comparison of this map with a physical map in the atlas, showing the major mountain and hill areas, will show that, in general, the highest rainfall is recorded in the highest relief areas, especially in the north-west of Scotland, the Lake District and the Cambrian Mountains of Wales. Again, the rainfall tends to be greater on the western areas than on the eastern areas. But the areas of maximum rainfall are precisely the areas of least population. Many of the greatest conurbations discussed in Chapter 1 (see Fig. 1.3) are to be found in the drier areas of the country.

We have discussed in several chapters the importance of water supplies to industry, some of which, such as steel-making, chemicals, and power stations require enormous quantities (the chemical industry of Teesside used 113,500 m^3 per day by 1970), and the growing demands by house-holders as living standards rise. But farmers, too, need much more water. What is significant to the farmer is the rainfall, or water supply, during the growing season, in the summer half-year. Harvest has often been spoilt by excessive rain but surprisingly often yields have been poor because of lack of rain or other water supplies. Yields of many crops could be greatly increased by irrigation during dry summers or dry spells at critical times in plant growth. The loss by evaporation is highest in summer and

Fig. 14.2 shows just how serious this is. The figures show those parts of the country which suffer an actual loss of water over the summer months: those in which irrigation would be of benefit to farmers. The greatest need is in the south and east, which is also where the greatest demands are made for water in urban areas.

In April 1974 a new water conservation system came into being, the supply of water in England and Wales being placed under the control of 10 regional authorities. Scotland had 13 in 1967.

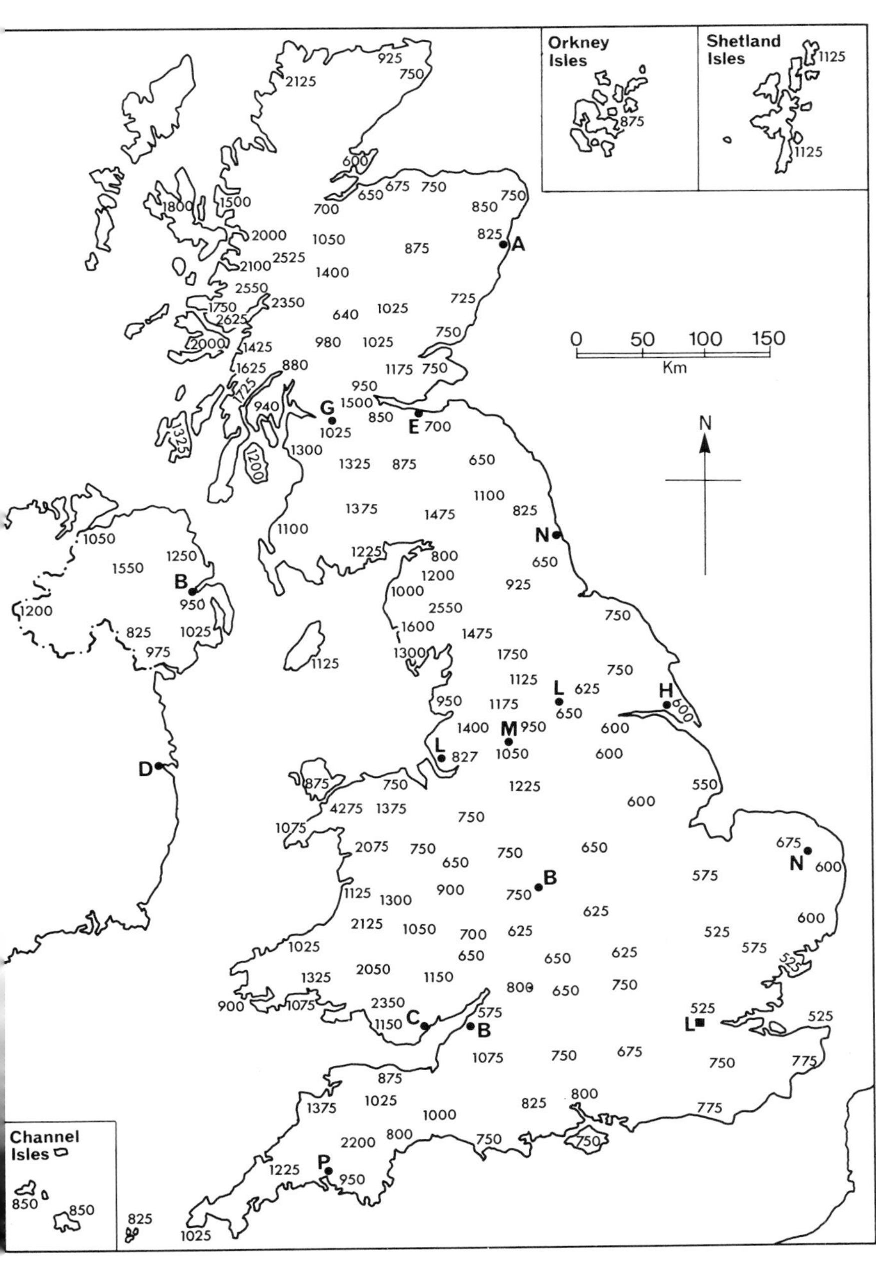

Fig. 14.1 Average annual precipitation (mm)

Fig. 14.2 Balance between precipitation and evaporation in the summer months (April to September) (mm)

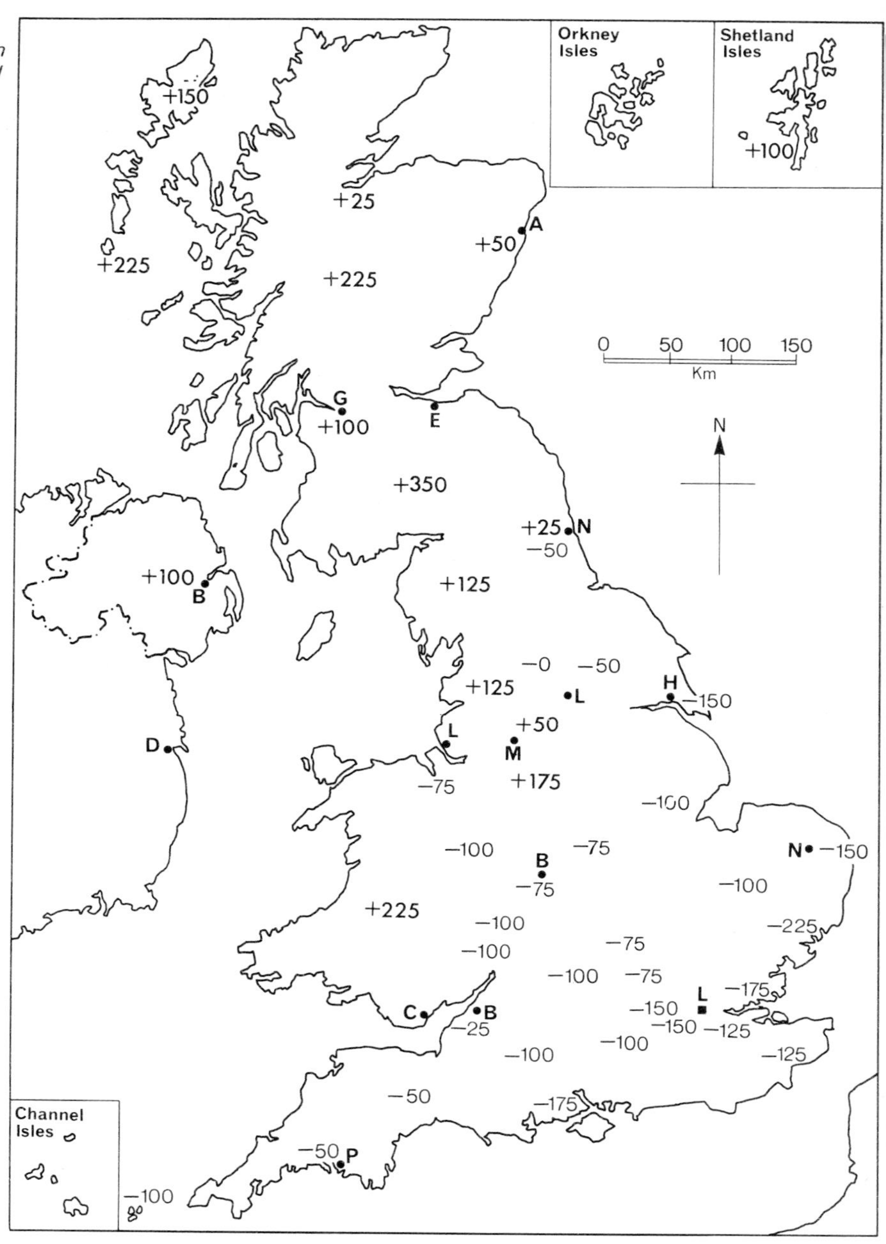

The task of each authority is:
(a) to control the rivers and prevent flooding, (b) to conserve water to supply needs, (c) to control sewage and to prevent pollution, (d) to develop fisheries and recreational facilities.

These tasks can be carried out most efficiently if the river authority controls the whole catchment area of the river i.e. the total land surface on which precipitation will find its way via tributaries into the main river. The pattern of a catchment area of a river is not unlike a tree with its trunk and branches. Fig. 14.3 shows the fairly regular

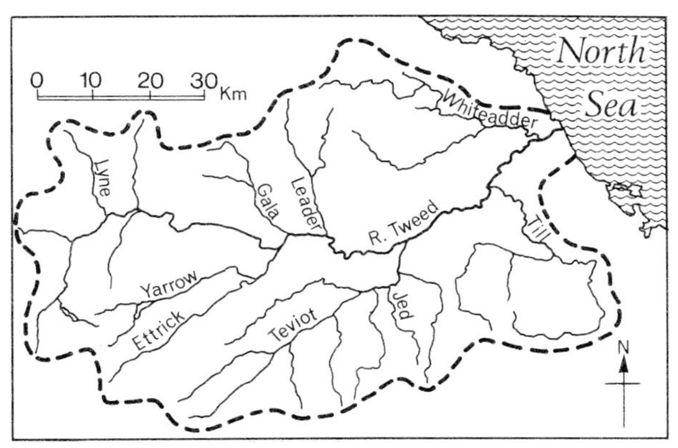

Fig. 14.3 Drainage in the Tweed valley

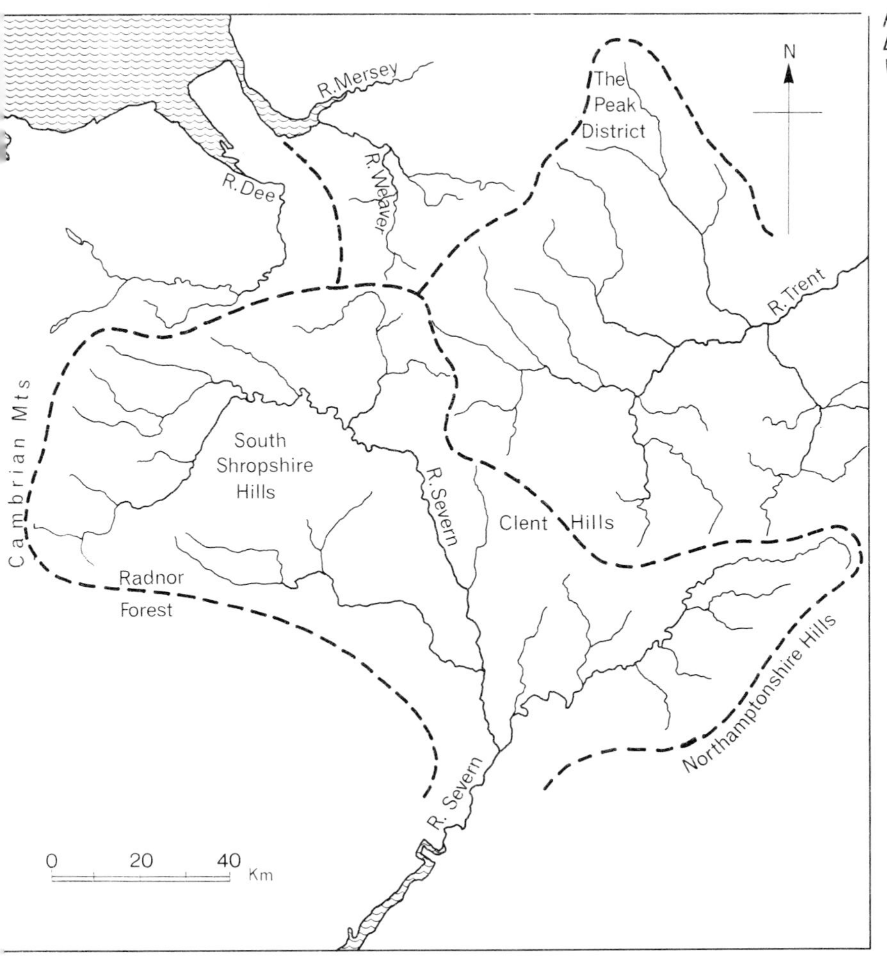

Fig. 14.4 Drainage in the West Midlands

pattern created by the various tributaries flowing from the Border hills into the river Tweed. Among the concerns of this river authority are the woollen industries' demands and the needs of the salmon. But catchment areas can be quite complicated. Fig. 14.4 shows the drainage pattern of the West Midlands. Rainfall in this region may reach the North Sea via the Trent, or the Bristol Channel via the river Severn depending on which side of the *watershed* it falls. The *watershed* is the name given to the boundary (usually of higher land) that divides one catchment area (or river basin) from another.

Birmingham, for 60 years, extracted enough water from comparatively local supplies in the Elan Valley for its needs, about 340,500 m^3 per day. By 1957, the needs of this great industrial city had far outgrown that supply and the water authorities looked to the wet hills to the west which fed the river Severn and gained the right to extract water from that river and pipe it to Birmingham. Unfortunately, a river does not have an even flow: it varies with the seasons, indeed, the level may fluctuate within hours. A water authority needs a steady, assured supply. The best way to control a river's flow is to build a reservoir up-stream so that water is held during times of surplus to be released during times of need. So a dam is constructed across the river and an artificial lake is created. But as the waters rise and the lake grows in size, a large land area, good valley land, farms and even villages are drowned beneath the rising waters. So the needs of water in the homes and industries of the Birmingham area and of the Liverpool area (which has also looked to the Welsh hills for its new supplies) have led to the loss of land in Welsh valleys. Here is a source of conflict of feeling.

Manchester, the city where test matches have the reputation of being rained off, also sought water far from the damp Pennine foothills surrounding it and gained the right to draw water from the lakes of the Lake District to the north. Local people were afraid that lake levels would be lowered and walkers and other users of the fells were annoyed by large areas being closed to them as the water boards feared that human beings would pollute the water. We have seen that the prevention of pollution is one of the duties of the water boards, but the Thames supplies nearly 1.4 million m^3 per day to London and it is hardly pure when it is taken out of the river. In fact, all authorities have to treat water, to purify it before it can be fed into the water mains for use. The lake surfaces are polluted anyway by birds, animals and the rain itself carrying particles from the atmosphere. So many authorities, supported by the Government, are encouraging the multiple use of lakes and reservoirs. Not only will they be a source of water but they will be recreational centres for boating, sailing, water-skiing, camping on the shores and the like. Haweswater, one of the first lakes to be used by Manchester has now been freed for other uses after 25 years.

Fig. 14.5 shows in detail a system of control of the upper reaches of the river Derwent in north Derbyshire creating the longest reservoir in England. Here was a case where farms and an entire village were lost under the water: the church steeple is sometimes seen peeping above the water after a long drought. But this illustrates an area suited to such water control. The high moorlands are very wet with a high rainfall and a thick peaty layer that holds the water like

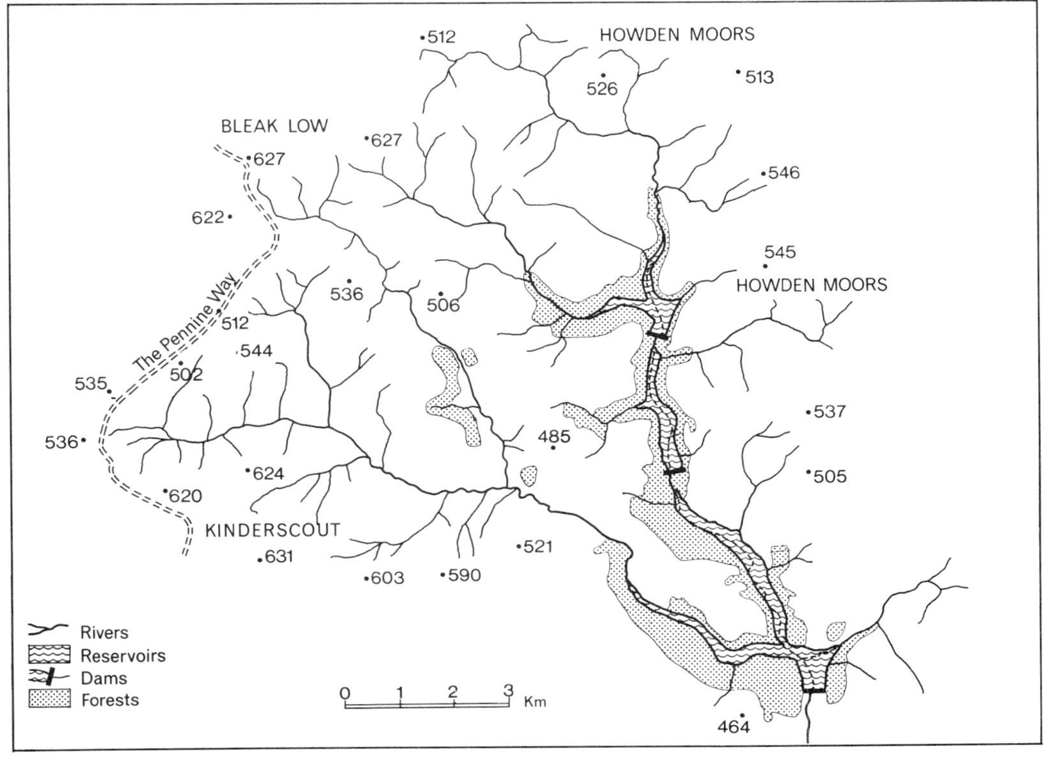

Fig. 14.5 The Upper reaches of the Derwent

a sponge and releases it slowly. The valleys are fairly narrow so that the water does not drown too wide an area, and the bed-rock, i.e. the solid rock that makes up the area, millstone grit and shales, gives a firm foundation to the dam (a dam-break can cause disastrous flooding down-stream) and the non-pervious rocks prevent the water draining underground. Even here, the dam builders found that water *was* draining away through small faults in the bedrock and liquid cement was pumped down to fill the gaps. A farmer complained that some of the cement starting coming up in his fields! The tree plantations along the lake sides helps to control run-off into the water and prevents soil being washed down to silt up the dam and block the sluice gates. The broken line running through the lakes shows the original course of the rivers before the reservoirs were constructed.

A new national plan for water resources published in 1975 emphasises the importance of inland reservoirs and a system of transferring water from one river basin to another (Fig. 14.6). Areas of surplus water would supply areas of deficiency on a national grid of water. Other sources may be tried. Why not the sea itself? Britain leads the world in the production of machinery for extracting salt from sea-water, known as desalinization: the most advanced research station in Europe was opened at Troon in Strathclyde in 1967. But it is, at the moment, more expensive than the conventional sources. Also, the water has to be pumped from the coast uphill to

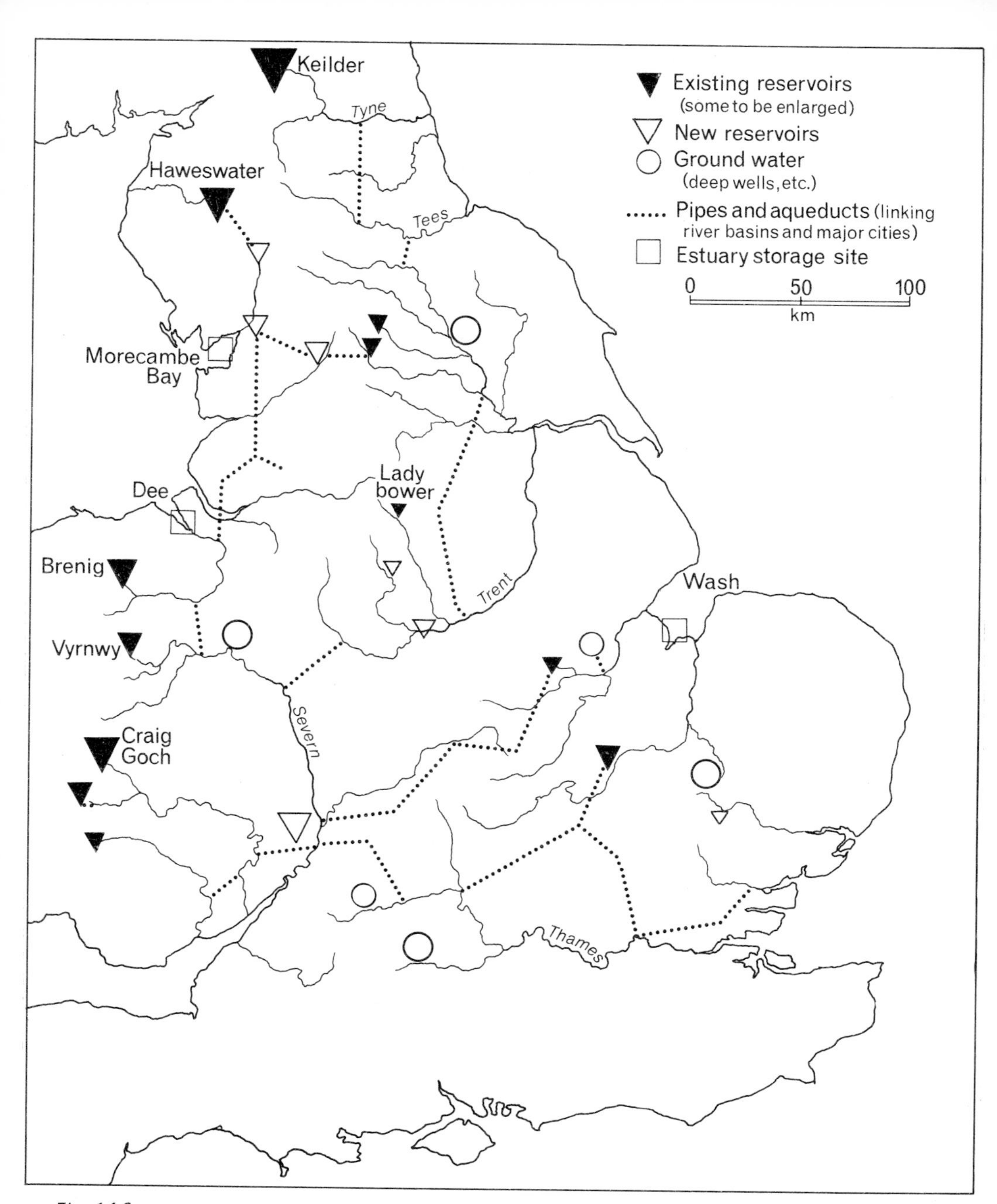

Fig. 14.6 A water strategy for England and Wales for the year 2000.

the urban areas: whereas water from the hills comes down to the urban areas on the lower land under the influence of gravity.

The construction of large barrages across bays such as the Dee Estuary and Morecambe Bay, shown on Fig. 14.6, are now being actively investigated. A barrage built across these shallow bays will keep out the sea water and the rivers flowing into them will gradually fill them with fresh water. Not only will large reservoirs of fresh water be constructed, much larger than any existing lake, but also fine areas for holiday makers fond of water sports.

There are many other possibilities. The Metropolitan Water Board is drilling 248 bore holes over an area of 2,300 square kilometres to supplement the river Thames water. The best place to store water is in natural *aquifers* underground: there is less pollution and no loss through evaporation. Authorities may have to use the same water many times, putting it through a process of purification each time. We may have to have two water systems, one of pure water for drinking and cooking and one of impure water, cheaper water (for purification is an expensive process) for other uses. Perhaps we may even pay for water, as many farmers and factories do, not by means of a flat water rate but by a metered supply, as with electricity and gas now.

1. *What uses does your household make of water? Why is it increasing every year?*
2. *Construct a simple diagram to show what happens to rainfall (and other forms of precipitation) when it falls on the earth's surface. Your diagram should illustrate, among other things, evaporation, seepage, an* aquifer, *a spring and surface run-off.*
3. *Make a simplified copy of the rainfall map, Fig. 14.1.*
   (a) Draw a line across it, dividing the areas receiving more than 750 mm from those receiving less than 750 mm.
   (b) Identify as accurately as you can, with the aid of an atlas map of the British Isles, three areas of very heavy rainfall, in the British Isles.
4. *Make a simplified copy of Fig. 14.2 and draw a line across it, dividing those areas with a surplus of rainfall in the six summer months from those areas with a loss of water in those months. This will show those areas in which farming would benefit from irrigation.*
5. *(a) What is the lowest rainfall registered on Fig. 14.1? In what area is it?*
   (b) Suggest reasons why the highest precipitation is to be found in the western parts of the islands.
6. *(a) What is meant by precipitation?*
   (b) What is the precipitation figure nearest your own area?
7. *Attempt to estimate the total catchment area of the river Tweed in square kilometres. (See Fig. 14.3.)*
8. *(a) Into what catchment area do streams from the south Shropshire hills flow? (See Fig. 14.4.)*
   (b) Into what catchment areas do streams from the Clent Hills flow? (See Fig. 14.4.)
   (c) Can you suggest reasons why the river Severn has more tributaries feeding from the west than from the east?
9. *Using Fig. 14.5:*
   (a) List the reasons why this part of the Peak District is suitable for the development of reservoirs.

(b) Why are there several reservoirs rather than one large reservoir on the Derwent?

10. *Study Fig. 14.6 and*
    (a) identify the regions in which the largest reservoirs are situated,
    (b) suggest reasons why there are many more reservoirs in the west than in the east,
    (c) suggest why it would be useful to be able to transfer water from one river basin to another, for example, from the Severn to the Thames.
    (d) work out if it would be possible to move water from the reservoir on Lake Vyrnwy in Wales to London,
    (e) name three coastal bays or river estuaries which might be developed for water supply by means of barrages.

B. The Raw Materials of the Construction Industry

In this section we come closer to geology than we have so far been in this book, except for the sections on coal, gas and oil. Most of the raw materials used in building and road construction are derived from rocks. You may remember from your previous work that a geologist defines any material which is mined, quarried or excavated as rock no matter how soft it is. Sand and clay are as much rock to the geologist as are limestone and granite. He does, however, omit from his list the top soil which he considers comes in a class on its own, since it is of a very different composition from the rock from which it was derived.

The materials we are concerned with are the following:

1. Clay which is used in brickmaking.
2. Limestone used for building stone and for cement manufacture.
3. Sand and gravel used in road construction and in the making of concrete for buildings.
4. Igneous and metamorphic rocks used for road metal.

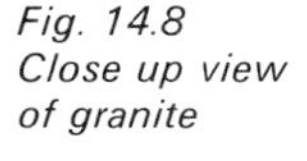

Fig. 14.8 Close up view of granite

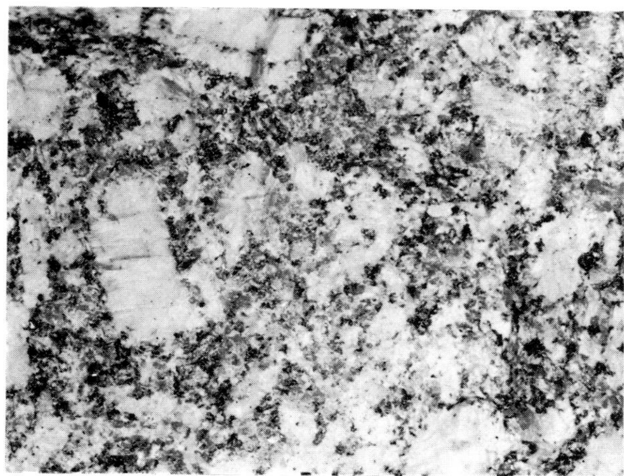

Fig. 14.7 Sedimentary limestone in a cliff

Clay, limestone, sand and gravel are rocks which belong to the group called *sedimentary rocks*. That is they were originally deposited as sediments at the bottom of a sea, lake, river or even glacier, or they were sediments dropped by the wind. Such sedimentary rocks are shown in Fig. 14.7.

Clay consists of minute particles of various minerals packed so tightly together that it will not allow water to pass through it and as such it is said to be *impervious*.

Sand on the other hand consists of coarser particles of such minerals as silica which are sufficiently loose to allow water to soak through rapidly. Sand is said to be *pervious*.

Gravel is a fairly loose term used to indicate small angular or rounded stones or pebbles which are found in some sort of a layer often mixed with other materials. The gravel pebbles are made of some resistant rock such as flint.

Limestone is a term used to describe rocks which have a considerable amount of calcium carbonate ($CaCO_3$) in them. This is because the rock is made up of the shells and skeletons of large and small sea organisms. Limestones vary considerably in their degree of purity, for at times much clayey or sandy material may have been deposited at the same time as the sea organisms. Consequently some rocks are sandy limestones but others may be limey sandstone, the lime (calcium carbonate) acting as a cement to bind the sand particles together. *Chalk* is the purest form of limestone available in the U.K.

Thus *sandstone* really consists of sand particles cemented together naturally. When you look at a sandstone, you can usually see the grains of sand of which it consists. Sandstones are used as building material, as grinding stones and as a basis for firebricks used in furnaces.

Granite is the best example of a rock of the igneous and metamorphic group. An igneous rock is one which was once molten, such as volcanic lava, and a metamorphic rock is one which has been changed or altered by heat and pressure. For example marble is really limestone which has been changed by heat and pressure. Its main chemical composition is much the same as limestone, but its physical appearance is different. Granite is usually classed as an igneous rock. It consists essentially of three minerals: quartz (silica in the form of crystals), mica (a transparent flakey substance) and felspar (a group of minerals made up of silicates of aluminium, potassium and sodium). It is often easy to recognize as it has a speckled appearance, for example black specks set in white quartz as shown in Fig. 14.8. The distribution of the main types of rocks in the British Isles is shown in Fig. 14.9. As you can see from the map, there is no apparent shortage of clay, limestone or granite in the British Isles. Areas where gravel is quarried are not shown, since these are mainly superficial deposits and do not appear on a map of solid geology. Let us first consider brickmaking.

Fig. 14.9
Main rock types of the British Isles

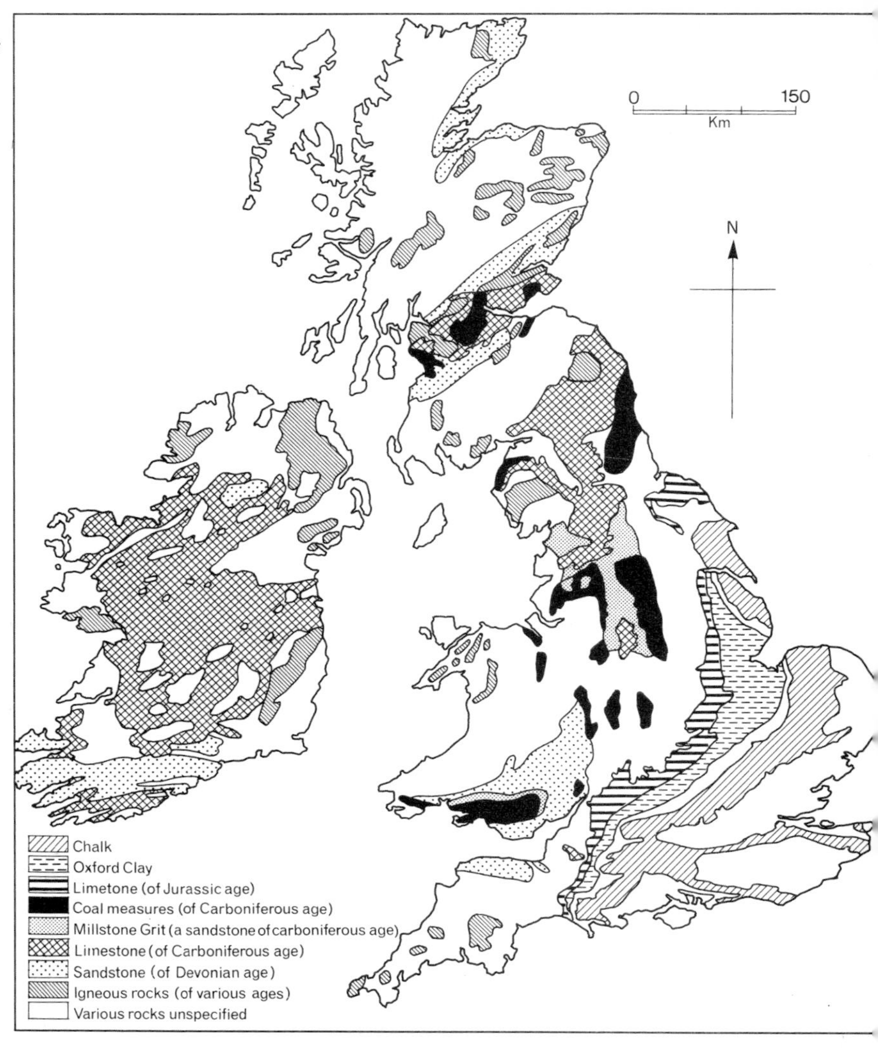

1. Brickmaking

The case of the London Brick Company's brick works at Stewartby will be taken as an example. Fig. 14.10 shows where Stewartby is located. The basic reason for this location is the existence of the Oxford Clay beds which are most suitable for making into bricks. The beds are thick, widespread and they do not change in composition to any extent. This is very important, because some sedimentary rocks change in type as one travels along the outcrop (the area where the rock is exposed on the surface). For example, the carboniferous limestone series shown in Fig. 14.9 as extending into Northumberland are often there composed more of sandstone than of limestone. As you can imagine it would cause much trouble to the brickmakers if they found that the clay they were using had gradually become very limey or sandy as quarrying was proceeding along the outcrop.

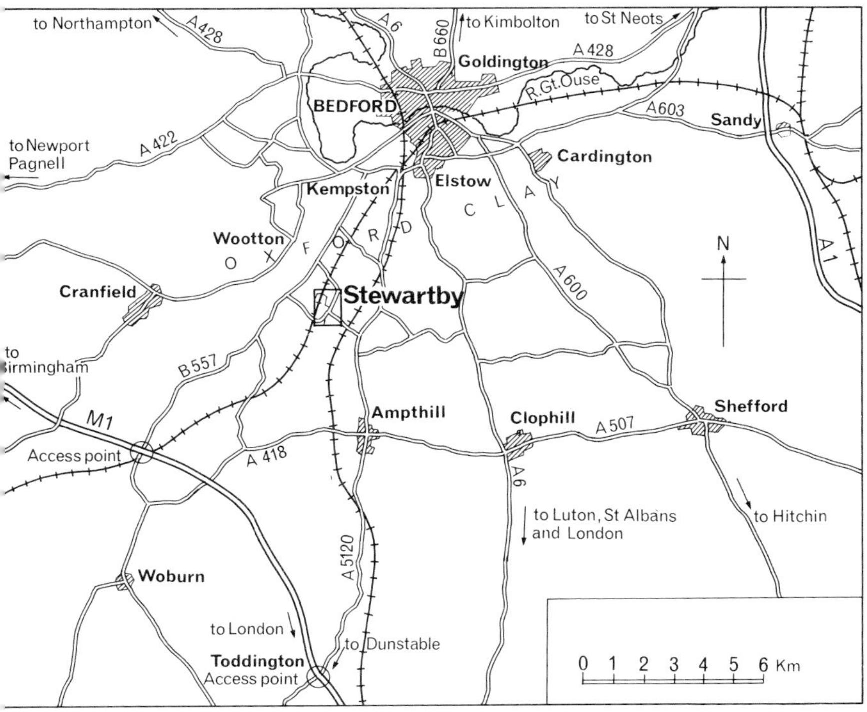

Fig. 14.10 Stewartby Brickworks

The first step in the making of bricks is to remove from 5 to 6 metres of surface clay which is too plastic for use in the kilns. This over burden is removed by a walking dragline (see Fig. 14.11 (a)) and then dumped into an abandoned clay pit. The next step is to remove the firm clay below the over burden. This is also done by walking draglines from a face which is 20 to 23 metres high. The clay is dropped onto a mile long conveyor belt which takes the clay to the brick works at the rate of 500 to 600 tonnes per hour. After being finely ground, the clay is pressed into the shape of a brick and heated or fired in kilns such as the one shown in Fig. 14.11 (b). Coal is used to heat the kilns which are kept at a temperature of over 900°C for 35 hours. As the Oxford clay contains some carbonaceous materials, less coal is required than when other clays are used.

The finished bricks are either distributed by road in the company's lorries (with the Phorpres trademark), or taken to the rail sidings from which they are transported by rail to various depots all over Britain. Lorries then make the final delivery to the building sites.

Stewartby village began to be built in 1926 to accommodate the employees of the company. Today more than 1,000 employees and their families live in nearly 300 houses. The village also has a church, a village hall, and a general store with a post office.

Other brickworks have developed along the Oxford Clay outcrop: in the Peterborough area, near Bletchley and near Calvert. About 45 per cent of all clay bricks made in the U.K. come from this area where costs are relatively low. This low cost of bricks is reflected in

Fig. 14.11(a) Clay excavations in Bedfordshire

the fact that only about 6 per cent of the selling price of a brick house is accounted for by the cost of bricks. Consequently the whole industry is dominated by a few giant producers. The typical brick made by the L.B.C. is used all over Great Britain with the result that distinctive types of brick in certain areas are seldom seen today in modern buildings.

Fig. 14.11(b) The London Brick Company works at Stewartby

2. Cement manufacturing

More and more large buildings and massive structures like viaducts, flyovers and bridges are made of prestressed concrete. For example, the Liverpool Roman Catholic and the Coventry Anglican Cathedrals were made of prestressed concrete. Such concrete is made with Portland cement. The output of Portland cement has been growing fast in recent years; in 1950 some 9,800 tons were produced, in 1966 output was 16,500 tonnes and in 1970: 20,000 tonnes.

Cement manufacture requires limestone or chalk and clay or shale (a hardened clay) as raw materials, and plenty of fuel and power. The main process, known as the wet process, consists of mixing clay, ground chalk, and water in the right proportion to form a slurry which is fed into a long rotating kiln which has coal, oil or gas fired burners within it. The clay and lime eventually fuse and the clinker as it is called is ground to a fine powder to which gypsum is added to control the rate at which the cement sets.

The distribution of cement manufacturing works is shown on Fig. 14.12. The concentration of cement works on the outcrop of chalk in south-eastern England is evident and particularly in those areas near a seaway.

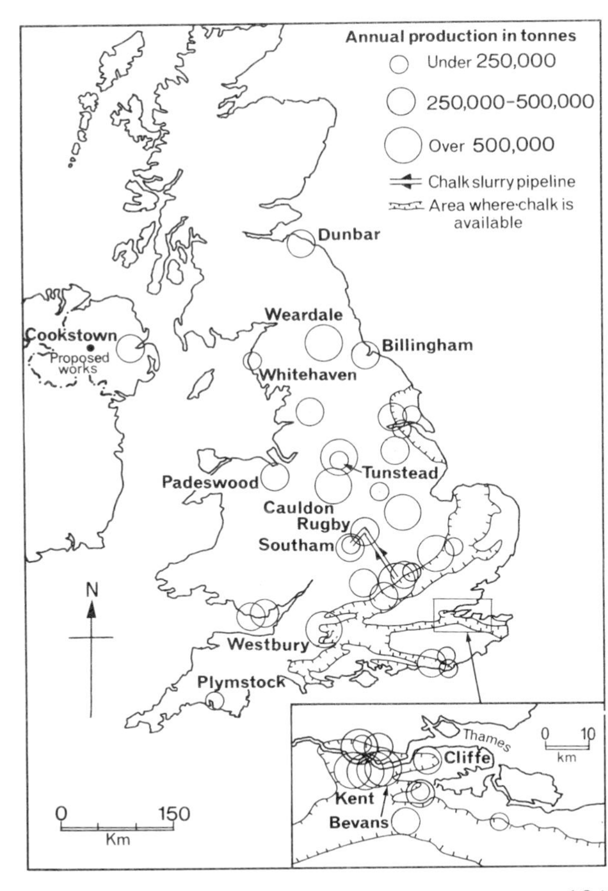

Fig. 14.12 Production at Portland Cement works 1966

3. Sand and gravel quarrying

Much of the sand and gravel needed in the building industry comes from superficial deposits: either gravels left by melting ice after the ice age or gravels left by rivers in the various *terraces* which may be found in river valleys. As it would be expensive to transport this gravel over long distances, most of it is quarried within 30 km of where it is used. The result is that large towns like London have large concentrations of gravel pits near to them. One such area is the Staines area west of London, part of which is shown on the map on the back end-paper. This map is on a scale of 1/25,000 (exactly 4 cm to 1 kilometre). You will notice that at Wraysbury where sand and gravel pits are marked (007 736) there are extensive areas of rather unusually shaped ponds or lagoons. These are the excavated quarries which have filled up with water. Why this should happen is easy to understand. Sand and gravel lie in beds. Owing to the various sizes and shapes of the gravel, a bed of sand and gravel will not only be *pervious* (i.e. let water through it) but it will also be *porous*, that is it will have spaces within the bed not occupied by rock (see Fig. 14.13). Consequently such a bed is able to hold large quantities of water within it.

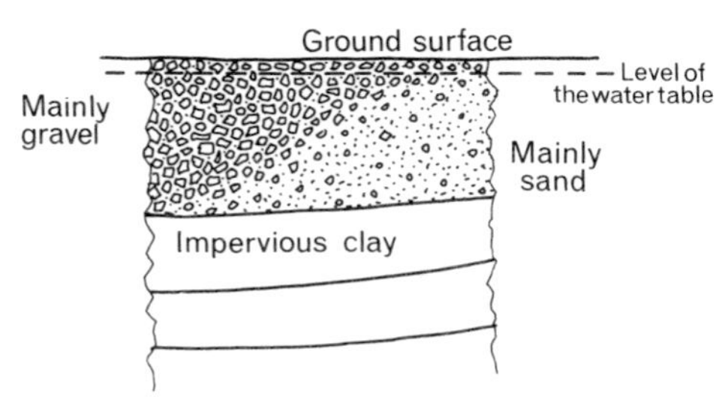

Fig. 14.13
A gravel bed

Now (a) since evaporation is not excessive in the British Isles, (b) since rainfall is usually adequate, and (c) since much of the London area is underlain by a thick bed of *impervious* clay (London Clay), the gravel beds are often saturated with water to a level which is very near the surface. This level to which a bed rock gets saturated is known as the 'level of the *water table*'. It follows from this that if the gravel and sand are excavated, the hollow created fills in with water in the same way as a well fills up with water when it is dug in *porous* rocks. Thus when gravel is dug out from the Thames river terraces, the areas of water created can never be used again for agricultural or building purposes unless they are filled in with other materials.

4. *Problems created by excavating raw materials for the building industry*

Whether granite is quarried for road metal, whether limestone is quarried for cement, whether clay is quarried for bricks, or gravel for concrete, the final result is a series of large holes in the ground, which are, in most cases, useless in the state in which the excavators have left them. Some fill up with water, some are just muddy, some are quite dry. But whatever their state they present a planning problem for the various county planning authorities. Should they be left in their present state or should something be done to alter them? It may be that some could be used as reservoirs for a town's water supply, some could be used as sailing lakes (see Fig. 14.14). Some might even be used as fish farms. But many could not be so used. If pits do not contain water or are not to be filled by water, then they must be filled with something else. The huge deep pits left by the London Brick Company's excavation in Bedfordshire are still unfilled, but it has been suggested that either domestic rubbish from London or waste rock from coal mines might be dumped into the pits. Eventually, when each pit was full, soil might be placed on top and the land restored to agriculture or to forestry. The trouble is that such schemes are costly and few of the firms or authorities concerned seem willing to pay for this filling up process. However, it is essential to do something about this problem if we do not want large areas of the U.K. to be permanently useless. About 4,800 hectares are required annually in England and Wales for mineral

Fig. 14.14 Sailing on a former gravel excavation

workings and only about 3,600 hectares are restored to other use once the minerals have been excavated. Thus a net loss of 1,200 hectares per year steadily builds up to a very large area.

11. (a) *What does a geologist mean when he talks about rocks?*
    (b) *Which of the following are* not *rocks: chalk, sand, clay, sandstone, peat, limestone, granite, soil, shale, marble.*
    (c) *Which of the following rocks are* pervious: *clay, sand, limestone, shale?*
    (d) *If a rock has many cracks or joints in it, is it* pervious *or* impervious?
12. (a) *What name is given to rocks which have been laid down as beds in seas, lakes or rivers?*
    (b) *Some rocks were once molten like lava; what general name is given to all such rocks?*
    (c) *What would you call rocks which have been transformed from one physical state to another by heat or pressure? Give an example of such rocks.*
13. (a) *What is the difference between sand and sandstone?*
    (b) *Why is it that limestones vary in composition in different areas?*
    (c) *What does granite consist of?*
14. *Study Fig. 14.9:*
    (a) *In which areas of Britain might granite be quarried?*
    (b) *In which parts of Britain might it be difficult to find limestone or chalk?*
    (c) *Are any of the main populated areas of Britain far from sources of clay or limestone?*
15. *Study Fig. 14.10. What are the advantages of the Stewartby location for the London Brick Company's works*
    (a) *from the point of view of the main raw material used?*
    (b) *for bringing in supplies of fuel?*
    (c) *for distributing the bricks?*
16. *Where else are there important brickworks in England?*
17. (a) *Where are most of the cement manufacturing works in England? (See Fig. 14.12.)*
    (b) *What explains this location?*
18. (a) *Why are gravel pits usually close to large towns?*
    (b) *What happens to most gravel pits once the gravel has been excavated?*
19. (a) *What is meant by the 'level of the* water table*'?*
    (b) *What do you think will determine whether in a gravel bed the level of the* water table *will be high or low?*
    (c) *Could a rock like granite be saturated with water? Give reasons for your answer.*
    (d) *If a rock can be saturated with water, is it* porous *or* pervious *or can it be both* porous *and* pervious*?*
20. (a) *Why do mineral workings create a problem for land use planning authorities?*
    (b) *What suggestions have been made for using these hollows?*
    (c) *Why is the demand for these minerals increasing?*

REVISION EXERCISES

21. *Why do some people get angry about proposals to provide towns with a greater water supply?*
22. *Suggest reasons why the consumption of water in Great Britain is increasing?*
23. *(a) From which three immediate sources does most of our water supply come?*
    (b) What determines the total amount of water available for distribution in one year?
24. *(a) Why is it that all the water derived from the precipitation over Great Britain in any year is not available for use?*
    (b) What is the estimated amount of moisture falling on England and Wales on one day in an average year.
25. *(a) What is an* aquifer*?*
    (b) Give examples of three rocks which can be good aquifers.
    (c) Must an aquifer *be* pervious *or* porous*?*
26. *(a) What is meant by a* river basin *or* river catchment area*?*
    (b) What name is given to the boundaries between various catchment areas?
27. *(a) Should the rock surrounding and under a reservoir be* porous, pervious *or* impervious*? Give reasons for your answer.*
    (b) Why is it an advantage to build reservoirs even in a country like England where rainfall is generally adequate?
    (c) What are (i) the disadvantages (ii) the advantages to the country-side of building dams to impound water for storage?
    (d) Why is it no longer considered important to keep people away from reservoirs?
28. *Why should irrigation be a good thing for certain farmers in Britain?*
29. *Describe what is meant by and give examples of*
    (a) a sedimentary *rock*
    (b) an igneous *rock*
    (c) a metamorphic *rock.*
30. *Select house No. 3 in 10 roads in your neighbourhood and note in each case what building material was used to construct it. What conclusion do you come to about the most popular building material in your area?*
31. *What would you do with an old gravel pit if you owned it? Give reasons for your answer.*

Part IV

Communications between Cities and Industries

Chapter Fifteen

Road and Rail Transport

Introduction

In the Middle Ages goods were seldom transported very far and very few people travelled much beyond the next village which might be 10 kilometres away. People travelled on foot or horseback and goods were transported by human or 'horse power'. In the 18th century heavy goods often travelled by canal, but the power used was still 'horse power'. In the 19th century, and especially in the second half of the 19th century, more and more goods and people travelled by rail. In the second half of the 20th century, many people and a large proportion of goods travel by road and air. The changes which have occurred since the Middle Ages have been brought about by technical progress, that is by the invention and development of new means of transport accompanied by a rise in the demand for these new means of transport. This has meant that today not only is travel much faster, but we have a much greater choice in the way we travel than our forefathers had. For example, very soon when you and your family take a holiday on the continent, you will have the choice of:

(a) using a car ferry and driving off on to continental roads
(b) using a car ferry and putting your car on a train (car-sleeper) to take you and your car to your destination (or part of the way)
(c) using an air-ferry and driving off from wherever the air-ferry lands
(d) travelling by train and ship as a foot passenger
(e) going by air as a foot passenger
(f) using a hovercraft.

Similarly a manufacturer wishing to send goods from Glasgow to London can choose between road, rail, air and even sea transport. Such a choice is useful since the manufacturer may choose which form of transport suits him best.

The patterns of links established between cities by the various means of transport are called *networks*. Thus today in the U.K. we have a road, rail, air and canal network. We shall only study the first two in this chapter and the third in the next chapter. The canal network is relatively unimportant today and will not be considered.

A. The Road Network: the problems

The main roads in the United Kingdom are often called the country's 'arteries'. This word, borrowed from biology, implies that like the arteries in the human body, the roads supply the country with vital substances, in this case goods of various kinds. Just as the arteries in the body are adapted to the needs of the body by going in the right direction and being of the right size to carry the amount of blood required in various areas of the body, so the road network ought to be adapted to the needs of traffic between towns. Unfortunately we know that this is not always so – why? The answer is relatively simple but the remedy is not so easy.

The first reason is that the network of roads which grew up in the U.K. was largely unplanned except for the roads which the Romans built when they occupied Britain. During the Middle Ages, tracks grew up linking nearby villages. Eventually, as the country developed and became unified, some of the more important towns became linked together largely by the process of joining together tracks linking a town to a village, that village to another village and so on until the other town was reached. Fig. 15.1 gives the example of the road (the A12) linking Ipswich with Lowestoft in East Anglia.

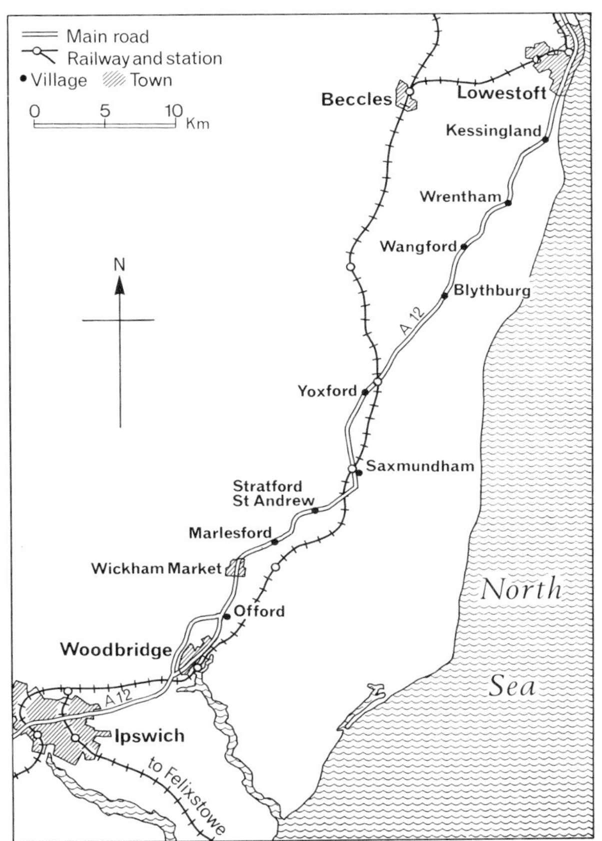

Fig. 15.1 The A12

It seems clear that the road was not planned as a single unit, but evolved out of a series of short tracks between villages which were gradually widened and improved as the traffic on them increased. One result is that unlike the planned Roman roads, most British roads seldom follow the shortest distance between two important towns.

The second reason why many of our roads are ill-adapted to the traffic they have to carry, is that until recently little work was done to enable the Department of the Environment to forecast how fast traffic would grow along certain roads. Thus the road builders and road improvers never seem to catch up with the traffic situation. An indication of how quickly traffic has grown is the number of vehicles which have been licensed in recent years, shown in Table 15.1.

Table 15.1

	Million licensed vehicles
1947	3.4
1952	4.9
1957	7.5
1962	10.6
1967	14.1
1972	16.0
1973	17.0

(Source: Annual Abstract of Statistics)

Further, even though estimates of how traffic is likely to increase between certain towns now exist, the time taken to improve or cut new roads is very long. Consider for example what is implied in straightening and widening an existing road: first the new route has to be surveyed to see how much land is required; and where it could be acquired without having to demolish too many buildings; secondly an estimate of the total cost involved has to be prepared and approved; thirdly negotiations involving legal proceedings have to be undertaken so that people whose land has been acquired for the road improvements are properly compensated. If many landowners object to the scheme, these proceedings can take a very long time; fourthly, plans have to be made for re-routing existing traffic or making temporary roads whilst the contractors are working on the road; fifthly all the services following the road: sewage, drainage, communications, gas pipes, electric cables, etc have to be displaced; sixthly the foundations and surfacing of the new road have to be laid. It is easy to see why road improvements often take so long to put into effect even though everyone has agreed upon the need for such improvements for a long time.

One of the eternal problems of traffic engineering is a kind of vicious circle, brought about by people reacting to road improvements by using the improved road more than it was used before. For example, the London to Portsmouth road (A3) crosses the south-western suburbs of London through Wimbledon, Kingston-upon-Thames until it reaches Esher (see Fig. 15.2). Originally this road passed through the centre of Kingston-upon-Thames. During the 1930s traffic increased to such an extent that an attempt to remove congestion from Kingston was made by building a by-pass which branched off from the old road at the Robinhood roundabout and rejoined it at the Scilly Isles roundabout. At that time most of the area through which the by-pass was cut was open country. Unfortunately, there was then little control over the building of private houses, and one effect of the new by-pass was to attract builders to set up new housing estates along the by-pass and near it (Fig. 15.3). This is known as *ribbon development*. Today such *ribbon development* is not possible owing to the Town and Country Planning laws which discourage the extension of housing along main roads. Such laws were passed to prevent the difficulties which arise when *ribbon*

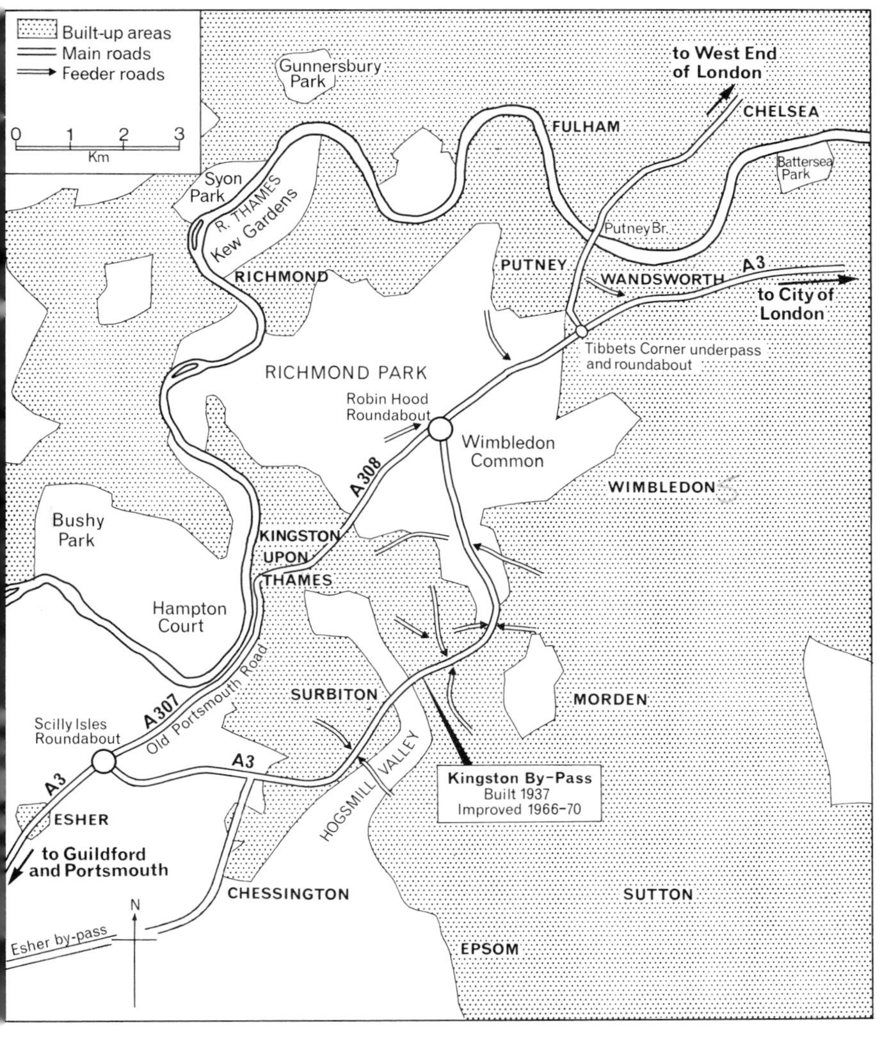

Fig. 15.2 The Kingston By-pass

Fig. 15.3 Ribbon development along the Kingston By-pass (A3)

development occurs. For not only is *ribbon development* unpleasant for those driving along the roads, not only does it increase the risk of accidents, but by making the by-pass a road used by people in the local housing estates for travelling to work and for local journeys, the by-pass soon becomes as congested as the road it was meant to relieve.

Thus the A3 Kingston by-pass, in the 1950s, was being used by long distance traffic, by people doing local journeys for example between Kingston and Morden, and by all suburban dwellers who travelled to work in London by car. As a result it became hopelessly over-crowded, especially at certain times of the day, and at road crossings and junctions. Consequently in the late 1960s certain improvements were made to the Kingston by-pass section of the A3 involving widening certain stretches to convert them to dual carriageways and the construction of bridges, underpasses and overpasses to prevent congestion at road intersections (Fig. 15.4). This improvement may have solved the problem of traffic flow along this particular section of the A3 for the time being. But what happens when all the cars and trucks arrive into the Wandsworth area? Traffic jams once more. The effect of clearing congestion along one stretch of road is often to shift it along to the next stretch of unimproved road. Thus traffic jams will not disappear until such times as our road 'arteries' are all large enough and numerous enough to take all the cars and lorries likely to use them. But this, as we have seen, is a long and expensive enterprise. It is also possible, that unless measures are taken to discourage people from using their cars for commuting, traffic will always expand to fill the roads to capacity.

Fig. 15.4 The overpass at Shannon Corner on the A3 near Raynes Park

B. The Road Network: one solution

When in 1953 the Government of Great Britain finally decided that more resources should be devoted to improving our road network, it was clear that just improving existing roads would not be enough. So a decision was taken to plan a series of motorways, linking the main conurbations of Great Britain. These motorways, now partly in existence, were conceived as fast roads mainly for through traffic. The main differences therefore between a motorway and an ordinary trunk road are that motorways:

1. Are limited to motor traffic.
2. Have dual carriageways with at least two lanes but often three per carriageway.
3. Have a limited number of access points; in other words, most roads which cross a motorway usually go under or over the motorway.
4. Have access points specially designed to enable traffic to leave or enter the motorway without disturbing the flow of traffic along the motorway (see Fig. 15.5).
5. Have no buildings along their flanks except at special points where petrol pumps, restaurants, toilets and other services are provided as shown in Fig. 15.6.
6. Have no steep gradients and no sharp bends.

The motorways of Great Britain have been designed around six major trunk motorways – linking

(a) London, the Midlands and the north-east (M1)
London and Dover (M2)
London and Exeter (M3)
London and South Wales (M4)

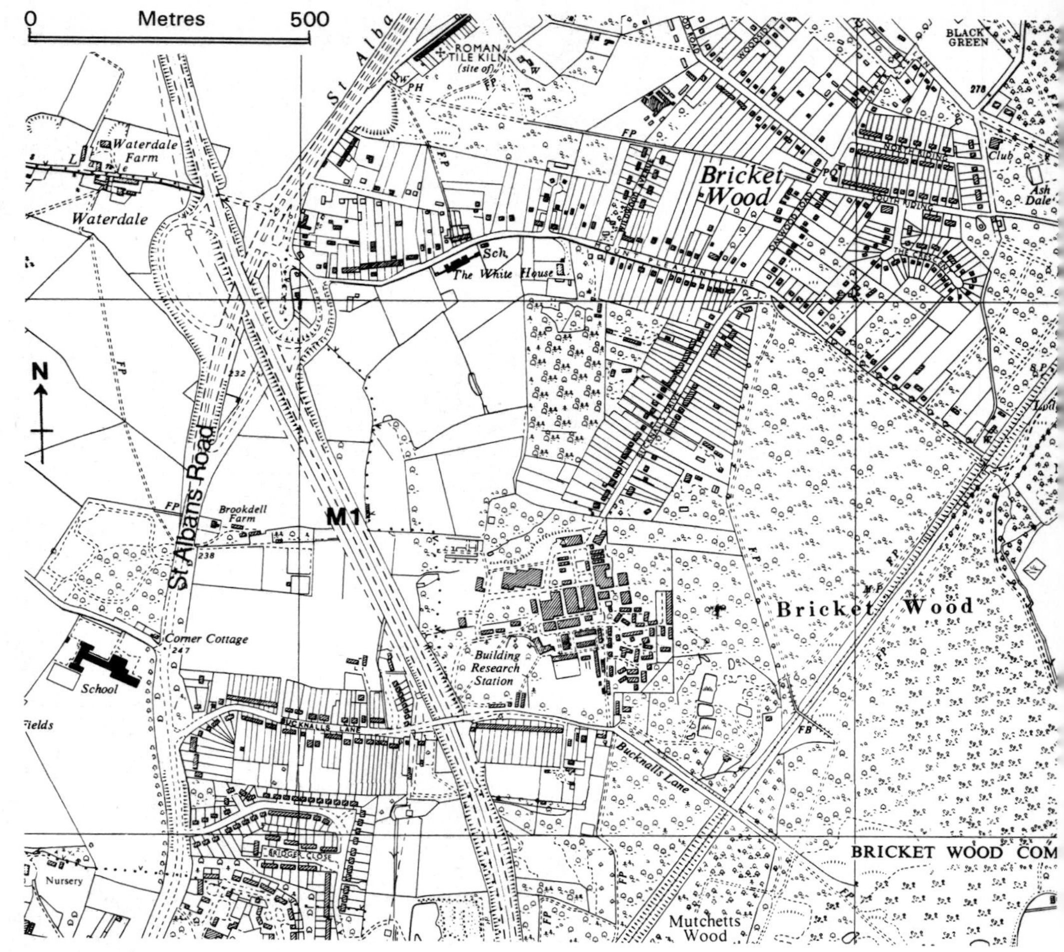

Fig. 15.5
A motorway intersection

(b) Birmingham and the north-west (M6)
Birmingham and the south-west (M5)

All other motorways built as spurs to main motorways or as supplementary motorways are labelled in double figures. For example the spur from the (M5) to south Wales is the M50, the London to Brighton motorway (between the M2 and M3) is to be called the M23.

The present extent of motorways in Great Britain is shown in Fig. 15.7.

Although it was intended that about 1,600 kilometres of motorway would be open to traffic by 1970, this was not realized until 1972 owing to lack of resources which have led to a cutting down of new road building. On the other hand, many ordinary trunk roads like the A1 have been so considerably improved that travelling along them is very much faster than it was in the 1950s. Thus in general the combined road improvements and motorway building have resulted in inter-city road transport being more efficient today than it was ten years ago.

Building a motorway has its problems and many people are incon-

Fig. 15.6
A motorway service centre

venienced. The following extract from *The Times** illustrates this in the case of the M4.

'This 11 mile stretch of the M4 (see Fig. 15.12) to the south of Swindon has brought its crop of attendant problems to the neighbourhood. At Chiseldon, just off the Marlborough road, it has cut a tomato farm in two and put six people out of work. At Wroughton, on the Devizes road, tractors brushing mud from the road have caused a traffic jam which on one notable occasion stretched for more than a mile and lasted two hours.

'At Badbury, also off the Marlborough road, the village has been halved and the residents are so incensed by the division, the noise, the mess, and the danger from lorries in country lanes that they have formed an association to look after their interests. The chairman, Mr Roland Champagne, a Swindon estate agent, said: "It has been hell.

* *The Times*, Dec. 2, 1969.

They even work in the evening under floodlights and a water pump goes on all night, keeping us all awake. The other morning I found my eight-year-old daughter sleeping with a pillow over her head to try to shut out the noise."

'People in Lower Badbury have to make a detour of nearly a mile to drive to the village shops. "The road is driving us all potty", Mr Champagne said. On the other hand the road has helped Swindon's unemployment situation – even to the extent of worrying some farmers whose workers have in some cases "swung over" in search of more money.

' "We like to get farmworkers because they are usually very strong, healthy, and used to being out of doors", a spokesman for the consulting engineers, Sir Alexander Gibb and Partners, said. The motorway has brought more trade to the town. There are 280 men here working seven days a week in the summer season so that in some places the work is several months up on schedule. "The rainy season", as they romantically call it, has cut them back a bit".'

1. *(a) Why were most of the roads in Great Britain not suitable for fast motor transport when they began to be used by motor-cars?*
   (b) Why had there been little incentive to straighten and widen roads in the 19th century?
2. *(a) What does the course of the A12 road in Fig. 15.1 illustrate about many British roads?*
   (b) Suggest why the road gradually gets further away from the coast south of Lowestoft.
3. *Explain*
   (a) Why insufficient work was originally done to improve the roads in Britain and fit them to the traffic likely to develop on them?
   (b) Why progress in road improvement is very slow?
4. *Name a road in your locality which requires improvement and state*
   (a) why it needs improving
   (b) what difficulties lie in the way of improving it.
5.* *(a) Suppose you had to estimate by how much traffic would increase in the next ten years along a road between two towns, what sort of factors would you have to take into account? In your answer mention such things as (i) past growth in traffic (ii) population growth in the towns (iii) number of feeder roads and their origin (iv) industrial development.*
   (b) (i) what has been the rate of growth in number of licensed vehicles for every five years since 1947?
   (ii) estimate what the rate of growth might be between 1972 and 1977.
6. *(a) What is the purpose of a by-pass such as the Kingston by-pass?*
   (b) Why did the building of by-passes before 1940 only solve the traffic problem for a short time?
7. *(a) Using information in the text and Fig. 15.3 describe what is meant by* ribbon development.
   (b) Why is ribbon development *not possible today?*

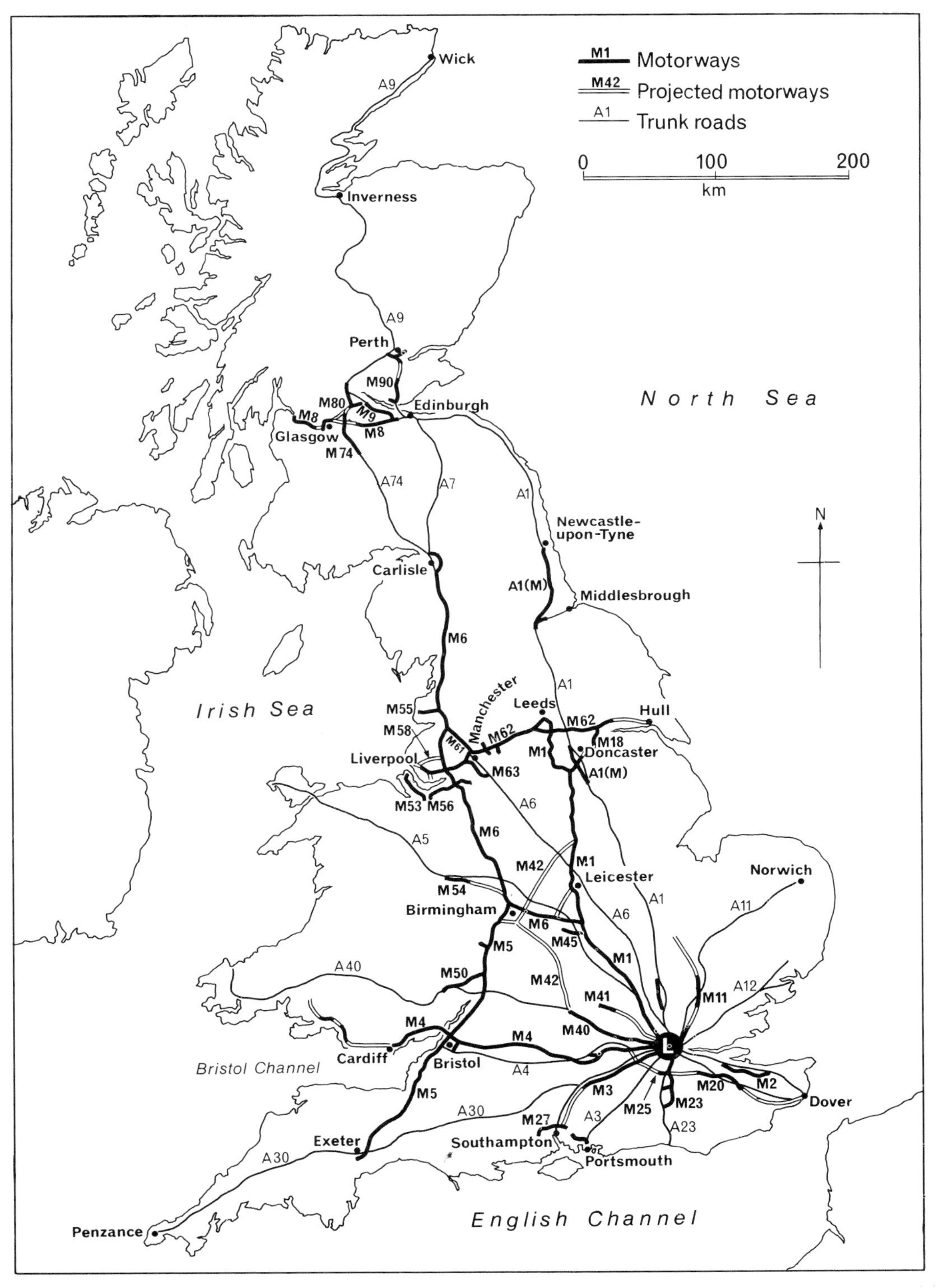

Fig. 15.7 The motorway system

8. *(a) What measures are taken to overcome congestion at road crossings such as on the A3 near Raynes Park? (Fig. 15.4.)*
   (b) (i) why is it often said that improving one stretch of road merely shifts the traffic jams to another section of the road?
   *(ii) * does this mean that it is useless improving one stretch of road unless the whole road can be improved?*
   (c) Improving and widening the Kingston by-pass section of the A3 was enormously costly. From the text and from Fig. 15.2, suggest why this was so. Would it have been so costly had the major Town and Country Planning laws been passed before instead of after the 1939–45 war? Give reasons for your answer.
   (d) Why is the built up area in Fig. 15.2 not continuous?
9. *(a) In what ways are motorways designed to make possible a smooth uninterrupted flow of traffic?*
   (b) Study Fig. 15.5 and describe the movements of a car
   (i) whose driver is travelling north along the M1 and wishes to leave it to go south along the St Alban's road.
   (ii) whose driver travelling north along the St Alban's road wishes to join the south-bound carriageway of the M1.
   *(c) * Draw a map to show how two motorways may merge so that cars may enter or leave each motorway without crossing each other's paths on the same level.*
   (d) Describe the layout of the motorway services in Fig. 15.6.
10. *(a) Suggest, in view of what we learn in Chapter 10 on the distribution of industry in Great Britain, why the first important motorways to be built were the M1 and M6? (See Fig. 15.7.)*
   (b) Compare Fig. 15.7 with an atlas map of Great Britain showing relief and towns and explain why:
   (i) the Lancashire to Yorkshire Motorway (Manchester to Leeds) proved difficult to construct
   (ii) the link between the M6 and M1 took a long time to complete
   (iii) certain short stretches of motorway have been built e.g. west of Middlesbrough along the A1, along the A2 and along the A20.
   (c) When the M3 eventually stretches to Exeter it may be considerably under used except during part of the year. Suggest why.
   (d) Why are there no immediate plans for motorways in central Wales and northern Scotland?

C. The Railways

Great Britain was the first country to develop its railway system in the 19th century and to help other countries to develop theirs. At that time, once people came to accept speedy transport on rails, the railways became very popular. There were no other means of transport on land which could compete with the attraction of railways: no motorised road transport and no air transport. As a result, more and more railways were built, mostly as a substitute for roads. For example Fig. 15.1, shows how the railway connecting Ipswich and Lowestoft goes through the same villages for a good deal of the way as the A12 road. No one at that time could foresee that road transport by car and lorry would develop as it has done in the 20th century. But enthusiasm for railways was so great that many railway companies duplicated lines already built by other companies. Here are two examples:

1. London to Scotland; there were three possible routes:
   (a) eastern route through Peterborough, York, Newcastle and Berwick
   (b) Midland route through Leicester, Leeds and Carlisle
   (c) western route through Rugby, Crewe, Preston and Carlisle
2. London to Exeter; there were two possible routes:
   (a) via Reading, Newbury, Westbury and Taunton
   (b) via Basingstoke, Salisbury and Yeovil

Figure 15.8 gives some indication in diagrammatic form of the extent of this duplication of tracks as it existed in 1964. It could not be said that such duplication was unnecessary if all tracks were being fully used, but in fact this was certainly not the case in the

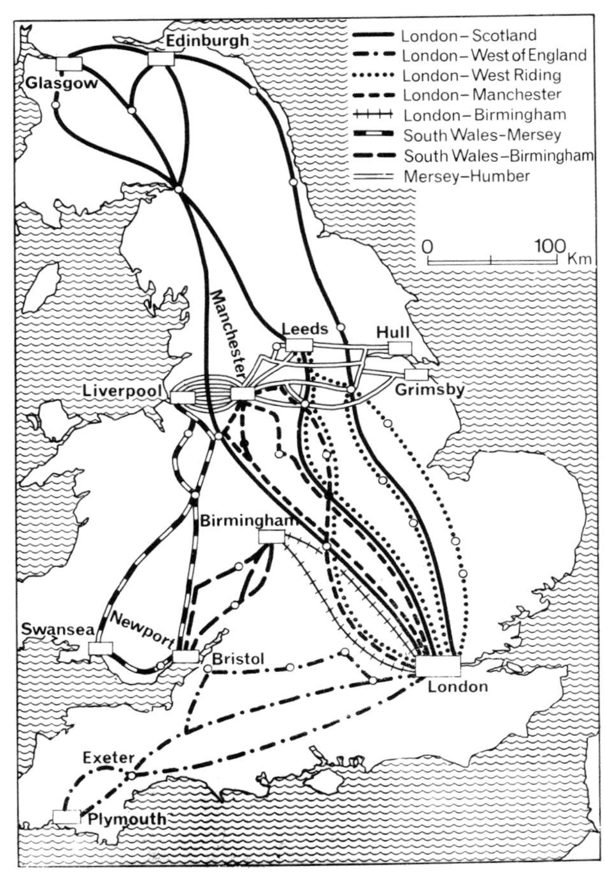

Fig. 15.8 Duplication of rail routes

second half of the 20th century. Consequently the railway authorities were having to maintain tracks, stations and signalling equipment along little used stretches of line. This was very costly and was one reason why the railways could not make any profit, but in fact made heavy losses. The other reason was, of course, the fact that road transport became very popular for carrying passengers and goods. Table 15.2 shows an estimate for the distribution of passenger kilometres among the various forms of transport. A passenger kilometre is a unit formed by multiplying the number of passengers travelling by the number of kilometres they have travelled. For example:

20 passengers travelling 10 kilometres produce 200 passenger kilometres

1 passenger travelling 200 kilometres produces 200 passenger kilometres

Table 15.2

Method of Transport	Passenger kilometres in thousand millions for 1973 in Great Britain
Air	2.4 (includes Northern Ireland and Channel Islands)
Rail	35.0
Road	
Public vehicles	54.1
Private vehicles	357.6
Total	449.1

(Source: Annual Abstract of Statistics.)

Table 15.3 makes the same comparison for goods in tonne-kilometres.

Table 15.3

Method of Transport	Goods transported in thousand million tonne-kilometres for 1973 in Great Britain
Road	89.6
Rail	25.0
Coastal shipping	20.2
Inland waterway	0.2
Pipe lines	3.4
Total	138.4

(Source: Annual Abstract of Statistics).

These tables seem to indicate that there is no point in maintaining a vast railway network which may be little used. But why is road transport apparently so attractive both for passengers and goods? The answer can probably be given in one word: flexibility. In the case of goods, they need only be loaded and unloaded once – at the beginning and end of the journey, if they are taken by road. However, if taken by rail, they will at least have to be loaded and unloaded twice unless there are railway sidings at the sending and receiving end which applies only in a few cases. For passengers the advantages of road transport by private car are very obvious especially for cross country journeys.

We might then ask whether there are any advantages in using the

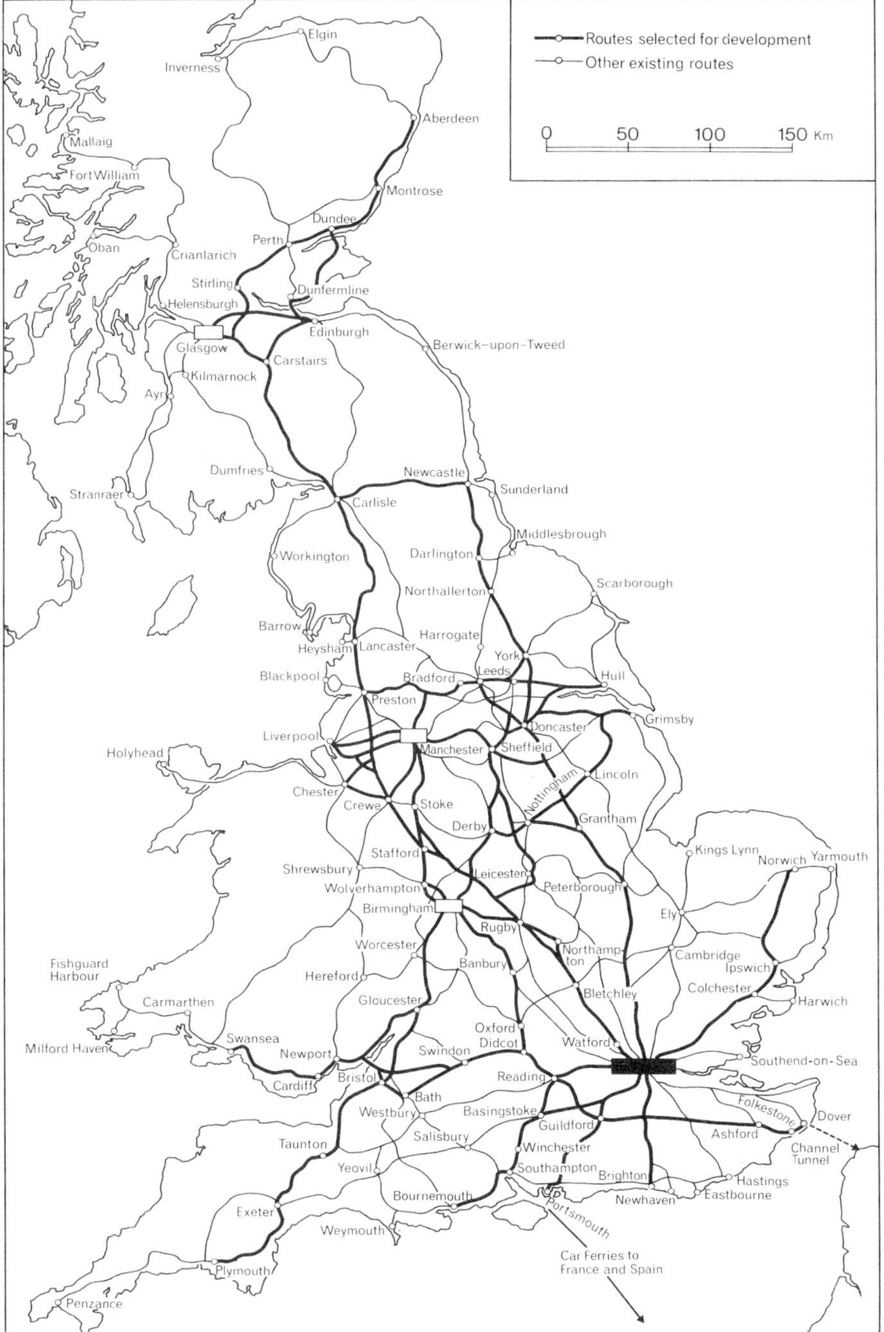

Fig. 15.9 Railway Development

railways at all. It is largely when long distances are involved that the railways offer the advantage of higher speed and therefore shorter time in delivery. With long distance transport, time spent in loading and unloading at both ends of the line does not seem so important.

It is because of the relative advantage of railways in dealing with fast long distance traffic, that the British Railway authorities decided to concentrate on using and modernizing a few selected railway routes and gradually closing or limiting services on the others. These selected railway routes are shown on Fig. 15.9.

The process of closing little-used tracks began among the thousands of kilometres of small branch lines. This caused some difficulties for some people; for certain villages were left with no public transport and not everyone has a private car. Thus in certain cases additional bus services had to be run.

The process of modernization on the railways has involved:

1. Improvement of tracks and signalling (electric lights instead of semaphore signals).
2. The electrification of certain heavily used lines, such as the London – Manchester – Liverpool lines.
3. The introduction of new carriages and waggons and of powerful electric, diesel-electric and diesel-hydraulic locomotives.
4. The improvement of freight handling facilities so that quick loading and unloading may take place. For example, the freightliner service illustrated in Fig. 15.10 (a) & (b) enables ready packed containers to be easily loaded and unloaded from lorry to railway truck, and to travel by a regular scheduled train to certain specified destinations. Containers may hold solids, liquids or gas and be insulated for goods requiring a controlled temperature. The routes on which freightliners run are shown in Fig. 15.11.

All plans for modernization have to be based on estimates of how the British economy will change in the years to come. Thus the railway planners assumed the following changes between 1964 and 1984 in the U.K.:

1. That population would increase from 54.2 m. to 62.5 m.
2. That the Gross National Income would rise from £28,000 m. to £51,000 m. (1964 prices).
3. That industrial output would rise from £12,000 m. to £25,000 m. (1964 prices).
4. That electric power generation would rise from 145,000 m. kilowatts to 390,000 m. kilowatts.
5. That steel production would rise from 26 m. tonnes to 38 m. tonnes.
6. That car ownership would rise from 8 m. vehicles to 19 m. vehicles.

On these assumptions Table 15.4 compares freight and passenger traffic as it was in 1964 with what British Rail hope it will be in 1984. All these figures also assume that there will be no radical alteration in the distribution of population and industry in the U.K. Experiments are also going on with trains capable of speeds of over 160 kph – the 'Advanced Passenger Trains' – to make intercity transport rapid and attractive.

11. *Why was there such a dense network of railways in Great Britain at the beginning of the 20th century?*

Fig. 15.10(a) Freightliner container being loaded

Fig. 15.10(b) Freightliner container and lorry

Fig. 15.11 The freightliner routes

Table 15.4

Type of traffic	Million tonnes or Passenger kilometres/year 1964	Million Tonnes or Passenger kilometres/year 1984
Coal	7,200	5,600
Iron and Steel	4,000	6,400
Oil	800	3,200
Other freight	7,200	24,000
Passengers	8,000	7,200

12. (a) (i) state between which towns the duplication of railway tracks occurred in Great Britain in the 19th century. (See Fig. 15.8.)
    (ii) how did this duplication arise?
    (b) Explain why this duplication was wasteful.
13. What do Tables 15.2 and 15.3 tell you about
    (a) the relative importance of road and rail transport today (i) for passengers (ii) for goods.
    (b) the ratio of goods travelling by inland waterways and by coastal shipping. What do you conclude about our inland waterways?
14. Explain what a ton-kilometre is.
15. (a) Make a table to compare the advantages and disadvantages of road and rail transport (i) for passengers (ii) for goods. Begin as shown below:

Passengers		Goods	
Road	Rail	Road	Rail
1. Door to door transport	1. Need to change to another form of transport	1.	
2. Relatively slow for very long journeys	2. Fast for long journeys	2.	
3. Tiring for driver	3. Passenger does not drive!	3.	

    (b) Describe (i) how the freightliner service works (see Fig. 15.10) (ii) between which centres freightliner services operate (see Fig. 15.11).
16. Why are British Rail concentrating on developing a few long distance trunk routes?
17. The Liverpool to London route is electrified, but the Exeter to London route uses diesel engine to pull trains. Why was the Exeter to London line not electrified?
18.* Study Fig. 15.9 and
    (a) suggest what is expected to happen to the port of Southampton as the Southampton – Winchester – Reading – Didcot – Birmingham line is being improved.
    (b) given that petroleum refineries are developing along the Solent what type of freight may increase along this line?
    (c) What sort of products might be carried from Birmingham to Southampton? (See Chapter 6)

(d) *Which way would a Birmingham to France train be routed assuming the Channel Tunnel were constructed?*

19. *Study Table 15.4 and the text carefully and*
   (a) *suggest why coal and passenger traffic are expected to decline between 1964 and 1984.*
   (b) *Which type of traffic is likely to have the greatest proportional increase?*

20. (a) *Why is it stated in the text that the plans made by British Rail 'assume that there will be no radical alteration in the distribution of population and industry in the U.K.'?*
   (b) (i) *what would British Rail have to do if it were decided to found a city of 250,000 people near Fort William? (See Fig. 15.9)*
   (ii) *why is this unlikely?*
   (c) *Would it be advisable to close commuter railway lines around London if these proved unprofitable? Give reasons for your answer.*

Conclusion

In this chapter we have examined the pattern of Great Britain's road and railway network and seen some of the problems faced by both. In particular we have learnt how Britain's roads from being ill-adapted to 20th century motor transport are gradually being modernized especially with the development of motorways both inter-city and urban. Of Britain's railways, we have noted how from being the only form of rapid transport available in the 19th century they have come under severe competition from motor roads and from air transport. With growing knowledge about future trends in the economy it would seem that the best solution is co-operation so that roads and railways help to provide the best transport service. Like everything else, it is easier said than done!

REVISION EXERCISES

21. (a) ***If you could choose between the various methods shown on page 6 of getting to a continental holiday resort, which one would you choose and why?***
   (b) ***Starting from your home town indicate your route by listing about six main towns you would pass through if you were going by surface transport most of the way.***

22.* ***The railways have been loosing money for many years. This money has been made up by taxing people more. Does this mean that if we closed all the railways we should all be better off because we would have slightly lower taxes to pay? Give reasons for your answer.***

23. ***Why are roads and railways sometimes called the arteries of trade?***

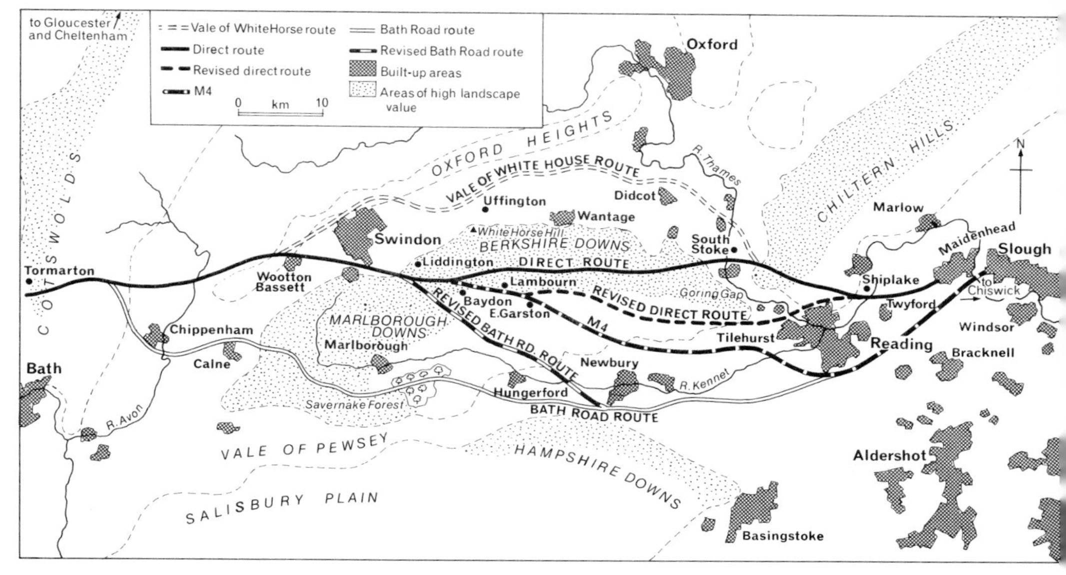

Fig. 15.12
The M4

24. ***(a)*** ***Choosing an appropriate route for a motorway whose two ends are known is a difficult task. Fig. 15.12 shows various routes for the M4 suggested in 1963. Explain as far as you can the advantages and disadvantages of***
(i) The Vale of White Horse Route
(ii) The Direct Route
(iii) The Bath Road Route.
Bear in mind the influence of relief, of towns near the route and of the total length of the road.
(b) Find out which route was in fact chosen (e.g. from an AA Book).
(c) What problems face those people who are living in the area through which a motorway is built?

25. ***If a lorry carrying goods which it was necessary to deliver to London as quickly as possible were to start from Newcastle-upon-Tyne, which way would you route the driver? (See Fig. 15.7.)***

26.* ***Design an access point for a motorway so that a road joins a north to south motorway from the west. Remember that traffic coming onto or off the motorway must not disturb traffic on the motorway.***

27. ***Write a short essay describing how relief has influenced the road and railway networks in Great Britain.***

28. ***Bad weather conditions tend to influence traffic on the railways less than on the roads. Suggest reasons for this.***

29. ***A former to bring the M1 into north London to join a new urban motorway is shown in Fig. 15.13.***
(a) Is it important to have urban as well as inter-city motorways?
(b) The 30 kilometre stretch it is proposed to build will cost £250 m. This compares with an average cost of £0.6 m per

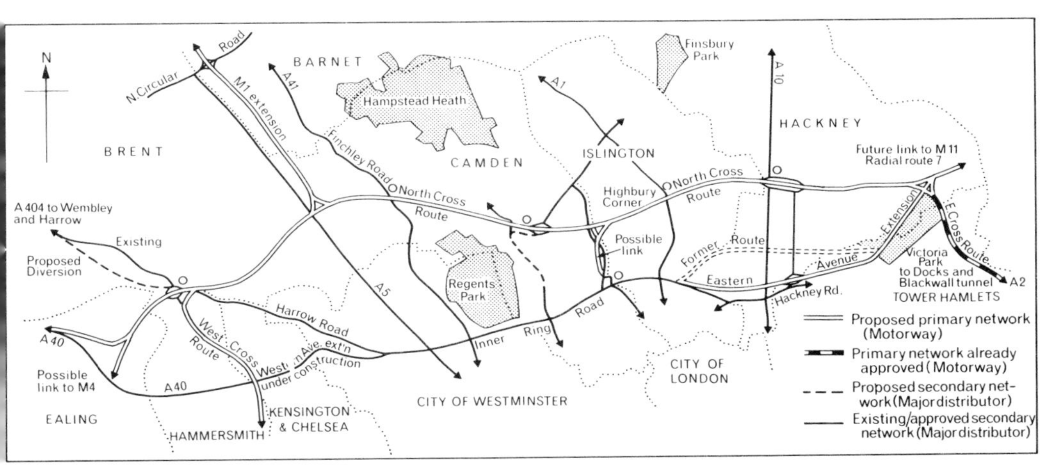

Fig. 15.13 Motorway plans in North London

kilometre for inter-city motorways. Why is the cost so much higher?

(c) ***Much of the urban motorway linking east to west across north London could be built next to railways. Can you suggest why it would be convenient to do this in such an area?***

(d) ***A good deal of the area through which this motorway will be cut was built up in the 19th century. On the whole do you think this is an advantage or not? Give reasons for your answer.***

(e) ***Urban motorways are often stated to be 'damaging to the environment'. What is implied by this?***

(f) ***The plans for the North and West Cross routes have been abandoned. Can you suggest why?***

Chapter Sixteen

Air Transport and Airports

A. Saving time

You do not need to be told that air transport has effectively shortened the *time-distance* between any two places. With the *Concorde* in operation it is possible to go from London to New York in three hours. But what about the use of aircraft within the British Isles? The following two experiences which happened to one of the authors will illustrate some of the advantages and disadvantages.

When I was living in Liverpool, it was occasionally necessary for me to spend a day in central London. I happened to live close to Speke Airport and it was possible for me to rise at 07.00 hrs, be on the 08.00 hrs airplane (Viscount) which reached London airport at 08.45 hrs and then travel to central London by coach and tube to reach it by 09.30 hrs – no later than many suburban dwellers reach their offices. It was also possible to catch an evening plane back to Liverpool and be home for dinner.

On another occasion, this time when I was living in London, I had cause to go to Edinburgh in June, but decided to travel by air to Newcastle in order to call on some friends and to travel on to Edinburgh the next day by train. The flight to Newcastle was due to leave at 10.00 hrs and to land at Newcastle airport approximately one hour later. At 13.00 hrs we were still waiting to take off because Newcastle airport was fogbound, although in London the weather was fine. At 14.00 hrs conditions had sufficiently cleared to enable the aircraft to leave. By 15.00 hrs we were over Newcastle, but by that time the fog had returned to the airport. The pilot decided to 'hold it' by circling over the airport in the hope that the fog would clear. The plane circled for nearly one hour and a quarter before the pilot decided regretfully that he could not land. We therefore flew south-westwards and landed at Manchester airport. Coaches were then used to take the passengers from Manchester to Newcastle where we arrived at 23.00 hrs . . . 12 hours late!

Clearly, air travel even within the British Isles can be a great boon. When one is travelling for business reasons rather than for pleasure, any cutting down of time spent in going from one place to another is to be welcomed, even if the saving is in the order of a few hours. But the shorter the distance between two points the greater is the risk that abnormal weather conditions at either end will completely cancel out the time saving advantage of going by air. For example, in the second experience quoted above, it would have been far quicker for me to travel by car, since the fog was a local 'sea fret' which had crept over the Northumberland coast. Similarly, if the travelling time from the airport to city centre is long, then this may well diminish the advantage of travelling by air. Since the electrification of the Manchester to London and Liverpool to London railway lines which has cut travelling time from city centre to city centre to approximately $2\frac{3}{4}$ hours, the relative advantage of going by air is small given the time taken to get to the airports at either end.

B. The growth in air traffic and the nature of air routes

Nevertheless the amount of domestic traffic has grown substantially in recent years as shown in Table 16.1.

The air routes used over the United Kingdom are shown in the map on Fig. 16.1. Not all these air routes are of equal importance. The routes from London to Edinburgh and London to Belfast have far more traffic than the routes from Newcastle to Belfast or from Manchester to Bristol. On some routes, the traffic is very light, for instance between Glasgow (Renfrew) airport and Stornoway, or on the Services to the Shetland islands. Some are very busy in summer only, as on the routes from London or Birmingham to the Channel Islands.

The pattern of the air routes depends partly on the position of the airports, but also on the position of the various radio beacons which are used by the pilots to help them navigate their aircraft. A B.A. jet aircraft flying from London to Glasgow will tend to fly in a series of straight lines from one radio beacon to the next. Thus instead of flying in a straight line from London to Glasgow, the course of the aircraft will appear as a series of minor zig-zags. There are two reasons for this. First most aircraft fly above cloud and frequently fly at night when navigation with reference to surface features would be impossible. Consequently pilots have radio equipment which enables them to set the aircraft on a course between two radio beacons. Secondly in an area like the British Isles where the density of domestic and international air traffic is very high, it is necessary to know exactly where each aircraft is at any given time. Consequently pilots are given, before take off, a flight plan in which they are told along which airlane they are to fly and at what altitude. The airlanes are 16 kilometres wide and 8,000 metres high and different aircraft are set at different altitudes to prevent collisions. When an aircraft is close to an airport, the airport control is responsible for directing the movements of the aircraft until it lands. Around important airports, however, large areas are under the guidance of 'approach control'. These are the flight control zones shown on Fig. 16.1.

C. Physical conditions affecting air traffic

In the U.K. physical factors are not overwhelmingly important in influencing air traffic. If we consider relief, we must admit that most of our so-called 'mountains' are much too low to be a great hindrance to aircraft flying at heights up to 10,000 metres. This is illustrated in

Table 16.1 U.K. airways – Operations and traffic on scheduled services

	1964	1965	1966	1967	1968	1969	1970	1971	1972	1973
Aircraft Stage Flights Number	127,581	129,594	140,649	143,932	138,021	151,145	151,506	149,839	158,698	172,636
Average length in kilometres	265	268	281	290	290	258	264	272	281	284
Aircraft kilometres flown (000)	33,872	35,024	39,640	42,738	39,974	38,946	39,692	40,656	44,539	49,079
Number of passengers carried (000)	4,216	4,669	5,122	5,314	5,041	5,159	5,366	5,367	5,890	6,513
Passenger kilometres flown (000)	1,612,000	1,672,000	1,832,000	1,930,000	1,859,000	1,897,000	1,980,000	1,960,395	2,166,984	2,441,211
Cargo carried (tonnes)	43,218	54,314	77,143	73,907	79,204	78,774	64,661	58,490	72,343	79,162
Freight carried in tonne kilometres (000)	11,202	14,847	22,110	22,766	25,931	25,486	19,822	17,634	21,755	24,690

(Source: Annual Abstract of Statistics)

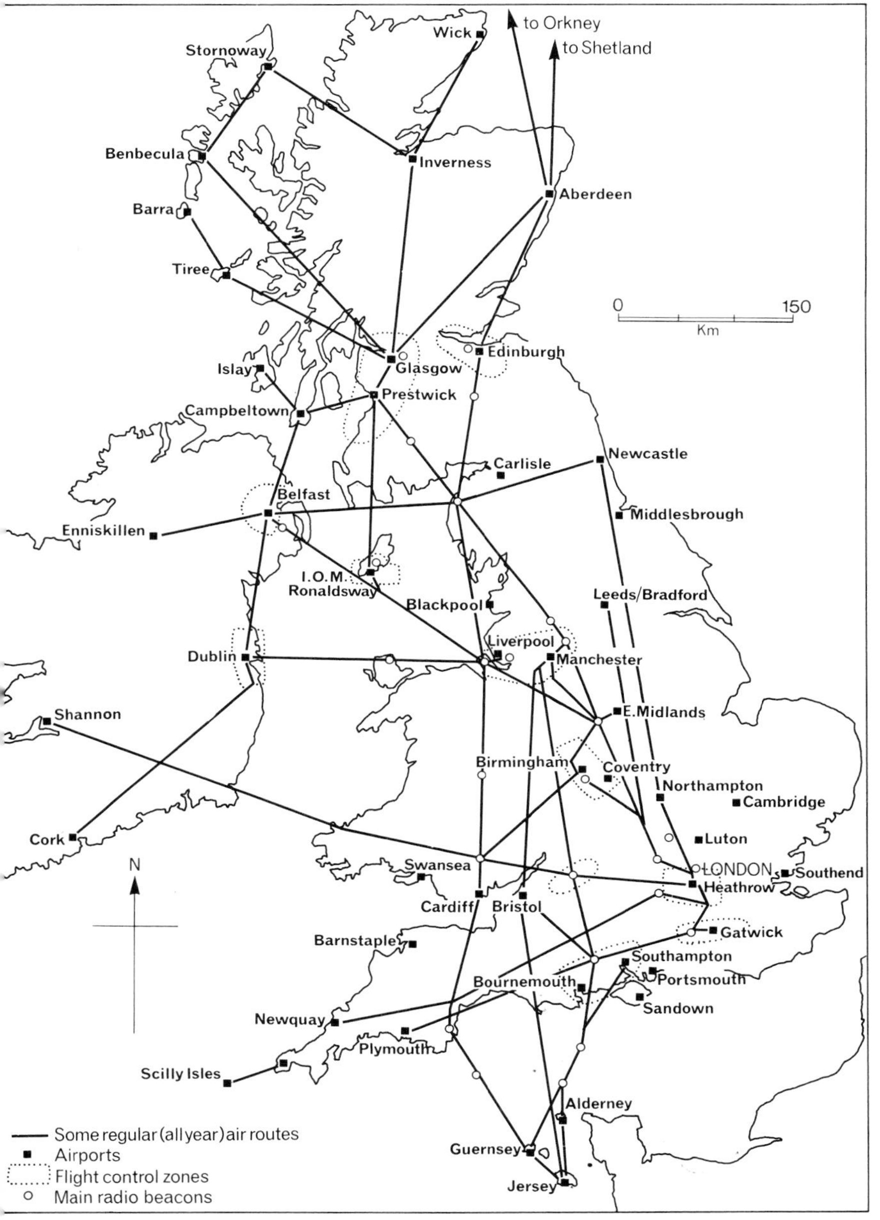

Fig. 16.1 United Kingdom air routes

Fig. 16.2. Only if an airport were sited close to a mountain would the relief constitute a great hazard to aircraft coming in to land. In fact, however, airports in Britain are near large towns and these are not to be found in highland areas. Even in Scotland the large towns are in the lowland and not in the highland zone. Small airfields are sometimes found in valleys in highland areas, but these are only used by smaller aircraft needing less room to manoeuvre.

The weather in Britain is more of a hazard than the relief. It is not so much the weather that pilots encounter when flying, for they

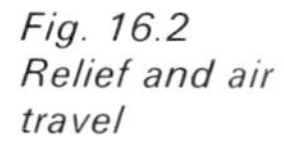

Fig. 16.2
Relief and air travel

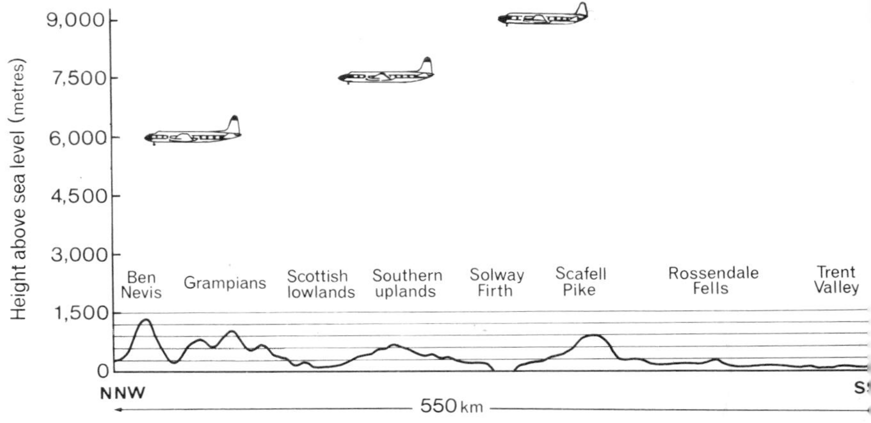

can usually fly above the clouds and fog and they can avoid storm clouds by flying round them. It is the weather when taking off and when landing which affects aircraft and in particular, fog and poor visibility, and snow. Although great progress has been made with automatic landing equipment, most aircraft are still landed by their pilots who rely on their eyesight to put down one hundred tonnes or more of 'ironmongery' as gently as possible on the runway. Consequently any weather conditions which limit visibility tend to prevent aircraft from landing.

Fog. Most foreigners who have never travelled to these islands tend to think of Britain as a land shrouded in mist and fog. The map in Fig. 16.3 shows that this is a much exaggerated view of the climate

Fig. 16.3
Average year: days of fog

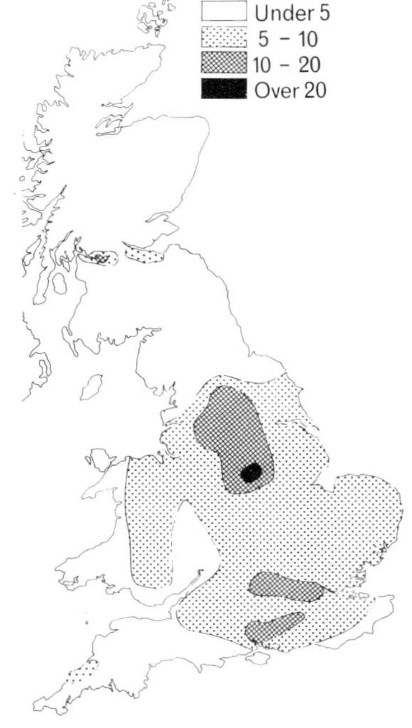

of Britain today. Most places in Britain have on an average fewer than five days of thick fog each year. You will notice that in this respect southern Britain is worse off than northern Britain. The map only refers to thick fog. There are many more days when mist or thin fog lies over Britain.

What is fog? Basically it is condensed water vapour lying in the atmosphere close to the ground. It is the millions of water droplets in the air which reduce visibility. Sometimes the condensed water vapour is associated with particles of soot dust and other materials which pollute the atmosphere especially in or near industrial cities. In this case visibility is still further reduced and we have *smog*. *Smog* is becoming rarer in industrial Britain because of the setting up of smokeless zones in towns where people must either use smokeless fuels or electrical energy for heating purposes.

Fig. 16.4 shows a weather map in which for a change fog is shown over parts of France, West Germany and northern Italy, but not over

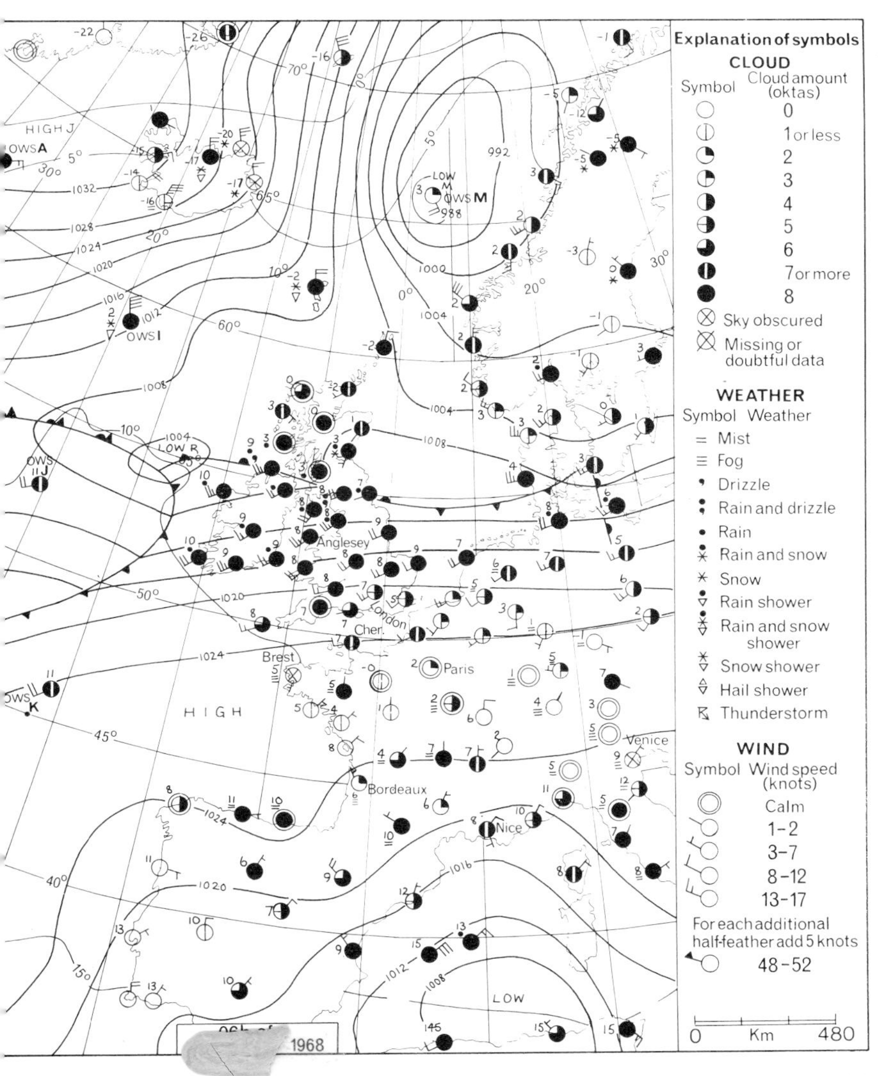

Fig. 16.4 North West Europe weather map

the British Isles. You will notice that the other differences between the weather in France and Britain are:

1. Winds are generally light or non-existent over France, but somewhat stronger over Britain.
2. Temperatures are in general slightly higher in southern Britain than in central France or West Germany.

Thus fog tends to exist where the air is calm or the winds light and when temperatures are relatively low. In fact if temperatures of the air several hundred metres above the surface of central France had been shown, you would have noticed that the temperatures were higher than at ground level. This condition, known as *temperature inversion* makes it very difficult for fog once formed to lift, as shown on Fig. 16.5.

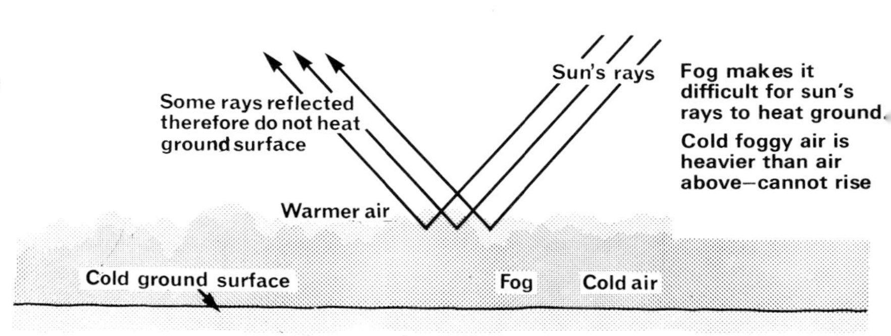

Fig. 16.5 Temperature inversion

The fog is formed in the first place because a mass of relatively humid but still air is cooled, usually at night when the ground becomes cold. It follows from this that fog is more common in the cooler rather than the warmer seasons and can only occur in relatively still air (usually 1 km per hour or less).

Now the fact that the air in the British Isles is not often still explains why, whatever others say about our climate, the number of foggy days in each year is relatively small, and the number of times that aircraft are prevented from landing is also relatively small.

There is, however, one further complication. Since cold foggy air tends to sink into low ground, fog is often unevenly distributed over even quite a small area. Motorists are familiar with the sort of condition on a cold winter's day when they seem to be continually driving in and out of fog.

1. (a) *Two travellers found themselves fogbound at London airport. One was travelling to Manchester, the other to Cape Town. The Manchester bound passenger decided to leave the airport and go by train, but the Cape Town passenger stayed on to wait for the fog to clear. What do you think influenced each traveller's decision?*

(b) Why would it not be worthwhile under present conditions to have regular passenger flights between London and Bristol or London and Norwich?

2. *Study Table 16.1.*
   (a) Roughly by what multiple has the number of aircraft kilometres increased between 1964/1973?
   (b) Why has the average length of aircraft stage flights not increased very much between 1964/1973?
   (c) Roughly by what multiple has the number of passengers increased between 1964/1973?
   (d) Approximately how many times has the number of passenger kilometres flown increased between 1964/1973?
   (e) What does the difference between your answer to (a) and (d) suggest?
3. *(a) Certain air routes are fairly popular with passengers although the distances are not great. e.g. Liverpool to Dublin, Liverpool to Belfast, Glasgow to Belfast. Can you suggest a reason for this?*
   (b) Certain routes have heavy summer traffic only. Which routes are they and state why the traffic is unevenly distributed throughout the year?
   (c) Some routes have very few passengers, but are considered essential. Give an example and explain why the routes are maintained despite the limited number of passengers.
4. *Study Fig. 16.1.*
   (a) What similarity do you find between the pattern of air routes shown in Fig. 16.1 and the maps of the distribution of industry shown in Chapter 10 and the maps of other forms of land transport shown in Chapter 15?
   (b) How can you explain the similarities you find?
   (c) What are 'flight control zones'? Why are there no such zones around airports such as those at Cardiff or Newcastle?
   (d) Why do aircraft not fly in a straight line between, for example, London and Edinburgh?
5. *(a) Why is the relief of Great Britain not a great hazard to aircraft? (Fig. 16.2.)*
   (b) When might relief cause difficulty for aircraft?
6. *(a) What type of weather gives most difficulty to aircraft pilots. State the reasons for this.*
   (b) (i) Describe the average distribution of thick fog over Great Britain. (Fig. 16.3.)
   (ii) What cities seem to have the greatest amount of fog per year on an average? (Compare Fig. 16.3 and an atlas map of Great Britain.)
   (iii) Why should cities be particularly susceptible to fog? (Water vapour needs particles around which to condense.)
   (iv) Can you suggest why the west coast of Britain is generally free of thick fog?
7. *(a) Describe carefully the conditions under which fog develops.*
   (b) What is meant by 'temperature inversion'*?*

Fig. 16.6 (facing page) Layout of London Airport

(c) *Why is it that once fog is established, if there is no wind it does not clear easily? (Fig. 16.5.)*

8. *Study Fig. 16.4*
   (a) (i) *What is the state of sky over Great Britain?*
   (ii) *Which has the greater cloud cover, northern or southern Britain? Where is it raining?*
   (b) *What is the speed of the wind in knots (i) over Anglesey (ii) over London (iii) over the Cherbourg Peninsula in France (iv) over Paris?*
   (c) (i) *If you had wanted to see the sun on April 1st, 1968, would you have had a better chance in London or Venice?*
   (ii) *Find another place where the sky was completely obscured.*
   (d) *Aircraft usually land facing the wind. In what direction would the nose of an aircraft have pointed which landed at (i) London airport (ii) Nice airport (iii) Paris airport?*
   (e) *Would you have expected that aircraft could land at Bordeaux airport in south-western France?*

D. Airport location

In a country like Britain, airport location is a great problem, not just because weather conditions are not as good, as for example in Egypt, but simply because finding the space for them is becoming increasingly difficult. You will notice from Fig. 1.3 that there appears to be a lot of open space left for airports in the British Isles, but if you think for a moment, you will notice that many empty areas are mountains or hills, and also that many empty areas are far from towns from which the passengers and the freight come. So one of the prime requirements of an airport site is that it should be reasonably near the town it is meant to serve.

The second main requirement is that there should be a large area of flat land, easily drained, and offering firm foundations for the runways. The speed and weight of modern jet aircraft make these requirements essential – Fig. 16.6 is a map showing the site of London airport (Heathrow) and Fig. 16.7 (a) an aerial photograph of this site. This site is on a fairly flat terrace underlain by gravels, which makes for good drainage and good foundations. The runways are, of course, built of several metres of concrete and other materials to withstand the impact of airliners on landing and when taxiing. The longest are about 3,300 metres long.

The number of runways provided depends on how much traffic the airport can expect. The position of the top twelve British airports is shown in Fig. 16.8.

The dominating position of London airport is evident, which is one reason why it has several parallel runways. Another reason for having more than one runway is that wind direction is not constant, and if possible aircraft try to land and take off facing the wind. In practice this is not always possible and most aircraft can stand a certain amount of crosswind. But in general the main runways will be aligned in the direction of the prevailing wind. Thus in the United

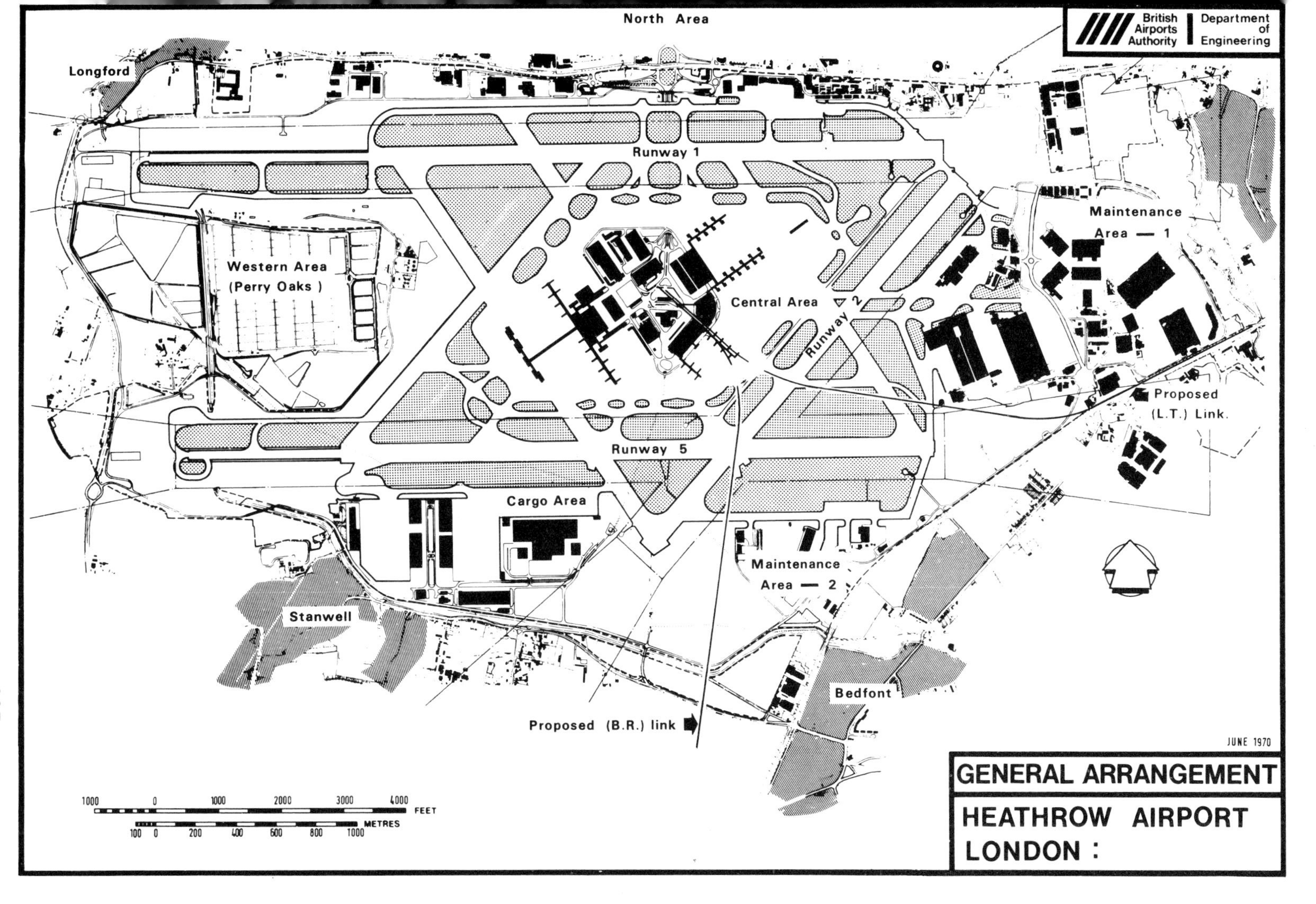
North Area
British Airports Authority
Department of Engineering
Longford
Runway 1
Western Area (Perry Oaks)
Central Area
Runway 2
Maintenance Area — 1
Proposed (L.T.) Link.
Runway 5
Cargo Area
Maintenance Area — 2
Stanwell
Bedfont
Proposed (B.R.) link
JUNE 1970
1000 0 1000 2000 3000 4000 FEET
100 0 200 400 600 800 1000 METRES
GENERAL ARRANGEMENT
HEATHROW AIRPORT
LONDON :

Kingdom, east-west runways may be used for 84 per cent of landings and take offs. Occasionally crosswinds may be too strong and the aircraft must either land on a different runway or at another airport.

London airport's (Fig. 16.6) parallel runways are arranged in such a way that the two longest are the east-west runways, since our prevailing winds are from the west, but there are also two north-west to south-east and two north-east to south-west runways. In such a case the service buildings need to be in the centre of the airport and are reached by an access road tunnel. The photograph in Fig. 16.7 (a) shows the two main east-west runways at the top and bottom, with an aircraft on the top (northern) runway. In the centre is the control tower building (Fig. 16.7(b)) with the various passenger handling

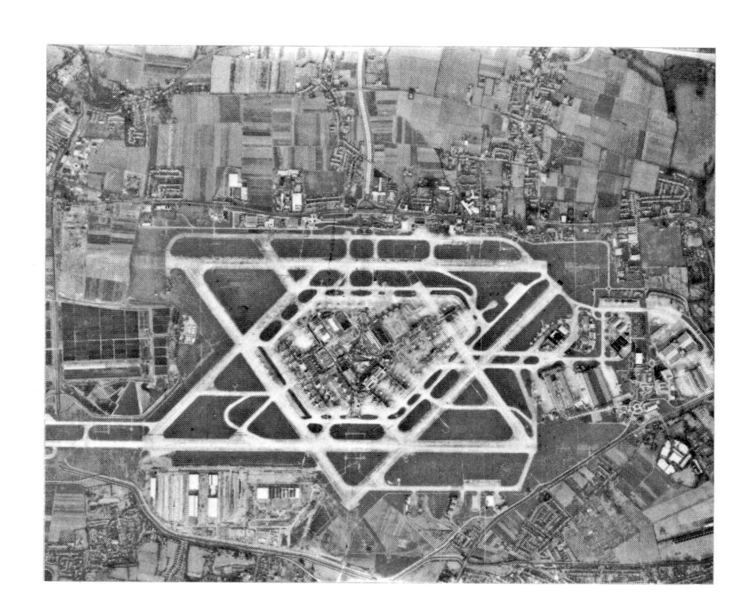

Fig. 16.7(a) Aerial direct view of London Airport (Heathrow)

Fig. 16.7(b) The control tower at Heathrow with a VC10 airliner

and freight buildings around it. The tunnel leading to the M4 motorway and A4 road is seen just north of centre.

As may be seen from Fig. 16.6, London airport is as close to the built up area of London as it can safely be, even though it is still

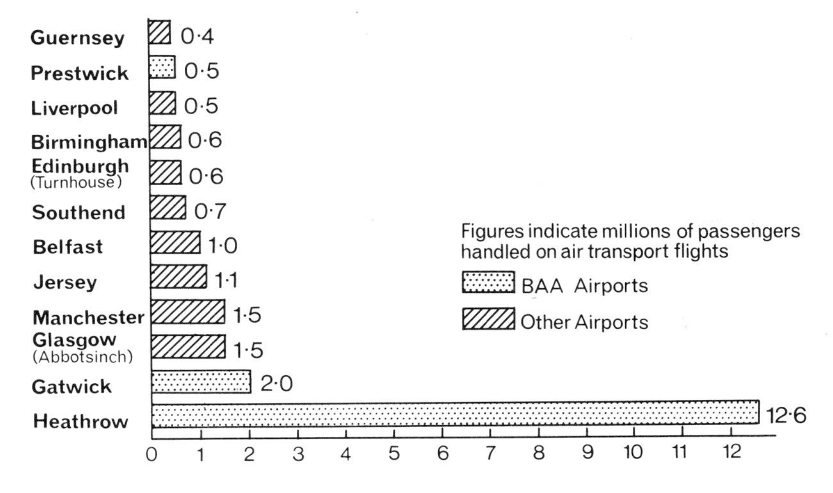

Fig. 16.8 Britain's main airports

25 kilometres from central London. However, this also brings the disadvantage of noise for the inhabitants of the surrounding houses, and many have had to have their houses sound proofed to minimize the effects of noise. Schools in the Ashford and Hounslow areas often have their lessons disturbed by aircraft noise.

One advantage of having an airport west rather than east of London is that industrial smoke and polluted air tends to be blown eastwards, thereby lessening the possibility of fog or smog forming over the airport.

One of the major features of air traffic is its steady increase, around 15 per cent per year. One result is that airports get busier and busier and there comes a time when they can no longer handle more traffic. For example it had been calculated that in the mid 70s London airport (Heathrow) would reach its maximum capacity. This means not only that all ground facilities will be in full use, but that the rate at which aircraft land and take off cannot be increased. As it is, during peak periods aircraft have to be 'stacked' to await their turn in landing, and for a large jet airliner this is expensive in fuel and in wasted travel time. Consequently most large cities have more than one airport – London has two: Heathrow and Gatwick and a third one is required. Finding a site has proved one of the most difficult problems the British Airport Authority has had to tackle, largely because the noise created by modern aircraft has led to much opposition from the inhabitants of areas where it is proposed to site the airport. Fig. 16.9 shows the extent of the 'noise carpet' for various sites. This noise might be supplemented by a sonic boom if the *Concorde* were to fly above the speed of sound over land. Sites near the North Sea like Sheppey and Foulness island (Maplin) would lessen the noise nuisance. On the other hand they are farther from London, would require new road and rail links to London, and might well be more affected by sea fog.

Stansted, which already has an aerodrome, is being used on a temporary basis. After great local opposition to the Stansted site the Roskill Commission pronounced in favour of a site at Cublington

Fig. 16.9
Noise carpet for London airport sites

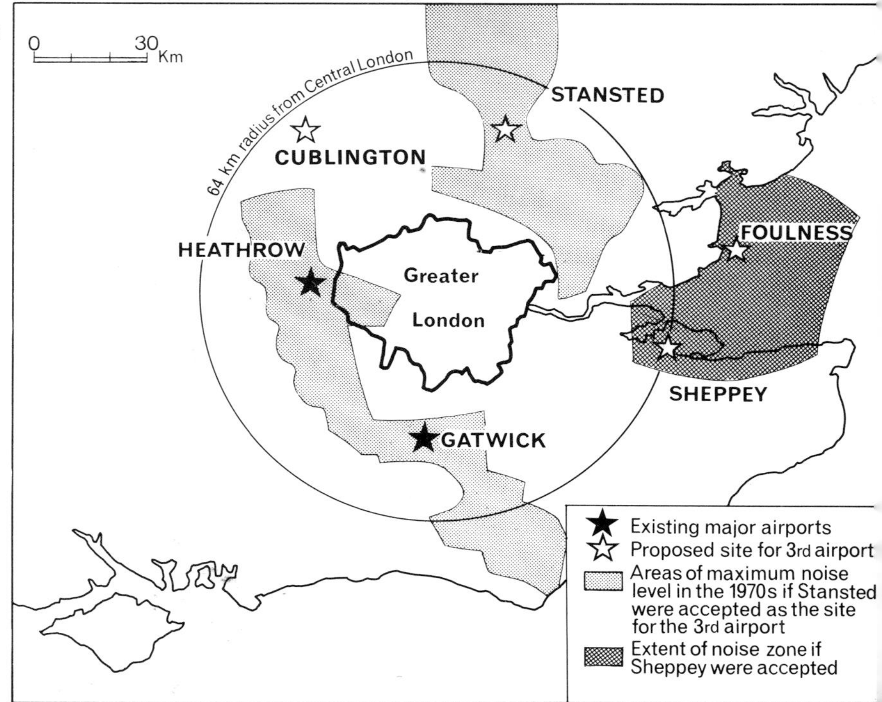

near Bletchley in 1970. However, the government rejected the commission's advice and decided to develop the Maplin site on the grounds that damage to the environment would be less than at Cublington. Owing to the advent of large aircraft capable of transporting over 300 passengers each, the need for a third airport for London is now being questioned and no development is to take place at Maplin for the time being.

9. *(a) What is the name of the nearest civil aerodrome to your home?*
   (b) Describe its position in relation to the town it serves.
   (c) What are the advantages of this position?
   (d) Draw a simple sketch map of its runway or runways and its associated taxiways and buildings.
10. *State in words what the diagram in Fig. 16.8 shows.*
11. *(a) Liverpool airport extended its runway in 1965. Why do you think this was necessary?*
   (b) What would be the effect on airport construction if vertical take-off and landing aircraft became extensively used for civil aircraft?
12. *(a) Draw a plan for an airport where two runways are required. The prevailing wind is from the north but strong winds from the west occur for at least 30 per cent of the year. Show where you would put the terminal buildings and the approach road.*
   (b) On what side of the town would you build the airport? State your reasons.

13. *Study Fig. 16.6*
    (a) What are the advantages of the site of London airport (Heathrow) (i) for runways (ii) for passengers travelling to and from London?
    (b) (i) Why would it be difficult to extend the area of Heathrow airport? (ii) In which directions would extension be most difficult?
    (c) Using the scale in the map as a guide, what is the length of the northern runway shown on the photograph in Fig. 16.7 (a)?
14. *Study Fig. 16.9*
    (a) What can you tell about the main movement of aircraft from the noise zone around Heathrow and Gatwick airports?
    (b) Does a large proportion of the aircraft coming to land at Heathrow fly over London's built up area? Give reasons for your answer.
    (c) What would be (i) the advantages (ii) the disadvantages of siting another airport on Sheppey or on Foulness islands?
    (d) Why might fog be more of a hazard on Sheppey or Foulness islands?

E. Analysing Networks

Whether a network is one of air-routes, roads, rail or canals, there are certain ways of describing these networks which can be useful and make possible certain comparisons. Let us take a simple case, namely, the network of air-routes within Scotland (Fig. 16.1). It may be simplified to look as in Fig. 16.10. As you can see, it is a network

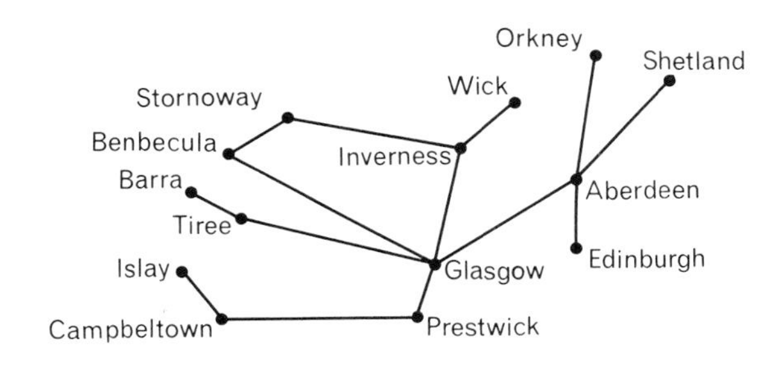

Fig. 16.10 A simplified network of air-routes in Scotland

along which you can fly from Glasgow to Aberdeen and Orkney, and *vice versa*, but you cannot fly from Orkney to Wick or from Orkney to Stornoway, or from Orkney to Barra and so on, without first going to Glasgow. Such a network is not very well connected. The degree to which a network is connected is called its *connectivity* and this can be measured by a simple index known as the β (*beta*) index. All you need do is count up the airports (the *nodes*) and count up the airlanes (the *links*) and then divide the links by the nodes:

$$\beta \text{ index} = \frac{\text{Links}}{\text{nodes}}$$

In the above case, this works out to:

$$\beta \text{ index} = \frac{14}{14} = 1$$

Now suppose British Airways decided to start services between Orkney and Shetland, Orkney and Wick, Wick and Stornoway, Benbecula and Barra, Barra and Islay, Islay and Glasgow, and Tiree and Islay, then the network would look like that in Fig. 16.11. The connectivity would clearly be increased and we would have a β index of:

$$\frac{21 \text{ links}}{14 \text{ nodes}} = \frac{3}{2} = 1.5$$

In other words, the connectivity would have been improved by 0.5.

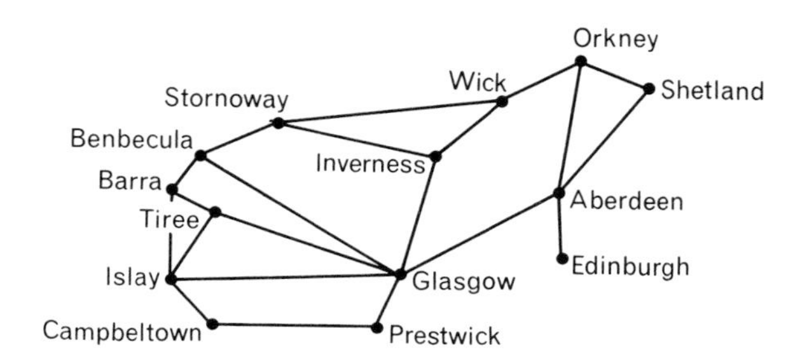

Fig. 16.11 An imaginary network of air-routes in Scotland

If you want to find out which is the most accessible plan in Scotland by air, then the simplest method is to count the number of air-routes which come into (or go out of) each airport. From Fig. 16.10 it seems clear that Glasgow has five routes converging on it whereas Aberdeen has only four and Inverness three; so Glasgow has the highest *accessibility*.

If you want to work out the exact order of accessibility of places in a network, then you need to do a little more work. You draw up a table as in Table 16.2 in which you count up the smallest number of links between each airport and every other airport in the network (Fig. 16.10). The airport with the smallest number is the most accessible, and that with the biggest number is the least accessible, in this case Islay.

If you were manager of an airline network, and you want to find out whether putting in an extra link would considerably improve the gross accessibility of the network, then you could draw up several tables or *matrices* like Table 16.2, one for each new link you proposed to put in to see what difference it would make to the whole network. For example, would it be better to link Benbecula and Barra or Tiree and Islay? Of course, you would also need to take account of possible traffic on each link. The ideal network from the user's point of view is usually also the most expensive. Some balance has to be sought between accessibility and cost in relation to revenue.

Table 16.2

	Aberdeen	Barra	Benbecula	Campbeltown	Edinburgh	Glasgow	Inverness	Islay	Orkney	Prestwick	Shetland	Stornoway	Tiree	Wick	Accessibility index	Rank order
Aberdeen	0	3	2	3	1	1	2	4	1	2	1	3	2	3	28	2
Barra	3	0	3	4	4	2	3	5	4	3	4	4	1	4	44	13
Benbecula	2	3	0	3	3	1	2	4	3	2	3	1	2	3	32	5
Campbeltown	3	4	3	0	4	2	3	1	4	1	4	4	3	4	40	7
Edinburgh	1	4	3	4	0	2	3	5	2	3	2	4	3	4	40	7
Glasgow	1	2	1	2	2	0	1	3	2	1	2	2	1	2	22	1
Inverness	2	3	2	3	3	1	0	4	3	2	3	1	2	1	30	3
Islay	4	5	4	1	5	3	4	0	5	2	5	5	4	5	52	14
Orkney	1	4	3	4	2	2	3	5	0	3	2	4	3	4	40	7
Prestwick	2	3	2	1	3	1	2	2	3	0	3	3	2	3	30	3
Shetland	1	4	3	4	2	2	3	5	2	3	0	4	3	4	40	7
Stornoway	3	4	1	4	4	2	1	5	4	3	4	0	3	2	40	7
Tiree	2	1	3	3	3	1	2	4	3	2	3	3	0	3	33	6
Wick	3	4	3	4	4	2	1	5	4	3	4	2	3	0	42	12
Gross accessibility index or dispersion value =															513	

Fig. 16.12 A simplified and modified motorway network for England and Wales

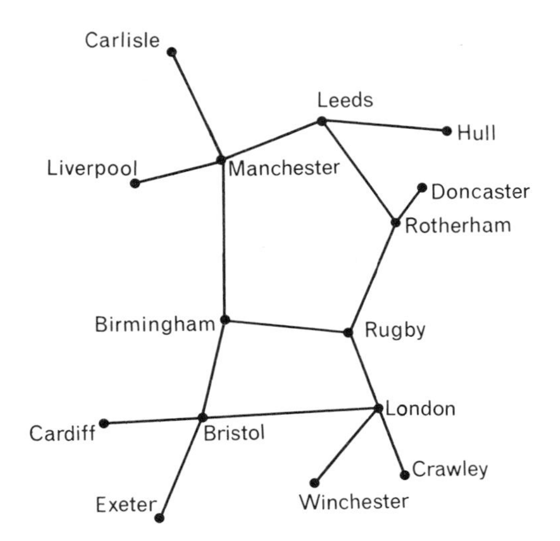

15. *If Fig. 16.12 represents the simplified motorway network in England and Wales,*
    (a) What is the β index for that network?
    (b) rank the various towns on the network for their accessibility according to the number of links which reach them.
    **(c) work out an accessibility index for each town and then rank them in order.*
    **(d) what is the gross accessibility index for the network?*
    **(e) where would you put in another motorway to improve the accessibility of the whole network?*
16. *(a) In Table 16.2, Edinburgh the capital of Scotland did not rank high in its accessibility in the airline network. Why do you think this was?*
    (b) Would there be any advantage in having an air link between Glasgow and Edinburgh?

Conclusion

The difficulties in finding sites for airports are inevitable in a country where land is very scarce and most people live in towns – unless vertical landing and take off aircraft can be developed, the amount of land used up by airports catering for heavy and fast jet aircraft is likely to increase with a growth in air travel.

Part V

Food Supplies for the Cities

Chapter Seventeen

Agriculture

A. The General Pattern

The fact that farming is left to one of the later chapters of this book is a reflection of the urbanization and industrialization of the British Isles. Yet there are still more than 420,000 people employed in farming in the United Kingdom, that is nearly 2 per cent of the total labour force. This is a smaller percentage than almost any other area in the world. Most of our inhabitants live in urban areas but from the point of view of the land area itself, by far the largest amount is still devoted to farming of various types. An air flight from Lands End to the Shetland Isles will still leave an impression of the urban areas being islands of bricks, mortar and concrete surrounded by a sea of green and brown. Table 17.1 puts this point into factual form.

Table 17.1 The Use of Land in United Kingdom (m. hectares)

	1973
Agriculture	19.0
Woodland	1.9
Urban Areas	2.3
Other Uses	1.2
Total	24.4

(Source: Britain 1975)

Table 17.2 Types of Farmland, 1973 (m. hectares)

	England and Wales	Scotland
Arable land	5.6	1.3
Permanent Grass	3.9	0.4
Rough Grazing	1.8	4.5
Total	11.3	6.2

(Dept. of Ag., F. & F.)

These figures show that nearly 80 per cent of the land surface is used for agricultural purposes; but there is a loss of farming land each year, a process which is certain to continue with the growth of residential and industrial areas, motorways, sports-grounds and the like.

The farming land itself may be divided into three main categories, arable land (under the plough), permanent grassland and, thirdly, rough grazing (mostly on hilly and mountainous areas). Their distribution and the contrast between the north and south of Britain is striking, as Table 17.2 reveals.

It will be seen that rough grazing dominates the landscape of Scotland while most of England and Wales has improved farming land, whether for crops or grass, with only about 17 per cent rough grazing and much of that is on the Welsh hills. The actual crops grown on the arable land in terms of hectares are shown below in Table 17.3.

Table 17.3 The Use of Land in the United Kingdom (m. hectares)

	1939	1973
Wheat	0.7	1.1
Barley	0.4	2.3
Oats	1.0	0.3
Potatoes	0.3	0.2
Sugar Beet	0.1	0.2
Fodder Crops	0.5	0.3
Fruit	0.1	0.1
Vegetables	0.1	0.2
Total Arable	5.2	7.2
Permanent Grass	7.5	4.9

(Dept. of Ag., F. & F.)

There has been a great expansion of the area devoted to cereal crops, especially barley, which is now the most important single crop. This extension has taken place at the cost of permanent grass. Nearly 2.4 million hectares of grassland have been ploughed up since 1939. This does not give the whole story because each hectare of arable land is giving more foodstuffs by the use of new techniques such as the use of better fertilizers. For example, nearly twice as much sugar beet is grown on only 25 per cent more land (from 451,000 tonnes to 846,000 tonnes). Similarly, the potato area has not changed, yet the production of potatoes has gone up from 4,873,000 tonnes in 1939 to 6,763,000 tonnes in 1970. In other words the yield per hectare has increased considerably in the last 20 years.

The permanent grassland and rough grazing are the main support of our stock breeds which are among the most famous in the world: our cattle and sheep are exported in large numbers. So valuable are they that we slaughter livestock with such diseases as foot-and-mouth to prevent the disease becoming established in Great Britain and causing a decline in the quality and reputation of our livestock. In spite of the increase in arable land, the numbers of livestock have not been reduced, as Table 17.4 will show.

Of the cattle, about 3.3 million were for milk production in the pre-war years and in 1968, so that the main increases in cattle have been in the varieties reared for beef. In fact, it is not easy to separate the two main types as many farmers now prefer a dual-purpose beast and many beef calves are now raised from dairy herds.

It has been estimated that our farming land produces nearly half of the total requirements of our population. But this is a very generalized figure and the figures given in Table 17.5 of food produced at home will give a much clearer idea of the real position.

Table 17.4 Livestock in the United Kingdom (million)

	1936/8 average	1973
Cattle and Calves	8.7	14.4
Sheep	25.8	27.9
Pigs	4.5	8.9
Poultry	76.2	144.0

(Annual Abstract of Statistics)

Table 17.5 Home Food Supplies, 1974

Wheat and Flour	57%
Sugar	30%
Meat	75%
Bacon and Ham	45%
Milk	100%
Cheese	57%
Butter	22%
Shell Eggs	98%
Potatoes	94%

It is evident that we cannot grow all the food we need, even dealing with the crops and livestock that we can produce in our climate. There are only three items in the list that show nearly 100 per cent home production. There is a variety of other foodstuffs, that we must import because the conditions of our climate make it impossible for us to grow them. This would include many fruits, such as pineapples, oranges and lemons, drinks, such as tea, coffee and cocoa, foods, such as rice, grapes, olives; in other words, foodstuffs which are grown in tropical and sub-tropical lands.

1. *What proportion or fraction of the land surface of Great Britain is occupied by agricultural land? (Table 17.1.)*
2. *Using a sheet of graph paper, make a diagram*
   (a) To show the main types of farm land, constructing one block to represent England and Wales and one block to represent Scotland. Fill in two cm. squares for each one million hectares of land, using a colour code to differentiate between arable (brown), permanent grass (green) and rough grazing (yellow). (Table 17.2.)
   (b) Suggest reasons why a much greater proportion of Scotland's land surface is covered by rough grazing than that of England and Wales. Reference should be made to a physical map in the atlas and to the rainfall map. (Fig. 14.1.)
3. *(a) Which crops have increased in area since 1939? (Table 17.3.)*
   (b) Express the increase of arable land area between 1939 and 1973 as either a percentage increase or as a fraction.
4. *Make a graph or diagram of the information contained in Table 17.4 omitting poultry from the graph.*
5. *(a) Copy the list of foodstuffs given in Table 17.5 and place against each food the percentage of that food that must be imported (in 1973). For example, if 57 per cent of our wheat and flour are grown at home, then the amount imported must be 43 per cent. Give a title to your table.*

(b) *Make a list of 10 products that must be imported from tropical and sub-tropical areas.*

6. *List four of the main changes that have taken place in the general pattern of British agriculture since the 1930's.*
7. *Suggest some of the ways by which the total amount of home-grown food supplies could be increased. Look especially at the milk products shown in Table 17.5.*

B. The Structure of Farming

The revolution that is now taking place in British farming by which more crops are being grown and more livestock raised on less and less land with an ever-declining labour force is due to many factors, some of which have been mentioned, such as the use of fertilizers, insecticides, pesticides and other products of industry. But perhaps the most important factor is the great increase in mechanization, especially on big-arable farms. Many of the processes carried out by hand-labour are now carried out by machines. Where harvest time once involved many people cutting, stooking, carting, threshing, now the combine-harvester moves slowly through the fields doing all the jobs simultaneously. The degree of mechanization is illustrated by the next short table, 17.6.

Table 17.6 Horses and Tractors (thousands)

	1939	1965	1973
Horses	649	21	*
Tractors	117	480	506

*not recorded

The replacement of horse-power by petrol-power in the form of tractors, combines and other machines has led to many of the most progressive farms becoming factories for the production of food. The effect on the labour force, on the types of farm-buildings and on the size of fields is leading to dramatic changes in the face of the countryside. A recent newspaper article reported a farmer with 100 hectares who pointed out that a modern machine could operate most successfully in large, regular fields rather than in small, irregular parcels of land. He plans to tear out all the hedgerows from his farm and make five big fields. Fig. 17.1 shows one such field in diagram form. On the same scale, Fig. 17.1 shows a group of separate holdings that were still being farmed on the Isle of Lewis in the Outer Hebrides in 1959. Twelve families were still working this land. Eight of the 'crofters' (small farmers) had 108 separate plots of land between them. On one 'croft', the average size of a strip of land was only 0.06 hectares. There are more than 18,000 crofts still operating in north-west Scotland but less than 600 of them give full time work to one person (i.e. 275 standard man-days). Many crofts are, therefore, part-time holdings.

Fig. 17.1 Strip holdings in the Hebrides

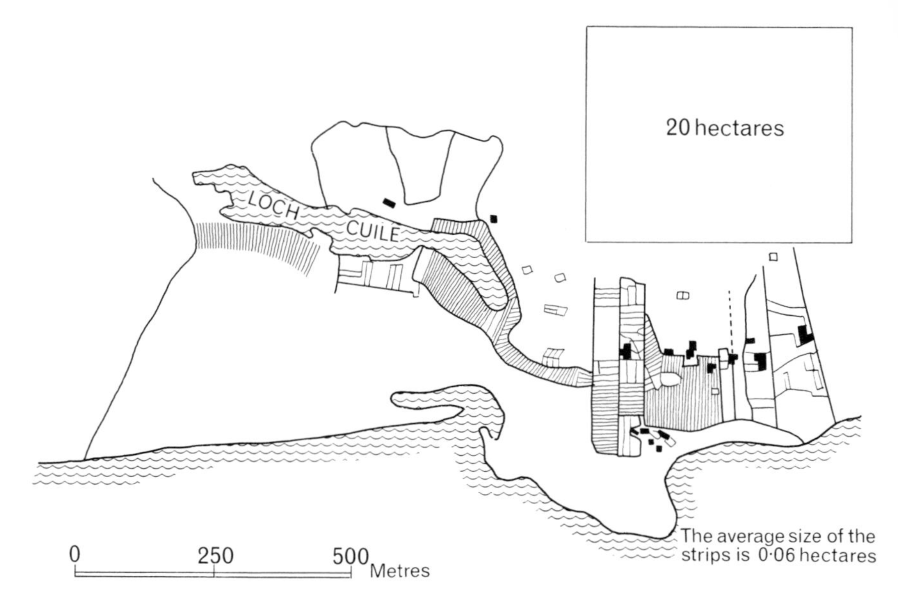

Another recent report spoke of a farmer who controls 8,000 hectares and operates 300 tractors and 43 combine harvesters. Farm labourers on a farm like this are really highly skilled drivers and technicians, capable of dealing with a variety of machinery as well as knowing all about crops and animals.

The actual pattern of British farms, their size and speciality has been studied in recent government publications; Table 17.7 is made up of some of the available material. The use of the measurement of Standard Man Days (SMD) is interesting and the experts regard 275 SMD as the equivalent of a year's work for one fully-employed man.

Table 17.7 The Size of Farms in Britain

Type of Holding	Av. size of holdings (in hectares)	Number of Holdings	% of Total Number of Holdings	SMD required to operate the farm	Speciality
Large	120	40,000	10	1,200 or more	Grain crops
Medium	52	65,000	15	600–1,199	Dairy/ livestock
Small	24.8	95,000	25	275–599	Dairy/ livestock
Very Small	6.4	200,000	50	Less than 275	Pigs/ poultry
All holdings	30				

The 40,000 large farms produced nearly half of the total farm output and are particularly on the lowland, grain-growing areas of Britain. One half of the farms are very small, having less than 275

SMD. In other words, according to official measurement, they do not represent a full-time occupation for one man.

The structure of modern farming is increasingly affected by government policy and now, as a full member of the European Community, Britain has to bring its regulations into line with the Common Agricultural Policy (CAP), in stages until 1979. This plans a common market for all the main agricultural produce so that goods from one country can move freely to another. Import duties are imposed on produce of countries outside the Common Market. This includes many of Britain's traditional suppliers. Farmers interests are protected by 'support buying' to make sure that the price of a product, such as meat or wheat, does not fall below an agreed level. This is similar in intent to the British government's system of guaranteed prices. The government buys some produce such as milk, wool, sugar and potatoes through its marketing boards which may also regulate the amount farmers may grow. In addition, subsidies are given to farmers on poorer hill land for their sheep and cattle, for example. Drainage, liming of land and improvement to buildings may also qualify for grants. Above all, the CAP seeks to increase the average size of farm holdings by encouraging smaller farmers to retire by special pensions.

The total pattern of farming that emerges as the result of climate, physical setting, historic growth and government policy is shown in Fig. 17.2, which is the distribution of the main types of farming in Britain. The rest of this chapter will be concerned with a series of short studies of certain farming areas in the country with emphasis placed on changes that are taking place. The location of the special study areas are shown on the generalized map.

8. *(a) Make a column graph to show the decline in the number of farm horses and the increase in the number of tractors between 1939 and 1965.*
   (b) List the changes that have taken place in the farming scene due to the replacement of horses by tractors.
9. *Given 45 hectares of land.*
   (a) How many very small farms with an average of 6.4 hectares could be fitted in?
   (b) how many houses could be built at a density of 35 houses per hectare?
10. *Why is the pattern of the British countryside likely to become one of large, regular fields?*
11. *In what ways does the Government influence the nature of farming?*
12. *Make a map of your own 100 hectare farm in which you are concentrating on grain crops. Lay out five large fields, put the necessary farm buildings in the most suitable place, build an access road and a series of wire fences where absolutely necessary.*

C. Beef-raising in the North East

The raising and fattening of cattle for beef production is one of the types of farming that government policy seeks to expand. Fig. 17.2

Fig. 17.2
British Isles: agriculture

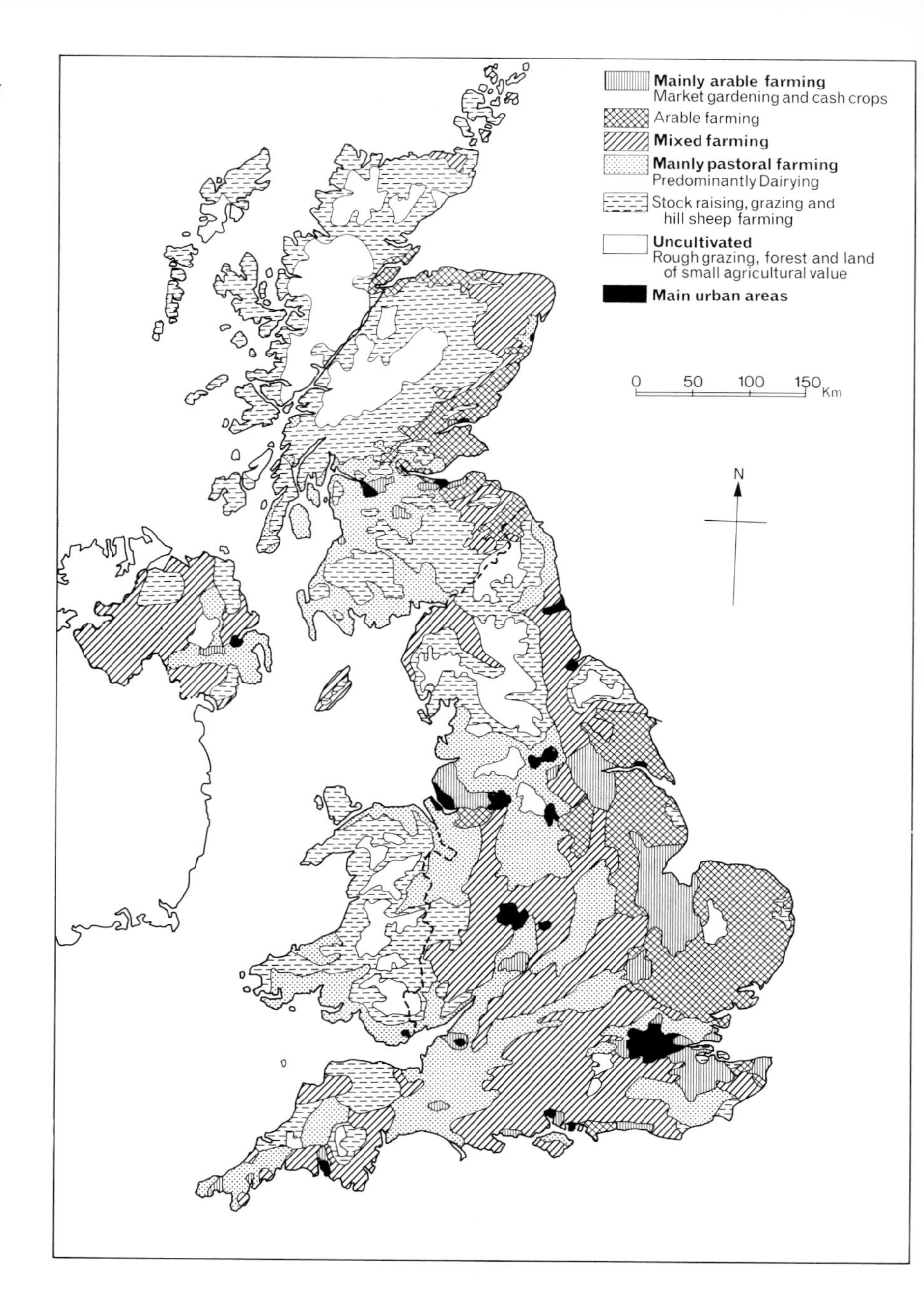

shows that the areas devoted to stock rearing and feeding are widespread but especially to be found on the lower slopes of mountainous areas. The greatest concentration of this type of farming, however, is to be found on the north-east coastlands, stretching from the Tyne up to the Pentland Firth and even beyond to the Orkney and Shetland groups of islands. The comparative dryness of the east coast, together with the late spring and distance from the greatest urban centres makes beef raising the more suited to the environment than, for example, dairy farming. The constant improvement of beef breeds such as the Aberdeen Angus by cross-breeding with other types such as the Hereford, the Shorthorn, the Highland and the Friesian and the increased production of high-quality grassland and winter fodder crops has led to a well-organized system of beef-production on large farm units, many of them being more than 400 hectares in extent. The layout of a fairly typical farm is shown in Fig. 17.3. The farm stretches from the moorland edge

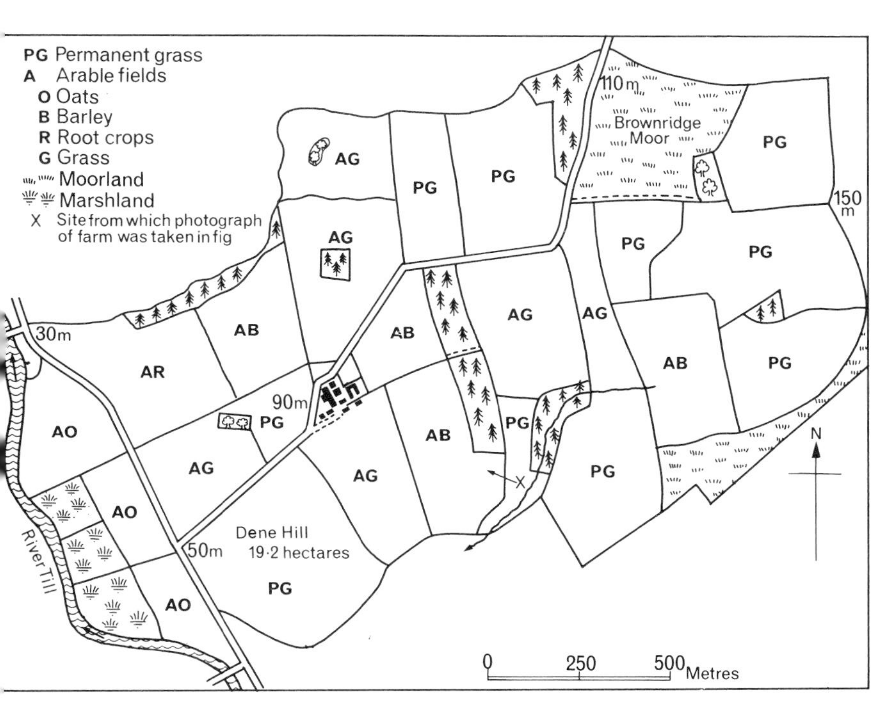

Fig. 17.3 Farm plan

at about 150 metres westwards to the river. Much of the higher land is left to grass while most of the fields adjacent to the farmbuildings are ploughed. The fields are fairly large, mostly between 8 and 12 hectares in size and regular enough in shape to suit mechanized farming methods. About 165 cows and 4 bulls are kept for the production of calves. Calving usually takes place in February on the moors and grasslands, as the cattle like a natural environment for dropping their calves. The calves are fattened throughout the summer, the biggest sales being in the autumn. The farmer buys in other bullocks for feeding, too. A large proportion of his arable crops and most of the hay crop is used for fattening but a lot of the barley is sold off the farm for malting. The more feedstuffs the farmer can grow, the less supplementary feed he has to buy in. The arable fields follow a seven-year rotation, wheat, roots, barley, clover, then three years of grass. This keeps the land in good heart and produces the right balance of crops. But the use of fertilizers is making the rotation less important and a nearby farmer is growing barley on 80 per cent of his land and growing it several years in succession. It is unwise for a farmer to 'have all his eggs in one basket' and this farmer diversifies his products by keeping a flock of 600 ewes, mostly Cheviots and Black-faced crossed with rams from the south, such as the Southdown and the Suffolk, so as to produce a fat, yet hardy, lamb. The cost of feeding livestock and the housewife's desire for a small, lean joint means that farmers are fattening animals for a shorter period and selling them off as younger beasts. Mutton, for example, is no longer as popular as it once was.

Fig. 17.4 shows some of the young bulls kept on the farm, an Aberdeen Angus, a Hereford and a Highland. Fig. 17.5 shows Black-face ewes strip-grazing turnips in winter, gaining strength be-

Fig. 17.4 Young bulls on a farm in Northumberland

Fig. 17.5 Black faced sheep grazing turnips in Northumberland

fore the spring lambing. Their wool-clip is sold to brokers in Kilmarnock.

Farmers are attached to traditional methods and do not change readily but the pressures of demand are such that they have 'to run to keep still'. If skilled farm labour is difficult to get then it is better to buy in livestock and fatten them rather than raise your own bullocks and lambs. Grass cannot just be left as grass: it must be improved by the application of lime and fertilizer so as to produce the maximum nutriment on each hectare. Animals are encouraged to graze more economically by strip-grazing or even by 'zero grazing', that is, by not letting the animals out on the grass but leading the fodder into their stalls. After all, the animals lose weight when they move, so the less they move, the quicker they fatten. This may sound rather harsh and unsentimental but only by modern methods can the farmer make a reasonable income from his hard work. Machines are taking the place of men; in terms of productivity per man, farming has made more progress than almost any other industry. One farmer in this same area now runs 112 hectares on his own, concentrating on barley growing and putting all the other farm jobs out to contract labour. This means that all big jobs like liming a field, harvesting a crop, ditching and fencing, are done by a gang of men with equipment who are employed on contract by a farmer for these specific tasks. The gangs are not attached to any particular farm, but travel from farm to farm. The following table, Table 17.8, will show how this farm compares with the six neighbouring farms.

Table 17.8 Seven North-Eastern 'Beef' Farms

	Hectares	Men 1971	Employed 1975
Farm A.	246	8	3
Farm B.	440	11	5
Farm C.	120	6	2
Farm D.	200	6	2
Farm E.	112	3	1
Farm F.	108	2	1
Farm G.	122	3	1

13. (a) What is the average size of the seven farms in Table 17.8?
(b) What is the average area per man?

14. (a) How many of the fields on the farm (Fig. 17.3) are (i) ploughed for crops and (ii) left to grassland or moorland?
(b) Make a list of the sources of income of the Northumberland farmer mentioned in this section, starting with BEEF.

15. Find out about the major beef breeds in the British Isles, especially the Aberdeen Angus and the Hereford, from an encyclopaedia or from Young Farmers Club booklets.

D. Changes in the Orkney Islands

As we have seen in Fig. 17.2, the major area devoted to stock rearing stretches as far north as the Orkney Islands off the north coast of

Scotland. It is in north and north-west Scotland that one finds man crofts. A croft is a smallholding from which the farmer obtains bare living sometimes supplemented by selling homespun wool, b fishing, or by providing tourists with bed and breakfast. The croftin area is shown in Fig. 17.6. The crofting areas are in a state of chang

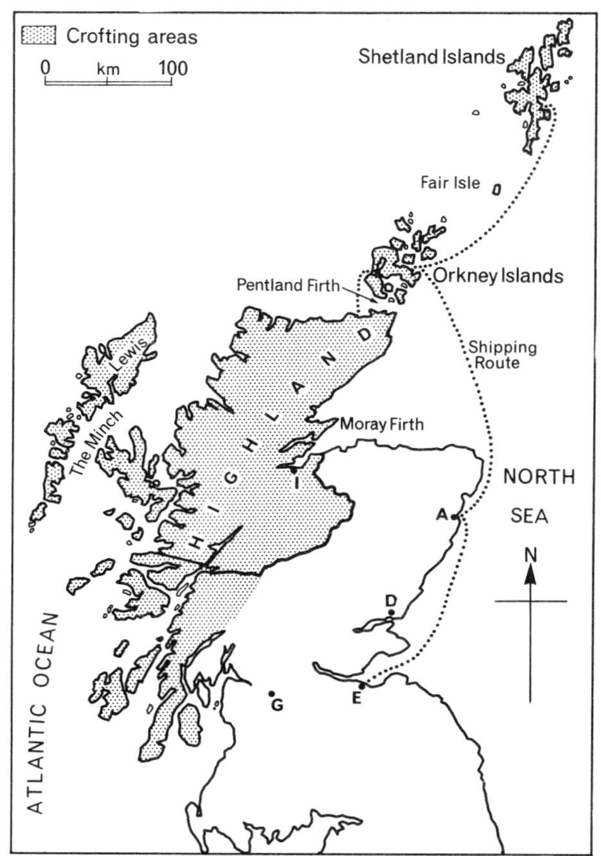

Fig. 17.6 The crofting areas

due to the impossibility of maintaining traditional farming method economically in such isolated areas. They are all suffering from th loss of people, especially the young. The deserted crofts tell thei own story. But the Orkney Islands show a much more successfu story of change that is still going on. Fig. 17.7 shows a part of th mainland of Orkney that is on the same scale as that of the beef farr in the previous section. Instead of one farm, however, there are n less than 18 holdings. Four of them, with their scattered fields ar mapped. It is quite impossible to talk about a 'typical' farm here they are all so different as Table 17.9 shows.

The only thing common to them all is the importance of raising beef cattle. Their sale on the mainland at Aberdeen is their most important source of income. The long distance from markets means that they are at a great disadvantage as compared with farmers

Farm or Croft	Size (hectares)	Cattle	Sheep	Poultry
No. 1	13.2	11	29	134
No. 2	21.6	20	—	—
No. 3	38.0	57	32	400
No. 4	4·8	16	22	600

Table 17.9 Four Orkney Farms

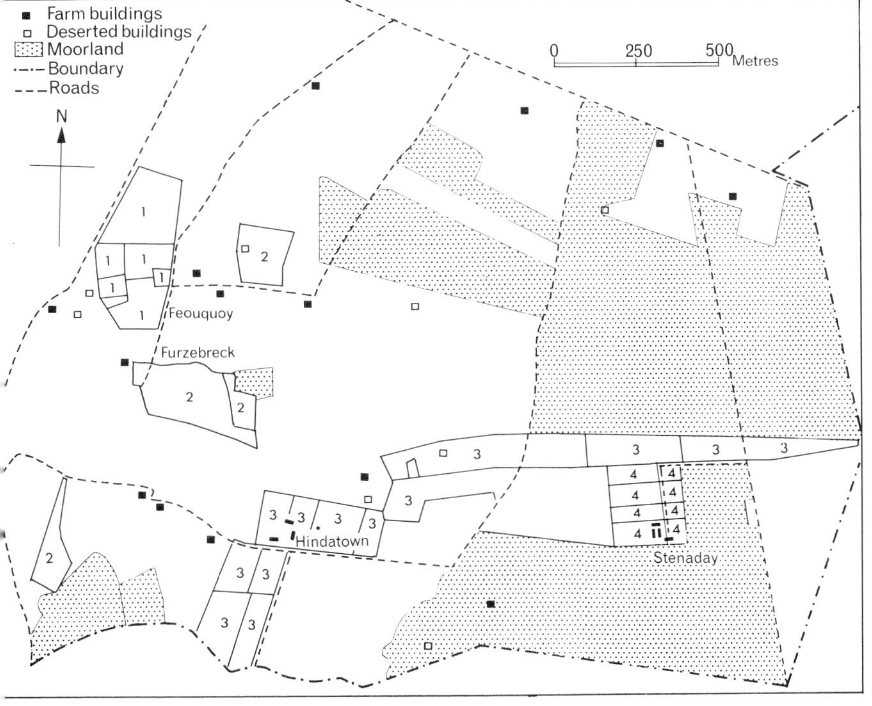

Fig. 17.7 Farm plan

on the mainland of Scotland but they make up for it with determination, hard work and a very heavy stocking ratio i.e. in beasts per hectare. None of them rely on cattle alone: they keep sheep though sheep numbers are declining as the farmers are attacking the moorlands to improve them as new intensively-farmed land. Poultry are kept in large numbers and the islands are amongst the most important egg-producing areas of the country.

All these farmers own their land and they also have common grazing rights on moorlands, which partly explains the heavy numbers of livestock. The type of cattle they prefer is an Angus/Galloway crossbreed. The moorlands also give them their source of fuel: they each have peat-cutting rights. The high transport costs of coal makes peat-cutting well worth while (Fig. 17.8).

A close study of Fig. 17.7 may explain the great variety of farm size and shape. It was once an area of many small crofts (generally crofts are under 30 hectares) and, as elsewhere, many crofters have left the land. The remaining crofters bought the land from those who left to increase their own land-holding. It is preferable to have all one's land in one parcel, as with the beef farm in Fig. 17.3, but this is not yet possible and may represent the developments of the years ahead. The map also shows new fields reclaimed from the moorland in the east of the area. The cool, damp climate means that the major crops are turnips, oats, potatoes and hay but a type of barley called 'bere' can also be grown.

The reorganization of the land-holdings is made particularly difficult in the Orkney Islands because the people are descended from Norse settlers and their land-holding laws are very complex. But a sign of the future may be seen in the north of the Orkney mainland where a farm has evolved, holding over 230 head of Ayrshire cattle on 400 hectares, entirely for the production of a special type of cheese which is shipped to Leith Docks for sale in Scottish cities.

Fig. 17.8 Peat-cutting on Harray (Orkneys)

16. *What is the distance by sea from the Orkney Islands to Aberdeen? (Fig. 17.6.)*
17. *(a) The area in Fig. 17.7 contains 18 farms on about 400 hectares. What is the average size of farm holding?*
    (b) How many deserted sites are shown in the area?
    (c) What difficulties would the farmer on Farm No. 2 face in working his land?
    (d) One of the numbered farms is a comparatively new one, sited on reclaimed moorland. Can you identify the farm?

8.* *Draw the outline of the area shown in Fig. 17.7 and reallocate the land to 18 farmers in the most efficient way you can devise. You may move the farm buildings if you wish.*

E. Hill Sheep Farming

The British Isles is the most important sheep-raising area in Western Europe. We have a long tradition of sheep farming; we were in effect the 'Australia' of the Middle Ages, exporting wool to the Continent where it was made up into cloth. The wool-clip is still a major source of income but the meat, especially of fat lambs, is increasingly important. The sheep of today are much larger and meatier than their ancestors due to selective breeding and improved feed stuffs especially during the winter, when grass is not available.

The main areas of sheep farming are very extensive, as shown in Fig. 17.2 and are found to dominate in the north and west, especially on the highlands and moorlands of Scotland, Wales, the Pennines and the Lake District. This is not because sheep prefer these 'hard' areas but because sheep farming has been driven from the 'softer' lands by the competition of more profitable types of farming. There are many lowland areas still famous for their sheep flocks, such as the Romney Marsh in Kent, but it is still generally true that sheep are retreating before the plough. Under the guaranteed price system there is more money in crop farming.

Fig. 17.9 Herdwick sheep near Coniston in the Lake District

One mountain area devoted to sheep rearing is the Lake District. The traditional sheep breed here is a small-framed tough animal, the Herdwick, able to survive the rigours of poor hill grazing and hard winters. The breed may have been introduced by the original Norse settlers (many of the place names of the district are Norse in origin, the most frequent 'thwaite' meaning 'a clearing'). Fig. 17.9 shows the Herdwick breed. Unfortunately, the breed doesn't suit modern taste in meat and Lake District shepherds are introducing other breeds such as the Gritstone from Derbyshire and the Swaledale to produce a larger, more economic carcase. Most of the open fell country is grazed in common: i.e. they are unfenced and shepherds are allowed a certain number of sheep (their 'stint') on the fell. In fact, flocks become attracted to a certain area (their heaf) and do not stray far from it. The better land in the lower slopes, containing comparatively rich pastures, is walled off into small irregular 'intakes' i.e. land taken in from the fell, which are owned separately and improved with good quality grasses and fertilizers. The best quality land, the flat alluvial areas of the valley bottoms, is called the 'inland' or 'inby' and it is on this level land that the few arable crops are raised. This low land can be subject to prolonged flooding.

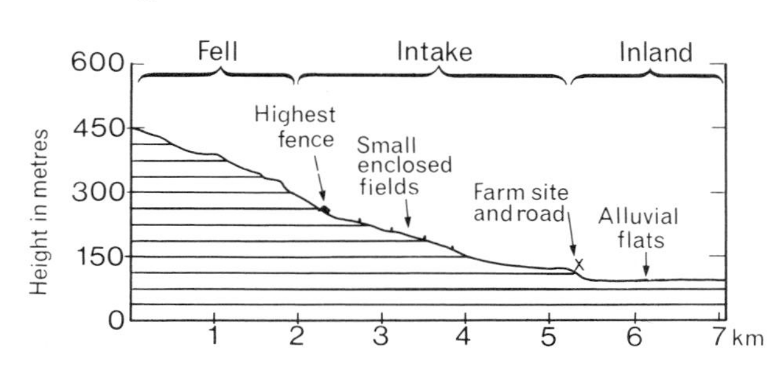

Fig. 17.10 Great Langdale cross section

This pattern of land use is illustrated in a simplified way by the diagram, Fig. 17.10, which is based on the valley of Great Langdale.

A clear picture of the dominance of sheep in the economy of Lake District farming is revealed by the agricultural statistics for one parish, as an example, that of Coniston. A map of the parish, with its lakes, main burns (streams) and highland is shown in Fig. 17.11.

*Table 17.10 The Parish of Coniston: Agricultural Statistics.**

		1955 (hectares)	1972 (hectares)
Crops:	Wheat	—	—
	Barley	—	—
	Oats	4.4	—
	Mixed Corn	2.4	—
	Potatoes	2.0	—
	Turnips	2.0	—
	Rape	0.9	—
	Cabbage, Kale etc.	2.0	—
	Total horticulture		0.5
Grasses:	Temporary	12.0	0.5
	Permanent	476.8	412.0
	Rough Grazing (not held in common)	754.4	571.0
Total Parish Area:		4,194.0	4,194.0
Livestock:	Cattle and Calves	511	571
	Pigs	152	176
	Sheep	5,472	8,077
	Horses	28	—
Total No. of Holdings:		33	16
Total No. of Farmers and Workers:		51	21

*These statistics are simplified from the sources available from the Ministry of Agriculture, Fisheries and Food.

Most of the farms in the parish, 27 in number according to the statistics, are situated on the land below 160 metres: the unshaded land contains most of the better, improved land, while the shaded hill area consists mostly of the open fell with some enclosed 'intakes' of rough grazing, very useful when gathering the flock together for lambing, dipping, shearing and marketing.

Table 17.10 shows the statistics supplied by the Department of Agriculture, Food and Fisheries for the years 1955 and 1972. They have been simplified for our purposes. They show that a very small proportion of the land is devoted to arable crops, that no wheat and barley were grown in 1972. The total area in crops and grass was 413 hectares. Add to this the 571 hectares of rough grazing held individually and we get a total of 984 hectares in the total parish area of 4,194 hectares. The balance of 3,210 hectares represents the open fell grazed in common: that is more than 75 per cent of the total parish area. Some of the fells are named on the map (Fig. 17. 1) such as the Coniston Fells and Little Arrow Moor.

This open fell grazing raises many problems today especially since farmers have, by law, to register their common rights in order to preserve them for the future. This has led to heavy stocking on the fells and will lead to a decline in the quality of the grazing. There is little incentive for a farmer to improve the hill grazing because he would not necessarily be improving the grazing for his own flock. Damage done to walls and gates, sheep-worrying by dogs are problems arising from the attractions of the area for holiday-makers. Many farmers would like to take advantage of these attractions and supplement their incomes by making facilities for camping and

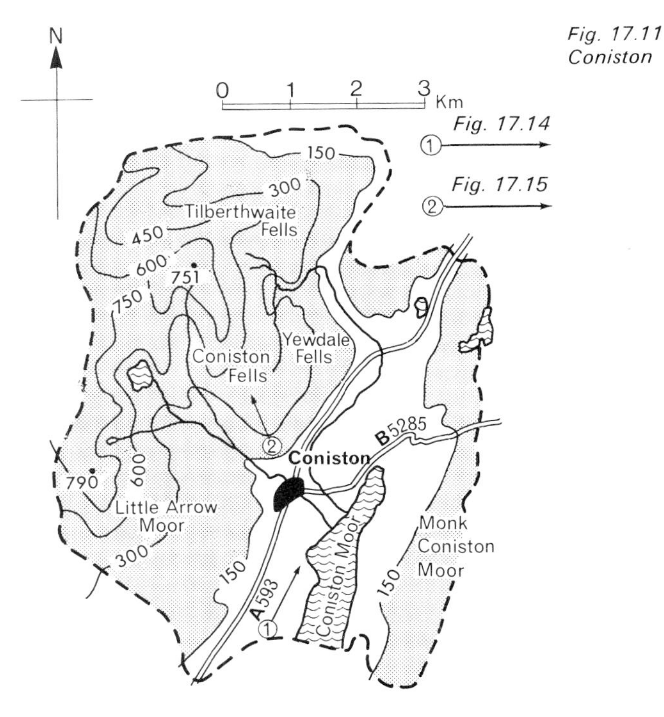

Fig. 17.11
Coniston

caravan sites and lake shore-pastimes. But there are strict controls over such developments due to the regulations in force to protect this area as a National Park. This aspect will be discussed further in Chapter 20. The very narrow, walled roads and the heavy tourist traffic make the movement of livestock and farm machinery difficult.

One farmer with 1,400 sheep and lambs has 74.4 hectares of 'inland' as well as his fell grazing. He winters some of his young sheep by renting pastures on the coastal area to the south where winters are less severe. He foresees the day when sheep farming will no longer be profitable and much of his interest is taken up with his herd of pedigree Ayrshire cattle and his prize Shorthorn bull. The milk goes to the Milk Marketing Board at Kendal, while the wool-clip goes to Bradford. The pedigree herd is shown in Fig. 17.12, grazing on pasture improved with special grasses. Dairying, forestry, and new tourist facilities – these are the uses to which he feels the fells could be put, to make a better living than sheep farming can supply.

19. *What proportion of the parish of Coniston is taken up with open fell land grazed in common?*
20. *What problems face the sheep farmer in his use of the fell country?*
21. *What is meant by a) intake,*
    b) inland?
22. *Why is so little land given over to the raising of arable crops? Reference to the rainfall map Fig. 14.1 will give part of the answer.*
23. *(a) Which items in the Agricultural Statistics show an increase in the ten years from 1955 to 1972?*
    (b) What is the average area of enclosed land for each of the farm holdings, assuming a figure of 984 hectares in 1972?

Fig. 17.12 Pedigree Ayrshire cattle near Torver in the Lake District

24. (a) *What methods are being used to improve the income from sheep farming?*
(b) *What methods are farmers using to supplement their incomes, apart from sheep farming?*

25. *Name four other areas of the British Isles dominated by hill sheep farming apart from the Lake District.*

F. Arable Farming and Dairy Farming

Figure 17.2 shows that most of the arable or cropped land is in eastern England particularly in East Anglia, that is mainly in the counties of Norfolk and Suffolk. This does not mean that the whole area is under wheat or barley, but rather that more land is under crops than under permanent pasture.

There are other crops besides grain crops, farmers also keep animals. Very few farms in Britain are solely crop farms—most are mixed farms keeping some animals and growing crops.

One of the questions which might be asked is why there is more arable land and grain growing land in East Anglia than in any other part of England. Farmers, like other business men, are out to make as large an income as they can. Consequently they will try to grow those crops and keep those animals which they can sell for a good price. But not all areas are equally suited to grain crops. If you compare the average rainfall figures for Norwich and Ilfracombe you will easily see why. In general in Britain, the greater the rain-

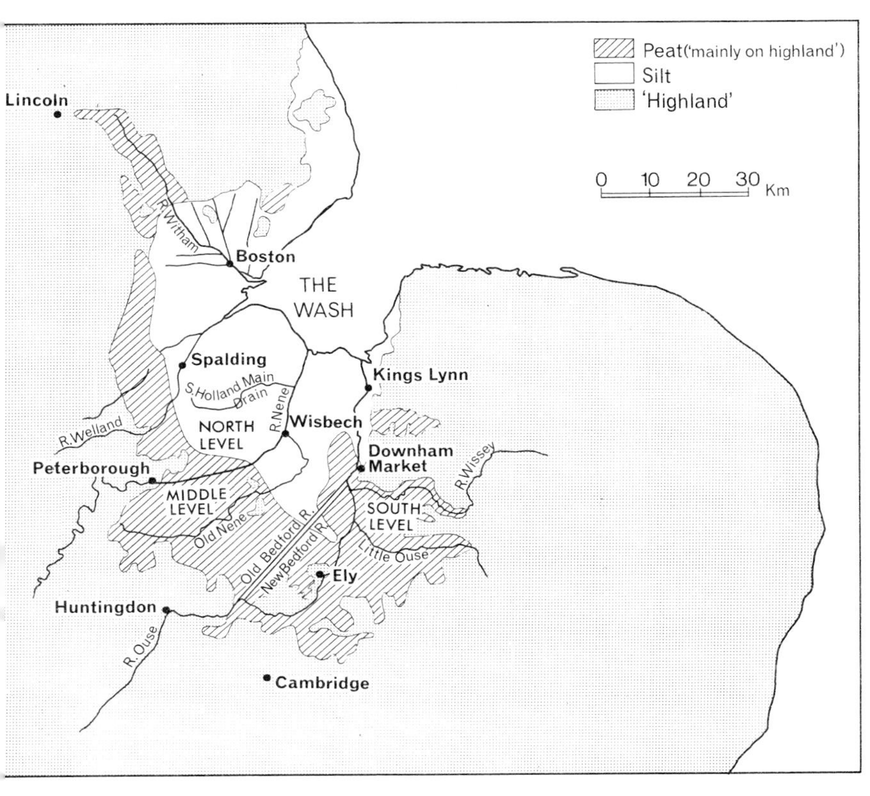

Fig. 17.13 Norfolk and the Wash

fall of a certain area, the greater the cloudiness of the sky, the les
sunshine, the less suitable it will be for growing grain crops. But Eas
Anglia is one of the drier parts of England, thus grain will have les
difficulty in ripening here than anywhere else.

Rainfall in Millimetres

	J	F	M	A	M	J	J	A	S	O	N	D	T
Norwich	60	45	48	47	47	65	52	50	60	62	65	63	664
Ilfracombe	100	70	66	60	62	50	75	77	78	110	111	112	971

Another influence is the soil, although this is of less importanc than it once was, because farmers can do much to improve their soil with fertilizers. They can also lighten them or make them heavier b adding various ingredients. East Anglia has many types of soils, bu much of the area is covered with clayey deposits left by the ice-sheet when they retreated after the Ice Age. These deposits, known as 'till or 'chalky boulder clays' (Fig. 17.14) are sufficiently heavy to provid a firm base for the wheat and barley roots but light enough to allo reasonable drainage of water. Further the area is sufficiently level fo farm machinery to run easily on its surface (see Fig. 17.15). In th Fens, to the west of Downham Market, there are good peat and sil soils (see Fig. 17.13).

Figs 17.16 (a) and 17.16 (b) show a very different part of England – the area of south Devon overlooking Bigbury Bay. Although o

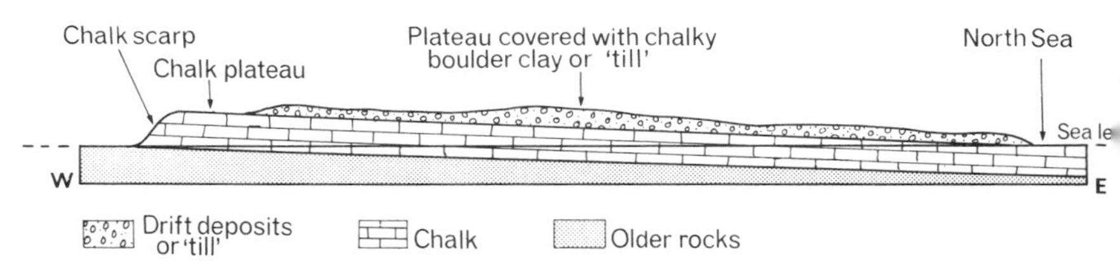

Fig. 17.14 Cross section to show 'till' deposits

Fig. 17.15 Arable landscape in Norfolk

SOUTH WALES
0 30 Km
Bristol Channel
Mendip Hills
Ilfracombe
Atlantic
EXMOOR
Quantock Hills
R. Exe
Ocean
Exeter
R. Tamar
DARTMOOR
BODMIN MOOR
Torquay
Plymouth
Yealmpton
Bigbury Bay
Penzance
Falmouth
English Channel

Fig. 17.16(a) South-west England

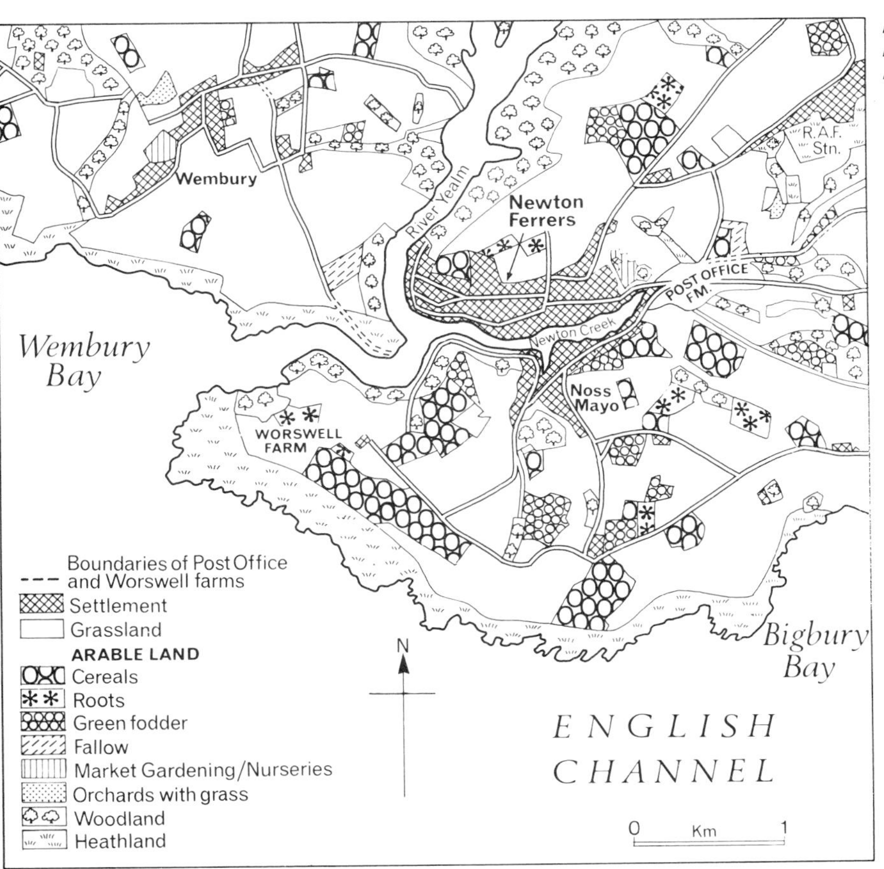

Fig. 17.16(b) Land use in the Lower Yealm valley

Fig. 17.2 this area is shown as being devoted to dairy farming, you will notice that again this does not mean that farmers are only concerned with keeping dairy cattle. There are many variations in land use.

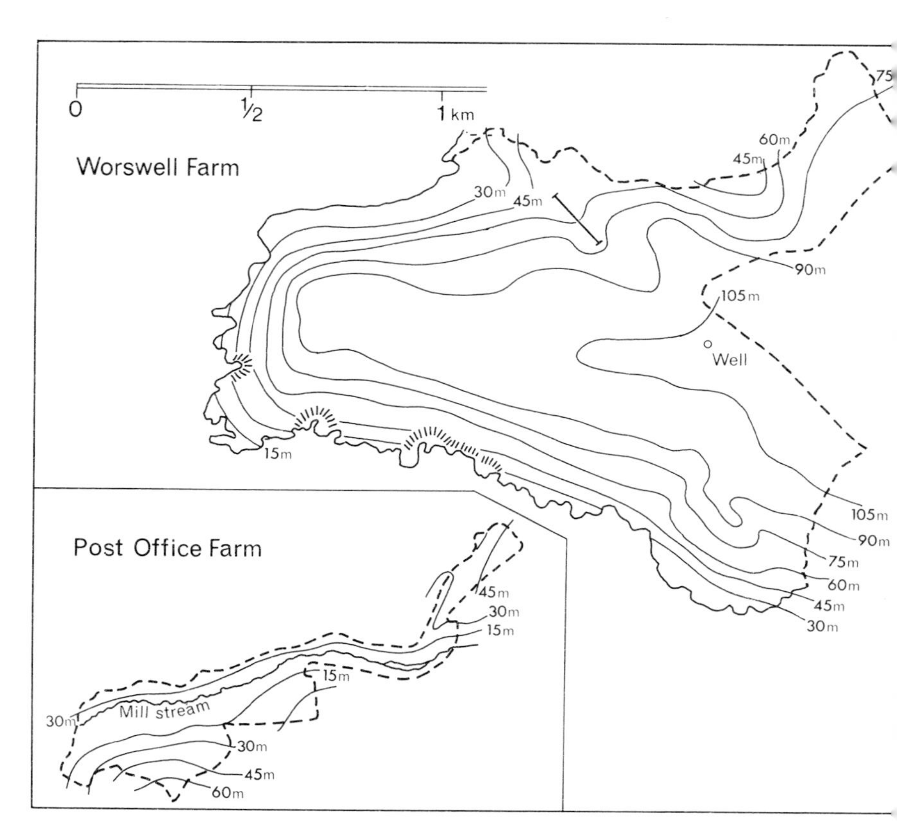

Fig. 17.17 Worswell and Post Office Farms

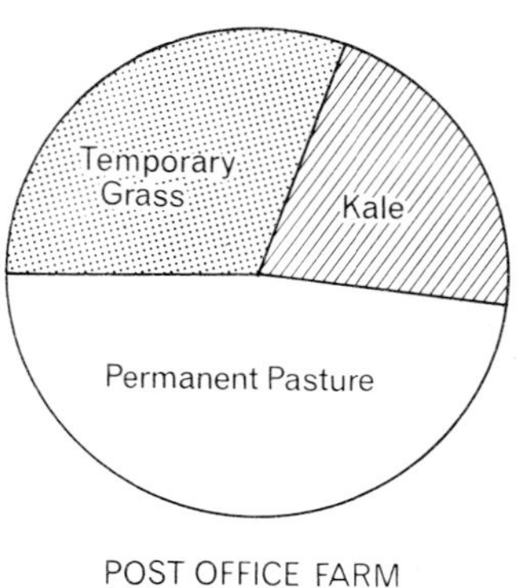

Fig. 17.18 Land use on Post Office Farm

Let us compare two farms in this area: Post Office farm in the valley bottom and Worswell farm on a plateau (see Fig. 17.17). On Post Office farm the soils derived from alluvial deposits are heavy and difficult to work, and only about 50 per cent of the farmland is ploughed as you may see from the diagram in Fig. 17.18. The farmer also needs to use a good deal of lime to help lighten his soil and prevent if from becoming too 'acid'. He keeps 25 Friesian cows for milk and about 15 calves which he sells for veal. He also keeps about 120 chickens.

On Worswell farm, the soils are lighter. They are derived from slate rocks and are about 20 centimetres deep, but like those of Post Office farm they tend to be 'acid' and have to be limed. This shows that the acidity of soils is often due to the climate rather than to the underlying rock. In areas like south Devon where rainfall is high and evaporation limited, soils tend to have some of their minerals washed out. This is called *leaching*. Luckily farmers can keep a check on their soils by having them analysed from time to time and feeding them with the required ingredients to keep them fertile. For example the farmer regularly spreads phosphates from North Africa on his land.

A note on soils

So far we have been studying soils incidentally in relation to particular farms or to areas like East Anglia. We have also mentioned in Chapter 14 that although geologists call sand or clay 'rocks', they leave out soils from their list. What is special about soils which puts them in a class on their own?

The main way to answer that question is to study a soil in some detail. There are several ways of doing this.

1. We can study the texture of the soil, that is we can find out whether it is a silky, coarse or sticky soil by feeling it with our fingers.

(i) If the soil feels sticky, then it is safe to say it is a clay soil.
(ii) If it feels gritty, it is probably a sandy soil.
(iii) If it feels silky, then it is probably a silt soil.

It is possible to have a number of combinations of these, and sandy soils can be of different degrees of coarseness according to the size of the particles which make up the soil. But we need not take this into account at present except to say that a soil in which clay, sand and silt are mixed in certain proportions, is called a *loam* and such a soil does not feel particularly gritty, silky or sticky.

2. We can also study the nature of a soil by looking at a soil profile, that is either by examining a soil exposed on the side of a quarry, or by cutting a small rectangular pit in the ground and looking at a cross-sectional view of the soil as shown in Fig. 17.19. Such a profile shows that the soil may be divided into various layers or *horizons*. It is by looking at the various *horizons* that we can see that the soil is different from the parent rock from which it is derived. For example, the top layer or *A. horizon* contains a good deal of decayed vegetation and bacteria, that is the humus content of the soil is very high. It is this topmost *horizon* which provides plants with most of their food. Thus the deeper the top *horizon* the better it is for the plants. How deep it is in fact depends on the climate. For example

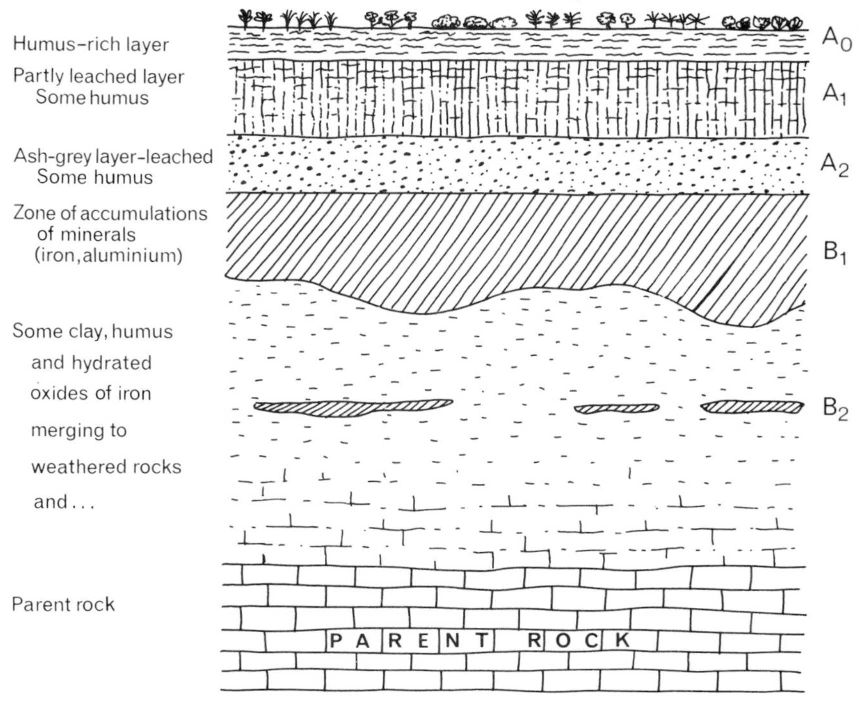

Fig. 17.19
Soil profile

in a wet, cool climate vegetation accumulation may not be very great and minerals get washed downwards (i.e. *leached*). This gives the *horizons* below the *A. horizons* a grey colour since aluminum and iron oxides (reddish in colour) will not be present. On the other hand in the *B. horizons*, the minerals and their oxides will accumulate often forming a solidified 'hard pan' which prevents further *leaching* downwards. Gradually these *B. horizons* merge into weathered rock and into the parent rock.

Just what sort of *horizons* will develop depends not only on the climate, but also on how long the soil has had to develop undisturbed. A soil which may have only recently been formed, for example on top of recently deposited alluvium, may have but one *horizon* or zone. Such a soil is called an *Azonal Soil*.

3. A soil may also be studied to find out whether it is acid or neutral or alkaline. An acid soil is one containing no lime (calcium carbonate) and an alkaline soil is one containing a good deal of lime. A means of finding out whether the soil is acid or not is to put a little barium sulphate and soil in a test tube, put some distilled water in the test tube to a certain level marked in the test tube, and pour soil indicator up to a further marked level on the test tube (see Fig. 17.20). If you mix up the ingredients and then let the mixture stand for a while, the soil indicator will turn a particular colour. You can then match this colour with one on a card and this will give you a indication of the pH value of the soil. The pH value is simply a number which varies from below 4.5 for extremely acid soils to above 9.0

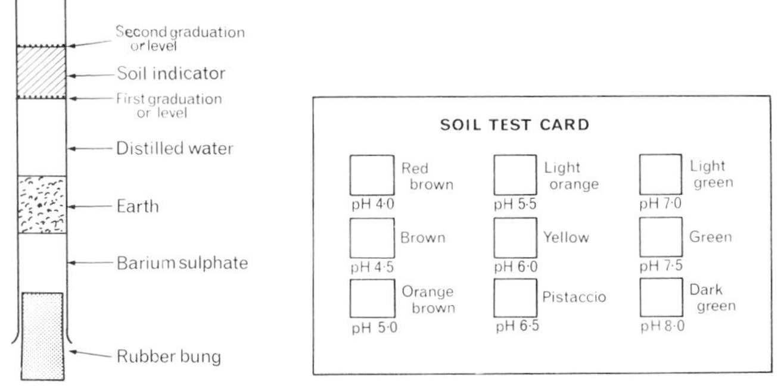

Fig. 17.20 Testing soil for acidity

for very alkaline soils. With most soil indicators the alkaline pH value is usually shown up by a green colouring and acid pH values by a yellowish colouring.

Both Post Office and Worswell farms had soils which tended to be too acid. Why is this? Post Office farm had soils which were derived from alluvial deposits from the stream passing through it and Worswell farm had soils derived from slates. It follows that neither were derived from chalk or limestone; there was no calcium carbonate to begin with, so the soils were bound to be very acid. But why is this a bad thing?

The answer is simply that no crops will grow in very acid soils and most crops prefer a slightly acid to neutral soils. Consequently if farmers want the plants they grow to do well they must prevent their soils becoming too acid. Hence the application of lime to the fields of both Post Office and Worswell farms.

Now let us attempt to answer the question we asked at the beginning of this note on soils concerning the special nature of soils. The distinguishing feature of soils is that they are an intimate mixture of rock particles, decayed vegetation, bacteria, animals like worms and beetles, and minerals such as iron oxides. Rocks on the other hand contain no living or recently decayed vegetable matter.

Conclusions on dairy and arable farming

Figure 17.21 shows that less than half of Worswell farm has been ploughed and that a good deal of unploughed land is rough pasture. Is this why the farmer keeps a herd of Friesian cattle which provide milk, so that he can use his pasture land? In fact his cattle are grazed on the improved pasture and temporary grass and sheep are allowed to roam over the rough pasture. The cattle are stall fed in winter with mangolds, hay and cattle cake. The main reason for keeping dairy cows is that the milk is sold to Plymouth Dairies and the farmer gets as a result a regular monthly income from the Milk Marketing Board. But it is also true that much of his land is steeply sloping towards the sea and would be difficult to plough and cultivate. This is particularly true of the northern and southern areas of the farm, which are further exposed to the winds from over the sea.

We can conclude that though farmers in East Anglia and in

Devon are both trying to make as good a living as they can and will plant those crops and keep those animals for which they can get a good price, certain physical conditions such as the rainfall, the wind, the height of the land, the slope of the land and the nature of the soils will influence what they in fact do. Thus though a Devon farmer will get the same price for his barley as the East Anglian farmer, he probably will not be able to grow as much. A recent tendency in East Anglia has been for farmers to produce certain crops under contract for a large frozen food organization like Birds Eye (a member of the Unilever combine). In such arrangements the buying firm usually specifies the quantity and quality of the crop it requires.

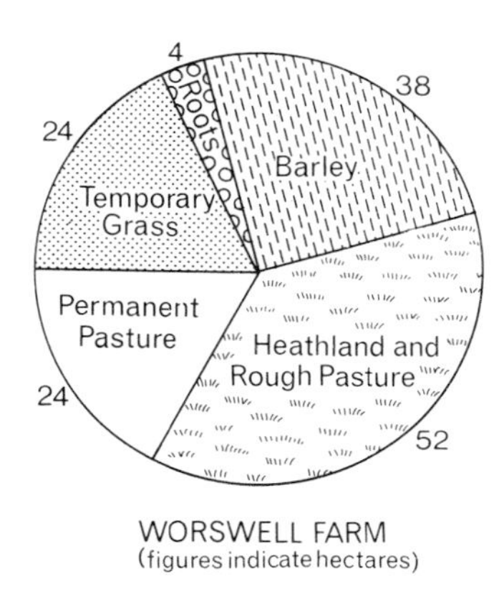

Fig. 17.21 Land use on Worswell Farm

26. *(a) If someone suggested that a particular area of East Anglia was 'arable land' what would be meant by this?*
    (b) Do East Anglian farms just grow grain crops?
    (c) Draw a sketch map of East Anglia to show (i) the coastline from Skegness to the Thames estuary (ii) the East Anglian Heights (iii) the rivers Nene, Welland, Great Ouse, Waveney, Yare, and Orwell (iv) the towns of Norwich, Bury St Edmunds, Yarmouth and Ipswich. Print 'Arable Farming' over the area east of the East Anglian Heights.
27. *Draw the table on page 261 in your note book and complete the information from figures 17.16, 17.17, 17.18, 17.21 and from information in the text.*
28. *Explain clearly and carefully why there is relatively more arable land in East Anglia than in western Britain.*
29. *What type of soil would you be handling if when pressing it between your fingers it felt*
    (a) gritty *(c) silky*
    (b) sticky *(d) neither sticky nor gritty nor silky*
30. *Ask for permission then dig a hole about 60 cm deep in your garden or in the school garden. Then*
    (a) draw a soil profile of the soil noting (i) the colour and depth of each horizon *(ii) the texture of the top 15 centimetres.*
    (b) borrow a soil testing kit and measure tne pH value of the soil.

31. *(a) What is meant by (i)* leaching *(ii)* acidity *in soils?*
(b) Why are very acid soils poor soils?
(c) Are the soils in the chalky boulder clay areas of East Anglia likely to be very acid soils? Give reasons for your answer.

32. *Using the examples of Post Office and Worswell farms, explain what physical factors (relief, slope, aspect and soil) influence the sort of farming done in South Devon.*

	Slate Farm	Post Office Farm	Worswell Farm
Position	3 kilometres west of Downham Market		
Relief – (height and variations in height)	Level — less than 8 m above sea level		
Evidence of Drainage	Ditches on field limits		
Land use	100% arable land	Just under half permanent 33 percent temporary grass. About 20 percent kale.	
Soils	Peat		
Animals kept	None		

G. Market Gardening and Fruit Growing

The main difference between arable farming in Norfolk and market gardening such as is practised in the Lea Valley in north London is that market gardening is more *intensive*. This means that the market gardener will spend much more money per hectare than an ordinary farmer. For example, in the Lea Valley much of the cultivation goes on in glass-houses – this may involve the investment of over £60,000 per hectare – that is money spent on the glass-houses, on heating plants and spraying equipment for insecticides. But even without glass-houses, many market gardens have much money spent on them. For example, not only will great quantities of fertilizer and manure be used, but equipment for irrigation by sprinklers will probably be installed and the number of hours of labour spent on the market garden will be high.

Now such intensive cultivation of the land will be in expectation of a high return; and indeed the yield per hectare of crops is very high.

The term market gardening is used in England (in North America truck farming) to indicate that the produce will be taken to a loca urban market to be sold to greengrocers who in turn will sell to th housewife. Consequently the sort of crops produced on market gardens are usually those of lettuces, brussel sprouts, cabbages, tomatoes (under glass) celery, soft fruit such as strawberries. Usually thes market gardens are small, a few hectares, and are situated near large town. This was important in the early days when the produc had to get to market fresh and would not stand a long journey. Toda with rapid transport, distance from the market is less important, bu many market gardens remain close to the cities they supply. Fo example, London is supplied by the Lea Valley, the Thames Valle to the west of London, north west Kent and the Biggleswade area o Bedfordshire. However, many vegetables are imported and it is no unusual to be eating Californian radishes, celery from Florida and from nearer home, Dutch lettuces and tomatoes. Clearly, however the local suppliers have an advantage in paying lower transport costs

A typical market garden landscape will look like that shown i Fig. 17.22. The small fields will seldom be empty except at the heigh of winter. In glass-houses cultivation can continue all the yea round. Similar to market gardens are the holdings of nursery-me

Fig. 17.22 Market gardens on the Foxall estate near Ardleigh in Essex

who provide plants and flowers for gardens and for the home. These are usually situated in or near city suburbs, since it is from the dwellers in the semi-detached and detached villas with gardens that the demand for these plants comes.

Owing to the intensive nature of the farming, soils can be made to the requirements of the market gardener. In the early days, however, many market gardens were set up on the lighter soils, for example on the 'brickearths' which are found on terraces in the Thames valley. These lighter soils were not only easy to cultivate and to drain, but they warm up more easily in the spring and summer. In areas where market gardens are not so close to the city they supply or where they are less intensive, the influence of type of soils is marked. Fig. 17.23 shows the distribution of market gardens and

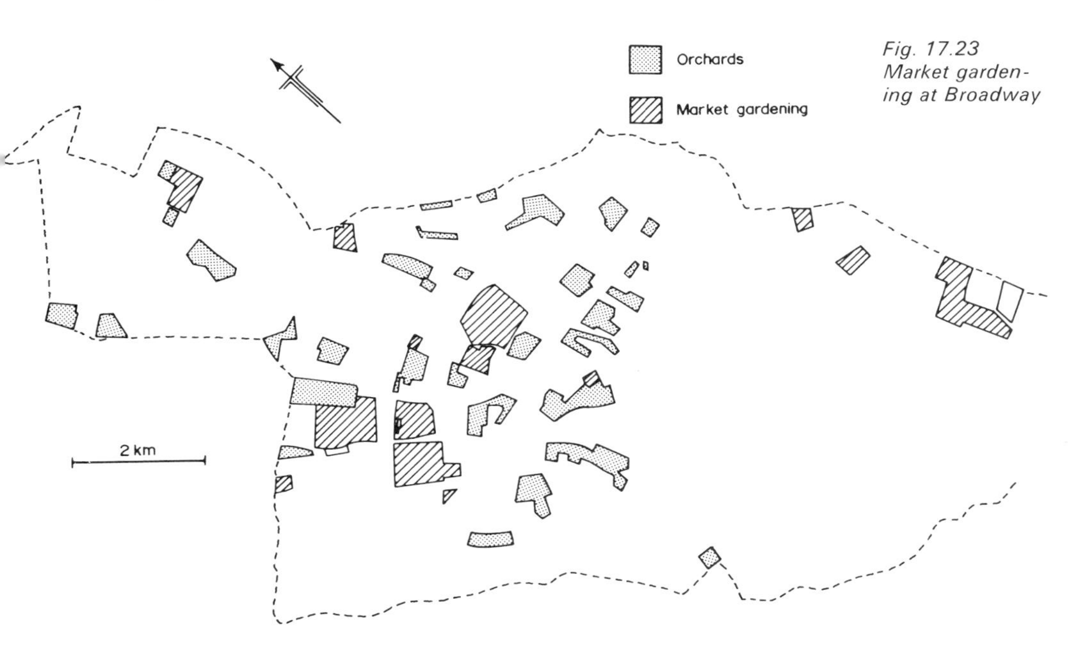

Fig. 17.23 Market gardening at Broadway

orchards in the parish of Broadway which spreads across the Cotswold scarp and part of the Vale of Evesham. It seems that there is some concentration of gardens on lighter soils and on river terrace gravel soils. As market gardening has spread, however, so heavier soils have been used and transformed into lighter workable soils by the market gardeners.

Orchards are similarly placed on lighter soils. Here a slope may be an advantage to allow frosty air to drain down to the bottom in spring when blossom might be damaged. A south facing slope would be an even greater advantage. But bearing in mind that the average number of days with frost in April may be no more than 3 or 4 days, the chance of a frost damaging a whole orchard is not very great. Further, farmers can light oil stoves to warm the air within the orchard if a frost is feared at blossom time. Conditions vary so much from place to place that it is difficult to generalize about the best position for an orchard. The main orchard fruits grown in Britain are apples, pears and plums, while soft fruit includes strawberries raspberries and black and red currants.

H. Patterns of Land Use

Of course, that costs influenced the pattern of agricultural land use was noticed as long ago as the late 18th and early 19th centuries by Johann Heinrich Von Thünen in Germany. He published a first outline of his theory in 1803. The main point of Von Thünen's theory was that, since transport costs would increase the further a farm was from its market town, only those forms of agricultural land use which would cover all costs, including transport costs, would exist at some distance from a market town. As a result, land-use rings would exist around a town indicating the effect of transport costs on types of farming as shown on Fig. 17.24. Beyond a certain radius the profits of farming would be absorbed by transport costs and land would not be used for commercial farming. Let us take a hypothetical case shown in Table 17.11 to illustrate Von Thünen's idea:

Fig. 17.24

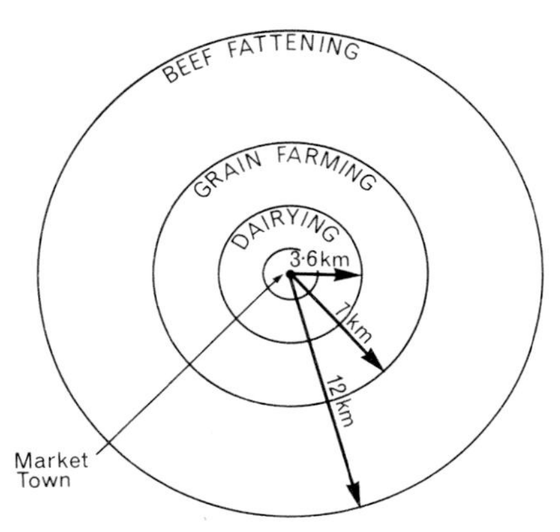

Table 17.11

Land use	(1) Market price per hectare of output per year (£)	(2) Production costs per hectare of output per year (£)	(3) Gross profit per hectare of output per year (£)	(4) Transport cost per kilometre per hectare of output (£)	(5) Limit of profitable production (km)
Dairying	150	50	100	20	5
Grain farming	85	35	50	5	10
Beef cattle fattening	55	19	36	3	12

If you ignore transport costs, dairy farming is most profitable, then grain farming and lastly beef cattle farming. But because transport costs are different for the products of each type of farming, a farmer who produces dairy products only just breaks even (i.e. makes no overall profit or loss) when his land is 5 kilometres from the market. In fact, he would be better off producing grain since he could make an overall profit of £25. Let us plot the overall profit for each land use at different distances from the market in Table 17.12.

Table 17.12

Distance from market (km)	Dairying (£)	Grain farming (£)	Beef fattening (£)
1	80	45	33
2	60	40	30
3	40	35	27
4	20	30	24
5	0	25	21
6		20	18
7		15	15
8		10	12
9		5	9
10		0	6
11			3
12			0

It follows from Table 17.12 that somewhere between 3 and 4 kilometres from the market (actually 3.6 km) it pays a farmer to undertake grain farming rather than dairying; beyond 7 kilometres from the market, it pays to undertake beef fattening rather than grain farming. Thus, if farmers seek to maximize their profits, dairying will be the dominant form of land use up to 3.6 kilometres from the market, then grain farming will take over until some 7 kilometres from the market when beef fattening will dominate, but at 12 kilometres even beef fattening will no longer be profitable. Hence the land use rings shown on Fig. 17.24.

Unfortunately, as we have seen before, reality is a little more complicated. A land use map will seldom reveal simple concentric rings of different uses of land. Many conditions will complicate the pattern: land will be more or less fertile; relief features will affect land use; various forms of transport with differing costs may be used for different products; railways, roads and canals only run along certain paths and therefore farms away from these paths will find transport more expensive, and so on. Nevertheless, Von Thünen was not entirely wrong, for in general, the farther one goes from a city, the less intensive is agricultural land use. For example, near to a city, one often finds market gardening where land is used intensively and costs per hectare are high but total transport cost low. Then, dairy farms may be fairly numerous a little distance out from the city, followed by arable farming, whilst more extensively used land for cattle or sheep rearing is usually some considerable distance from markets. But it is easier to see such patterns in less densely settled countries than it is in the U.K.

33. (a) What is meant by intensive cultivation*?*

(b) What kind of investment might a market gardener make on his holding that an ordinary farmer would probably not make?

Fig. 17.25

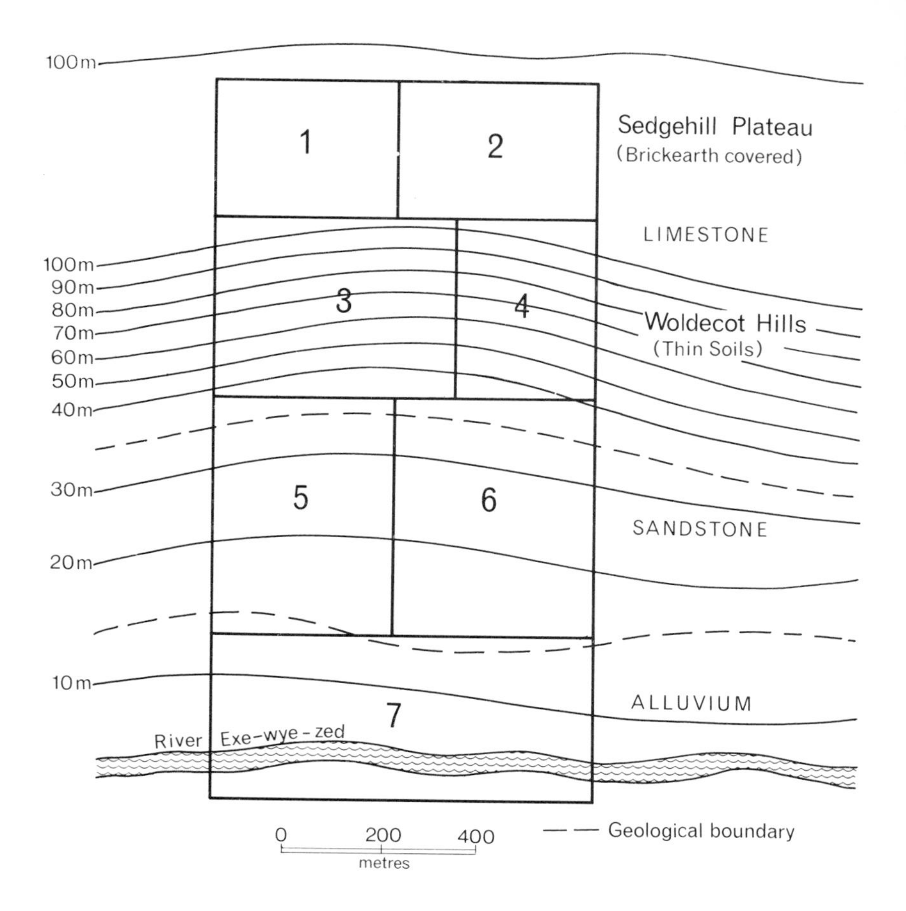

34. (a) *Study Figure 17.2 and list the main areas of Britain where intensive agriculture takes place.*
    (b) *What connection do you find between the location of these areas and that of the main cities of Britain.*
    (c) *What evidence is there in the text that market gardens no longer have to be close to their markets?*
35. *Which market gardens can produce food all the year round in Britain?*
36. *Study Fig. 17.22 and describe carefully the landscape of intensive cultivation shown in that photograph.*
37. (a) *Why are light soils no longer absolutely necessary for market gardening today?*
    (b) *Why are light soils preferred by market gardeners?*
38. (a) *Fig. 17.25 represents an area of land owned by you and on which you can grow vegetables, fruit, perhaps keep a cow or two and have some woodland. Suggest, with reasons, which fields you would use for various purposes.*
    (b) *Suppose the price of tomatoes shot up to a high level and was expected to remain at that level for a long time. What would you do to change the use of your land?*

Conclusions

In this chapter we have seen that there is still plenty of variety in the British rural landscape. From the wild treeless moors of the Highlands of Scotland to the flat intensively cultivated lands of the Fens; from the sheep runs of the Lake District to the orchards of the Vale of Evesham; from the rolling mixed farming landscape of Devon to the arable lands of East Anglia. Farms today, however, have more in common than they had 100 years ago. They are essentially businesses concerned with making a profit. This means that they have to be adaptable and ready to change from one crop to another, from one method to another, from one fertilizer to another. Farming is no longer a pleasantly slow way of making a living, where time hangs heavily between seed time and harvest, where animals pasture dreamily across wide acres of grassland. Rather it is an industry where every £100 invested must yield a return.

REVISION EXERCISES

39. (a) What percentage of the land in Great Britain is not used for agricultural purposes?

(b) From Table 17.2 work out what percentage of the agricultural land is (i) under rough grazing (ii) permanent grass (iii) arable cultivation.

40. (a) From Fig. 17.2 and an atlas map explain how relief and climate influence (i) the distribution of sheep farming areas (ii) the distribution of arable land.

(b) Does (i) relief and (ii) climate, have much influence on the distribution of areas of intensive agriculture? Give reasons for your answer.

41. (a) Make a list of the differences between beef farming and sheep farming (Section C and Section E).

(b) If you were in a position to buy a good arable farm, in which part of the country would you buy it and why?

42. (a) How could you tell whether a soil was clayey, sandy or silty?

(b) What would a pH value of 4.5 mean for a soil?

(c) If a soil is strongly alkaline what sort of rock is likely to underlie the soil?

43. When a city expands, it usually builds on what was good market garden land. Why is this?

44. Using the information on Fig. 17.13 describe and account for the differences you find in land use east and west of the River Ouse.

Chapter Eighteen

Fish Supplies

A. The Fishing Industry

Although the fishing fleets of the United Kingdom are facing a period of great difficulty due largely to the competition of foreign fleets with more modern organization, they still supply most of the requirements of the home market. Our fish is still basically a 'home' product. Some fresh fish are landed at British ports by foreign craft and a great deal of canned fish and fish products are imported.

Fish is a high protein food, yet it is still based upon men catching fish with a net, one of the most primitive methods of gaining a food supply. It is almost like obtaining meat by hunting wild animals. A great deal is being done to modernize our fishing fleet and its methods but fishing remains a dangerous and arduous occupation which requires men to spend weeks at sea in some of the most dangerous seas in the world and in seasons when storms and sub-zero temperatures are common. This was brought home to the public in a recent winter when three trawlers were lost within a few days off the coast of Iceland and only one man was saved. What are the basic facts about the industry? Table 18.1 shows the pattern of change.

Table 18.1 Fishermen in the United Kingdom

	1938	1973
Regular	39,380	19,110
Part-time	48,444	4,366
Total	87,824	23,476

(Dept. of Ag., F. & F.)

Yet although the number of men in the industry has nearly halved, the total weight of fish caught has remained fairly constant, 1.1 million tonnes in 1973 as compared with 1.15 million tonnes, in 1938. In other words, the productivity of each fisherman has gone up by nearly 100 per cent.

The main types of fish landed at the ports shown in Fig. 18.2, show the dominance of cod, accounting for nearly 44 per cent of all the fish landed (see Table 18.2). The pattern for Scotland is somewhat different (see Table 18.3), cod taking fourth place after herring, haddock and sprats (see Table 18.3).

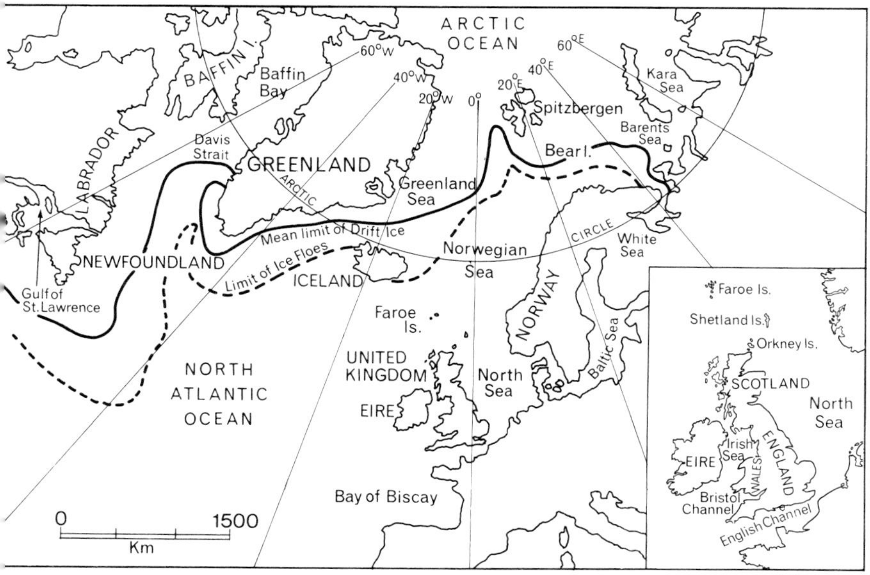

Fig. 18.1 The North Atlantic Ocean

The *demersal* fish, such as cod, are fished near the seabed by trawlers while the *pelagic* fish, such as herring, are caught by drifters fishing just beneath the sea surface.

Table 18.2 The Major Fish Landings in Ports of England and Wales during 1973 (in tonnes)

Demersal Fish:	
Catfish	4,350
Cod	215,400
Dogfish	6,950
Haddock	44,940
Lemon Sole	2,250
Plaice	32,300
Redfish	8,800
Saithe	27,900
Skate and Ray	4,100
Whiting	6,050
Pelagic Fish:	
Herring	5,600
Mackerel	17,900
Sprats	37,050

(Min. of Ag., F. & F.)

Table 18.3 Scottish Wet Fish Landings, 1973 (tonnes)

Cod	52,800
Haddock	97,700
Whiting	27,100
Plaice	4,850
Saithe	27,100
Herring	143,050
Sprats	58,900

(Min. of Ag., F. & F.)

Centuries of hunting has led to many wild animals becoming nearly extinct and, in the same way, the fierce competition between nations for fish has led to the exhaustion of nearby waters and fishing fleets have to go greater distances to find fish-rich waters. The old three-mile (4.8 km) limit has been replaced by a twelve-mile (19.2 km) limit which has led to a recovery of inshore fishing. Some countries such as Iceland have introduced a two hundred mile (320 km) limit in an attempt to preserve their national fish supplies. This limit could become general.

Table 18.4 The Major Fishing Grounds, 1973 (tonnes)

Grounds	Cod	All Wet Fish
Bear Island	8,150	12,400
Barents Sea	45,250	7,950
Norwegian Coast	9,650	19,500
North Sea	38,800	140,900
Iceland	99,500	127,000
Faroes	4,150	12,400
West Coast Scotland	1,700	7,250
English Channel	400	16,800
Bristol Channel	150	8,050
West Coast Greènland	400	450
Newfoundland	3,600	5,800
Irish Sea	2,600	12,150

(Min. of Ag., F. & F.)

The major supply areas for the important cod-fish catches are shown in Table 18.4. Most of them are in the North Atlantic Ocean and on the fringes of the Arctic Ocean requiring a round-trip in some cases of nearly 9,600 kilometres. For even the largest deep-sea trawlers, this means several weeks at sea. The grounds can be identified on the map of the North Atlantic Ocean, Fig. 18.1.

The search for fish has led to the search for new fishing grounds. The White Fish Authority, the main organization for advising the fishing industry, in conjunction with the Ministry of Agriculture, Food and Fisheries, has started to investigate fisheries off the south-west coast of Africa. The problem here will be not just to find enough fish to make such an enormous journey worthwhile but to find the type of fish that people at home will want to eat. People are very conservative in their eating habits and tend to be very suspicious of new types of food and fish.

B. Trawling

The major fishing ports of the United Kingdom are shown in Fig. 18.2 and their comparative importance may be judged by the number of fishing craft registered at each one, shown in Table 18.5. The modern trawler has to be a very specialized ship. Not only must it endure long journeys in very severe conditions, coping with storms, fog and ice. It must catch the fish, store them and deliver them to the home ports in first-class condition, otherwise no one will buy them. The trawler must be a floating factory. Fig. 18.3 shows one of the latest deep-sea trawlers and Fig. 18.4 shows the lay-out of the interior where the 'factory' work is carried on.

The fish trawls are brought in on the ramp at the stern of the vessel and stored in the 'pound'. Then the fish go through a series of processes on the 'factory deck' where they are beheaded, gutted, sorted and washed and are then stored in enormous refrigerators on the lower deck. In some craft, the fish livers are extracted and turned into liver oil and the inedible parts of the fish are turned into fish meal which has many uses in farming.

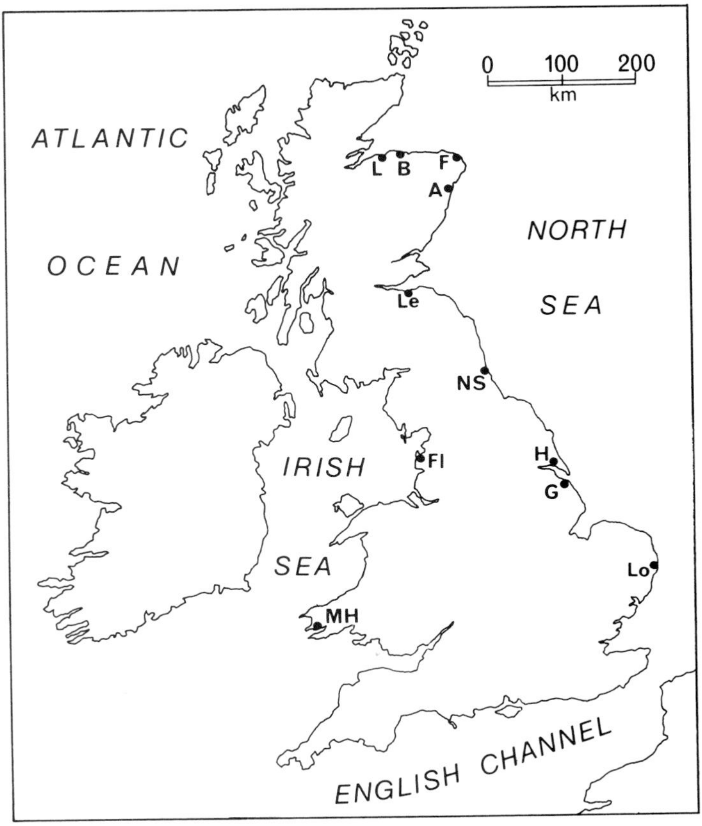

Fig. 18.2 The principal fishing ports

Port	Trawlers	Drifters	All Vessels
Fleetwood	107	—	116
Grimsby	158	—	282
Hull	100	—	111
Lowestoft	107	6	126
Milford Haven	23	—	30
North Shields	36	—	59
Others in England & Wales	926	67	2,888
Aberdeen	129	—	169
Buckie	80	—	131
Fraserburgh	74	1	180
Leith	56	—	91
Lossiemouth	28	—	115
Others in Scotland	369	3	2,003

Table 18.5 Trawlers and Drifters; Ports of registration, 1974

Hull	98
Grimsby	52
Fleetwood	11
Lowestoft	2
Aberdeen	2

Table 18.6 Home ports of 45-metre trawlers, 1974

Our fishing fleet is being equipped with more and more of the new 45-metre trawlers full of modern scientific equipment. The ports of registration of these new super-trawlers illustrates just how important are the Humber Estuary ports of Hull and Grimsby.

It would not be an exaggeration to say that these ports are the key to the home fishing industry. In fact, these 165 distant-water trawlers land no less than 40 per cent of all our wet fish.

Fig. 18.3 A modern freezer steam trawler

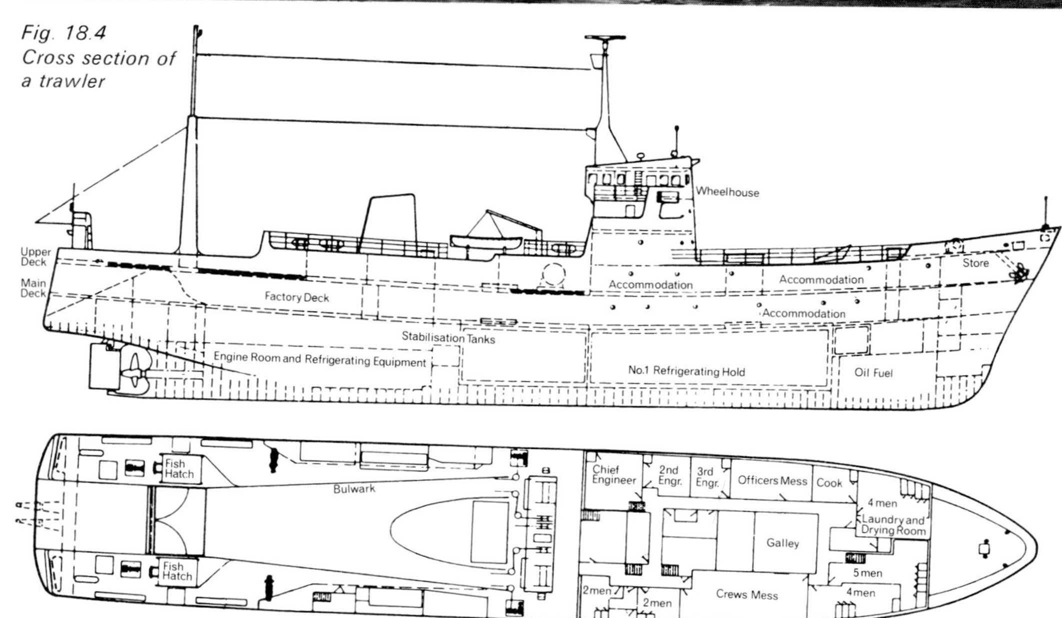

Fig. 18.4 Cross section of a trawler

Much of the research of the White Fish Authority is concerned with the design of these vessels. New methods of echo-sounding will enable skippers to pin-point large shoals of fish quickly. New machinery reduces hand-labour. The accumulated knowledge of skippers is being assembled in a series of 'Kingfisher' charts, designed especially to avoid obstructions and dangerous grounds.

Methods of keeping fish in good condition are shown in the cross-section of the trawler (Fig. 18.4). Different temperatures of the deep-freeze plants are being tried to see which is most suited to maintaining the freshness of the fish. But all these methods add to the total cost of fish and one of the problems for the industry is to reduce costs so as to encourage the increased consumption of fish.

C. Fish Farming

Ultimately, methods of fishing will have to change as much as those in farming. In other words, fish will have to be kept, as animals are, in special places, fattened up in special conditions and then sold off in batches in the way that cattle are. This is not as revolutionary as it sounds. Fish are already reared and fattened in the rice fields of the Far East and give a much-needed addition of protein to the diet of the people in those areas. Nearly every medieval monastery had its fish-pond in which fish were raised specially for eating. Farmers in France have experimented successfully with the same method using flooded fields in winter to grow a crop of fish. It is possible that a hectare of fish would give more nourishment than a hectare of wheat! Of course, there is no doubt that fish farming can be carried out but the problem is that of scale. Can it be carried out on such a scale as to make distant-water trawling unnecessary? Game fishing and angling are major sports in Britain but we could hardly solve our problems of fish supplies by giving everyone a rod and line or net! Special inshore beds are kept for special 'fish' such as oysters, lobsters and mussels. Attempts are now being made to use suitable inshore areas that could be enclosed, almost like a field in the sea, to breed and fatten other types of fish. Fig. 18.5 shows one of these research areas off the west coast of Scotland where an arm of the sea has been cut off from the open water. However, of the 200,000 plaice put into the enclosure in August, 1965 only 500 remained by November. Such disappointments are bound to occur with such a new idea and much more needs to be known about the exact biological conditions in which fish breed and thrive. Research to this end is being carried out at Port Erin on the Isle of Man.

Another possible site for fish farming is to be found, surprisingly, near power stations. The high temperatures of water due to the effluent from power stations have been found to cause fish to grow much more rapidly than normal in almost tropical conditions. Pilot schemes are being carried out in Carmarthen Bay and also by the

Fig. 18.5 A fish farm in North West Scotland

nuclear power station at Hunterston in Scotland. The C.E.G.B. has a salmon hatchery at Cynrig on the Usk. Similar research is being carried out by the Fisheries Laboratory at Lowestoft. There is no doubt that the decline of catches from the deep open seas will lead to a great increase in such research to improve home stocks of fish.

1. *Make a graph of the major fish catches shown in Table 18.2 in order of importance, expressing each figure to the nearest 5,000 tons. (Use a scale of 5,000 tonnes to 2 mm).*
   i.e. Catfish 4,350 equals 2 mm
   Cod 215,400 equals 86 mm
   Dogfish 6,950 equals 2 mm
2. *Superimpose the major cod catches shown on Table 18.4 on to the map of fishing grounds, Fig. 18.1. This can be done simply by tracing the map and inserting the appropriate figure. A more effective way is to invert a symbol for every 5,000 tonnes (e.g. a fish box or a blue dot) and put the right number of symbols in each sea area. North Sea, for example, would have 8 symbols for 38,800 tonnes whilst Barents Sea would have 9 for its 45,250 tonnes. Ignore all catches under 5,000 tonnes.*
3. *(a) How many degrees of longitude are crossed by fishermen on a journey from Hull to the Gulf of St Lawrence?*
   (b) Since crossing 360 degrees of longitude involves a time difference of 24 hours, what is the time difference between Hull and the Gulf of St Lawrence?

4. *(a) What is the difference in latitude between Hull and Bear Island according to your atlas?*
   (b) What other fishing grounds are within the Arctic Circle?
5. *On a tracing of the map of the British fishing ports shown in Fig. 18.2, add a series of symbols, each symbol (perhaps a trawler?) to stand for 20 craft shown on the table of registered craft, Table 18.5. i.e. Hull, Fleetwood and Lossiemouth, will each have six symbols. Aberdeen, with 169 will have 8 symbols.*
6. *Describe the major problems that the skipper of a trawler will encounter on a fishing trip to the Newfoundland fishing grounds.*
7. *What is meant by (a)* demersal *fish? (b)* pelagic *fish?*
8. *Why is super-chilling so important in modern trawling?*
9. *Make a flow-chart showing the processes a fish goes through after being brought on board a factory trawler.*
10. *What is meant by the '12 mile (19.2 km) limit'?*

REVISION EXERCISES

11. ***(a) Why is fishing considered a primitive way of obtaining food?***
    (b) What would be the advantages of large scale fish farming?
12. ***(a) The amount of fish caught in 1973 was no greater than in 1938, yet the*** **productivity** ***of the fishing industry is said to have gone up. Explain this.***
    (b) Is fishing now a **labour intensive** ***or*** **capital intensive** ***industry?***
13. ***Which of the fish shown in Fig. 18.6. are demersal?***
14.* ***Why do fishing vessels seem to trawl to northern rather than southern tropical waters?***

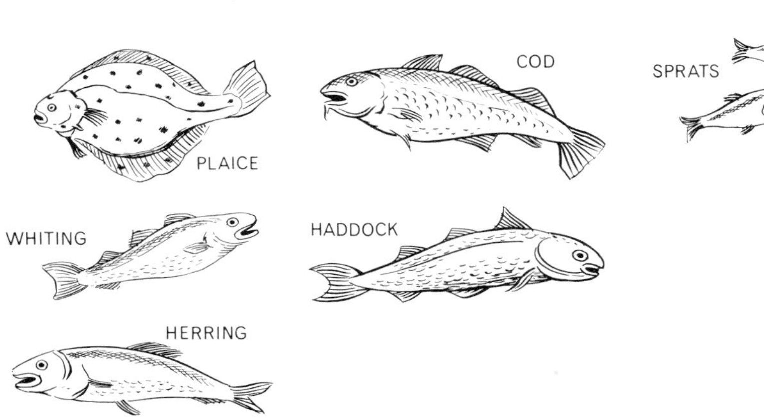

Fig. 18.6

Part VI

Playgrounds for Cities

Chapter Nineteen

Tourism, Coastal Areas and Resorts

The number of people who annually travel abroad for their holidays is growing. We can infer the increase in this holiday traffic from the following figures in Table 19.1.

Table 19.1 Movement of Passengers out of UK by sea and air to European Continent and Mediterranean Sea area.

Year	1963	1964	1965	1966	1967	1968	1969	1970	1971	1972	1973
Number in 000s	2,915	3,024	3,295	3,413	3,497	4,758	4,197	4,758	4,935	5,189	5,338

(Source: Annual Abstract of Statistics).

These numbers include people who are going on business trips, but the overwhelming majority are holiday makers. Why is the number going abroad increasing? The most obvious reason is that more people can afford to go abroad for a holiday. Other reasons are: the desire to spend some time in an area where the weather is reliably sunny, the attraction of different scenery and a different way of life, in other words curiosity about other nations. In spite of this growing tendency to travel abroad, the majority of Britons still take their holidays within the British Isles, though you must remember that this gives them the possibility of travelling to the Channel Isles, to the Irish Republic, as well as to the various areas of Britain. Thus in 1970 some 853,000 people went to the Irish Republic by sea and 826,000 went there by air. Again these figures include non-holiday makers.

A. Types of tourists

In general we tend to call people on holiday tourists even though many may not really tour round the area where they have settled for their holidays. It follows therefore that tourists are of many kinds. Let us attempt to sort out which way we can classify them.

In the first place there is the foreign tourist who has decided to spend his vacation looking at Britain. He is either a North American or European and seldom stays in one place for a great length of time. He wants to get a general impression of the British landscape and visit some of the main cities. He is often more interested in cities with historic buildings rather than those with industrial buildings and so may visit London, Edinburgh, York, Lincoln, Norwich, Stratford-on-Avon rather than Birmingham, Liverpool, Manchester or Glasgow. Such historic cities, then, need to provide comfortable ıigh standard accommodation for these tourists who are usually rom the upper income groups.

In the second place there is the British roving tourist who is ısually a motorist spending his time exploring various areas of the 3ritish Isles as yet unknown to him. For this type of tourist who may ɔe of more modest means than his foreign counterpart, small hotels ɔr boarding houses catering for 'Bed and Breakfast' are more ıppropriate. Since he has his own transport, the exact location of hese hotels is not so important and often a rural location is pre-'erred to an urban one.

In the third place, there is the traditional British tourist who wishes o spend a holiday in one spot, usually by the sea. He is often of nodest means, brings his family with him and consequently prefers ın inexpensive boarding house to a hotel or a self-catering flat which ıe can rent. If he wants many entertainment facilities, he may go to a holiday camp.'

3. Old holiday resorts

Most British holiday resorts were built up to cater for the last type ɔf tourist, though if one goes back to the 19th century or even earlier, ɔne finds that, of course, only relatively wealthy people could afford ı holiday, so that the early beginnings of such places as Scarborough ɔr Brighton were associated with the development of accommoda-:ion for the upper classes. Brighton, for example, acquired much ɔf its fame because it was patronized in the 18th century by the Prince ɔf Wales, later to become George IV. But why did the wealthy come :o such places?

Strangely enough, they did not really come for a holiday in the modern sense of the term, but they came for their health. A certain Dr Richard Russell who lived in Brighton from 1754 onwards, prescribed sea bathing and the drinking of sea water as a cure for most ills. This medical fashion caught on and many people came to Brighton to be cured of real and imaginary ills by the magical properties of sea water. To cater for these people hotels with ballrooms, banqueting halls and theatres were built and a race course established. These provided further attractions and more people came to Brighton irrespective of whether they wanted to try sea bathing or not. This explains why such old established holiday resorts as Brighton have elegant Georgian houses as well as ultra-modern tower blocks of flats as shown in Figs. 19.1 and 19.2 (a).

A similar story can be told for other holiday resorts like Scarborough and Blackpool in the north of England. Blackpool could only boast of one or two houses in 1735, but in the late 18th century bathing at Blackpool began to be advertised in Manchester newspapers and visitors began to arrive and once again inns and theatres were opened to cater for these. In most cases it was the building of a railway which brought in a flood of people to these bathing places. The London to Brighton railway opened in 1841 and Blackpool was connected to the main line in north-west England in 1846. As a

Fig. 19.1 A Georgian terrace house in Lewis Crescent, Brighton

result these places developed rapidly. Blackpool's population in 1876 rose to 10,000; today it is about 152,000.

C. The growth of holiday resorts

Fig. 19.3 shows the main seaside resorts of the British Isles in relation to the main towns and industrial areas. It may be seen that there are a large number of these towns, and that if the large number of smaller towns and villages which have summer visitors were marked on the map, there would be even more. We are sorry if your favourite holiday place is not marked but we had to limit the size of the map. You will notice that the distribution of these towns is uneven; for

Fig. 19.2(a) Brighton from the air

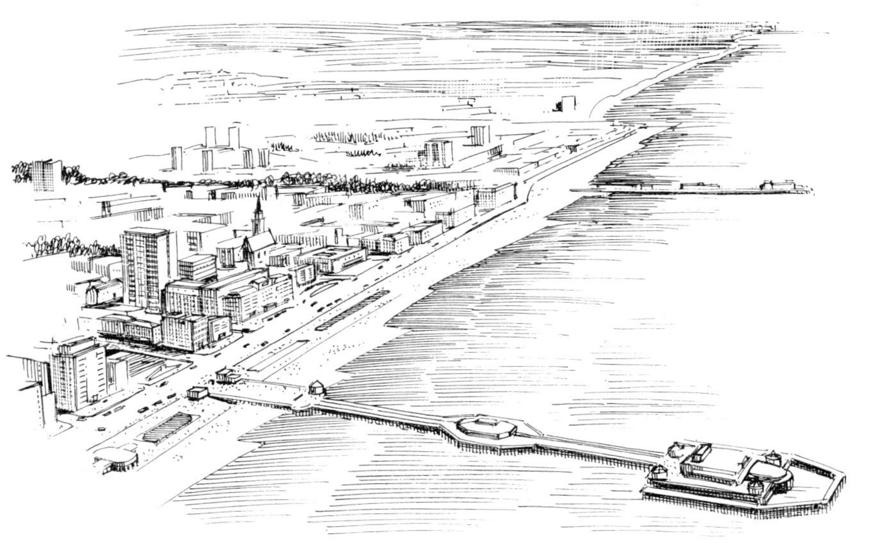

Fig. 19.2(b) Brighton: a sketch view

example none are marked in Scotland or Ireland, there are but a few in Wales but there are many in south-eastern England.

It is possible to divide these seaside holiday resorts into the following groups:

1. The South Coast resorts from Ramsgate to Swanage.
2. The South West Peninsula resorts from Lyme Regis to Weston-super-Mare.
3. The North Wales and Lancashire resorts from Llandudno to Morecambe.
4. The North Eastern resorts from Whitley Bay to Bridlington.
5. The East Coast resorts from Cleethorpes to Southend.

Now since these seaside resorts developed in the 19th and early 20th centuries, they needed to cater for a population which only had up to a fortnight's holiday per year, often less, and often without pay. They therefore had to be fairly close to the main towns from which the holiday makers came. Luckily the coast in England is never very far away, compared with, for example, North America where a citizen of Denver (Colorado) would have to travel at least 1,280 kilometres to see the sea. Thus people from the north Lancashire industrial towns need only travel 30 to 50 kilometres to get to Blackpool, Whitley Bay is very close to the Tyneside industrial area, Colwyn Bay to Merseyside, some of the east coast resorts like Southend are close to London, others like Cleethorpes to the Sheffield area. A recent count of enquiries about holidays in Great Yarmouth produced the following result:

Origin of enquiry	*Numbers*	*Origin of enquiry*	*Numbers*
Eastern Counties	6,761	Northern Ireland	
Eire	54	Scotland	2,785
London & Home Counties	10,227	Southern Counties	2,125
Midland Counties	17,376	Wales	884
Northern Counties	17,805	Western England	841

Fig. 19.3 Seaside resorts and the industrial centres

Another factor which had some influence on the number of seaside resorts in various areas is the weather. Table 19.2 shows the average monthly sunshine, temperature and rainfall records for various towns in the British Isles in the summer season.

It seems obvious why Inverness or Fort William have not developed as holiday resorts. The mean July temperature for both places (14°C) is very nearly as low as the mean December temperature

Table 19.2

	Mean number of hours of sunshine per day			Mean rainfall mm			Mean temperature °C		
	June	July	August	June	July	August	June	July	August
Blackpool	7.1	5.9	5.5	55	75	93	14	16	16
Bournemouth	7.7	6.8	6.6	40	55	63	15	17	17
Brighton	7.7	6.2	6.8	33	55	58	15	17	17
Cork	6.3	5.0	4.9	50	73	78	14	16	16
Dover	7.9	7.2	6.8	40	60	55	14	17	17
Felixstowe	7.6	7.1	6.6	30	45	45	15	17	17
Fort William	5.1	3.7	3.8	108	133	150	13	14	14
Ilfracombe	7.5	6.2	6.0	48	75	80	14	16	17
Inverness	5.6	4.5	4.4	50	73	78	12	14	14
Littlehampton	8.0	7.2	6.9	40	55	58	15	15	17
Llandudno	7.1	5.8	5.4	45	53	63	14	16	16
Penzance	7.4	6.4	6.4	50	68	75	15	17	17
Scarborough	6.5	5.7	5.2	43	63	65	14	16	16
Skegness	6.9	6.4	5.8	38	55	53	14	16	16
Southend	7.5	7.1	6.6	33	50	50	16	18	18
Torquay	7.8	6.8	6.7	45	55	65	15	17	17

for Marseilles (12°C) in southern France. The mean number of hours sunshine per day in the summer months is the lowest for all the stations listed in Table 19.2, even though the total number of hours of daylight is greater in Scotland than in southern England in summer. The rainfall is also high during the summer months at the two Scottish stations. So in spite of the supposed health-giving properties of sea water, not many Scots were willing to spend much money staying on the Scottish coast, though today plenty of Britons tour Scotland to admire its wild scenery.

For many people, one fact which influences their decision to go to a particular resort is the scenery to be found along the coast and in the area behind the coast. Fig. 19.4 illustrates this point.

Some people used to go to the extremities of Britain to get away from their fellow beings, to spend their holidays in peace and quiet. Today this is hardly possible in the summer season. Only Ireland still offers the opportunity of relatively uncrowded conditions and the Irish Tourist Board has been exploiting this fact to attract visitors to the Republic. The appeal is to the tourist who wishes to admire the landscape, to look at the relics of Ireland's past (Fig. 19.5), to fish in its seas or rivers, rather than to the holiday maker who wants to lie on sun drenched beaches – which is just as well because he will not find much sunshine (see figures for Cork – Table 19.2). Thus Ireland has few holiday resorts of a similar kind to Brighton or Blackpool. She has developed a series of hotels and inns in areas of great natural beauty, for example in the Killarney area of south west Ireland (Fig. 19.6). The graph in Fig. 19.7 shows how successful Ireland was in attracting British tourists.

The table on page 285 shows a sample of what investments are being made to improve facilities for holiday makers in Ireland.

Fig. 19.4
Scarborough

Fig. 19.5
The Skelligs in County Kerry, Republic of Ireland

Major resort development scheme

Resort	*Works Completed*	*Irish Tourist Board Contribution*
Achill	Keem Bay road and car parks, Caravanning facilities at Keel	£41,300
Arklow	Recreational Centre – additional facilities	£10,500
Ballybunion	Property acquisition. Caravan Park, pitch and putt course. Foreshore development scheme (South Beach.)	£67,600
Bray	Property acquisition. Recreation grounds. Bus shelter, shops and toilets. Beach pavilion with diving platform, dressing accommodation, toilets, cafe and shelters.	£100,600
Dingle Peninsula	Improvement of pier. Reconstruction of exhibition cottage at Feoghanagh. Improvement of access roads to beaches and provision of car parks and turning circles.	£6,000
Co. Donegal	(Whole County a Major Resort area) Bundoran – property acquisition; new golf clubhouse; car park. Buncrana – property acquisition; new golf clubhouse. Donegal – improvement works at golf club and castle. Greencastle – new golf clubhouse. Moville – foreshore scheme, including games area. Kerrykeel – new caravan park. Rathmullan – property acquisition. Bridgend Customs Post – improvement works. Narin/Portnoo-Golf Clubhouse and course extension. General improvement to beach accesses and scenic routes.	£157,000
Dun Laoghaire	Recreation centre at Moran Park. Floodlit tennis courts, pavilion and car parking. Improvement of swimming facilities at Forty Foot.	£32,900
Galway/Salthill	Property acquisition. Promenade extension, car park, groynes, public lighting. Park improvement. Golf clubhouse and course improvements. Improvements to tennis facilities. Redevelopment of Eyre Square. Information kiosk on promenade. Thoor Ballylee development works.	£200,110
Greystones	Shelters, pier and harbour improvements. Car park, beach access and landscaping. Tennis courts and pavilion. Property acquisition.	£20,250
Kilkee	Caravan park. Golf clubhouse and shelter. Promenade improvements. Access works. Property acquisition for East End Scheme.	£50,000
Killarney	Remodelling of Town Hall. Amenity works and car park at Muckross Estate. Landscaping at Kilcoolaght sandpit site. Property acquisition at Aghadoe and Gap of Dunloe. Shelter at Ross.	

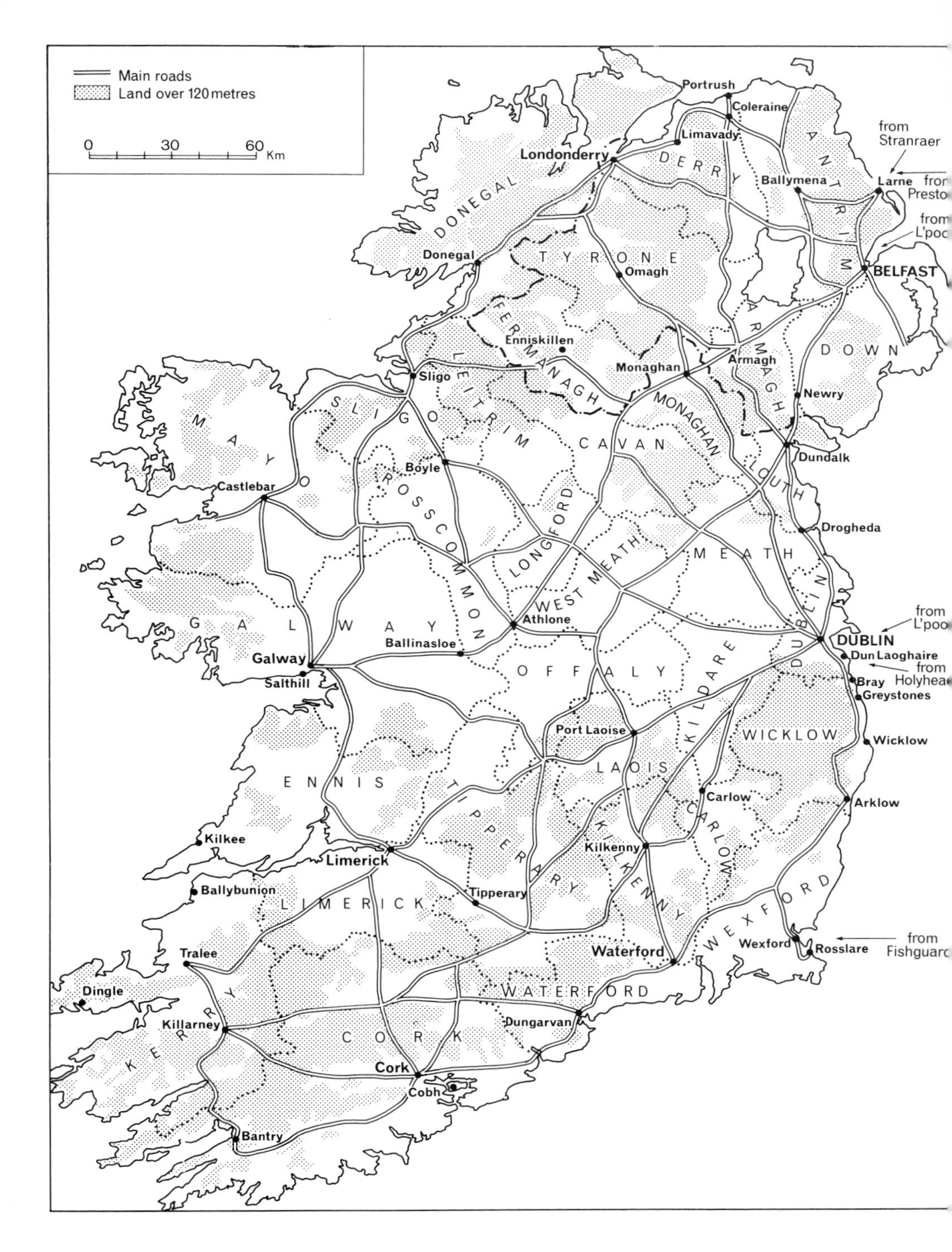

Fig. 19.6 Ireland

1. (a) *A hundred years ago few people went away on holidays; today most people go on holiday. Give two reasons why this change has happened.*

   (b) *(i) why do some people go abroad for their holidays? (ii) why do the majority of Britons not go abroad for their holidays? (iii which places in the British Isles are popular with holiday makers although they need to cross the sea in order to get to these places?*

2. *(a) Three types of tourists were mentioned on pages 278 and 279; what were they?*
   (b) Can you think of any other type of tourist?
   (c) Why does the government encourage foreign tourists to come to Britain?
3. *(a) Thirty years ago advertisements for particular resorts used to stress the healthy nature of the resort. Why do you think health was emphasized so much?*
   (b) Why was it that most holiday resorts came to be by the sea?
   (c) In which century did people begin to come to seaside towns?
4. *(a) What evidence is there in Fig. 19.1 that the first people who came to Brighton for their health were fairly well off.*

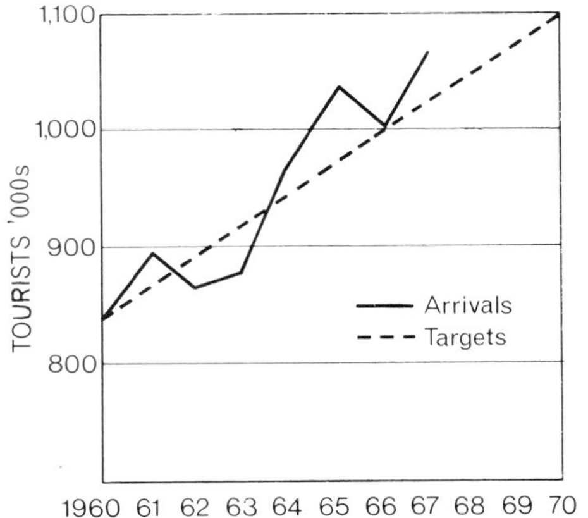

Fig. 19.7 Tourists from the United Kingdom to the twenty six counties

   (b) What evidence is there in Fig. 19.2 (a) that people are still keen to come to Brighton?
5. *(a) Study Fig. 19.2 (a) and Fig. 19.2 (b). Make a copy of Fig. 19.2 (b) in your note book and label the following features*
      (i) shingle beach
      (ii) groyne
      (iii) chalk cliff
      (iv) West Pier, Palace Pier
      (v) tower flats (one only)
      (vi) swimming pool
   (b) The groynes are fixed at right angles to the coast to limit the drifting of shingle. In which direction is the current causing the drift of shingle?
   (c) Why is there a swimming pool when the sea is so close?
6.* *(a) Both Figs. 19.1 and 19.2 show clear skies. If these photographs were taken in August, and there are 14 hours between sunrise and sunset, look up the mean number of hours of sunshine for Brighton in Table 19.2 and express as a fraction the likelihood of sunshine occurring on any one day in August.*
   (b) The mean number of hours of sunshine in January is 2 hours per day. If there are 8 hours between sunrise and sunset, what

is the likelihood of sunshine occurring on a January day? Express this chance as a percentage.

7. *Examine Fig. 19.3 carefully.*
   - *(a) State why there appear to be few resorts (i) in Scotland (ii) in Ireland (iii) in West Wales.*
   - *(b) Give at least two reasons why there should be a large number of resorts on the south coast of England*
   - *(c) During the summer season many Scots may be found in Whitley Bay. Why is this?*
   - *(d) What do the figures about enquiries for holidays in Great Yarmouth show about the possible origin of most holiday makers in this resort?*

8. *(a) Study Table 19.2. Which holiday resort seems to have the best record for (i) sunshine (ii) high temperature (iii) low rainfall.*
   - *(b) Is there much difference between these towns in (i) temperature (ii) rainfall (iii) sunshine average.*
   - *(c) Which resort would you go to from the weather point of view? Give your reasons.*
   - *(d) Supposing you chose to go to Bournemouth next August, would you be likely to get 6.6 hours of sunshine per day?*

9. *(a) Study Fig. 19.4 and make a sketch to show (i) the coastline (ii) the area of sandy beach (iii) the area of cliff coast (iv) the plateau on which Scarborough Castle stands (v) the built up area (vi) the harbour.*
   - *(b) Print the following names on your sketch (i) North Sea (ii) North Bay (iii) South Sands (iv) Castle (v) Peninsula, plateau, cliff, urban area.*

10. *(a) Why does Ireland appeal to some tourists? (See text and also Table 1.1.)*
    - *(b) Why is it stated that tourists don't come to Ireland to lie on sun drenched beaches? (See table 19.2.)*
    - *(c) What can you tell about the appeal of Ireland from the photo in Fig. 19.5?*

11. *(a) Using an atlas and the map in Fig. 19.6 state from which port in Britain you would embark to go to Ireland if you lived (i) in central Scotland (ii) in Lancashire (iii) in Bristol.*
    - *(b) Which Irish port would be nearest to your destination if you wanted to visit (i) Antrim (ii) Kerry (iii) the Wicklow Mountains.*

12. *(a) Give an example of three sorts of improvements that the Irish Tourist Board is helping to finance to attract tourists to Ireland.*
    - *(b) What evidence is there that they are being successful or unsuccessful in attracting tourists? (Fig. 19.7)*

D. The resorts and their economy

Because of their location along coastlines and their function as holiday resorts, towns like Blackpool, Brighton, Cleethorpes and

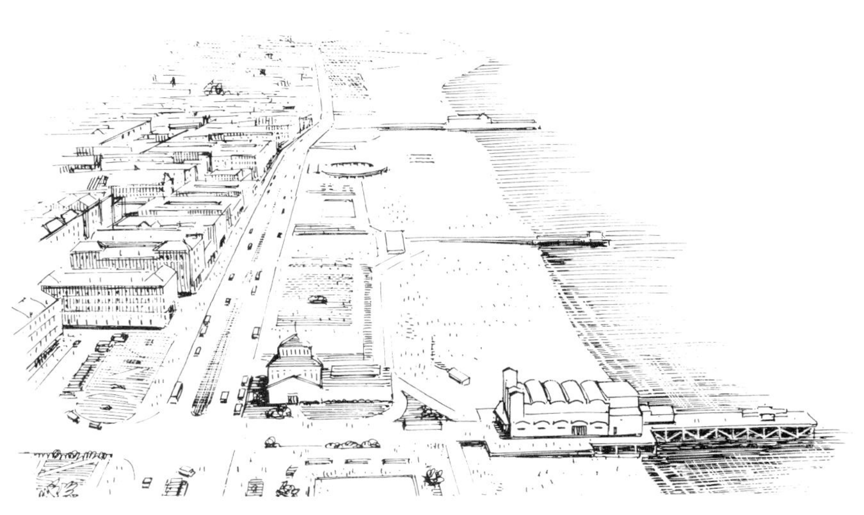

Fig. 19.8
Great Yarmouth

Great Yarmouth tend to have a rather special shape. In the first place their boundary on one side is the coast line, which in the sandy coast resorts tends to be straight or gently curved as shown in Fig. 19.8.

In the second place, because closeness to the sea is sought after by holiday makers and by residents, the town tends to expand along the coast. Consequently such towns tend to be long in one direction and relatively narrow in another. This often results in neighbouring settlements along the coast merging into one another.

In the third place, the functions of various areas of the town tend to differ from those of an ordinary town. For example the 'central business district' tends to be near the coast rather than in the centre of the built up area. Also the area of the town immediately next to the sea tends to be highly specialized, catering for holiday makers and day trippers, as may be seen in Fig. 19.9 (b).

One problem which is peculiar to holiday resorts is the lack of balance which exists between the opportunities for earning money between the summer and other seasons. Most people take their holidays in the months of June, July, August and September, July and August being by far the most popular months partly because of school holidays and partly because the weather is thought to be better in these months. It follows therefore that many hotels, boarding houses, amusement houses, ballrooms, restaurants, theatres and cinemas are considerably under-used during most of the year. In fact many of them close during the winter season. Now this is a waste of capital – the money invested in these facilities is not earning any income during the winter months. Some attempt has been made to overcome this problem recently by getting big organizations like political parties, trade unions, professional associations, etc to hold their conferences in these resorts in the off-season, thereby using to some extent hotels and other facilities which would otherwise have been empty. Another way of using accommodation more fully is to site new universities and colleges in such a town so that students take up lodgings when there are no holiday makers. This is the case at Brighton.

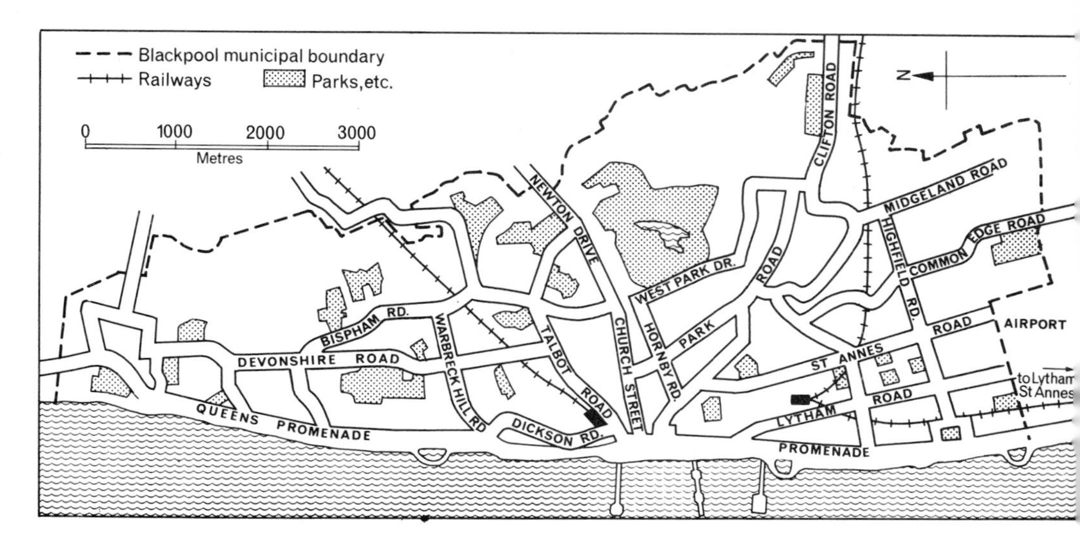

Fig. 19.9(a) Blackpool

Another related problem is that at peak holiday time, there is a need for much temporary labour to work in the hotels and places of entertainment. Some of this labour is provided by the employment of local people who are not normally in full time employment, for example, housewives. Other labour comes to the resort for the season, for example, use is made of students who are on vacation, or who have finished their courses and are waiting to start a permanent job. But it is realized that for a town to exist wholly on the tourist industry is not very satisfactory. Consequently attempts have been made to develop light industry in these towns so that a more permanent source of employment is available. Great Yarmouth for example has a large number of light industries ranging from shirt manufacturers to liftmakers. There are of course many industries connected with

Fig. 19.9(b) Great Yarmouth

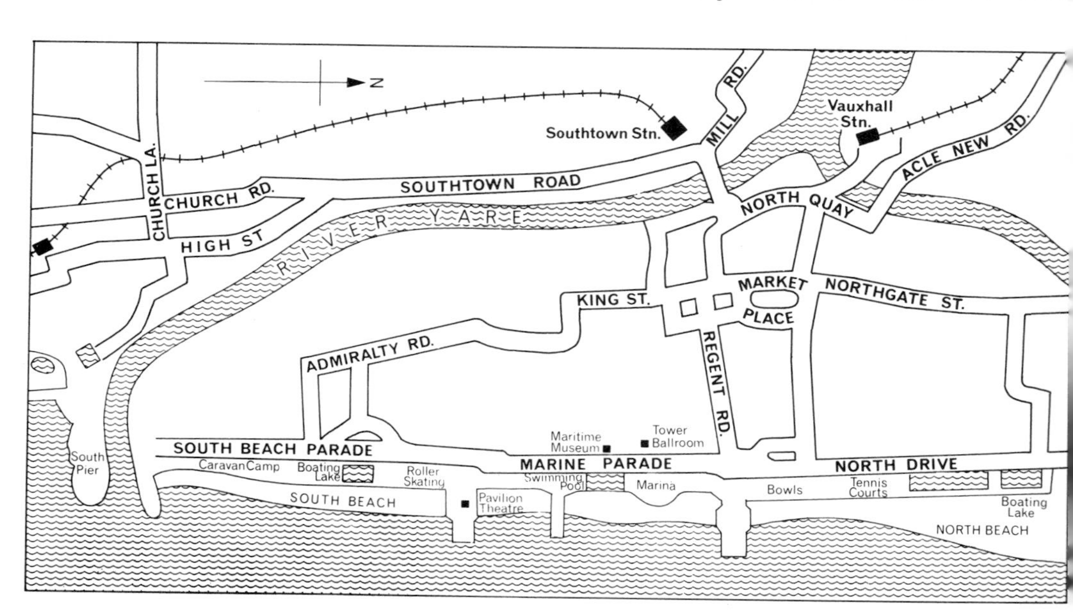

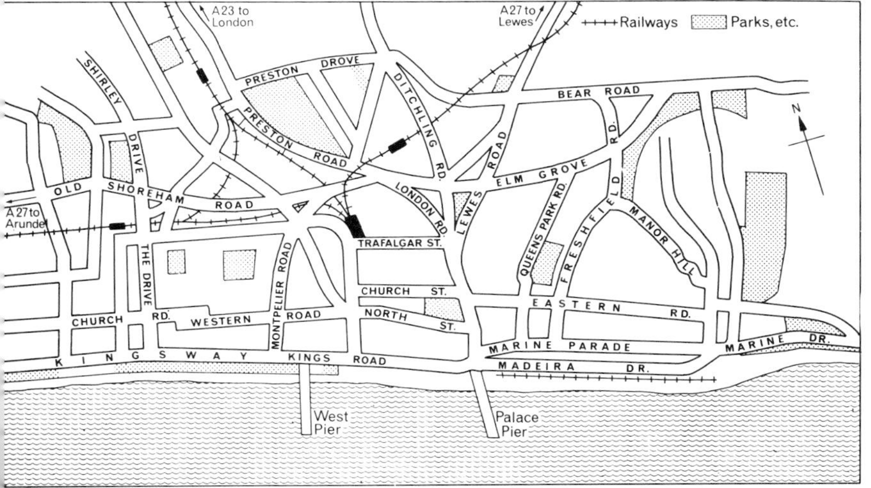

Fig. 19.9(c) Brighton

the port of Yarmouth such as boatbuilding and marine engineering for small boats. The aim is the diversification of employment.

13. *(a) Study Figs. 19.8 and 19.9(b)*
    (i) give names to the three zones which run parallel to the coast.
    (ii) why are these parallel zones common to many seaside resorts?
    (b) Compare Fig. 19.8 with Fig. 19.2 (b).
    (i) Which of the two resorts, Brighton or Great Yarmouth, appears to be the more prosperous from the evidence provided by the photographs?
    (ii) Can you give reasons for the apparently greater prosperity of one resort over the other? (Bear in mind their respective positions in England.)

14. *(a) From Figs. 19.9 (a), (b) and (c) state which features are common to the built up area of (i) Blackpool (ii) Great Yarmouth (iii) Brighton.*

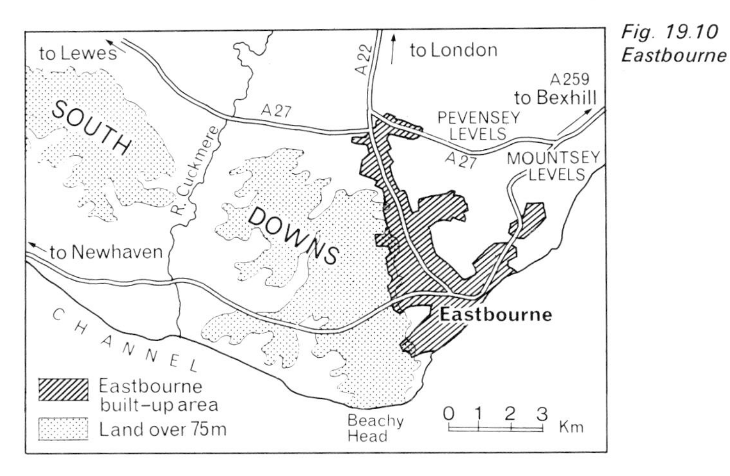

Fig. 19.10 Eastbourne

(b) *What prevents Blackpool and Lytham St Annes from linking up?*

(c) *What is the length of the built up area along the sea front from the northern to the southern end of Blackpool?*

15. *Fig. 19.10 shows the site of Eastbourne. Suggest why its shape is different from that of the other seaside resorts considered.*
16. *Most people choose August as their holiday month. From Table 19.2 state from the weather point of view whether they are wise to do so.*
17. (a) *Explain carefully why it is said that capital is wastefully used in holiday resorts.*

    (b) *What attempts are made to use capital more efficiently in these resorts?*
18. *What other difficulties are met in holiday resorts by those earning their living there?*

Conclusion

We have seen that from being health resorts for the wealthy, the seaside resorts of England became places where all Britons could relax and enjoy themselves during their annual holidays. Recently there has been a trend towards taking holidays in the Mediterranean area, partly because of the more reliable sunshine. As a result British holiday resorts can expect a gradual falling off in summer bookings in the years to come, though tourism as a whole is increasing and the number of foreign tourists coming to Britain each year is growing larger.

REVISION EXERCISES

19. (a) ***Draw an approximate plan for a seaside resort known to you and shade differently the 'promenade-beach' area, the 'amusement-theatres' area, the 'hotel and boarding house area', the central business district and any industrial area.***

    (b) ***Describe the advantages and disadvantages of the place for holidays by the sea.***
20. ***Few American tourists spend any time in English seaside resorts. Why is this?***
21. (a) ***If you wanted a seaside holiday with imposing scenery along the coast, which areas of the British Isles would you choose?***

    (b) ***Would you be more likely to find resorts with spectacular scenery in western or eastern Britain? Give reasons for your answer.***
22. ***Suppose your family decided to go on a touring holiday by car in Ireland. Describe the route you would take to a port in Britain, where you would arrive in Ireland and what you would like to see in Ireland.***

Fig. 20.2 The Lose hill, Mam Tor ridge in Derbyshire above Castleton

Fig. 20.3 The Whin Sill near Housesteads in Northumberland

scape and way of life that is becoming all too rare in the modern world. But, of course, the people who live in these 'parks' do not see them in this way. They want work; they want the same benefits of 'modern' living that the people in the cities enjoy. To give but one example, farmers in the dales want electricity but the authorities responsible for the parks fear that overhead pylons carrying electric power will spoil the landscape. Unfortunately, it costs a great deal more to put the electric supply underground than in overhead cables. So the electricity would be much more expensive. Who pays the additional costs? The local people or the people for whom the area is 'protected' i.e. you and I?

The general drift from the rural areas is affecting many of the national park areas and one of the reasons is lack of employment. If you stop the development of new industries in these areas, you encourage their depopulation. The great growth of the tourist industry in the parks has increased employment of a certain type, hotels, cafes, garages, souvenir shops, but this is seasonal employment and rarely offers a job for the whole year round.

It is part of the responsibility of the national park authorities to make provisions for visitors. Think of what this means in terms of car-parks alone: the growth of camping and caravanning, the need for shops and cafes and toilets. In the Peak District National Park alone there were about 4,000,000 visitors in 1965 with about 3,000,000 cars. This number had more than doubled by 1972. The danger is obvious: if all these people have to have facilities supplied

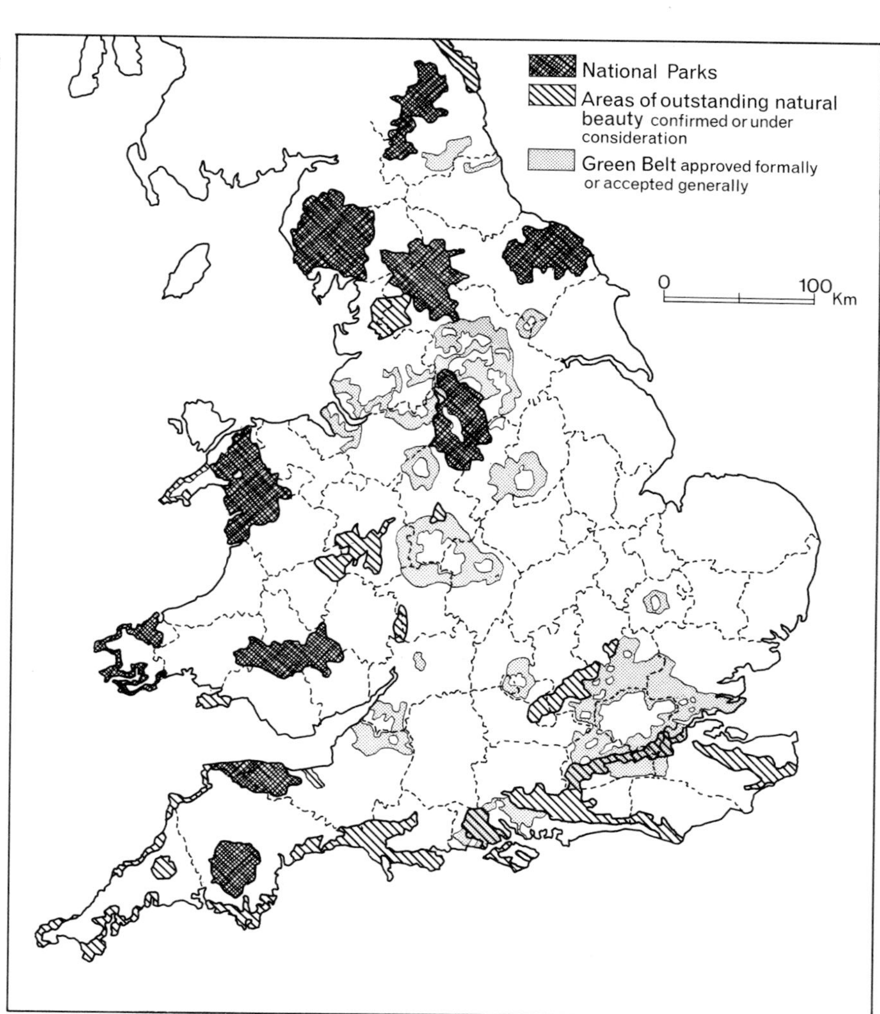

Fig. 20.4 The protected areas

for them, the very countryside that we are seeking to preserve will be altered beyond recognition. Indeed, summer traffic jams can be as bad in the national parks as they are in the cities; and many beauty spots cannot be seen for cars. The problem of limited space and a large population, the congestion of life in the British Isles, is no more obvious than in the new parks at certain times of the year, especially summer week-ends.

The city dweller is not always appreciative of the countryside he is visiting; the damage he does, often by sheer lack of understanding of country life, and the litter he leaves behind cause bad feeling among the local people. The National Parks Commission has produced a 'Country Code' with ten suggestions for visitors to follow. Wardens have been appointed to advise and assist visitors and, in some cases, by-laws have had to be introduced to enforce regulations, about litter, for example. Broken walls, gates left open, sheep-worrying by dogs, damage to farm property, camping in fields of growing crops: all these activities cause concern and undermine the whole idea of the national park.

Government departments themselves have also caused concern by giving permission for large-scale developments of an industrial nature which are out of keeping with the preservation of the countryside. New power stations in Snowdonia, a radar station on the North Yorkshire Moors, limestone quarrying in the Peak District, oil tank-farms and refineries on the Pembroke coast are among recent examples.

The national parks and the green belts are not the total area under protection. Other areas set aside for conservation are so-called 'Areas of Outstanding Natural Beauty' and other smaller areas are set aside for special scientific study, especially of their plant and animal life. All these areas together amount to nearly 25 per cent of the land surface of England and Wales. 32 more such areas have been designated in 1973/74. This country is one of the pioneers of this type of protection and experts from many countries come here to study our conservation measures. The total protected areas is shown in Fig. 20.4.

1. *After studying the photographs (Fig. 20.2, 20.3) of the Peak and Northumberland areas, suggest (a) reasons why these areas should be chosen for preservation as national parks and (b) the types of employment already available to people who live in these areas.*
2. *Why do you think it has been unnecessary so far to set up national parks in Scotland?*
3. *Draw a simple outline map of England and Wales, put in the national parks, then draw a straight line dividing the map into two areas, one containing all the national parks, the other containing none of them. What do you notice about the distribution of the parks.*
4. *(a) Fig. 20.1 not only gives the distribution of the national parks;*

it also shows radii 80 kilometres and 160 kilometres around two major cities, London in the south-east, Manchester in the north-west.

(i) How many parks are within 80 kilometres of London?

(ii) How many parks are within 80 kilometres of Manchester?

(iii) How many parks are within 160 kilometres of London?

(iv) How many parks are within 160 kilometres of Manchester?

(b) Can you suggest why the answer to 4a (i) and 4a (iii) should be so disappointing for Londoners?

5. *(a) The same map, Fig. 20.1 also marks several other major cities. By constructing your own map (which you have already done for Exercise 3 above) and drawing in your own series of radii around the marked cities, work out which city is most favoured in its position regarding national parks i.e. which city has most parks within (i) 80 kilometres radius and (ii) within 160 kilometres radius? (iii) Which great city is the worst off, being least accessible to the national parks?*

   (b) Which national park is nearest to most big cities and therefore likely to be the most visited?

6. *Why are these areas called national parks?*

7. *Make two lists on a page, one giving arguments in favour of power stations being built in the Snowdonia National Park (see Chapter 13 Section C) and the other giving arguments against such a development.*

8. *(a) Which was the first national park to be set up?*

   (b) Which is the largest of the national parks?

   (c) How many national parks are in Wales?

9. *What other types of land are set aside for 'protection' by the nation other than national parks?*

B. Forestry

During the reign of Queen Elizabeth I, so little of the original woodland cover of England remained that the Queen introduced strict laws against the cutting of timber. Cleared for farming, cut for fuel and for building, grazed by livestock, the forests remained only in small patches. The shortage of timber led to the development of coal as a fuel and, ultimately, other materials were used for construction, such as iron, steel, bricks and concrete. But timber is always in demand. The 18th and 19th centuries saw a renewed interest in trees and many of the finest plantations and parkland trees in our countryside are due to the activities of private landowners during these centuries. But Great Britain became almost entirely dependent on imported timber and the difficulties of getting such supplies during wartime led to a renewed interest in large-scale afforestation. The Forestry Commission was set up to purchase suitable land throughout the islands and to plant trees, especially of the quick-growing soft-wood variety. In place of the oak and beech woods of Britain,

Fig. 20.5 Beech woodland near Ide Hill in Kent (Greensand ridge)

large dark areas of conifers were planted, dominated by the Scots pine and varieties of spruce and larch. Coniferous trees are generally called softwoods, whilst deciduous and tropical trees are termed hardwoods.

By 1971, the areas planted by and managed by the Forestry Commission totalled 0.78 million hectares and privately-owned forests covered another 1.1 million hectares giving a total of 1.9 million hectares of managed woodland as compared with 19.0 million hectares classified as agricultural land in a total land surface in the U.K. 24.4 million hectares. The Forestry Commission is planning a further 180,000 hectares. Many of the early plantations of the Forestry Commission are now reaching maturity (conifers grow much more quickly than the oak or the beech) and are now being used for pit-props, for chipboard manufacture, for paper

Fig. 20.6 Forestry Commission forest Byrness in Northumberland

pulp and for timber. The largest factory in Hexham, for example, which was mentioned in Chapter 2, is one of the most up-to-date in Europe, making a variety of products from the forests in northern England.

It is now a major problem for the Forestry Commission to find suitable land for planting as the land must be taken from other uses such as agriculture. Much afforestation is on hill land and has led to a loss of land available especially to sheep grazing. On the whole it is poor agricultural land that has been transferred to forestry but trees grow best in good soils with adequate rainfall, so the decision has to be made as to which use of the land is most profitable for the nation as a whole.

Young coniferous trees are grown in nurseries sometimes from seeds from the local cones but more often from seeds from other areas. The seeds may be extracted by heating cones in an oven. After two years in a specially prepared bed of fine soil protected against wind-blow and birds by coverings of brushwood and other devices, the young trees are then transplanted to give them more room for growth and also to develop their rooting system. After four years they are ready for transplanting to the forest proper, sometimes under the shelter of more mature trees but sometimes in the turned-up sod, very demanding on labour and time. Young trees may be planted as closely as two metres apart and only after several years of growth is the plantation thinned out, perhaps as many as every other tree being cut. This still gives a much greater density of trees than a traditional oak or beech forest could give. The rooting system of a mature oak may take up as much as 50 square metres, whereas a mature conifer may not need more than about 10 square metres. Although the timber value of a hardwood is higher than that of a softwood, the latter lends itself more easily to modern forestry which, to a large extent, regards trees as a type of crop which must give a regular yield in the way that other crops do.

One of the advantages of forestry as a land-use is that it can be used for recreation also. Safeguards are needed against damage to trees especially by fire but the Commission is required by law to open up forests to the enjoyment of the public by supplying camping and caravan sites, and other methods of helping public understanding and appreciation by laying down 'nature trails' which people can follow and have various aspects of the countryside pointed out and explained. These trails have proved very popular: one has been laid out in the area shown in Fig. 20.3 and was followed by 10,000 people in one month. In the Grizedale Forest in the Lake District it is now possible not only to follow a nature trail but also to observe wild life from specially constructed 'hides'. Many forest parks and national parks have information centres.

The first forest park was set up in Argyllshire as early as 1935. The nine existing parks are shown in Fig. 20.7. The Country Code, as applied to the national parks is just as important in the forests for their major purpose is to supply much needed timber for the nation.

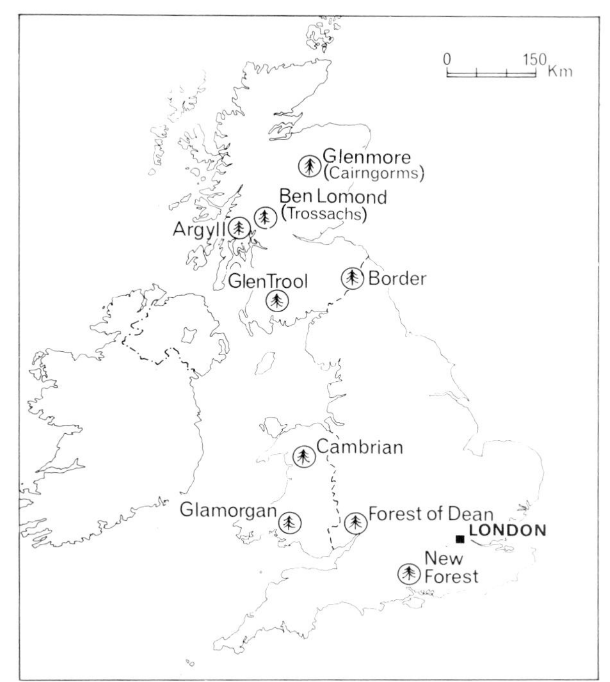

Fig. 20.7
Forest parks

C. The Countryside Commission

The extent of land under some type of conservation has led the Government to introduce new legislation to replace the National Parks Commission with a new Commission for the Countryside whose job is to 'encourage the provision, development and improvement of facilities for the enjoyment of the countryside and of open-air recreation in the countryside'. This may not sound any different from the existing order but in fact the emphasis has changed from one of protection and conservation to one of actively encouraging people to use the countryside and follow outdoor pursuits. Local authorities are setting up 'parks or pleasure grounds': the use of the word 'park' in this context is more like the traditional view of a park, such as Battersea Park in London, now a pleasure ground with fun-fair, than a national park. One of the first of these new style 'parks' has been set up on old coal workings on the Northumbrian coast and another in a disused quarry in Kent.

Famous sites like Ironbridge on the Severn and the Seven Sisters on the chalk shore line of East Sussex are further examples.

One of the new-style parks which is now under active construction is the Lea Valley park to the north of London. An area once devoted to the production of market-gardening under glass, it will now create an open lung for Londoners, with a long chain of lakes and reservoirs available for water sports. Together with Epping Forest to the east, it will supply a major playground for London's millions.

Car access, camping and picnic sites are encouraged and particular attention is paid to water surfaces, such as lakes, flooded gravel pits, reservoirs, canals, for boating, sailing and other increasingly popular water sports. Provision is made to protect agricultural land and forests but public footpaths and rights-of-way will be better signposted. The essence of this new commission is to regard the entire countryside as a source of new richness; beyond its capacity to grow crops, feed livestock, grow forests, is its power to give health and pleasure to a public which has to spend more and more of its life divorced from the countryside. But already over-use is causing problems of erosion of paths and loss of vegetation as at Pitch Hill and the Frensham Ponds in Surrey.

10. What led to the loss of the forests that once covered the British Isles?

11. What proportion or fraction of the land surface of Great Britain is now covered with forests?

12. (a) What is meant by (i) softwoods? (ii) hardwoods?
(b) What are the main uses of softwoods?

13. (a) How many of the forest parks are (i) in Scotland? (ii) in Wales? (iii) in England?
(b) Which is the nearest forest park to London?

14. What are the main dangers in making forests available for public recreation?

15. You may be able to verify or disprove some of the information given about the amount of ground needed by certain types of tree. If there is parkland nearby, it will certainly contain some mature trees and it may be possible for you to assess the amount of space each tree requires for its sustenance. A good way of doing this in open woodland is to measure out a square, fifty metres each axis, and count the number of trees within that area. A 50 metre axis gives a total area of 2,500 square metres, so you might anticipate about 50 trees in that area.

REVISION EXERCISES

16. Why is there an absence of national parks and forest parks near London?

17. What are the nearest areas of outstanding beauty to London?

18. Examine Fig. 20.3 and assess whether you consider it to be pleasant scenery or not. Express your feelings about it.

19. Why should city dwellers need to have 'lungs' in the form of parks and national parks?

20. If you were asked to set up a new 1,000 hectare forest for the Forestry Commission, what trees would you grow and where would you buy land to grow them? Give reasons for your answers.

21. Find out from your local authority the schemes they have for countryside parks.

22. Make a study of a local area that you think could qualify as a Countryside Park and show how you would develop it to cater for visitors.

Chapter Twenty-one

The British Isles: General Conclusions

In this book we have examined various aspects of life in the British Isles with special emphasis being given to certain of the problems of urban life since most people in these islands live in towns.

We have found out that the growth in the urban population of Britain is one which is associated with the development of industry in the 18th and 19th centuries. But though we now have many large *conurbations* which have populations of over one million, there are still many towns which remind one of the time when Britain was not an industrial nation but essentially an agricultural country with small towns serving the needs of the surrounding countryside. Thus were born such towns as Hexham, (Chapter 2) Market Weighton, Market Drayton and many others like Banbury whose name does not immediately conjure up a market. Present-day market towns are much smaller than their industrial neighbours simply because they usually only cater for a limited number of *functions*. They enable farmers to come and sell their livestock and buy some of their needs, but they are not necessarily large shopping centres, in this they are often overshadowed by much bigger industrial centres not far away. For example Hexham would be overshadowed to a large extent by Newcastle upon Tyne.

Another type of town which reminds one of a bygone age is the cathedral city (Chapter 3). Such towns as Wells in Somerset, Worcester, Salisbury, Winchester, Lincoln and Durham are dominated by cathedrals, all of which were built at a time when the Church as an organization was very much more powerful than it is today and when church activities influenced a much greater percentage of the population than they do today. Consequently, where these towns have not become large industrial centres, the cathedral and its surrounding buildings seem to overawe what is often a very quiet country town. Although a few, like Lincoln, have developed into industrial centres, they are still dominated physically by their cathedrals because these are situated on a hill overlooking the lower town. But modern cathedral cities have no special character and can hardly be said to be dominated by their cathedrals, even though the buildings themselves may be imposing. Liverpool (Chapter 5), for example, is a 'double' cathedral city with a large, solid Anglican cathedral and a Roman Catholic cathedral of ultra-modern design;

neither, however, can be said to dominate the city, which is so large that the cathedrals within it are just two among many large buildings. In fact as we have seen (Chapter 5), Liverpool's main *function* is that of a large port, and industries connected with its port *function* have developed in and around the town.

The Birmingham *conurbation* (Chapter 6) is an example of a small market town which developed into a large industrial area, partly because of various successful enterprises which were launched there and partly because of its association with the coalfields of the Black

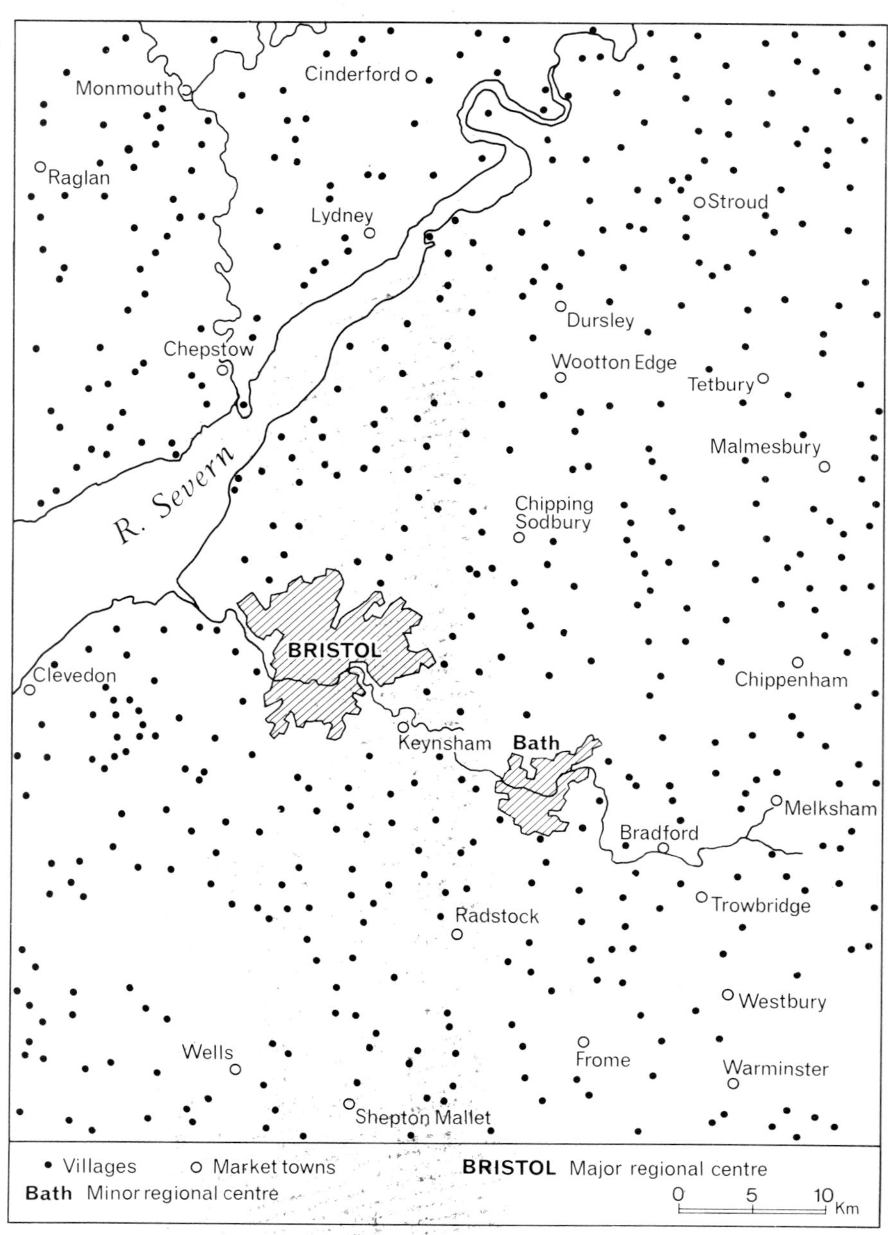

Fig. 21.1(a) Hierarchy of settlements

Country. Such a town as Birmingham may be called a *regional capital* because it performs many services for a large area around it. Other similar towns are Manchester, Sheffield, Leeds, Newcastle upon Tyne, Bristol and Norwich. Not only are these towns major shopping centres where almost anything which is required may be bought, but they are also centres of local administration, centres where important courts of justice are held and, of course, major *nodes* of communication.

Where a town performs services for a whole country, then it becomes a *national capital*. These services are usually those performed by government departments, courts of justice and the Church; though such national capitals are usually also centres of commerce and industry. London, Edinburgh, Cardiff, Belfast and Dublin are examples of such national capitals. London is necessarily the dominant capital (Chapter 7) since it is the capital of the United Kingdom of Great Britain and Northern Ireland, and since it is also a huge industrial town and the biggest seaport in the kingdom.

Thus it is possible to arrange towns in order of increasing importance according to the *functions* which they perform. This arrangement is known as a '*hierarchy*'. In practice, it is easier to use the population of a town to gauge its position in the *hierarchy* since this gives a simple direct measurement of size and usually the greater the size of a town's population, the greater is the number of *functions* it performs. Conversely, the greater the population of a town, the smaller the number of such towns in existence.

A typical *hierarchy* of settlements in the U.K. might be that shown in Table 21.1. One interesting fact about towns of various sizes is that they tend to be distributed in a country according to a definite pattern. Villages will tend to be close together, market towns somewhat further apart, regional centres are the furthest apart. National capitals are unique in any one country, but on the international scale they are clearly further apart than regional centres.

On a map, therefore, towns appear in clusters, with large towns in the centre and smaller towns clustered round them, while each smaller town will have a cluster of villages around itself. This pattern is shown in Fig. 21.1 (a).

The bigger towns are usually known as *central places* largely because they are central in relation to the surrounding smaller towns and the countryside and because communications tend to converge towards them.

Geographers such as Christaller in 1933 and Lösch in 1954 published theories about how towns and their *fields of influence* might be spaced out over a country. Their countryside would be divided up into hexagonal areas as shown in Fig. 21.1 (b). Each town would draw its customers and send out its goods and services to an hexagonal area because such areas 'nest' into one another, whereas circular areas do not (Fig. 21.1(c)). Of course, hexagonal areas will be large or small according to whether the central town is a large town covering many functions or a small town having but a few functions. Let us take the example of a small town serving a few surrounding

Figs. 2.21(b)–2.21(g)

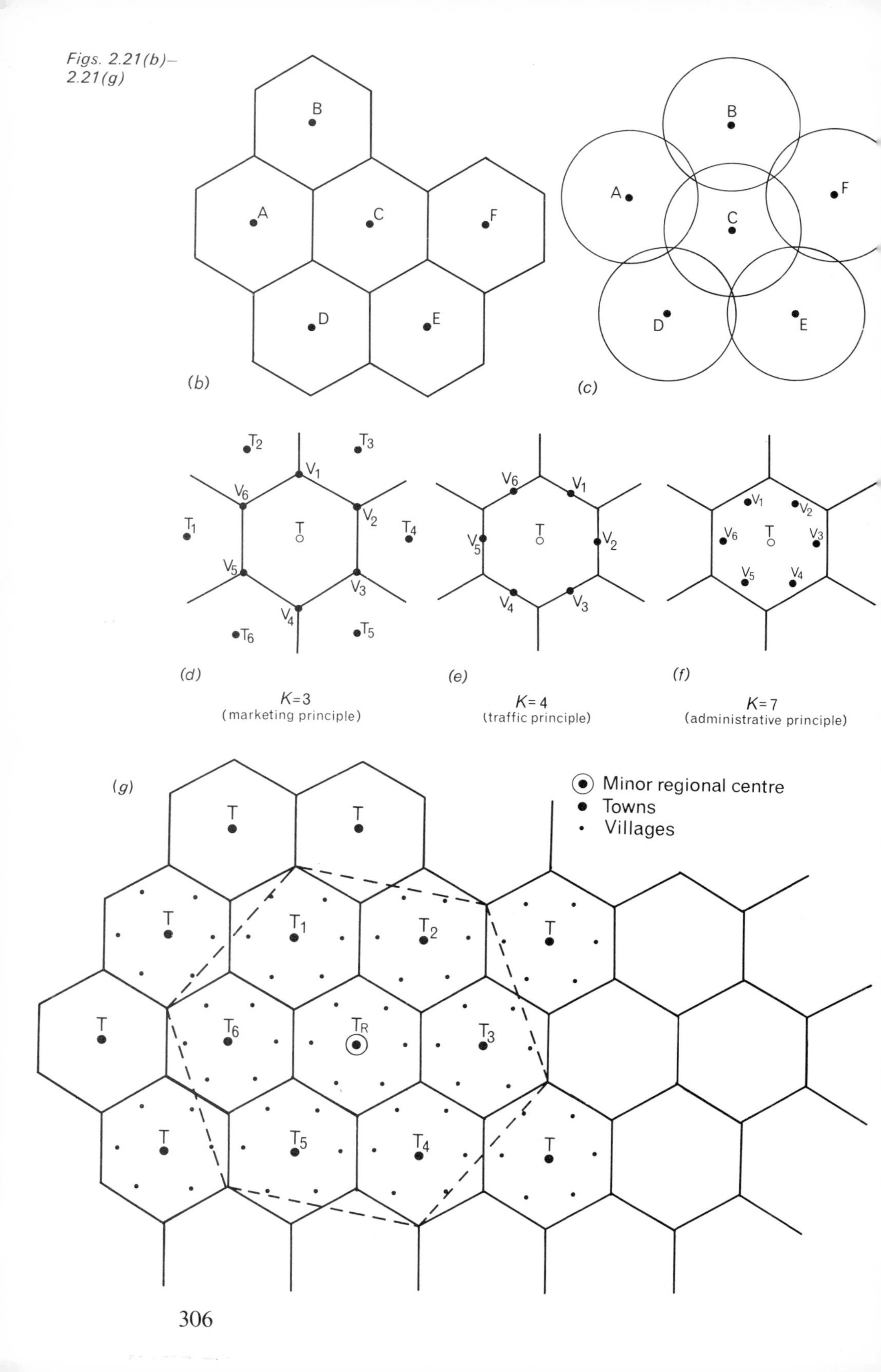

villages. The arrangement could be as set out in Fig. 21.1(d). Town T serves villages V_1, V_2, V_3, V_4, V_5 and V_6, but in fact since those villages also border on two other areas each, it is reasonable to suppose that only $\frac{1}{3}$ of the village will be served by town T_1. So the town only serves $\frac{1}{3}$ of six villages or effectively 2 villages and itself, that is a total of 3 settlements. So Christaller called this the $K = 3$ system or marketing principle. Other arrangements might be those shown in Fig. 21.1(e) where $K = 4$ (the traffic principle) and in Fig. 21.1(f) where $K = 7$ (the administrative principle). If you consider the whole hierarchy of settlements you might get a pattern like that in Fig. 21.1(g). Here town T_R is a minor regional centre and towns T_1, T_2, T_3, T_4, T_5 and T_6 are market towns, whilst all the small dots are villages. So each market town serves 6 villages and itself and each minor regional centre serves the areas containing 6 market towns, 42 villages (6×7) and itself – that is, a total of 49 settlements (7 areas $\times$ 7 settlements). In the real world, it is unlikely to be as simple as that, but you might try to find out how towns are arranged in your local area.

One thing which is happening in the real world is that bigger towns are taking over functions which were once catered for by smaller towns in the area. For example, villages may now find themselves without a general store because people can go to the supermarket in the nearest town which offers a better range of goods.

We have also seen that towns tend to be divided internally into various *districts* or *zones*, with usually one major *central business district* (C.B.D.) and a number of other districts such as residential areas and industrial areas, though the larger the town, the greater the number of very specialized areas as was seen in the case of London (Chapter 7). The tendency for the residential areas to be on the outskirts of towns is due partly to the high cost of land in central areas when business organizations are competing for sites. In Chapter 8 we studied some of the problems of large urban areas, problems due to buildings getting old and having to be rebuilt, problems due to old buildings often being inhabited by people of relatively low income who had to be rehoused in more expensive accommodation, and problems due to the enormous growth of motor traffic which lead to a need to redesign city centres and the roads leading to them. But the growth of *conurbations* is causing many to wonder whether the countryside itself may not rapidly disappear in England. So attempts have been made to limit the spread of towns by surrounding them with green belts or wedges (Chapter 9) and instead of extending old towns, building new ones at some distance from the old towns. So towns like Basildon, Crawley, Cumbernauld and Peterlee have come into being. All this requires foresight and planning and all large local authorities now have planning departments which work with the central government departments which deal with the planning of towns in the United Kingdom.

It is realized now that town and country are not really separate and independent forms of life but that they are intimately linked.

Table 21.1

Type of Town	Examples	Population (1973)
National capital (Provides all services and specializes in central government services. Usually an industrial and commercial centre).	London (G.L.C.) Edinburgh Belfast Cardiff Dublin	7.3 million 453,000 359,000 278,000 650,000
Regional capital (Provides most services except some central government services).	Birmingham Bristol Manchester Newcastle-upon-Tyne Glasgow	1,004,000 422,000 535,000 212,000 836,000
Minor regional centre (Provides good shopping services, local administration. Usually an industrial town).	Ipswich Preston Worcester Perth	123,000 133,000 741,000 43,000
Market town (Provides moderate shopping facilities and some local administration. Not usually an industrial centre, but specializes in selling and buying for agriculture).	Hexham (Northumberland) Romsey (Hants) Bury St Edmunds (Suffolk) Malton (Yorks) Elgin (Morayshire)	10,000 11,000 26,000 4,000 17,000
Village (Provides for immediate shopping needs only, few services apart from post office).	Hovingham (Yorks) Knowl Hill (Berks) Saxthorpe (Norfolk) Brodie (Morayshire)	326 978 657 240

Source: Britain 1975 H.M.S.O.

After all, not only do farmers sell their produce to towns, but many industrial undertakings are set up in country districts, for example, example: coal and iron ore, roadstone, gravel and clay; further, many industrial undertakings are set up in country districts, for example, power stations; also town dwellers often stream out to the country during weekends and holiday periods (Chapters 19 and 20). Consequently the idea that country areas should be administered by one authority (county councils) and towns by other authorities (county boroughs) is no longer thought to be a good one and the new administrative structure of Great Britain includes local authorities dealing with cities and their surrounding regions as shown in Fig. 21.2. The new administrative areas are to be counties and metropolitan countries, the latter being made up of the conurbations. The government has however, decided that some services should be

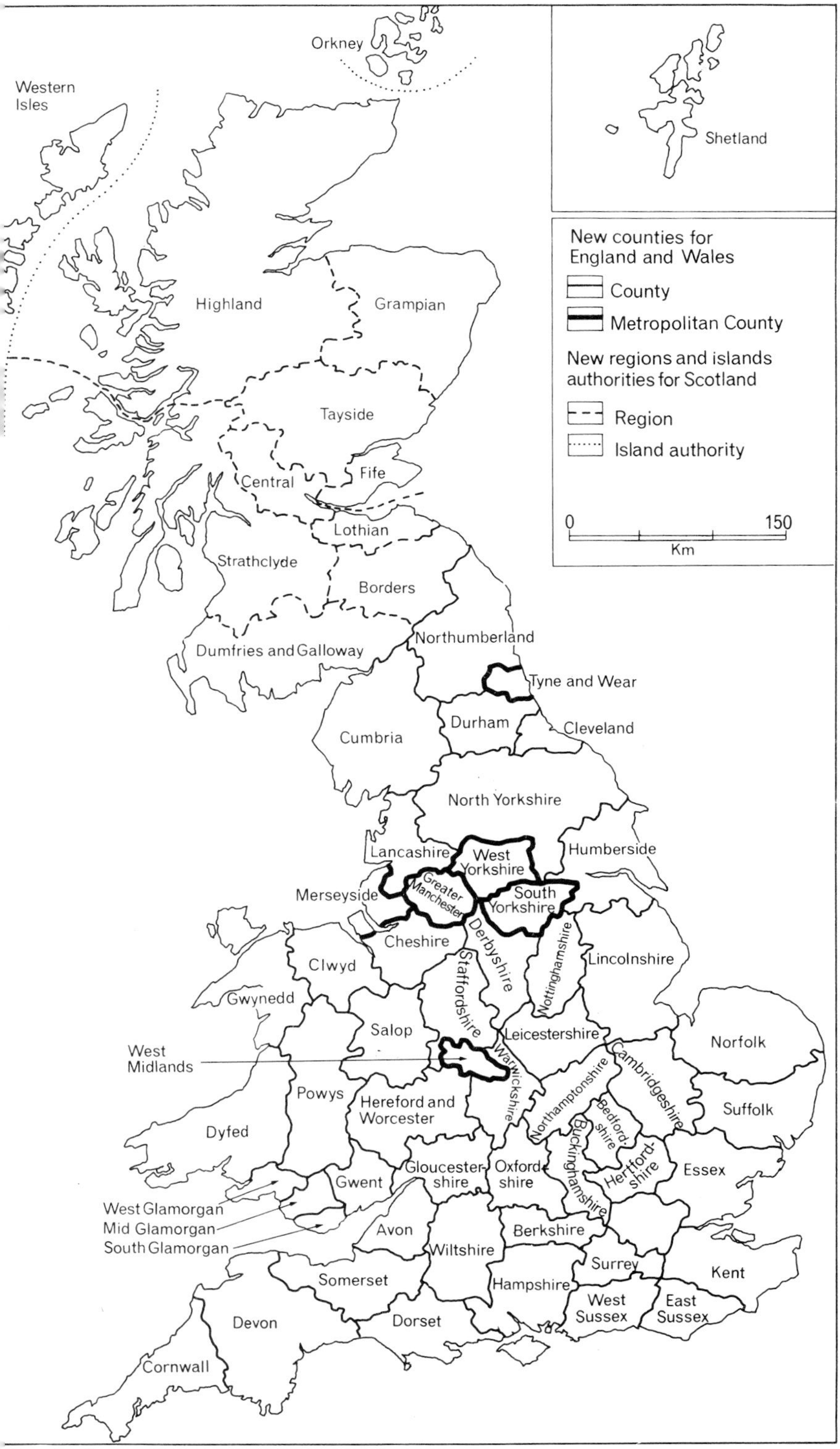

Orkney
Western Isles
Shetland
New counties for England and Wales
County
Metropolitan County
New regions and islands authorities for Scotland
Region
Island authority
0
150
Km
Highland
Grampian
Tayside
Central
Fife
Lothian
Strathclyde
Borders
Dumfries and Galloway
Northumberland
Tyne and Wear
Durham
Cleveland
Cumbria
North Yorkshire
Humberside
Lancashire
West Yorkshire
Merseyside
Greater Manchester
South Yorkshire
Cheshire
Derbyshire
Nottinghamshire
Lincolnshire
Clwyd
Gwynedd
Staffordshire
Salop
Leicestershire
Norfolk
West Midlands
Warwickshire
Cambridgeshire
Northamptonshire
Powys
Hereford and Worcester
Suffolk
Dyfed
Bedfordshire
Buckinghamshire
Hertfordshire
Essex
Gloucestershire
Oxfordshire
Gwent
West Glamorgan
Mid Glamorgan
South Glamorgan
Avon
Berkshire
Wiltshire
Surrey
Kent
Somerset
Hampshire
West Sussex
East Sussex
Devon
Dorset
Cornwall

Fig. 21.2 Reorganisation of administrative areas into counties and Metropolitan counties

Table 21.2 Estimated Populations and Rateable Values of the Counties

Part I

Metropolitan Counties

Name of county	1973 Census Population (thousands)	Rateable value at April 1974 (£m)
Greater Manchester	2,730	303
Merseyside	1,621	185
South Yorkshire	1,319	122
Tyne and Wear	1,198	115
West Midlands	2,785	369
West Yorkshire	2,080	187

Part II

Non-Metropolitan Counties

Name of county	1973 Census Population (thousands)	Rateable value at April 1974 (£m)
Avon	914	107
Bedfordshire	481	69
Berkshire	651	102
Buckinghamshire	496	77
Cambridgeshire	533	63
Cheshire	896	114
Cleveland	567	68
Clwyd	369	35
Cornwall	391	38
Cumbria	474	42
Derbyshire	888	137
Devon	921	99
Dorset	566	72
Durham	610	50
Dyfed	317	27
East Sussex	658	87
Essex	1,398	204
Gloucestershire	482	56
Gwent	441	42
Gwynedd	222	19
Hampshire	1,422	178
Hereford & Worcester	577	72
Hertfordshire	940	149
Humberside	847	87
Isle of Wight	110	12
Kent	1,435	159
Lancashire	1,363	128
Leicestershire	824	95
Lincolnshire	512	49
Mid Glamorgan	536	34
Norfolk	644	74
Northamptonshire	488	57
Northumberland	283	26
North Yorkshire	645	61
Nottinghamshire	984	107

Table 21.2 (continued)

Name of county	1973 Census Population (thousands)	Rateable value at April 1974 (£m)
Oxfordshire	529	68
Powys	99	7
Salop	345	36
Somerset	399	42
South Glamorgan	392	45
Staffordshire	985	106
Suffolk	562	64
Surrey	1,012	155
Warwickshire	468	57
West Glamorgan	373	35
West Sussex	630	82
Wiltshire	501	50

Source: Municipal Authorities Year Book.

administered at the district level, for example refuse collections, but others, for example, education, at the county level. The districts are sub-divisions of the counties. The populations of these areas are shown in Table 21.2. The separation between metropolitan and non-metropolitan counties, presents difficulties for such counties as Northumberland which now has no large town within its boundaries. Its income earning capacity is limited as you may see from its low rateable value in Table 21.2.

In Chapters 10 to 14 we examined the way in which industry was distributed over the British Isles and discovered that the pattern is now somewhat different from what it was in the 19th century or even from what it was in the 1940s. In particular there is a 'manufacturing belt' from London to Liverpool. We also found that no regions in Britain are as highly specialized as they once were and that service occupations are dominant in nearly all regions. Some areas, however, compared with the U.K. as a whole, do have relatively more people employed in certain industries. For example, there is still some degree of specialization in textiles in Lancashire, and we saw how this degree of specialization could be measured by an index or coefficient called a *location quotient* in Chapter 10. Important developing industries were those concerned with engineering and chemicals, particularly those chemicals based on petroleum, as on Teesside. No industries would function without transport, and we have seen how rail transport is concentrating on high-speed trunk routes, how motorways are being built to link up the main centres of population in the U.K., while feeder roads are improved (Chapter 15). The scope for air transport is more limited because of the relatively small area of the U.K., so that little time is saved between such cities as London and Birmingham if the traveller goes by air (Chapter 16). The enormous growth in international air traffic has posed certain problems such as whether and where new airports should be located in this crowded island and this problem is particularly acute in the London area, where not only is land in short supply, but the noise made by aircraft is a considerable nuisance.

Lastly, but not least, a growing population needs to be fed and if the country is not to depend entirely on imported food, then steps must be taken to develop agriculture and fisheries. In Chapters 17 and 18 we have studied the nature of these activities in the U.K. and we have seen that though farmers can do much to improve their soils and techniques of farming, basically they are still dependent on the weather, and the type of farming carried out in various parts of Britain still reflects to some extent the differences in climate between east and west, north and south. Man works with nature to improve upon it, but he cannot yet afford to neglect nature. It still does not pay to grow bananas or oranges in Britain!

The future of the British economy is now linked to that of Europe since Britain and Ireland are now part of the European Economic Community.

REVISION EXERCISES

1. *Describe the main* functions *of*
   (a) a village *(c) a minor regional centre*
   (b) a market town *(d) a major regional centre*
2.* *Supposing that the U.K., France, West Germany, Belgium, Luxembourg, Netherlands and Denmark became one federal state with the federal capital in Paris. What would happen to the* functions *of London?*
3. *(a) What is meant by a* hierarchy *of settlements?*
   (b) Pick out examples of settlements which are in order of size from Fig. 21.1 (a).
   (c) Roughly how far apart are most (i) villages (ii) market towns.
4. *What possible methods are there of preventing a complete take-over of the country by the towns?*

Index